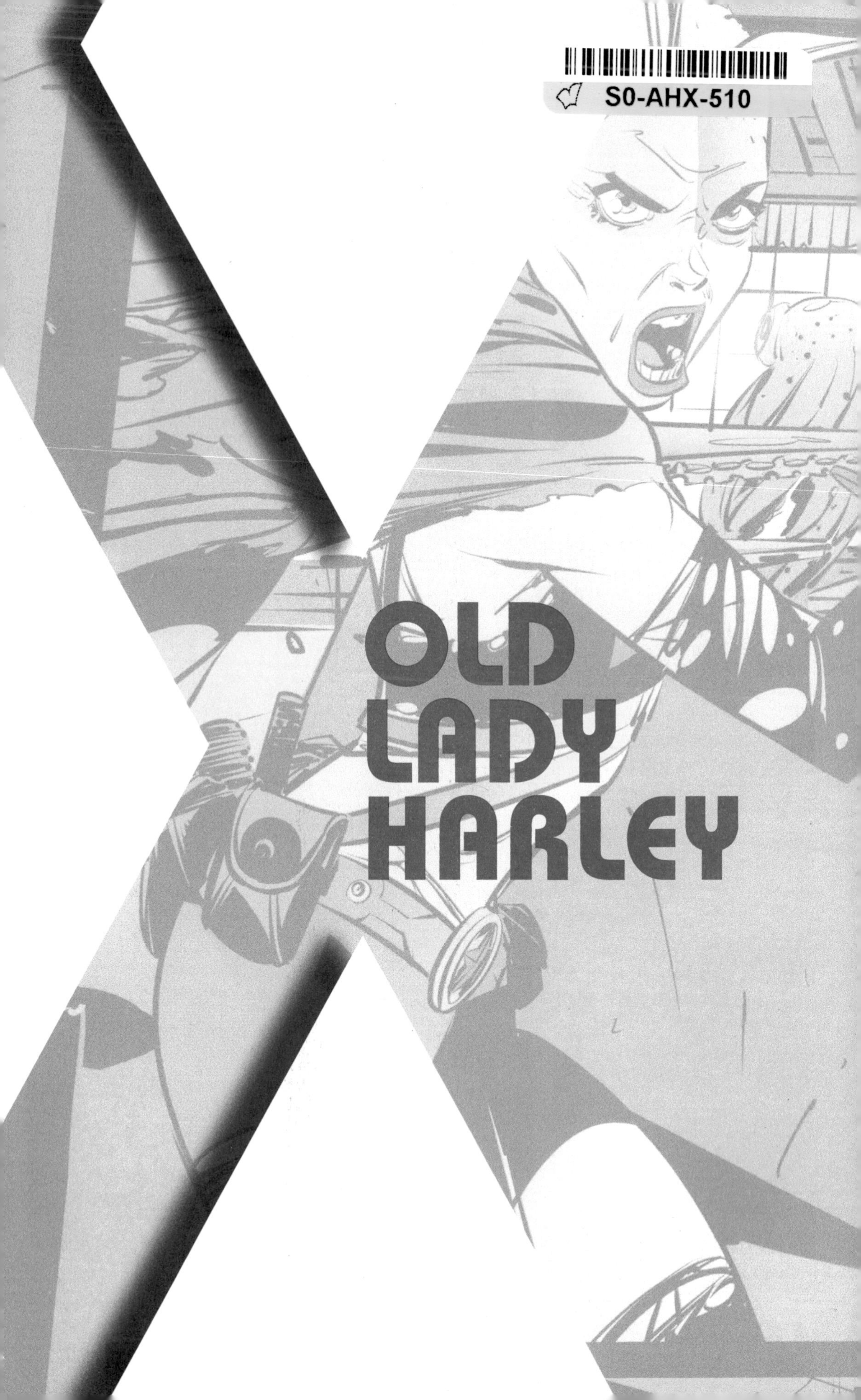
OLD
LADY
HARLEY

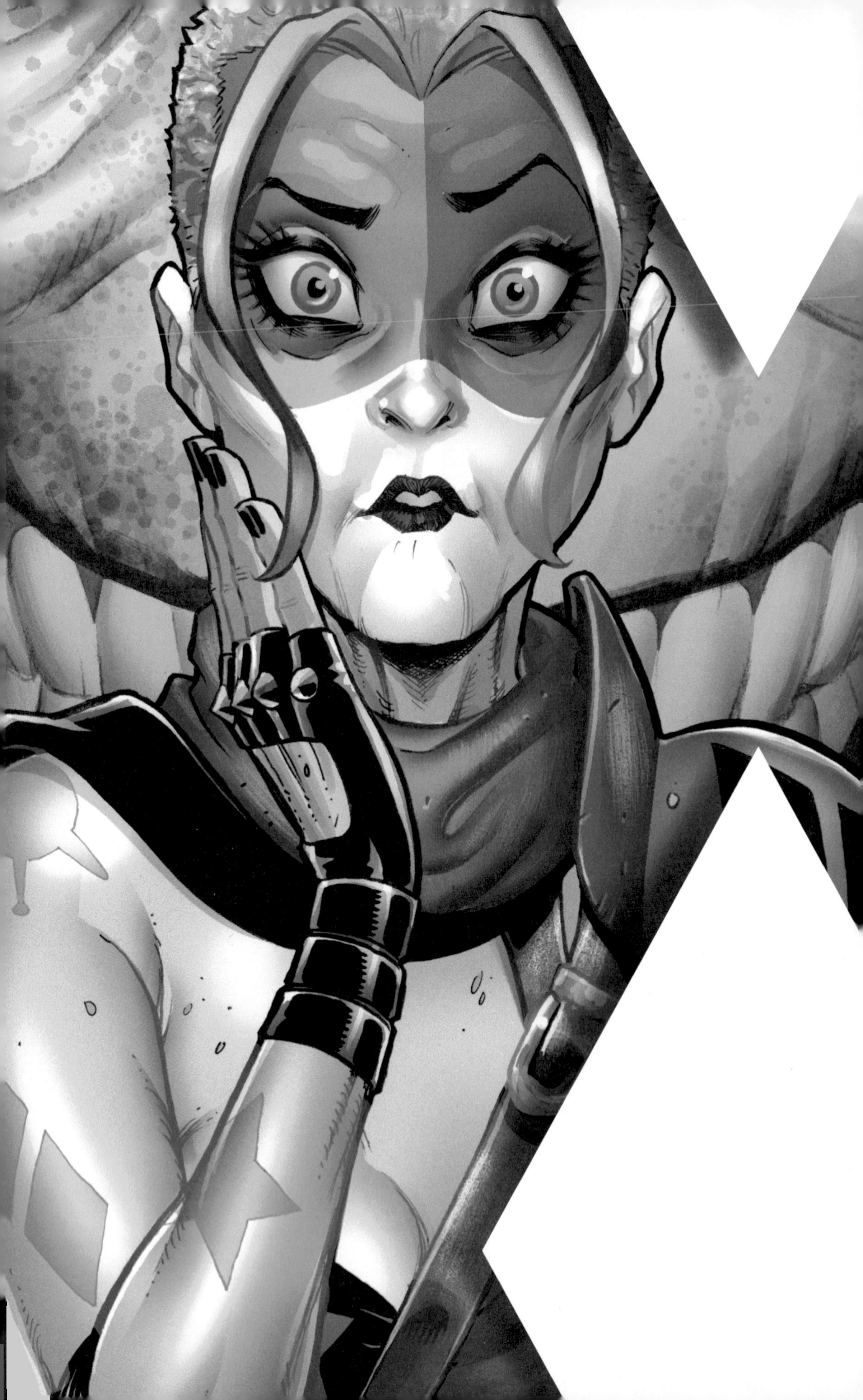

OLD LADY HARLEY

FRANK TIERI
writer

INAKI MIRANDA

MAURICET | TOM DERENICK
artists

EVA DE LA CRUZ

PAUL MOUNTS
colorists

DAVE SHARPE
letterer

**AMANDA CONNER
and PAUL MOUNTS**
collection cover artists

HARLEY QUINN created
by PAUL DINI and BRUCE TIMM

CHRIS CONROY Editor – Original Series
DAVE WIELGOSZ Assistant Editor – Original Series
JEB WOODARD Group Editor – Collected Editions
ROBIN WILDMAN Editor – Collected Edition
STEVE COOK Design Director – Books
MONIQUE NARBONETA Publication Design

BOB HARRAS Senior VP – Editor-in-Chief, DC Comics
PAT McCALLUM Executive Editor, DC Comics

DAN DiDIO Publisher
JIM LEE Publisher & Chief Creative Officer
AMIT DESAI Executive VP – Business & Marketing Strategy, Direct to
               Consumer & Global Franchise Management
BOBBIE CHASE VP & Executive Editor, Young Reader & Talent Development
MARK CHIARELLO Senior VP – Art, Design & Collected Editions
JOHN CUNNINGHAM Senior VP – Sales & Trade Marketing
BRIAR DARDEN VP – Business Affairs
ANNE DePIES Senior VP – Business Strategy, Finance & Administration
DON FALLETTI VP – Manufacturing Operations
LAWRENCE GANEM VP – Editorial Administration & Talent Relations
ALISON GILL Senior VP – Manufacturing & Operations
JASON GREENBERG VP – Business Strategy & Finance
HANK KANALZ Senior VP – Editorial Strategy & Administration
JAY KOGAN Senior VP – Legal Affairs
NICK J. NAPOLITANO VP – Manufacturing Administration
LISETTE OSTERLOH VP – Digital Marketing & Events
EDDIE SCANNELL VP – Consumer Marketing
COURTNEY SIMMONS Senior VP – Publicity & Communications
JIM (SKI) SOKOLOWSKI VP – Comic Book Specialty Sales & Trade Marketing
NANCY SPEARS VP – Mass, Book, Digital Sales & Trade Marketing
MICHELE R. WELLS VP – Content Strategy

OLD LADY HARLEY

DC Comics, 2900 West Alameda Ave., Burbank, CA 91505
Printed by LSC Communications, Owensville, MO, USA. 5/24/19. First Printing.
ISBN: 978-1-4012-9216-4

Library of Congress Cataloging-in-Publication Data is available.

PEFC Certified

This product is from
sustainably managed
forests and controlled
sources

PEFC/29-31-337   www.pefc.org

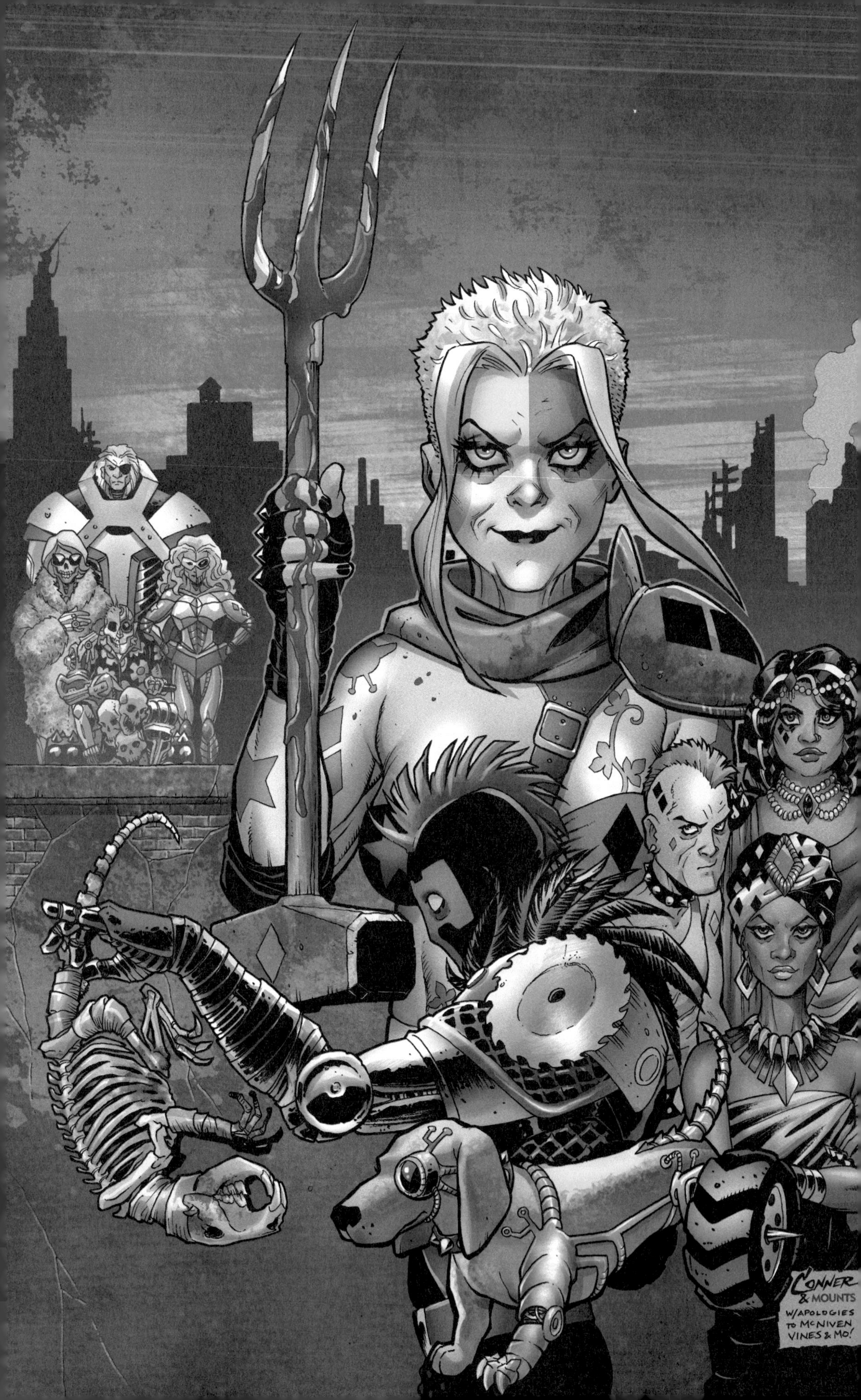
CONNER & MOUNTS
W/APOLOGIES TO McNIVEN VINES & MO!

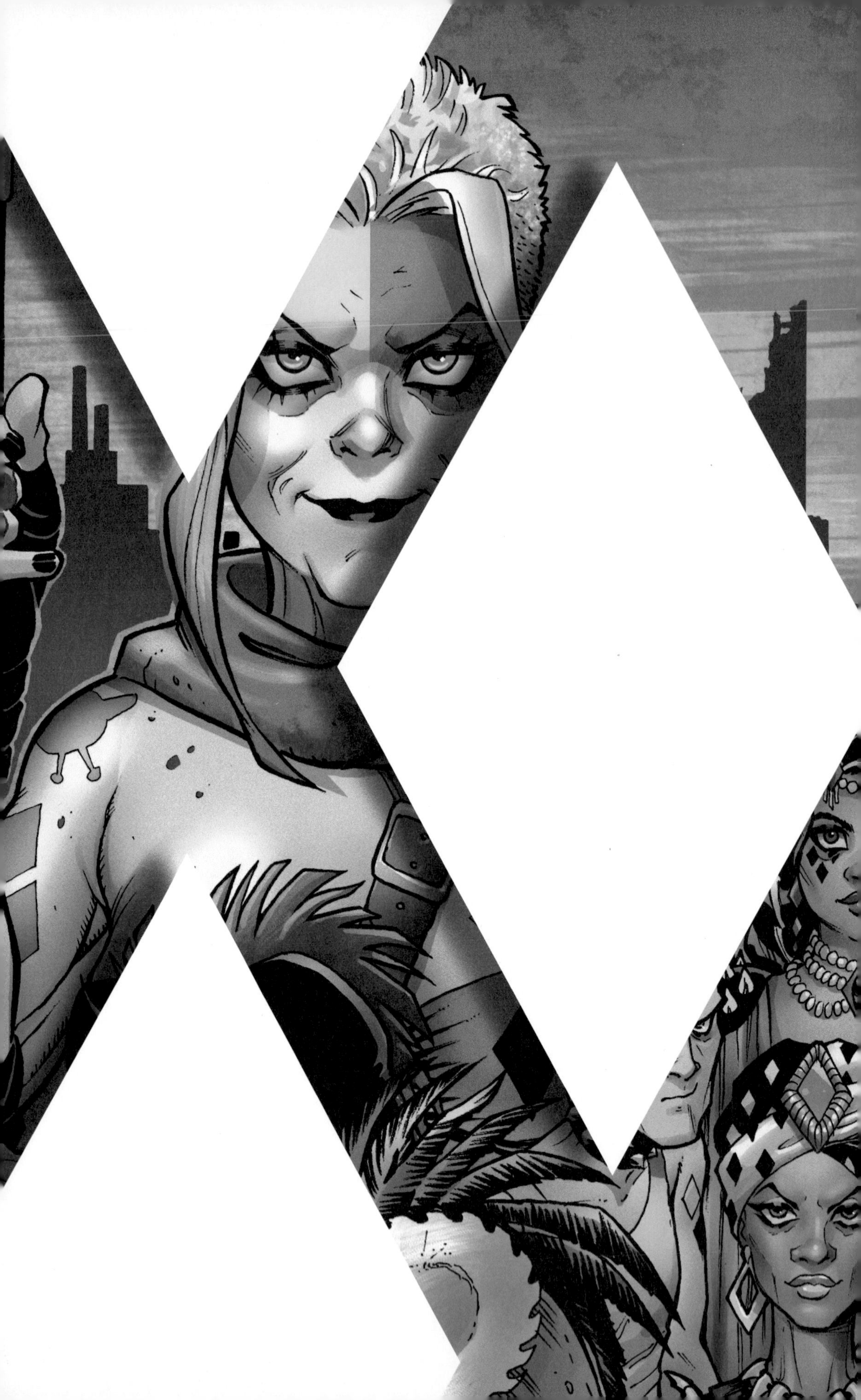

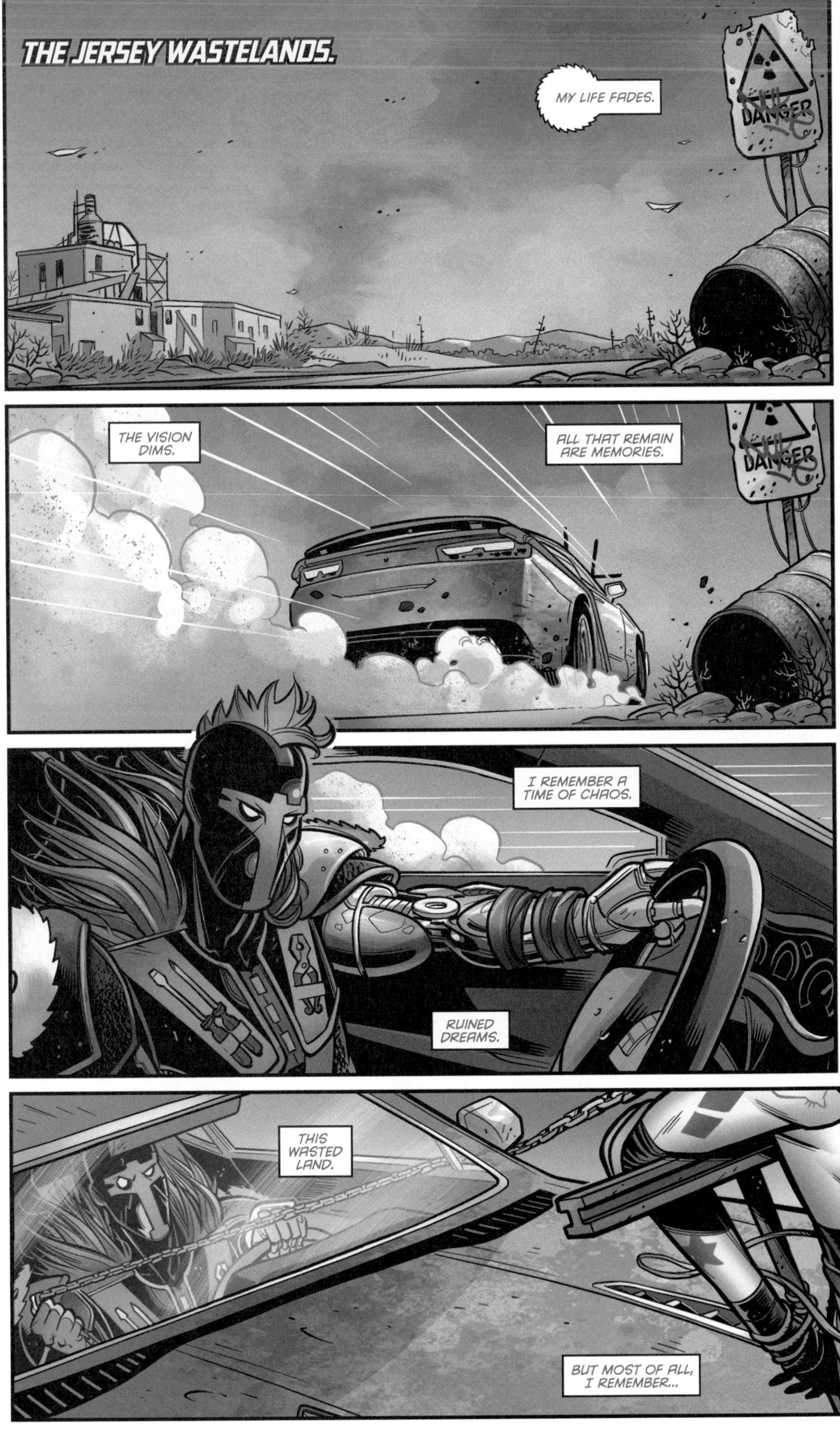
THE JERSEY WASTELANDS.
MY LIFE FADES.
DANGER
THE VISION DIMS.
ALL THAT REMAIN ARE MEMORIES.
DANGER
I REMEMBER A TIME OF CHAOS.
RUINED DREAMS.
THIS WASTED LAND.
BUT MOST OF ALL, I REMEMBER...

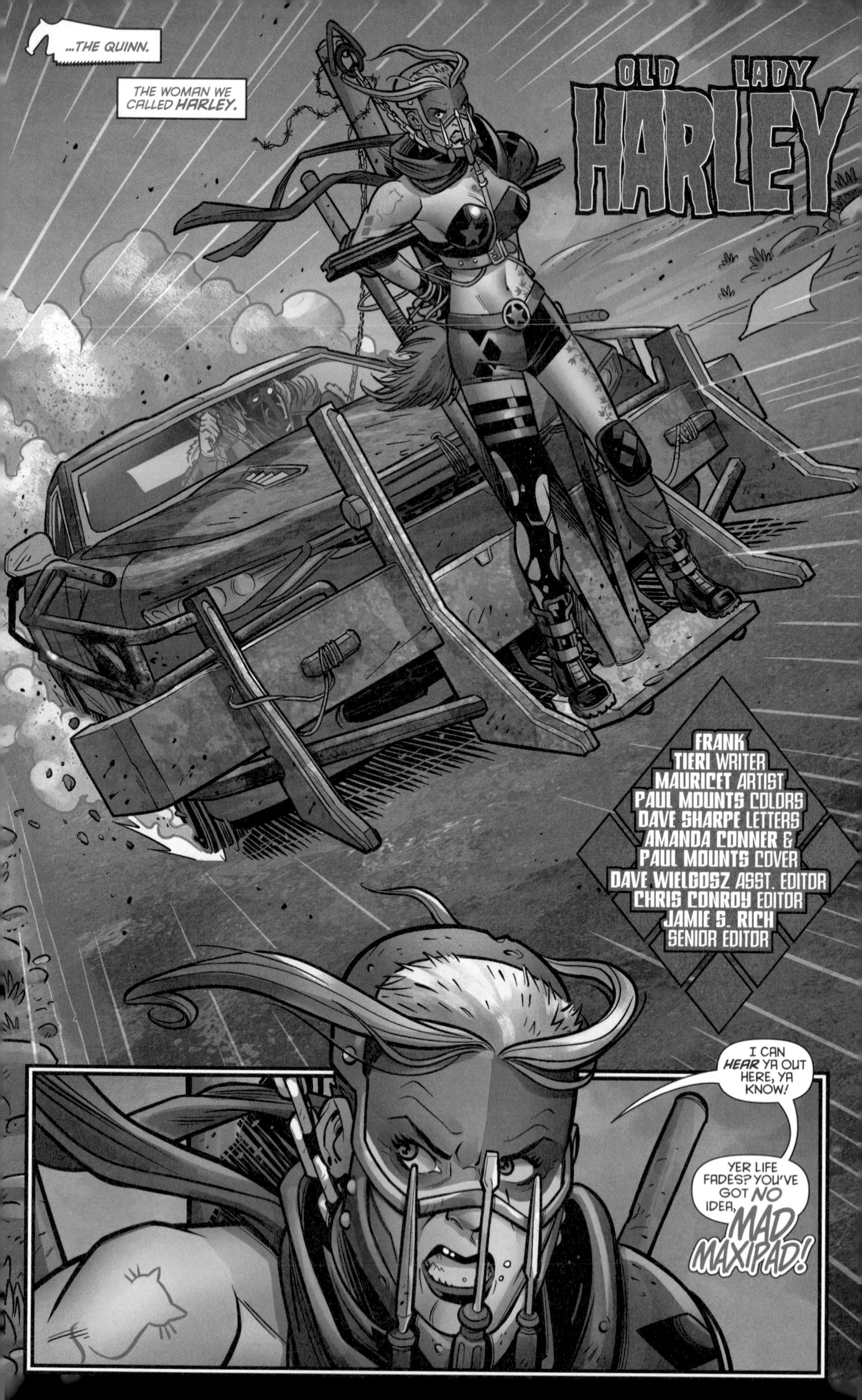
...THE QUINN.
THE WOMAN WE CALLED HARLEY.
OLD LADY HARLEY
FRANK TIERI WRITER
MAURICET ARTIST
PAUL MOUNTS COLORS
DAVE SHARPE LETTERS
AMANDA CONNER & PAUL MOUNTS COVER
DAVE WIELGOSZ ASST. EDITOR
CHRIS CONROY EDITOR
JAMIE S. RICH SENIOR EDITOR
I CAN HEAR YA OUT HERE, YA KNOW!
YER LIFE FADES? YOU'VE GOT NO IDEA, MAD MAXIPAD!

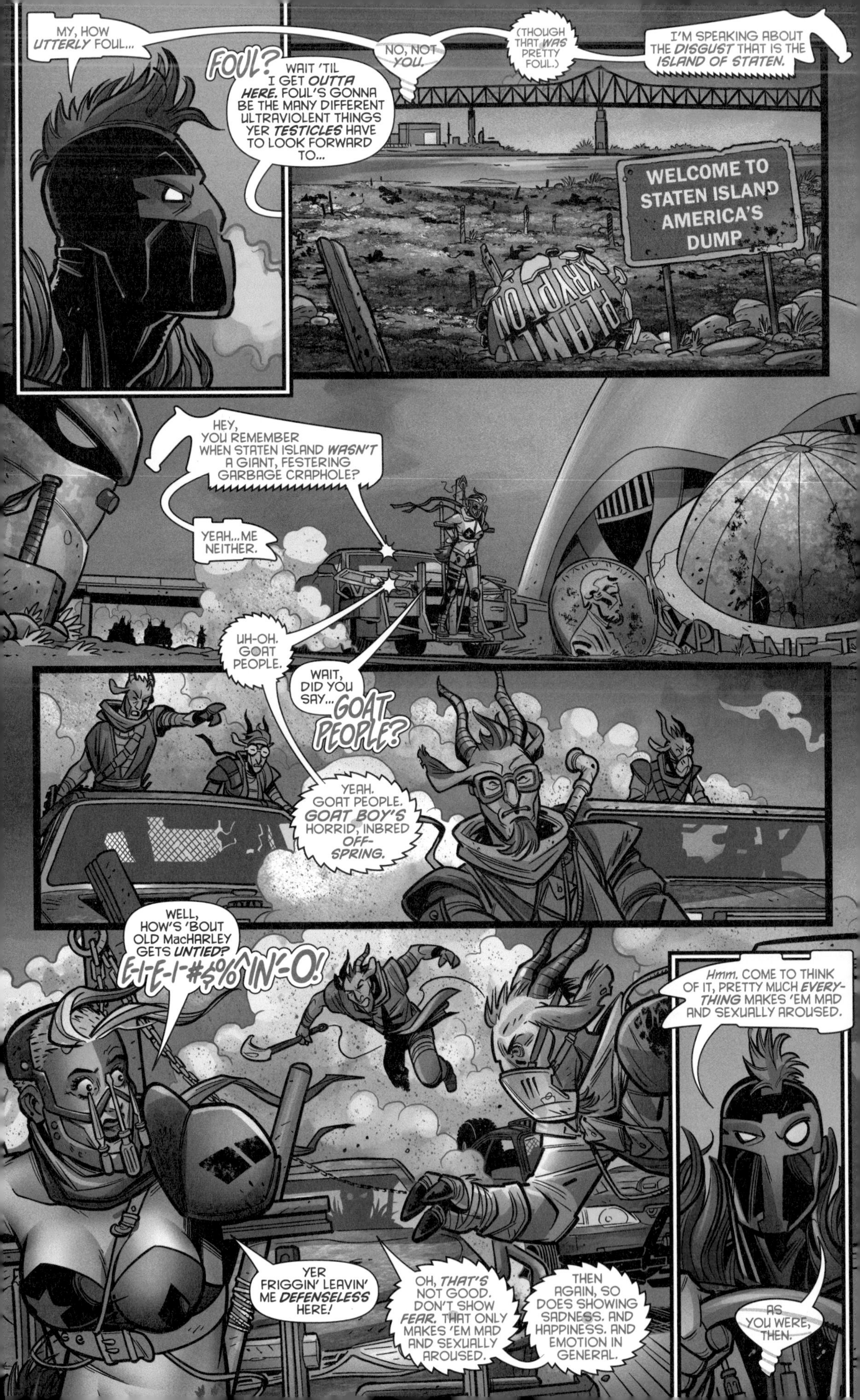

MY, HOW UTTERLY FOUL...
FOUL? WAIT 'TIL I GET OUTTA HERE. FOUL'S GONNA BE THE MANY DIFFERENT ULTRAVIOLENT THINGS YER TESTICLES HAVE TO LOOK FORWARD TO...
NO, NOT YOU.
(THOUGH THAT WAS PRETTY FOUL.)
I'M SPEAKING ABOUT THE DISGUST THAT IS THE ISLAND OF STATEN.
WELCOME TO STATEN ISLAND AMERICA'S DUMP
PLANET KRYPTON
HEY, YOU REMEMBER WHEN STATEN ISLAND WASN'T A GIANT, FESTERING GARBAGE CRAPHOLE?
YEAH...ME NEITHER.
UH-OH. GOAT PEOPLE.
WAIT, DID YOU SAY...GOAT PEOPLE?
YEAH. GOAT PEOPLE. GOAT BOY'S HORRID, INBRED OFF-SPRING.
WELL, HOW'S 'BOUT OLD MacHARLEY GETS UNTIED? E-I-E-I-#$%^IN'-O!
Hmm. COME TO THINK OF IT, PRETTY MUCH EVERY-THING MAKES 'EM MAD AND SEXUALLY AROUSED.
YER FRIGGIN' LEAVIN' ME DEFENSELESS HERE!
OH, THAT'S NOT GOOD. DON'T SHOW FEAR. THAT ONLY MAKES 'EM MAD AND SEXUALLY AROUSED.
THEN AGAIN, SO DOES SHOWING SADNESS. AND HAPPINESS. AND EMOTION IN GENERAL.
AS YOU WERE, THEN.

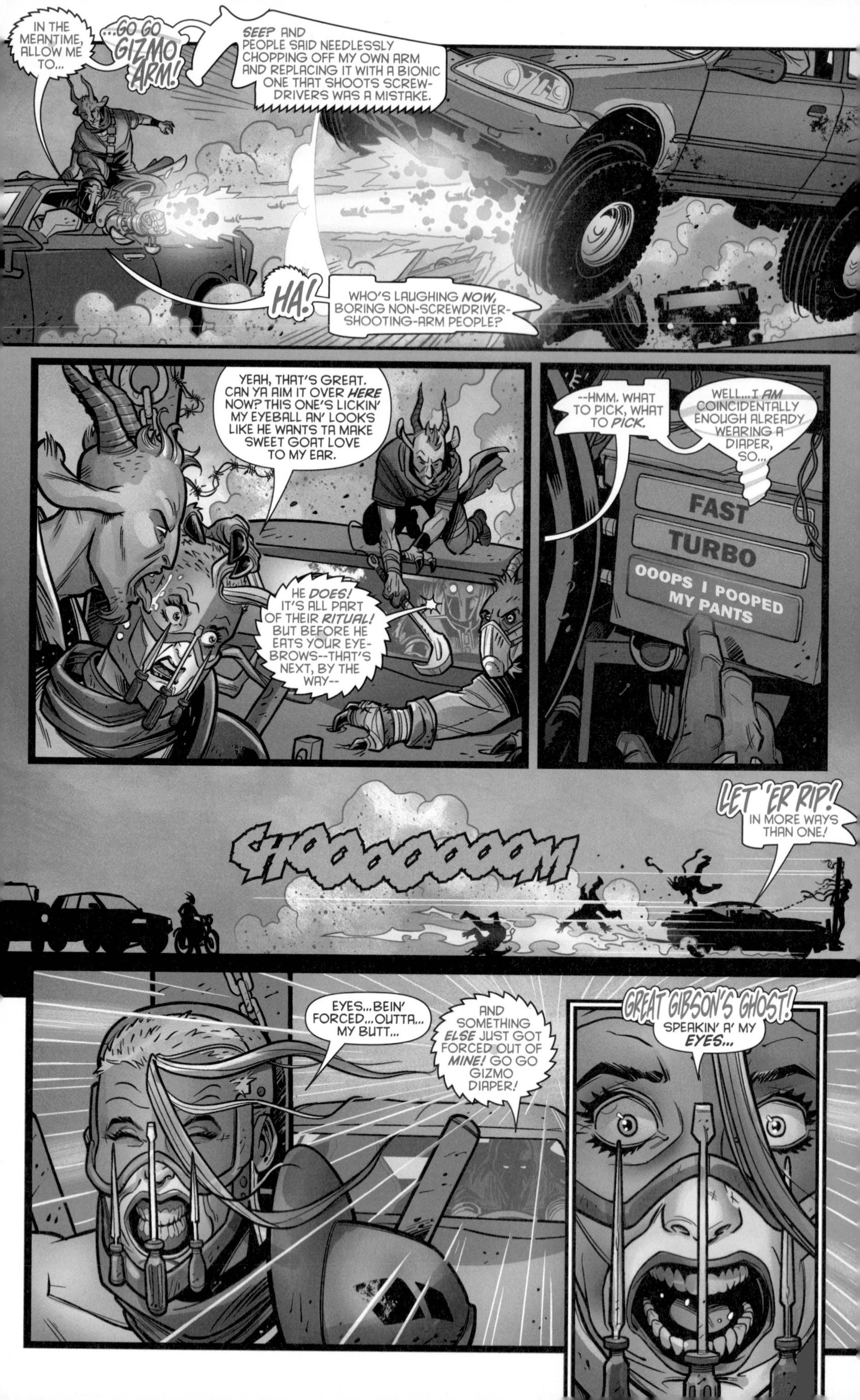
IN THE MEANTIME, ALLOW ME TO...
...GO GO GIZMO ARM!
SEE? AND PEOPLE SAID NEEDLESSLY CHOPPING OFF MY OWN ARM AND REPLACING IT WITH A BIONIC ONE THAT SHOOTS SCREW-DRIVERS WAS A MISTAKE.
HA!
WHO'S LAUGHING NOW, BORING NON-SCREWDRIVER-SHOOTING-ARM PEOPLE?
YEAH, THAT'S GREAT. CAN YA AIM IT OVER HERE NOW? THIS ONE'S LICKIN' MY EYEBALL AN' LOOKS LIKE HE WANTS TA MAKE SWEET GOAT LOVE TO MY EAR.
HE DOES! IT'S ALL PART OF THEIR RITUAL! BUT BEFORE HE EATS YOUR EYE-BROWS--THAT'S NEXT, BY THE WAY--
--HMM. WHAT TO PICK, WHAT TO PICK.
WELL...I AM COINCIDENTALLY ENOUGH ALREADY WEARING A DIAPER, SO...
FAST
TURBO
OOOPS I POOPED MY PANTS
SHOOOOOOOOM
LET 'ER RIP! IN MORE WAYS THAN ONE!
EYES...BEIN' FORCED...OUTTA... MY BUTT...
AND SOMETHING ELSE JUST GOT FORCED OUT OF MINE! GO GO GIZMO DIAPER!
GREAT GIBSON'S GHOST! SPEAKIN' A' MY EYES...

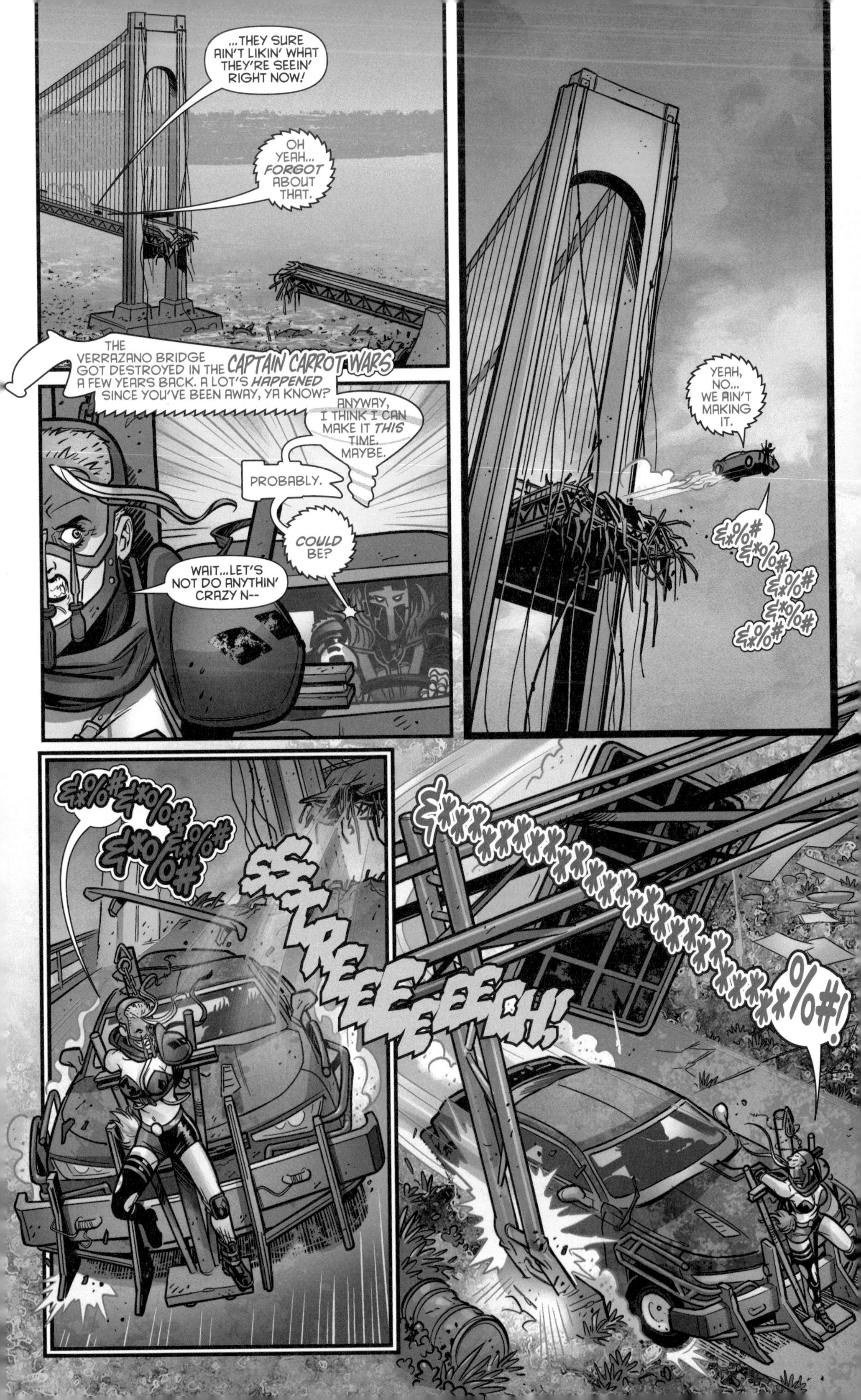
...THEY SURE AIN'T LIKIN' WHAT THEY'RE SEEIN' RIGHT NOW!
OH YEAH... FORGOT ABOUT THAT.
THE VERRAZANO BRIDGE GOT DESTROYED IN THE CAPTAIN CARROT WARS A FEW YEARS BACK. A LOT'S HAPPENED SINCE YOU'VE BEEN AWAY, YA KNOW?
ANYWAY, I THINK I CAN MAKE IT THIS TIME. MAYBE.
PROBABLY.
COULD BE?
WAIT...LET'S NOT DO ANYTHIN' CRAZY N--
YEAH, NO... WE AIN'T MAKING IT.
&*%# &*%# &*%# &*%# &*%#
&*%#&*%# &*%#&*%#
SSSCREEEEEEECH!
&***************************%#!

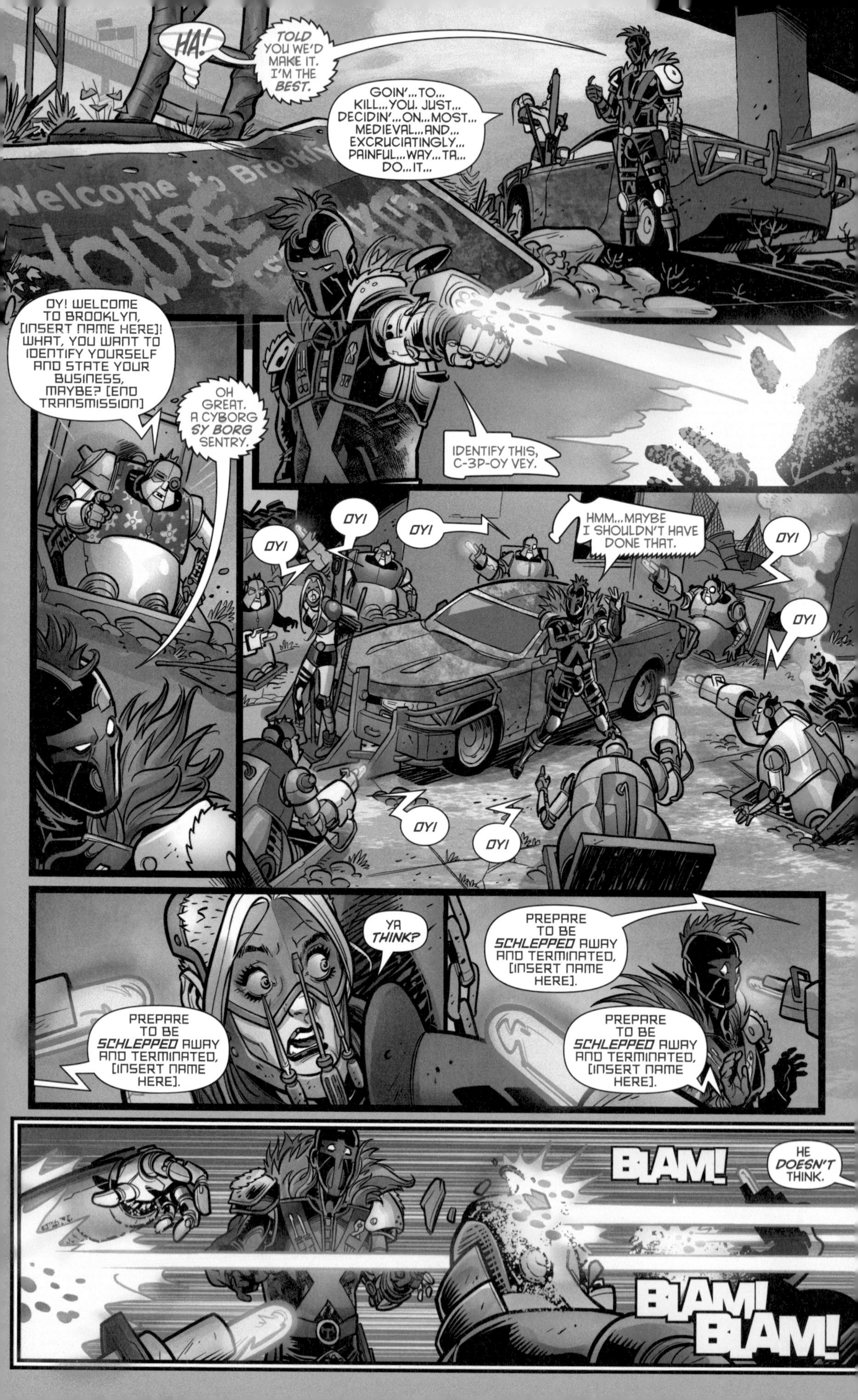
HA!
TOLD YOU WE'D MAKE IT. I'M THE BEST.
GOIN'...TO...KILL...YOU. JUST...DECIDIN'...ON...MOST...MEDIEVAL...AND...EXCRUCIATINGLY...PAINFUL...WAY...TA...DO...IT...
Welcome to Brooklyn
OY! WELCOME TO BROOKLYN, [INSERT NAME HERE]! WHAT, YOU WANT TO IDENTIFY YOURSELF AND STATE YOUR BUSINESS, MAYBE? [END TRANSMISSION]
OH GREAT. A CYBORG SY BORG SENTRY.
IDENTIFY THIS, C-3P-OY VEY.
OY!
OY!
OY!
HMM...MAYBE I SHOULDN'T HAVE DONE THAT.
OY!
OY!
OY!
OY!
YA THINK?
PREPARE TO BE SCHLEPPED AWAY AND TERMINATED, [INSERT NAME HERE].
PREPARE TO BE SCHLEPPED AWAY AND TERMINATED, [INSERT NAME HERE].
PREPARE TO BE SCHLEPPED AWAY AND TERMINATED, [INSERT NAME HERE].
BLAM!
HE DOESN'T THINK.
BLAM! BLAM!

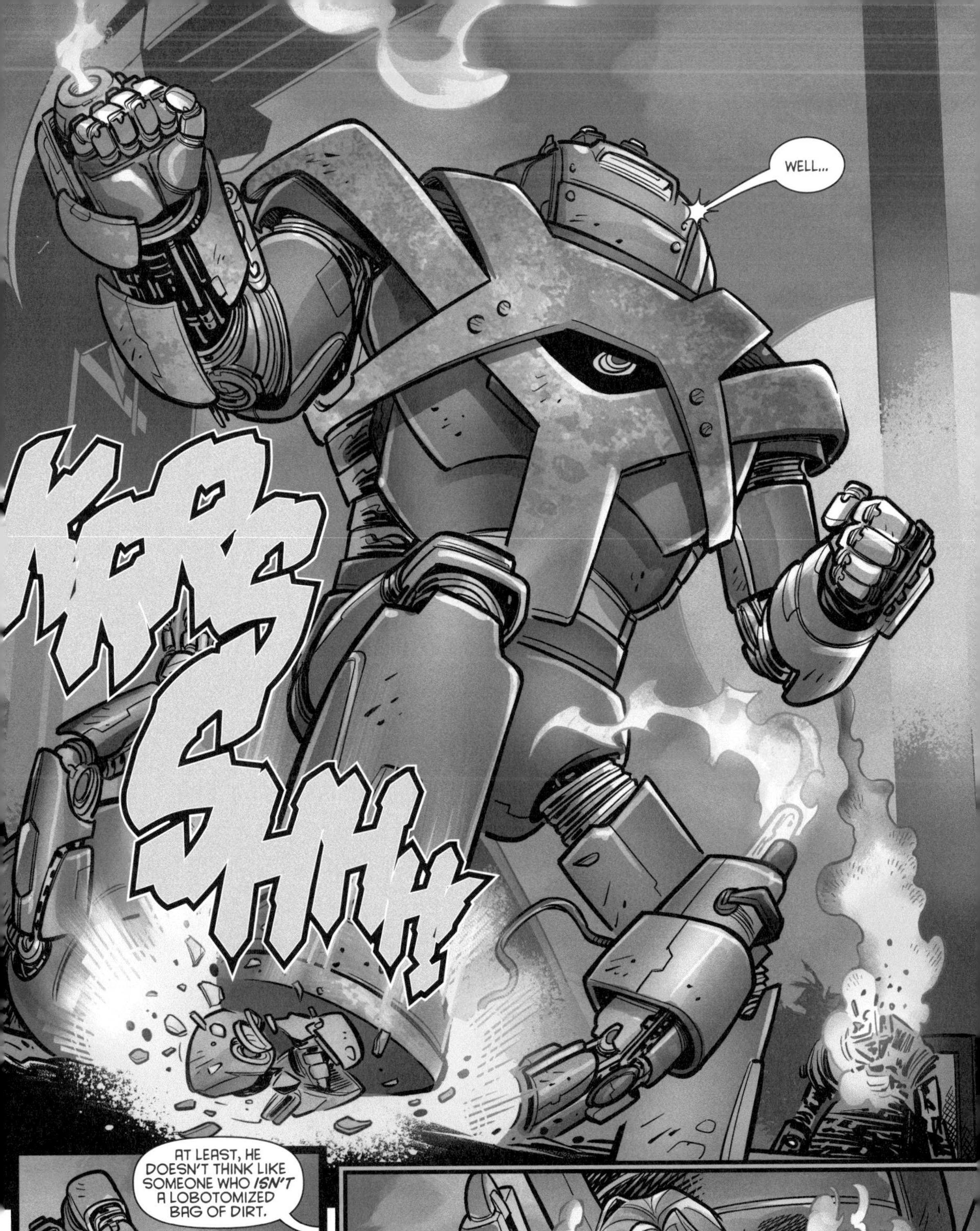
WELL...
KRRSHHH

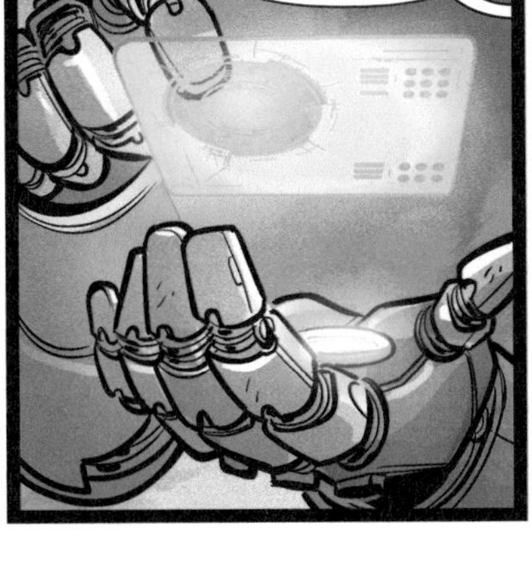
AT LEAST, HE DOESN'T THINK LIKE SOMEONE WHO *ISN'T* A LOBOTOMIZED BAG OF DIRT.

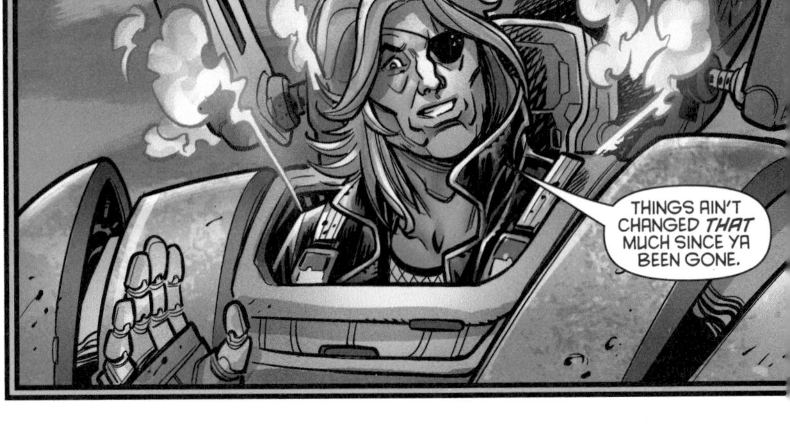
THINGS AIN'T CHANGED *THAT* MUCH SINCE YA BEEN GONE.

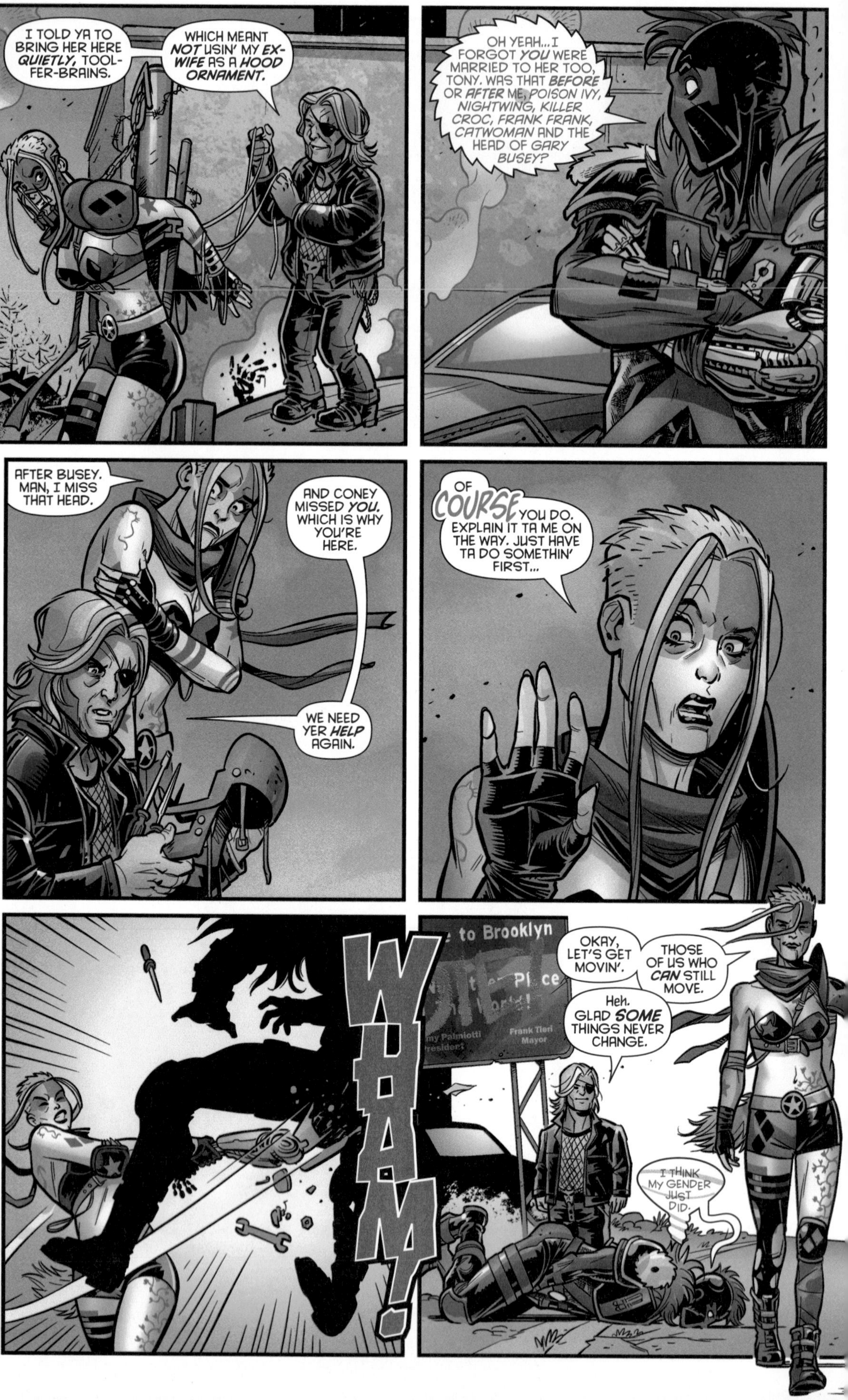
I TOLD YA TO BRING HER HERE QUIETLY, TOOL-FER-BRAINS.
WHICH MEANT NOT USIN' MY EX-WIFE AS A HOOD ORNAMENT.
OH YEAH... I FORGOT YOU WERE MARRIED TO HER TOO, TONY. WAS THAT BEFORE OR AFTER ME, POISON IVY, NIGHTWING, KILLER CROC, FRANK FRANK, CATWOMAN AND THE HEAD OF GARY BUSEY?
AFTER BUSEY. MAN, I MISS THAT HEAD.
AND CONEY MISSED YOU. WHICH IS WHY YOU'RE HERE.
WE NEED YER HELP AGAIN.
OF COURSE YOU DO. EXPLAIN IT TA ME ON THE WAY. JUST HAVE TA DO SOMETHIN' FIRST...
WHAM!
to Brooklyn
Frank Tieri
Mayor
OKAY, LET'S GET MOVIN'.
THOSE OF US WHO CAN STILL MOVE.
Heh. GLAD SOME THINGS NEVER CHANGE.
I THINK MY GENDER JUST DID.

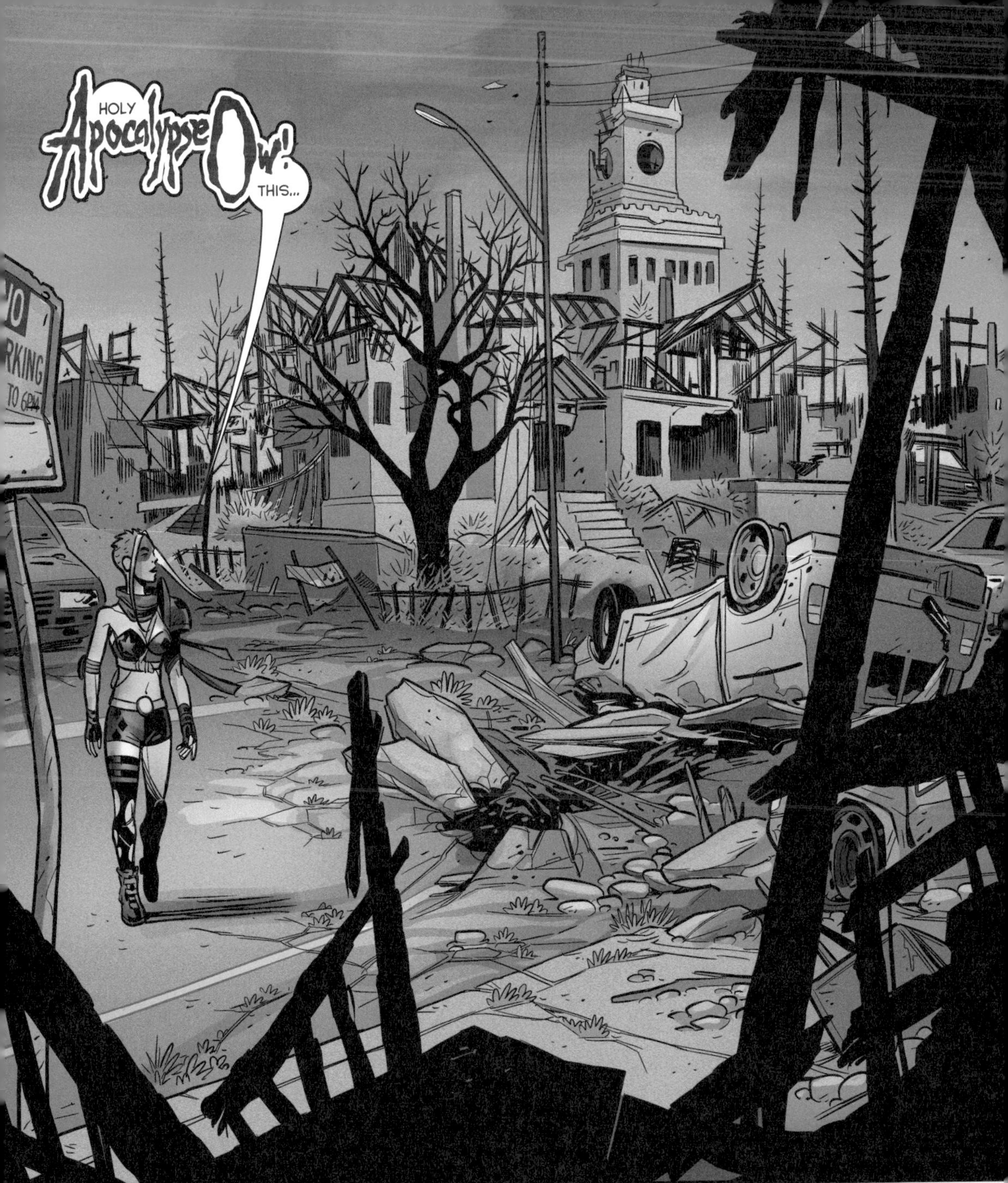
HOLY Apocalypse Ow! THIS...

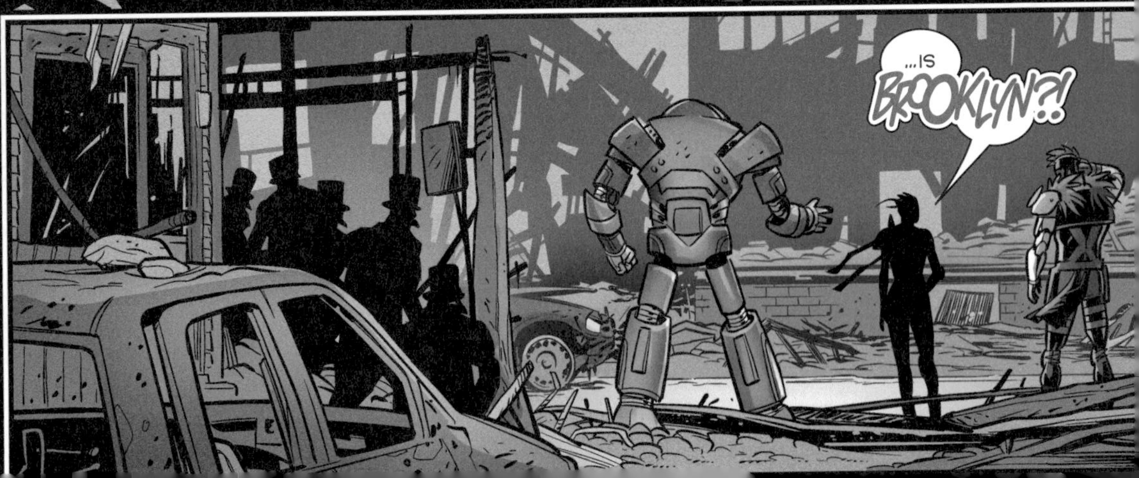
...IS BROOKLYN?!

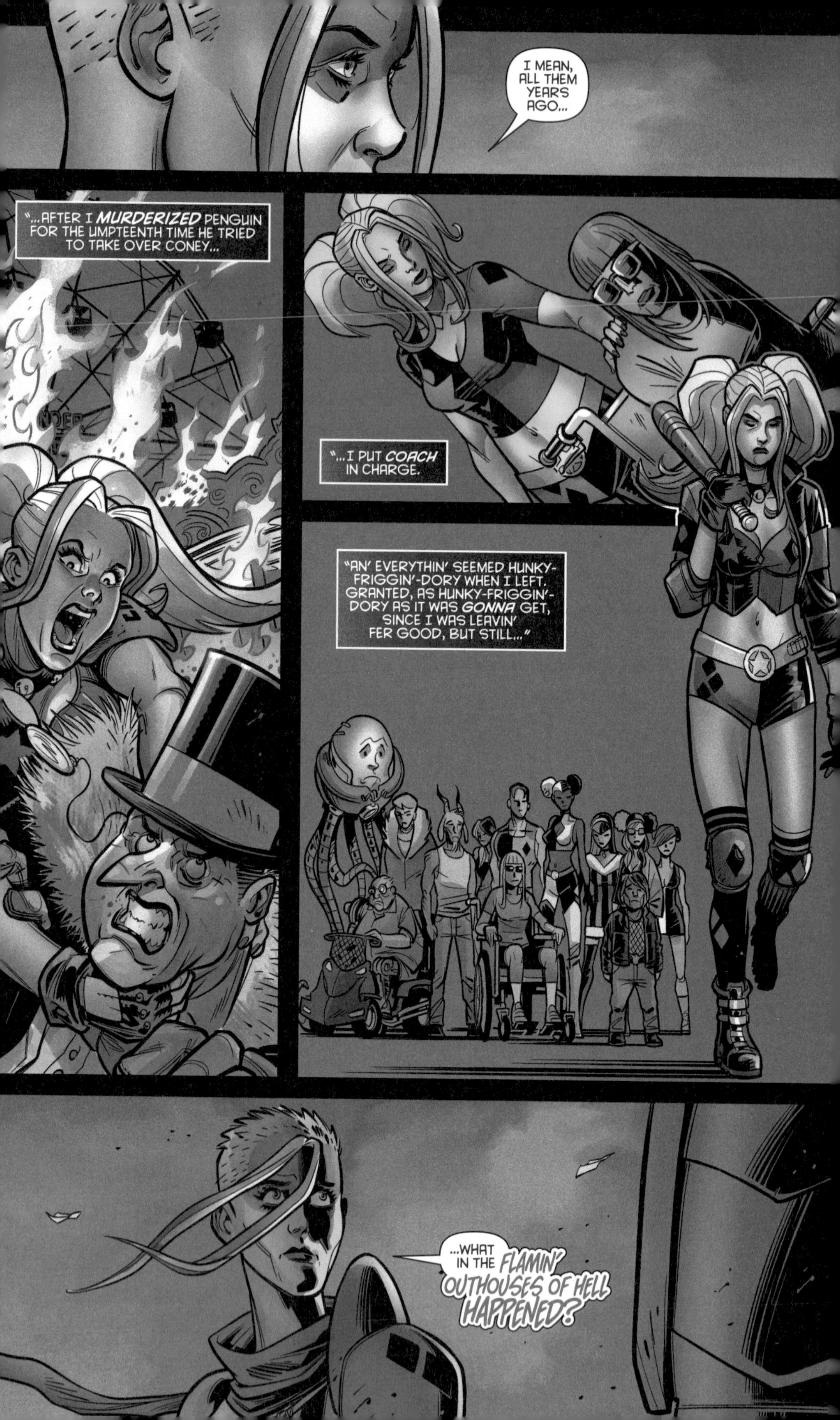
I MEAN, ALL THEM YEARS AGO...
"...AFTER I MURDERIZED PENGUIN FOR THE UMPTEENTH TIME HE TRIED TO TAKE OVER CONEY...
"...I PUT COACH IN CHARGE.
"AN' EVERYTHIN' SEEMED HUNKY-FRIGGIN'-DORY WHEN I LEFT. GRANTED, AS HUNKY-FRIGGIN'-DORY AS IT WAS GONNA GET, SINCE I WAS LEAVIN' FER GOOD, BUT STILL..."
...WHAT IN THE FLAMIN' OUTHOUSES OF HELL HAPPENED?

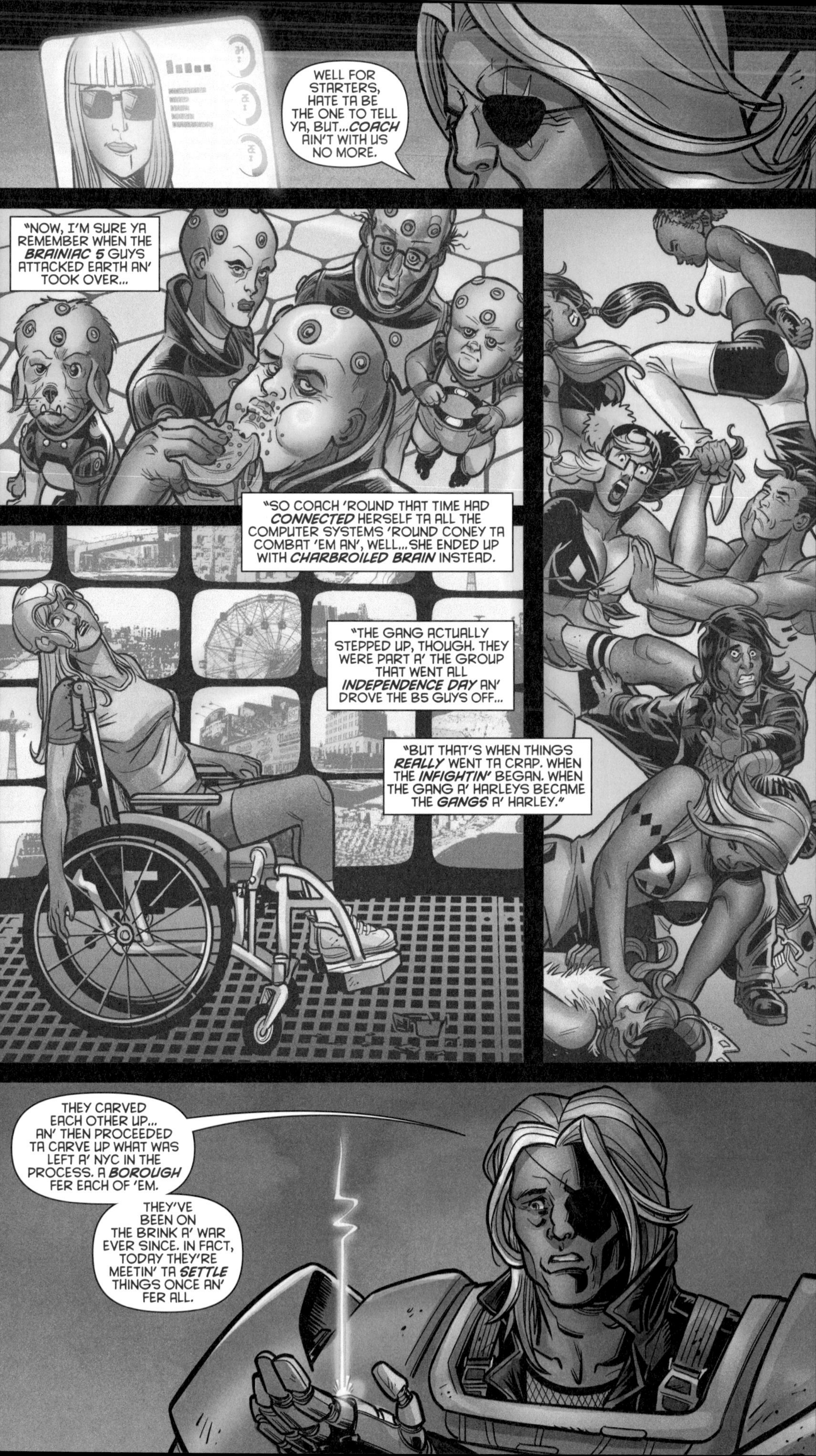

WELL FOR STARTERS, HATE TA BE THE ONE TO TELL YA, BUT...COACH AIN'T WITH US NO MORE.
"NOW, I'M SURE YA REMEMBER WHEN THE BRAINIAC 5 GUYS ATTACKED EARTH AN' TOOK OVER...
"SO COACH 'ROUND THAT TIME HAD CONNECTED HERSELF TA ALL THE COMPUTER SYSTEMS 'ROUND CONEY TA COMBAT 'EM AN', WELL...SHE ENDED UP WITH CHARBROILED BRAIN INSTEAD.
"THE GANG ACTUALLY STEPPED UP, THOUGH. THEY WERE PART A' THE GROUP THAT WENT ALL INDEPENDENCE DAY AN' DROVE THE B5 GUYS OFF...
"BUT THAT'S WHEN THINGS REALLY WENT TA CRAP. WHEN THE INFIGHTIN' BEGAN. WHEN THE GANG A' HARLEYS BECAME THE GANGS A' HARLEY."
THEY CARVED EACH OTHER UP... AN' THEN PROCEEDED TA CARVE UP WHAT WAS LEFT A' NYC IN THE PROCESS. A BOROUGH FER EACH OF 'EM.
THEY'VE BEEN ON THE BRINK A' WAR EVER SINCE. IN FACT, TODAY THEY'RE MEETIN' TA SETTLE THINGS ONCE AN' FER ALL.

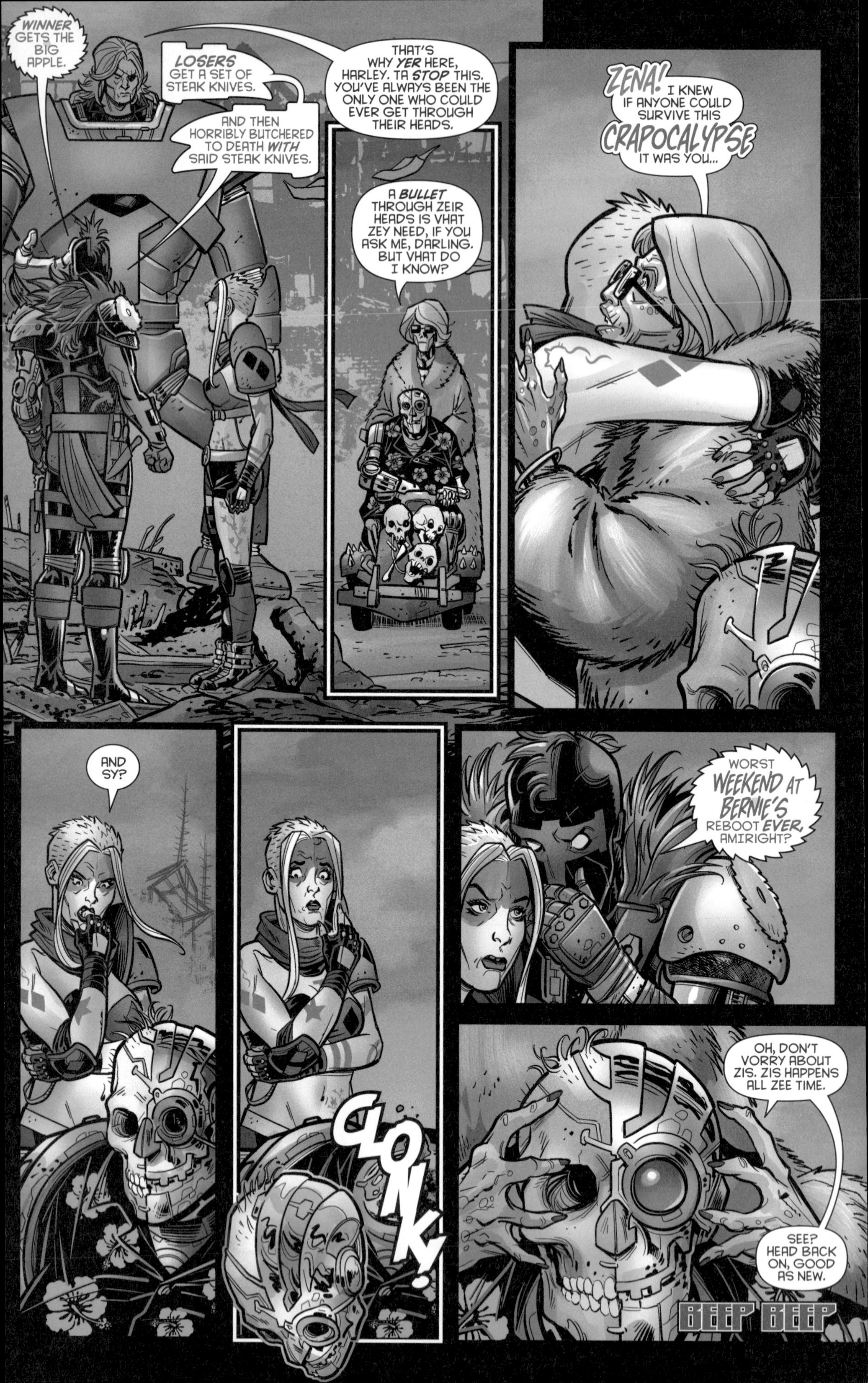
WINNER GETS THE BIG APPLE.
LOSERS GET A SET OF STEAK KNIVES.
AND THEN HORRIBLY BUTCHERED TO DEATH WITH SAID STEAK KNIVES.
THAT'S WHY YER HERE, HARLEY. TA STOP THIS. YOU'VE ALWAYS BEEN THE ONLY ONE WHO COULD EVER GET THROUGH THEIR HEADS.
A BULLET THROUGH ZEIR HEADS IS VHAT ZEY NEED, IF YOU ASK ME, DARLING. BUT VHAT DO I KNOW?
ZENA! I KNEW IF ANYONE COULD SURVIVE THIS CRAPOCALYPSE IT WAS YOU...
AND SY?
CLONK!
WORST WEEKEND AT BERNIE'S REBOOT EVER, AMIRIGHT?
OH, DON'T VORRY ABOUT ZIS. ZIS HAPPENS ALL ZEE TIME.
SEE? HEAD BACK ON, GOOD AS NEW.
BEEP BEEP

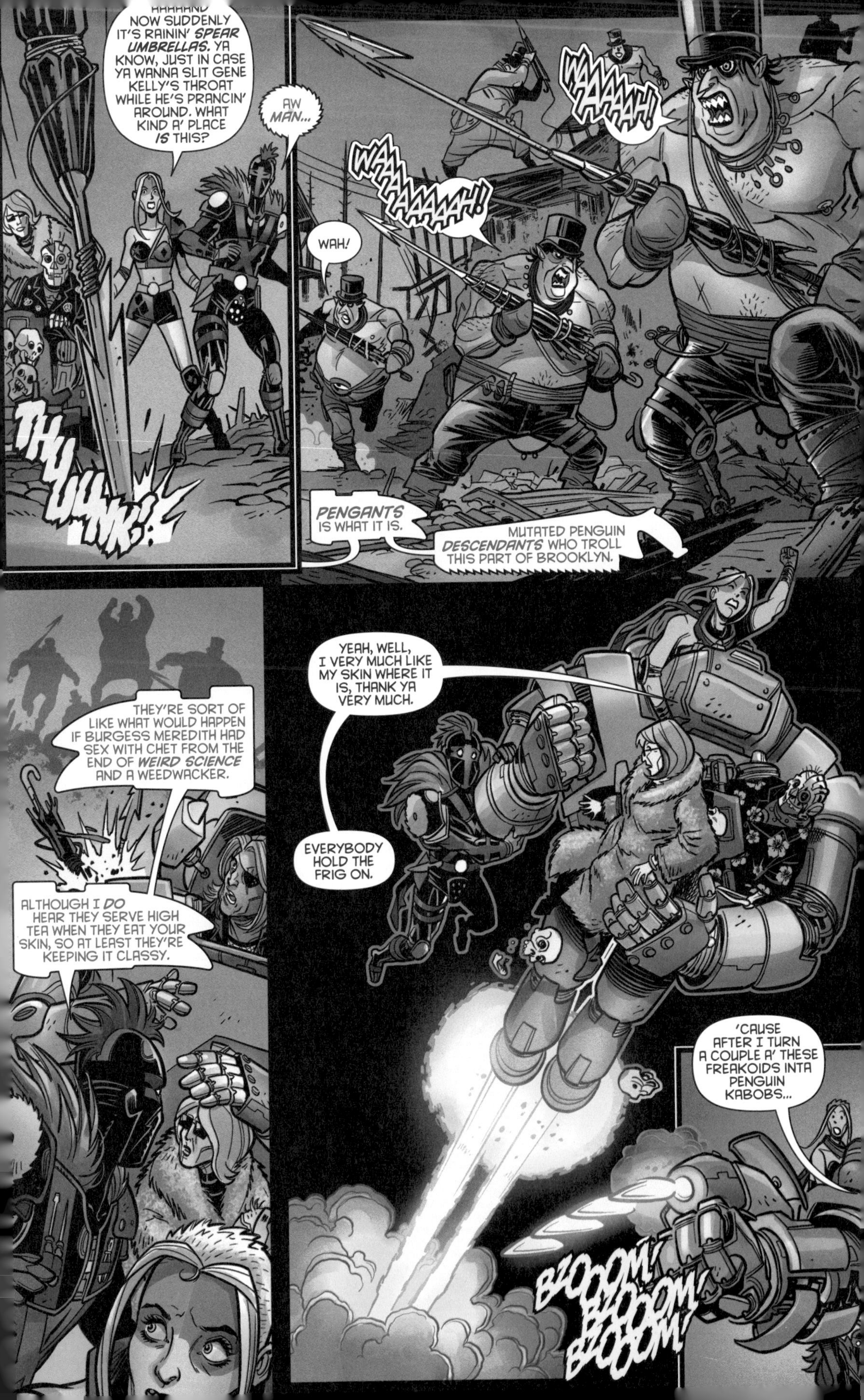
AAAAAAND NOW SUDDENLY IT'S RAININ' SPEAR UMBRELLAS. YA KNOW, JUST IN CASE YA WANNA SLIT GENE KELLY'S THROAT WHILE HE'S PRANCIN' AROUND. WHAT KIND A' PLACE IS THIS?
AW MAN...
THUUNK!
WAAAAAH!
WAAAAAAAAAH!
WAH!
PENGANTS IS WHAT IT IS.
MUTATED PENGUIN DESCENDANTS WHO TROLL THIS PART OF BROOKLYN.
THEY'RE SORT OF LIKE WHAT WOULD HAPPEN IF BURGESS MEREDITH HAD SEX WITH CHET FROM THE END OF WEIRD SCIENCE AND A WEEDWACKER.
ALTHOUGH I DO HEAR THEY SERVE HIGH TEA WHEN THEY EAT YOUR SKIN, SO AT LEAST THEY'RE KEEPING IT CLASSY.
YEAH, WELL, I VERY MUCH LIKE MY SKIN WHERE IT IS, THANK YA VERY MUCH.
EVERYBODY HOLD THE FRIG ON.
'CAUSE AFTER I TURN A COUPLE A' THESE FREAKOIDS INTA PENGUIN KABOBS...
BZOOOM! BZOOOM! BZOOOM!

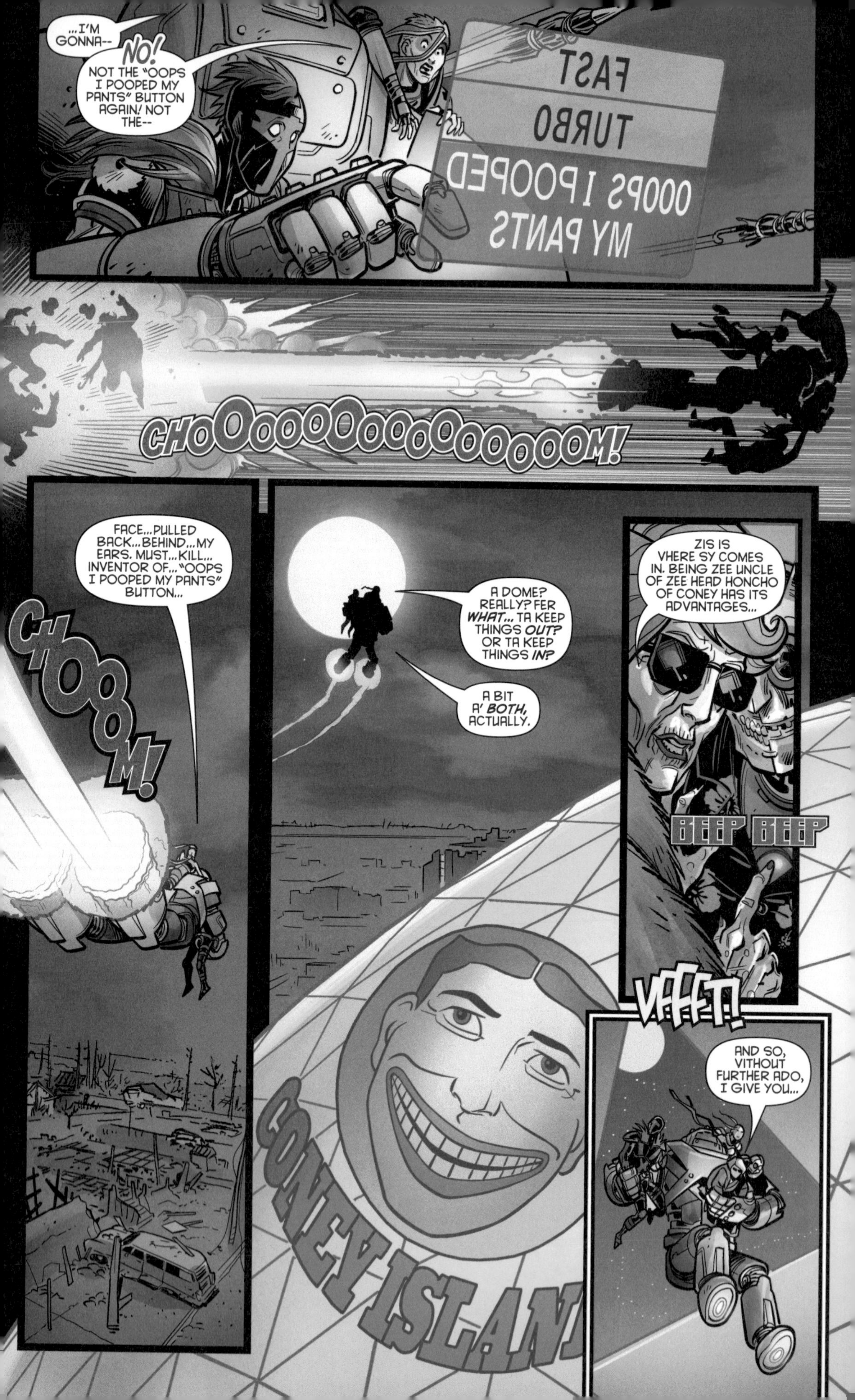
...I'M GONNA--
NO! NOT THE "OOPS I POOPED MY PANTS" BUTTON AGAIN! NOT THE--
FAST
TURBO
OOOPS I POOPED MY PANTS
CHOOOOOOOOOOOOOOOOM!
FACE...PULLED BACK...BEHIND...MY EARS. MUST...KILL... INVENTOR OF..."OOPS I POOPED MY PANTS" BUTTON...
CHOOOM!
A DOME? REALLY? FER WHAT... TA KEEP THINGS OUT? OR TA KEEP THINGS IN?
A BIT A' BOTH, ACTUALLY.
ZIS IS VHERE SY COMES IN. BEING ZEE UNCLE OF ZEE HEAD HONCHO OF CONEY HAS ITS ADVANTAGES...
BEEP BEEP
VFFFT!
AND SO, VITHOUT FURTHER ADO, I GIVE YOU...
CONEY ISLAN

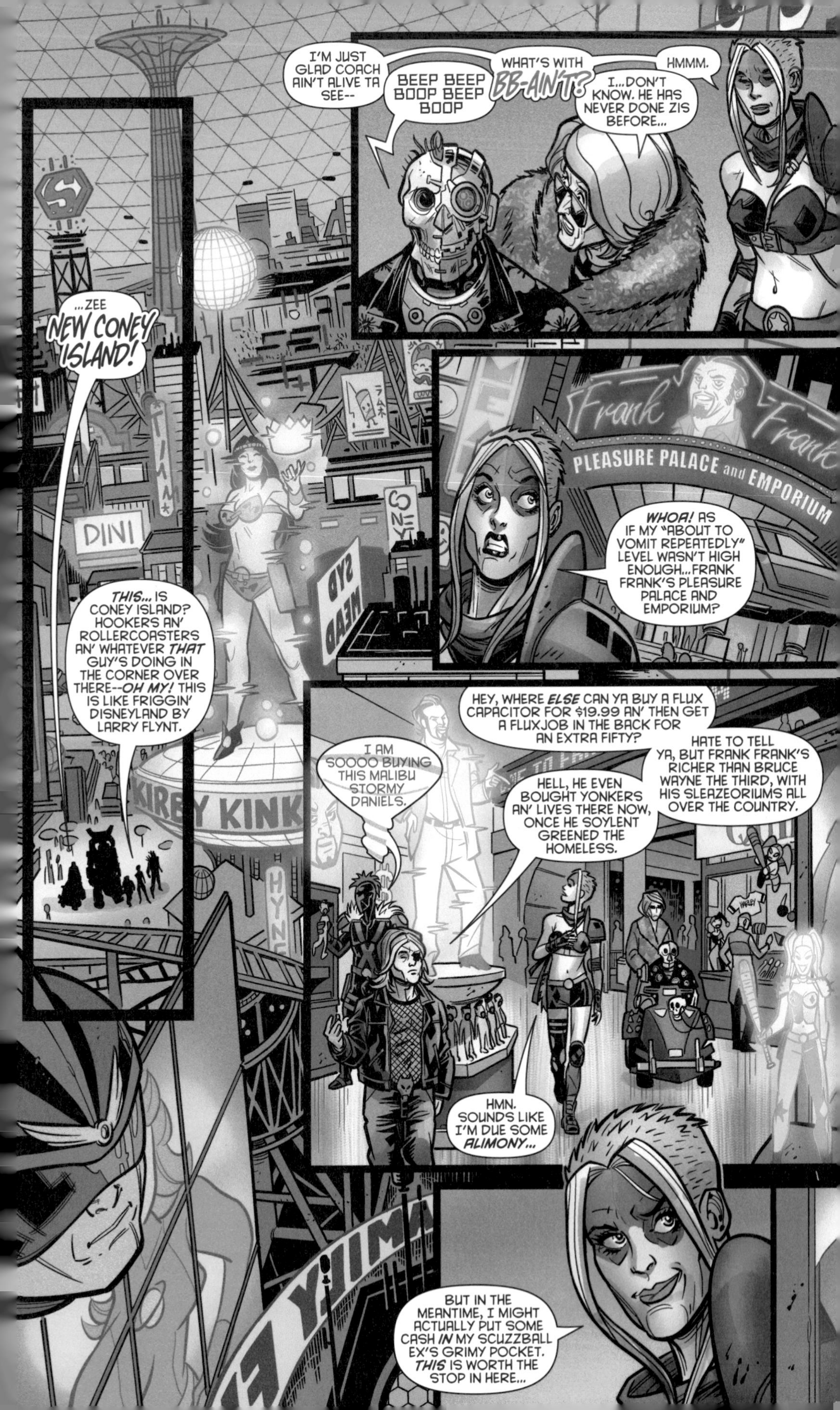
...ZEE
NEW CONEY ISLAND!
I'M JUST GLAD COACH AIN'T ALIVE TA SEE--
BEEP BEEP BOOP BEEP BOOP
WHAT'S WITH BB-AIN'T?
HMMM.
I...DON'T KNOW. HE HAS NEVER DONE ZIS BEFORE...
DINI
SYD MEAD
KIRBY KINK
Frank Frank
PLEASURE PALACE and EMPORIUM
WHOA! AS IF MY "ABOUT TO VOMIT REPEATEDLY" LEVEL WASN'T HIGH ENOUGH...FRANK FRANK'S PLEASURE PALACE AND EMPORIUM?
THIS... IS CONEY ISLAND? HOOKERS AN' ROLLERCOASTERS AN' WHATEVER THAT GUY'S DOING IN THE CORNER OVER THERE--OH MY! THIS IS LIKE FRIGGIN' DISNEYLAND BY LARRY FLYNT.
HEY, WHERE ELSE CAN YA BUY A FLUX CAPACITOR FOR $19.99 AN' THEN GET A FLUXJOB IN THE BACK FOR AN EXTRA FIFTY?
I AM SOOOO BUYING THIS MALIBU STORMY DANIELS.
HATE TO TELL YA, BUT FRANK FRANK'S RICHER THAN BRUCE WAYNE THE THIRD, WITH HIS SLEAZEORIUMS ALL OVER THE COUNTRY.
HELL, HE EVEN BOUGHT YONKERS AN' LIVES THERE NOW, ONCE HE SOYLENT GREENED THE HOMELESS.
HMN. SOUNDS LIKE I'M DUE SOME ALIMONY...
BUT IN THE MEANTIME, I MIGHT ACTUALLY PUT SOME CASH IN MY SCUZZBALL EX'S GRIMY POCKET. THIS IS WORTH THE STOP IN HERE...

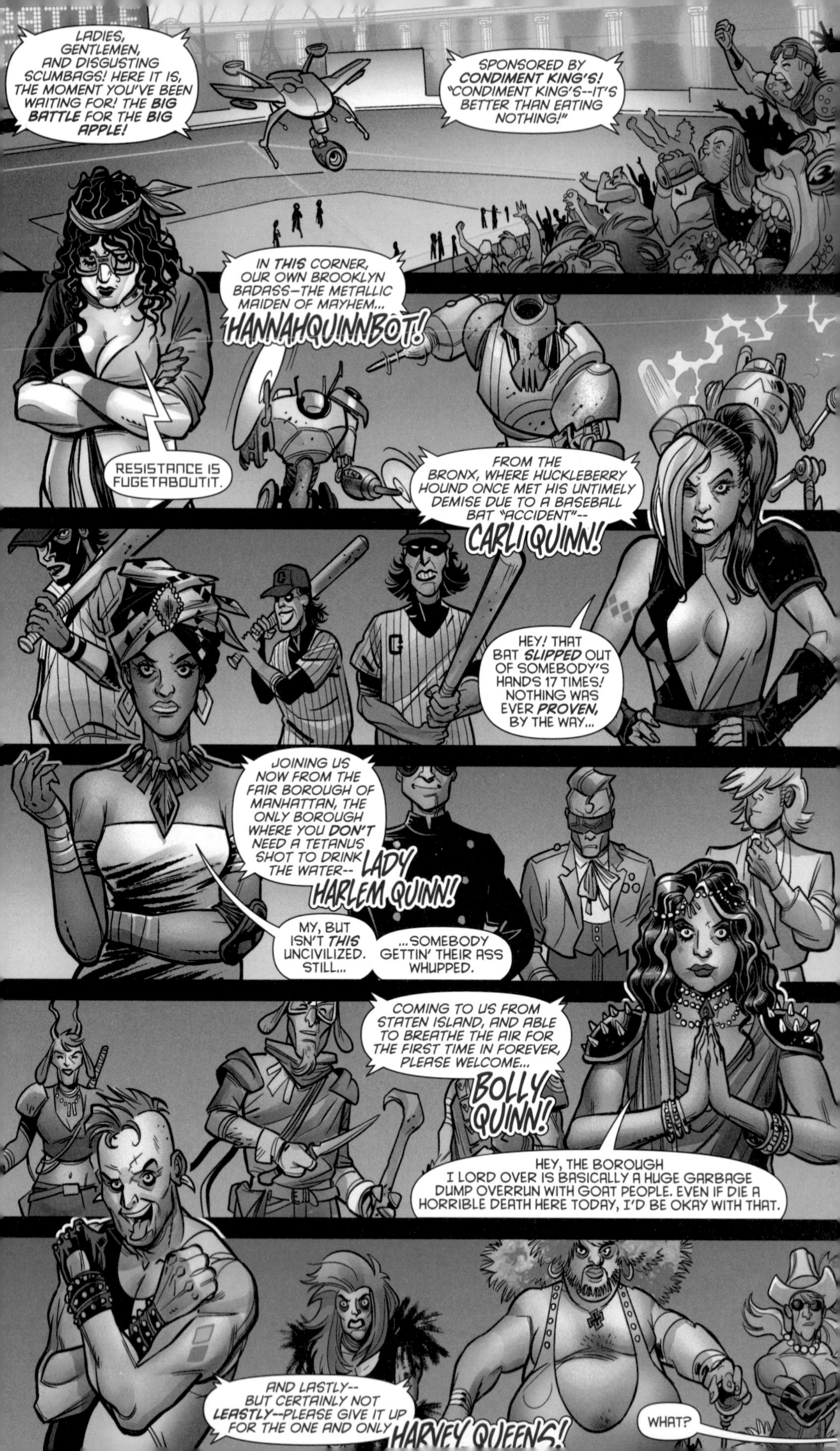
LADIES, GENTLEMEN, AND DISGUSTING SCUMBAGS! HERE IT IS, THE MOMENT YOU'VE BEEN WAITING FOR! THE BIG BATTLE FOR THE BIG APPLE!
SPONSORED BY CONDIMENT KING'S! "CONDIMENT KING'S--IT'S BETTER THAN EATING NOTHING!"
IN THIS CORNER, OUR OWN BROOKLYN BADASS—THE METALLIC MAIDEN OF MAYHEM...
HANNAHQUINNBOT!
RESISTANCE IS FUGETABOUTIT.
FROM THE BRONX, WHERE HUCKLEBERRY HOUND ONCE MET HIS UNTIMELY DEMISE DUE TO A BASEBALL BAT "ACCIDENT"--
CARLI QUINN!
HEY! THAT BAT SLIPPED OUT OF SOMEBODY'S HANDS 17 TIMES! NOTHING WAS EVER PROVEN, BY THE WAY...
JOINING US NOW FROM THE FAIR BOROUGH OF MANHATTAN, THE ONLY BOROUGH WHERE YOU DON'T NEED A TETANUS SHOT TO DRINK THE WATER--
LADY HARLEM QUINN!
MY, BUT ISN'T THIS UNCIVILIZED. STILL...
...SOMEBODY GETTIN' THEIR ASS WHUPPED.
COMING TO US FROM STATEN ISLAND, AND ABLE TO BREATHE THE AIR FOR THE FIRST TIME IN FOREVER, PLEASE WELCOME...
BOLLY QUINN!
HEY, THE BOROUGH I LORD OVER IS BASICALLY A HUGE GARBAGE DUMP OVERRUN WITH GOAT PEOPLE. EVEN IF DIE A HORRIBLE DEATH HERE TODAY, I'D BE OKAY WITH THAT.
AND LASTLY-- BUT CERTAINLY NOT LEASTLY--PLEASE GIVE IT UP FOR THE ONE AND ONLY
HARVEY QUEENS!
WHAT?

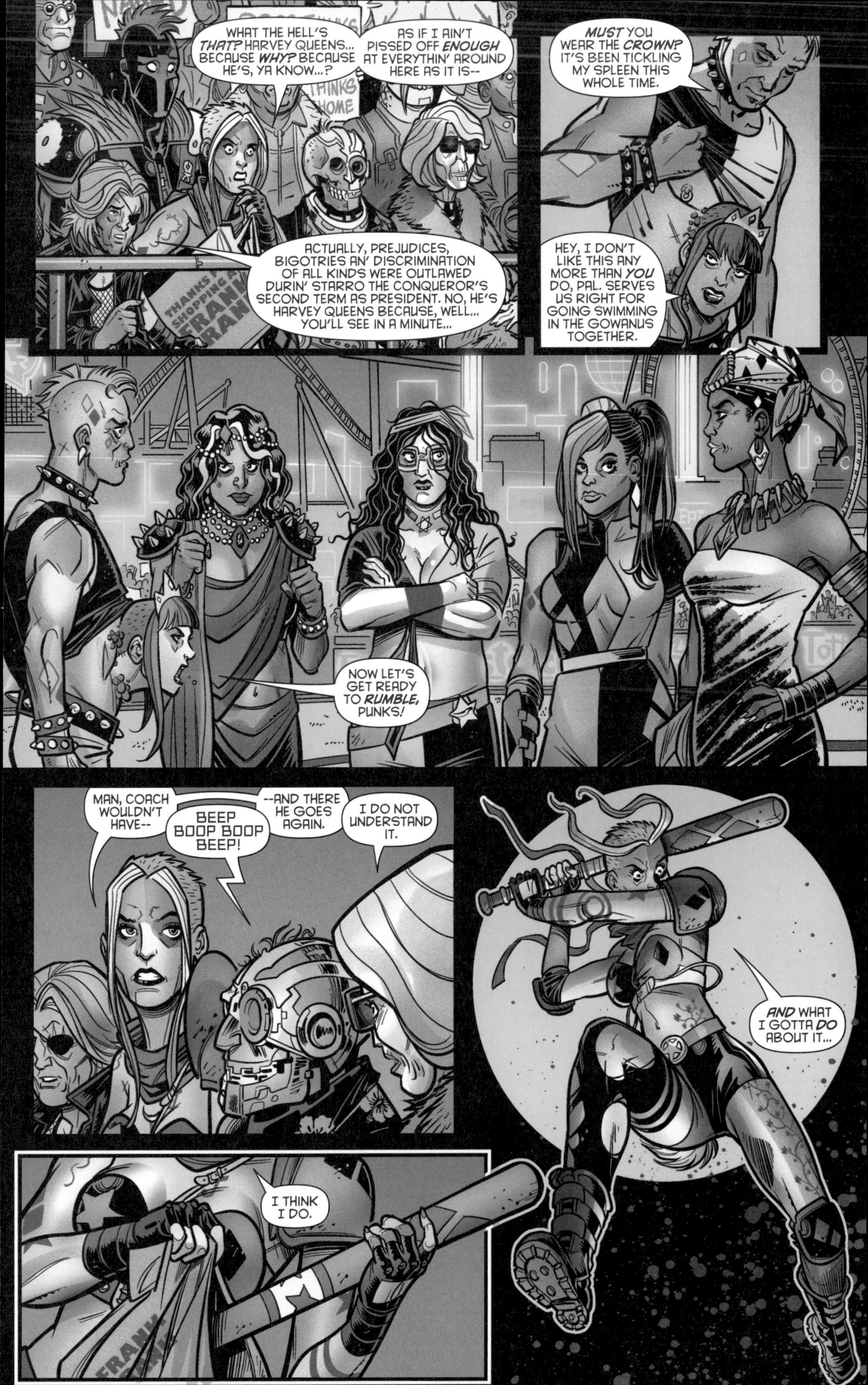
WHAT THE HELL'S *THAT?* HARVEY QUEENS... BECAUSE *WHY?* BECAUSE HE'S, YA KNOW...?
AS IF I AIN'T PISSED OFF *ENOUGH* AT EVERYTHIN' AROUND HERE AS IT IS--
ACTUALLY, PREJUDICES, BIGOTRIES AN' DISCRIMINATION OF ALL KINDS WERE OUTLAWED DURIN' STARRO THE CONQUEROR'S SECOND TERM AS PRESIDENT. NO, HE'S HARVEY QUEENS BECAUSE, WELL... YOU'LL SEE IN A MINUTE...
MUST YOU WEAR THE *CROWN?* IT'S BEEN TICKLING MY SPLEEN THIS WHOLE TIME.
HEY, I DON'T LIKE THIS ANY MORE THAN *YOU* DO, PAL. SERVES US RIGHT FOR GOING SWIMMING IN THE GOWANUS TOGETHER.
NOW LET'S GET READY TO *RUMBLE,* PUNKS!
MAN, COACH WOULDN'T HAVE--
BEEP BOOP BOOP BEEP!
--AND THERE HE GOES AGAIN.
I DO NOT UNDERSTAND IT.
AND WHAT I GOTTA *DO* ABOUT IT...
I THINK I DO.

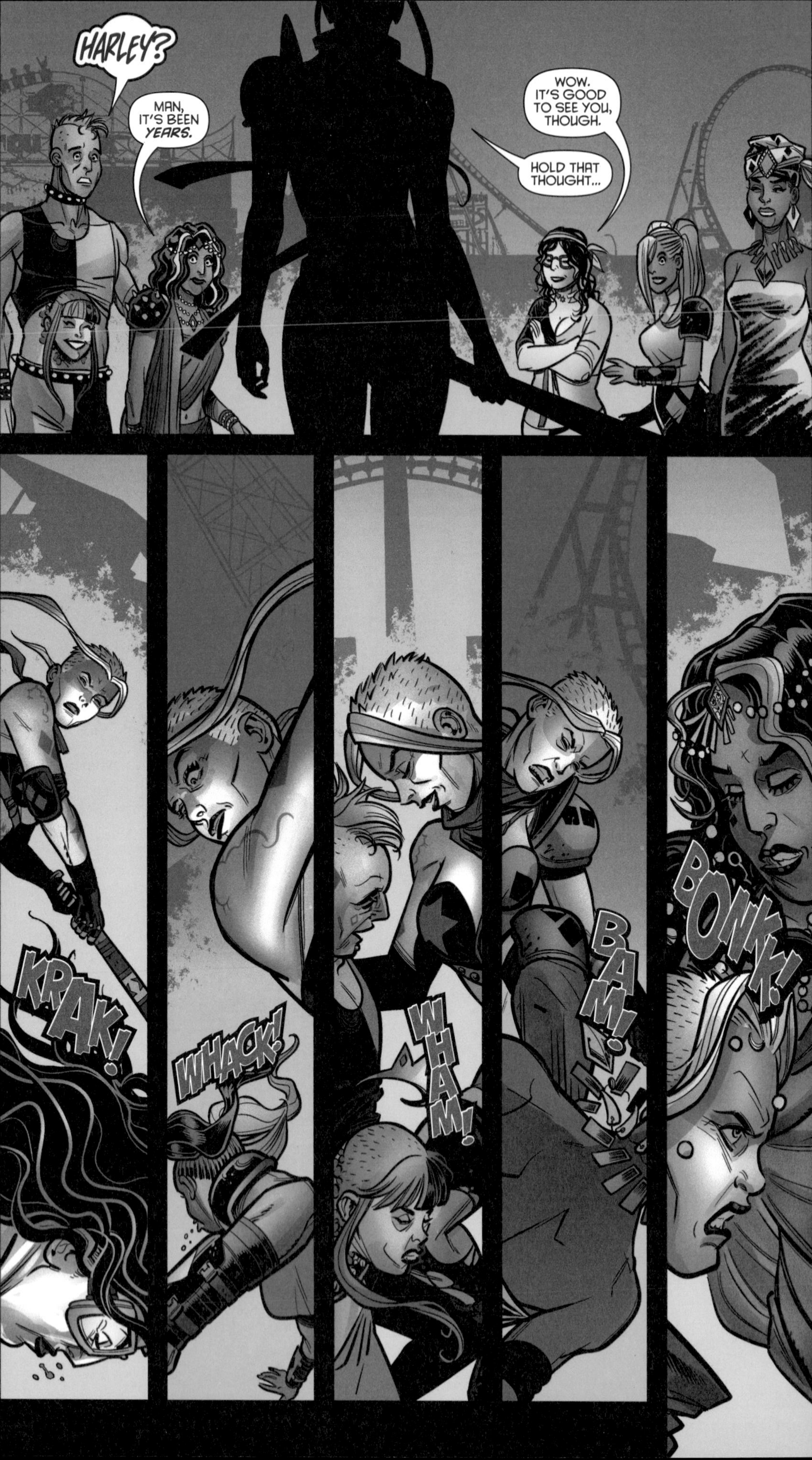
HARLEY?
MAN, IT'S BEEN YEARS.
WOW. IT'S GOOD TO SEE YOU, THOUGH.
HOLD THAT THOUGHT...
KRAK!
WHACK!
WHAM!
BAM!
BONKK!

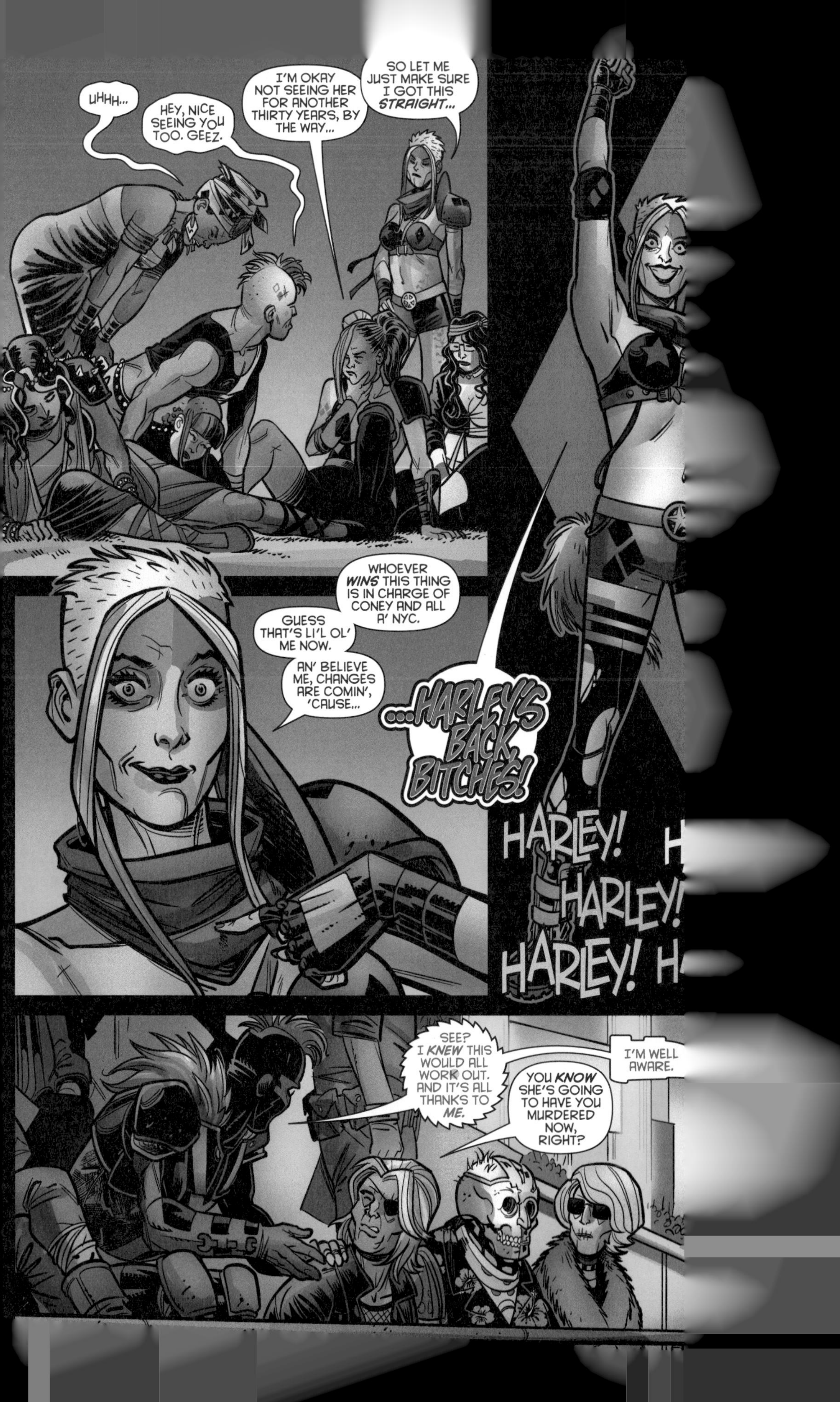
UHHH...
HEY, NICE SEEING YOU TOO. GEEZ.
I'M OKAY NOT SEEING HER FOR ANOTHER THIRTY YEARS, BY THE WAY...
SO LET ME JUST MAKE SURE I GOT THIS *STRAIGHT...*
WHOEVER *WINS* THIS THING IS IN CHARGE OF CONEY AND ALL A' NYC.
GUESS THAT'S LI'L OL' ME NOW.
AN' BELIEVE ME, CHANGES ARE COMIN', 'CAUSE...
...HARLEY'S BACK, BITCHES!
HARLEY!
HARLEY!
HARLEY!
SEE? I *KNEW* THIS WOULD ALL WORK OUT. AND IT'S ALL THANKS TO *ME.*
YOU *KNOW* SHE'S GOING TO HAVE YOU MURDERED NOW, RIGHT?
I'M WELL AWARE.

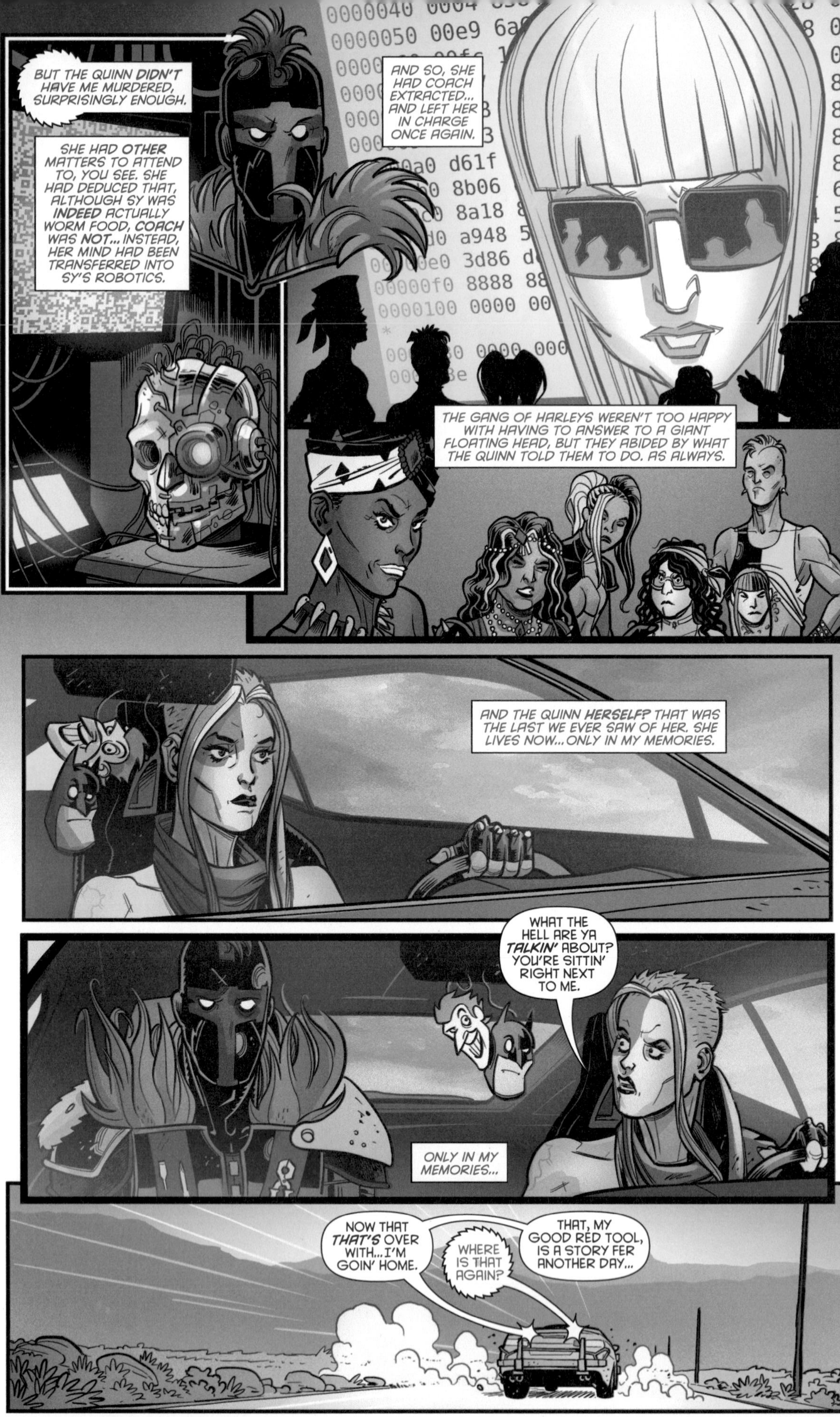
BUT THE QUINN DIDN'T HAVE ME MURDERED, SURPRISINGLY ENOUGH.
SHE HAD OTHER MATTERS TO ATTEND TO, YOU SEE. SHE HAD DEDUCED THAT, ALTHOUGH SY WAS INDEED ACTUALLY WORM FOOD, COACH WAS NOT... INSTEAD, HER MIND HAD BEEN TRANSFERRED INTO SY'S ROBOTICS.
AND SO, SHE HAD COACH EXTRACTED... AND LEFT HER IN CHARGE ONCE AGAIN.
THE GANG OF HARLEYS WEREN'T TOO HAPPY WITH HAVING TO ANSWER TO A GIANT FLOATING HEAD, BUT THEY ABIDED BY WHAT THE QUINN TOLD THEM TO DO. AS ALWAYS.
AND THE QUINN HERSELF? THAT WAS THE LAST WE EVER SAW OF HER. SHE LIVES NOW...ONLY IN MY MEMORIES.
WHAT THE HELL ARE YA TALKIN' ABOUT? YOU'RE SITTIN' RIGHT NEXT TO ME.
ONLY IN MY MEMORIES...
NOW THAT THAT'S OVER WITH...I'M GOIN' HOME.
WHERE IS THAT AGAIN?
THAT, MY GOOD RED TOOL, IS A STORY FER ANOTHER DAY...

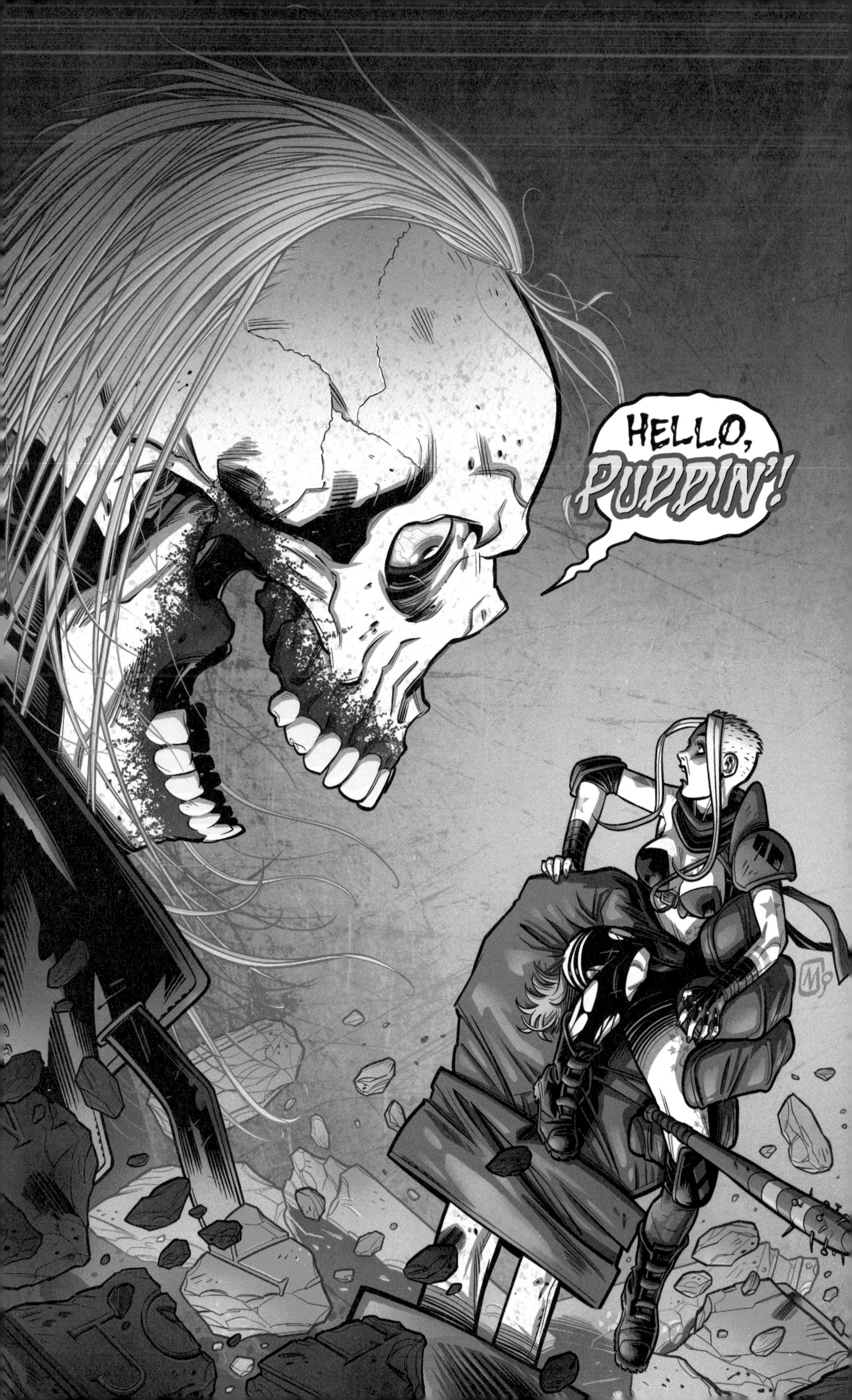
HELLO, PUDDIN'!

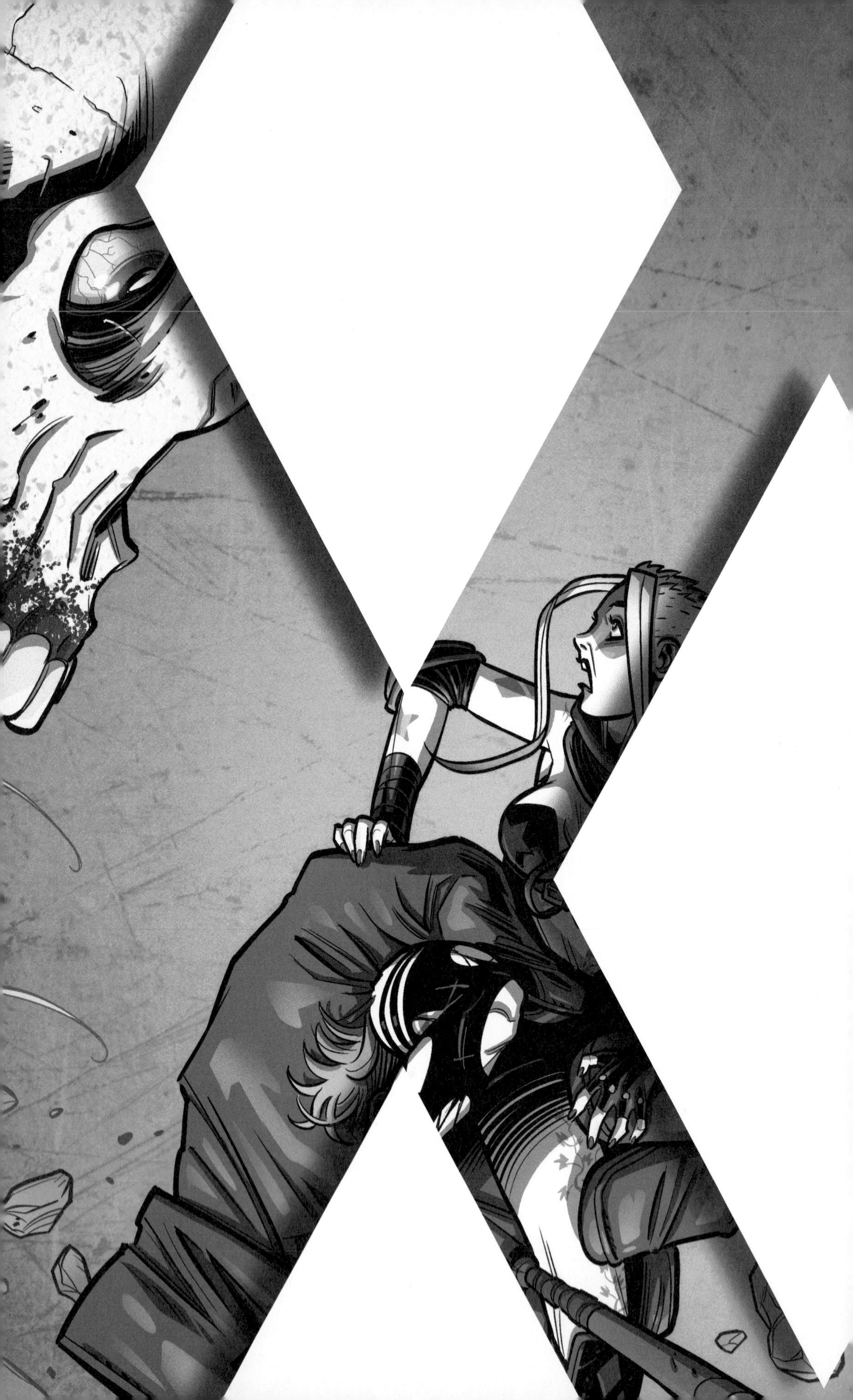

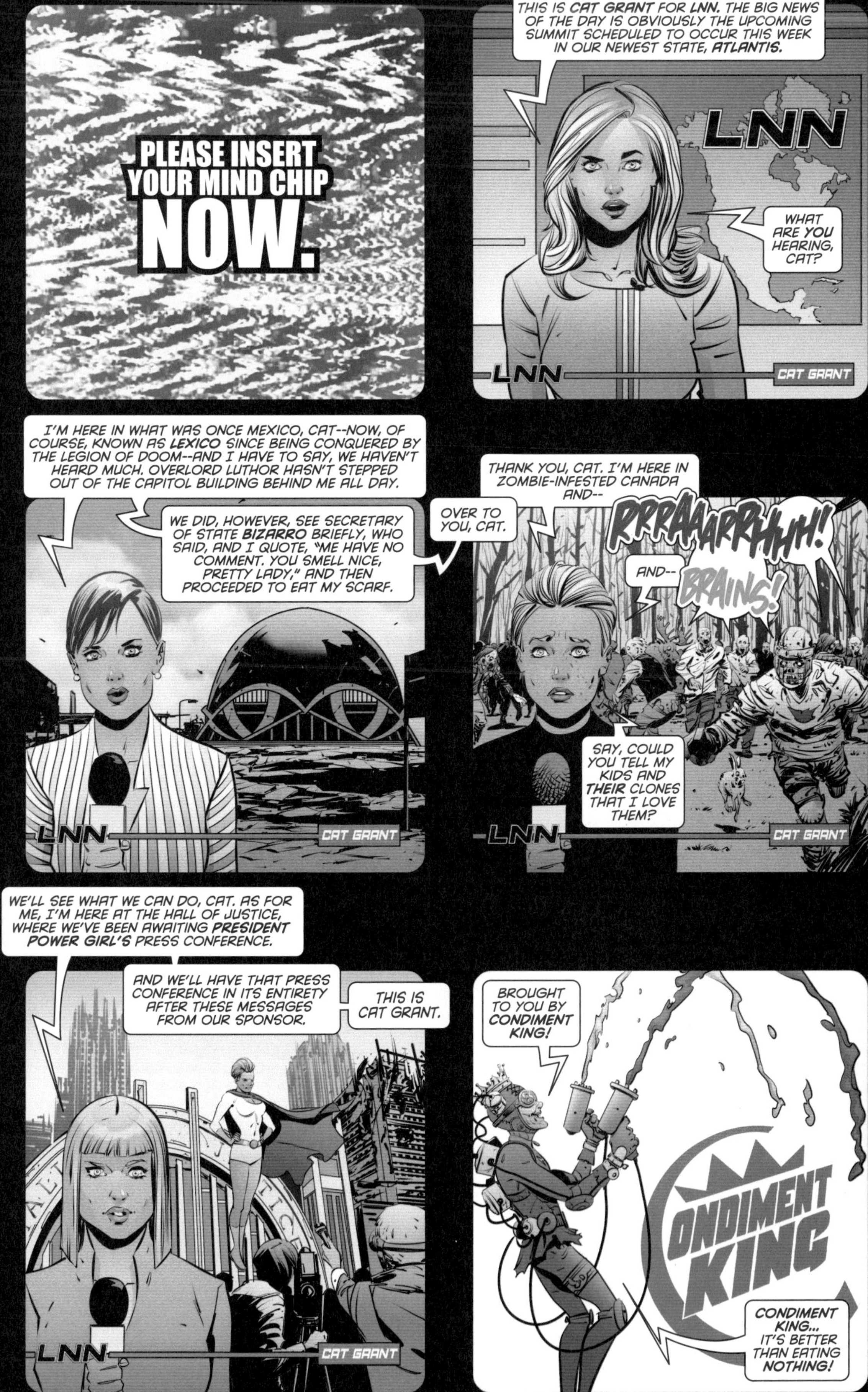
PLEASE INSERT YOUR MIND CHIP NOW.
THIS IS CAT GRANT FOR LNN. THE BIG NEWS OF THE DAY IS OBVIOUSLY THE UPCOMING SUMMIT SCHEDULED TO OCCUR THIS WEEK IN OUR NEWEST STATE, ATLANTIS.
LNN
WHAT ARE YOU HEARING, CAT?
LNN
CAT GRANT
I'M HERE IN WHAT WAS ONCE MEXICO, CAT--NOW, OF COURSE, KNOWN AS LEXICO SINCE BEING CONQUERED BY THE LEGION OF DOOM--AND I HAVE TO SAY, WE HAVEN'T HEARD MUCH. OVERLORD LUTHOR HASN'T STEPPED OUT OF THE CAPITOL BUILDING BEHIND ME ALL DAY.
WE DID, HOWEVER, SEE SECRETARY OF STATE BIZARRO BRIEFLY, WHO SAID, AND I QUOTE, "ME HAVE NO COMMENT. YOU SMELL NICE, PRETTY LADY," AND THEN PROCEEDED TO EAT MY SCARF.
OVER TO YOU, CAT.
LNN
CAT GRANT
THANK YOU, CAT. I'M HERE IN ZOMBIE-INFESTED CANADA AND--
RRRAAARRHHH!
AND--
BRAINS!
SAY, COULD YOU TELL MY KIDS AND THEIR CLONES THAT I LOVE THEM?
LNN
CAT GRANT
WE'LL SEE WHAT WE CAN DO, CAT. AS FOR ME, I'M HERE AT THE HALL OF JUSTICE, WHERE WE'VE BEEN AWAITING PRESIDENT POWER GIRL'S PRESS CONFERENCE.
AND WE'LL HAVE THAT PRESS CONFERENCE IN ITS ENTIRETY AFTER THESE MESSAGES FROM OUR SPONSOR.
THIS IS CAT GRANT.
LNN
CAT GRANT
BROUGHT TO YOU BY CONDIMENT KING!
CONDIMENT KING
CONDIMENT KING... IT'S BETTER THAN EATING NOTHING!

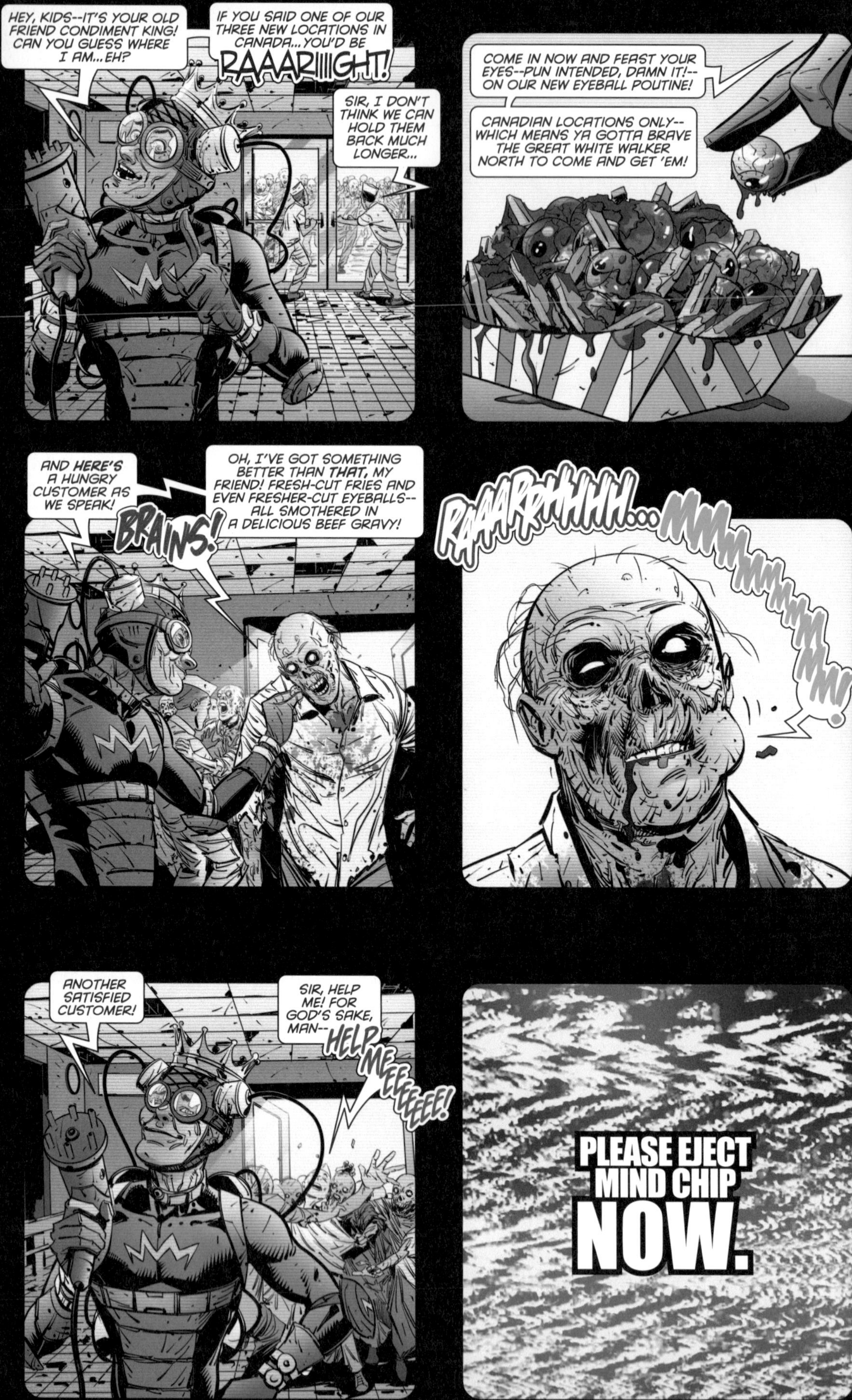
HEY, KIDS--IT'S YOUR OLD FRIEND CONDIMENT KING! CAN YOU GUESS WHERE I AM...EH?
IF YOU SAID ONE OF OUR THREE NEW LOCATIONS IN CANADA...YOU'D BE
RAAARIIIIGHT!
SIR, I DON'T THINK WE CAN HOLD THEM BACK MUCH LONGER...
COME IN NOW AND FEAST YOUR EYES--PUN INTENDED, DAMN IT!--ON OUR NEW EYEBALL POUTINE!
CANADIAN LOCATIONS ONLY--WHICH MEANS YA GOTTA BRAVE THE GREAT WHITE WALKER NORTH TO COME AND GET 'EM!
AND HERE'S A HUNGRY CUSTOMER AS WE SPEAK!
BRAINS!
OH, I'VE GOT SOMETHING BETTER THAN THAT, MY FRIEND! FRESH-CUT FRIES AND EVEN FRESHER-CUT EYEBALLS--ALL SMOTHERED IN A DELICIOUS BEEF GRAVY!
RAAARRHHHH...
MMMMMMMMMMMM!
ANOTHER SATISFIED CUSTOMER!
SIR, HELP ME! FOR GOD'S SAKE, MAN--
HELP MEEEEEEE!
PLEASE EJECT MIND CHIP NOW.

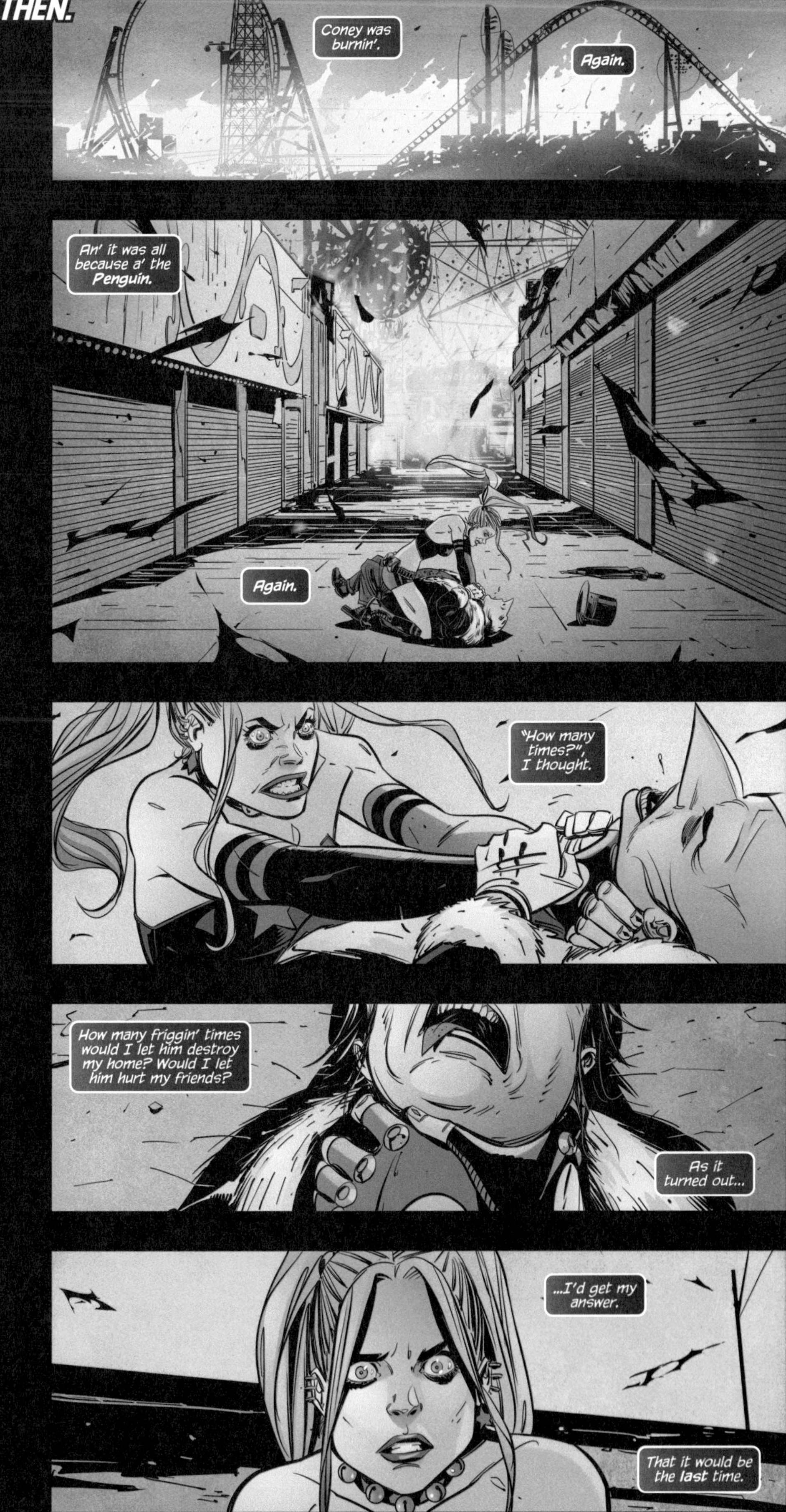
THEN.
Coney was burnin'.
Again.
An' it was all because a' the Penguin.
Again.
"How many times?", I thought.
How many friggin' times would I let him destroy my home? Would I let him hurt my friends?
As it turned out...
...I'd get my answer.
That it would be the last time.

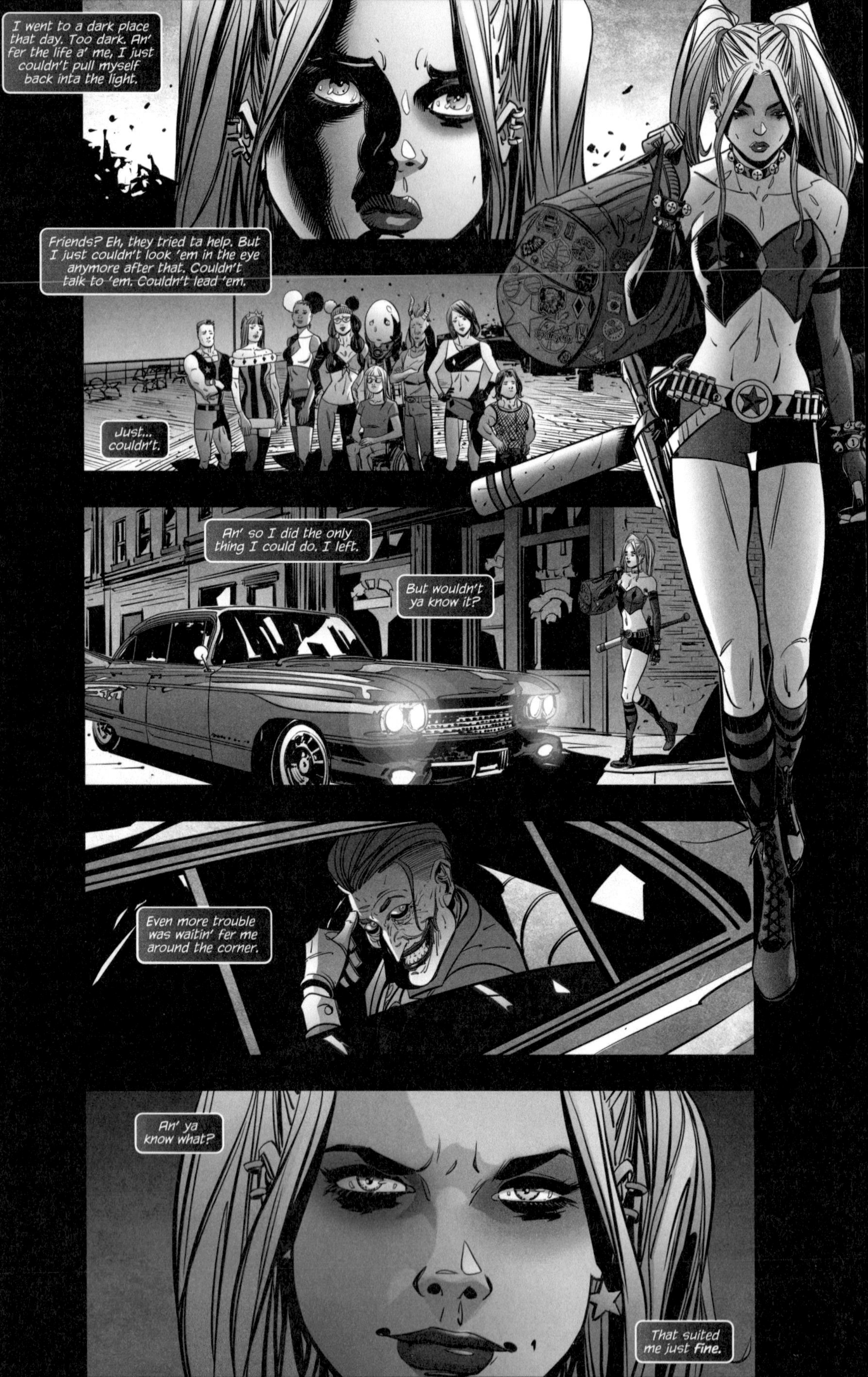
I went to a dark place that day. Too dark. An' fer the life a' me, I just couldn't pull myself back inta the light.
Friends? Eh, they tried ta help. But I just couldn't look 'em in the eye anymore after that. Couldn't talk to 'em. Couldn't lead 'em.
Just... couldn't.
An' so I did the only thing I could do. I left.
But wouldn't ya know it?
Even more trouble was waitin' fer me around the corner.
An' ya know what?
That suited me just **fine.**

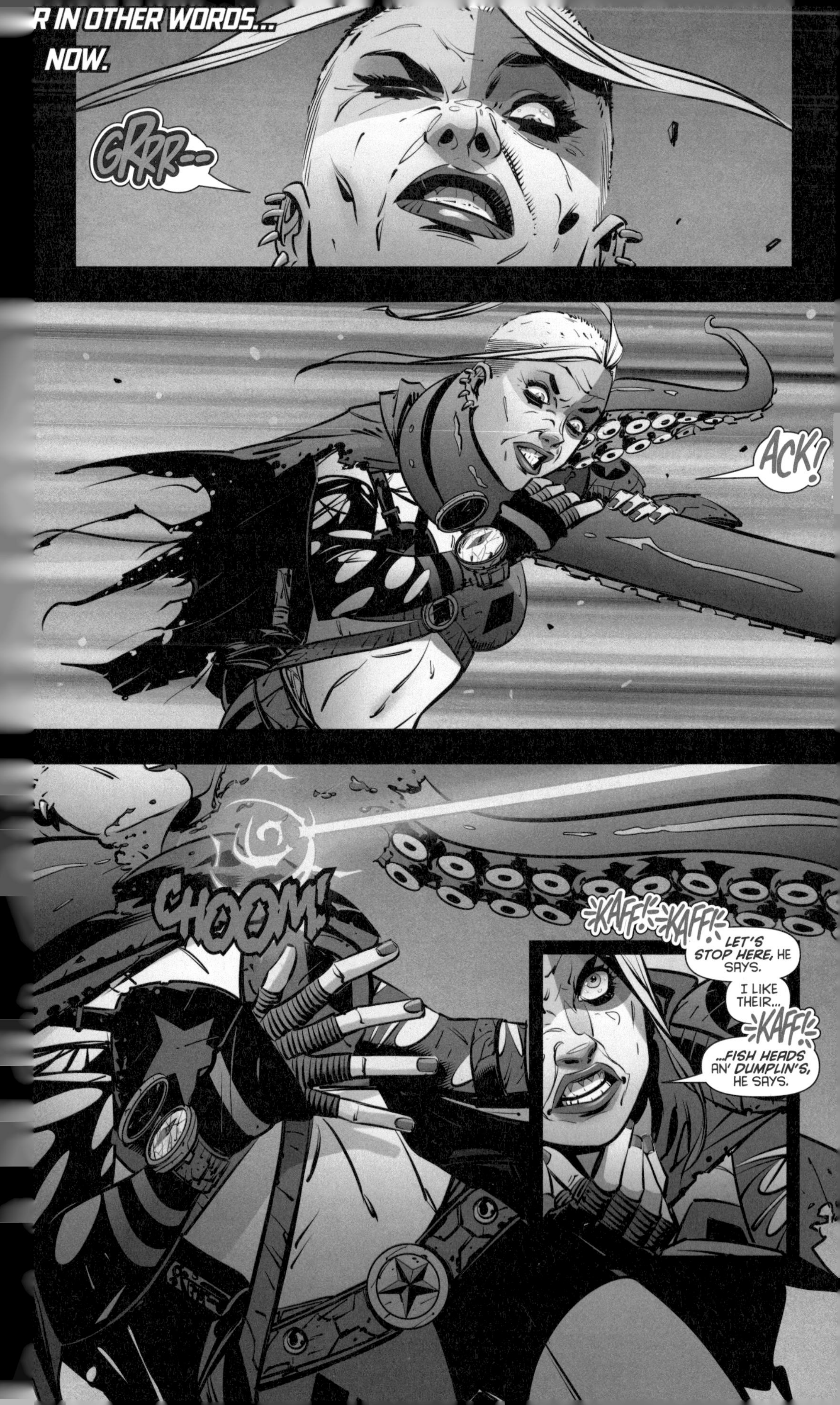
R IN OTHER WORDS...
NOW.
GRRR--
ACK!
CHOOM!
KAFF! KAFF!
LET'S STOP HERE, HE SAYS.
I LIKE THEIR...
KAFF!
...FISH HEADS AN' DUMPLIN'S, HE SAYS.

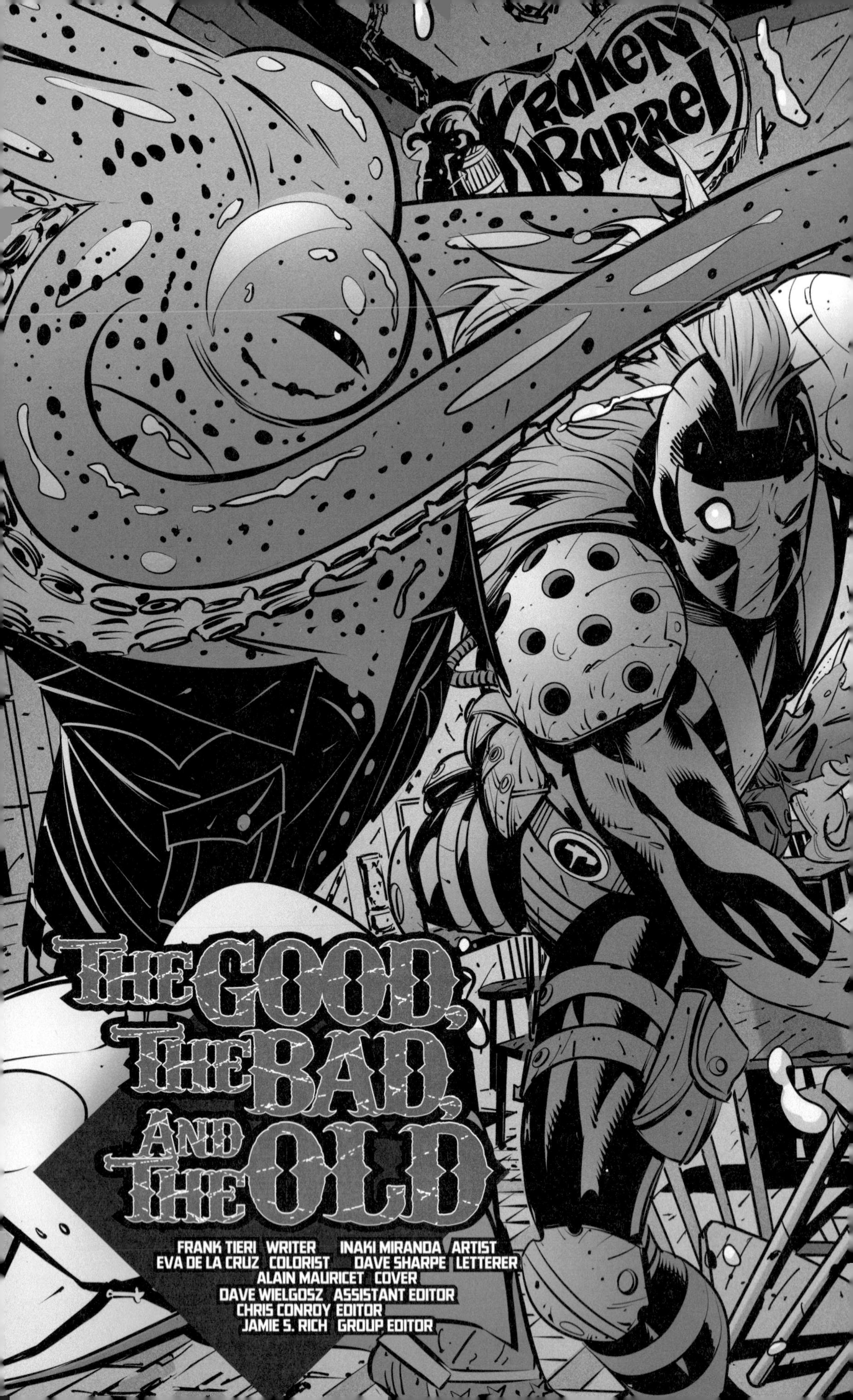
Kraken Barrel
THE GOOD, THE BAD, AND THE OLD
FRANK TIERI WRITER INAKI MIRANDA ARTIST
EVA DE LA CRUZ COLORIST DAVE SHARPE LETTERER
ALAIN MAURICET COVER
DAVE WIELGOSZ ASSISTANT EDITOR
CHRIS CONROY EDITOR
JAMIE S. RICH GROUP EDITOR

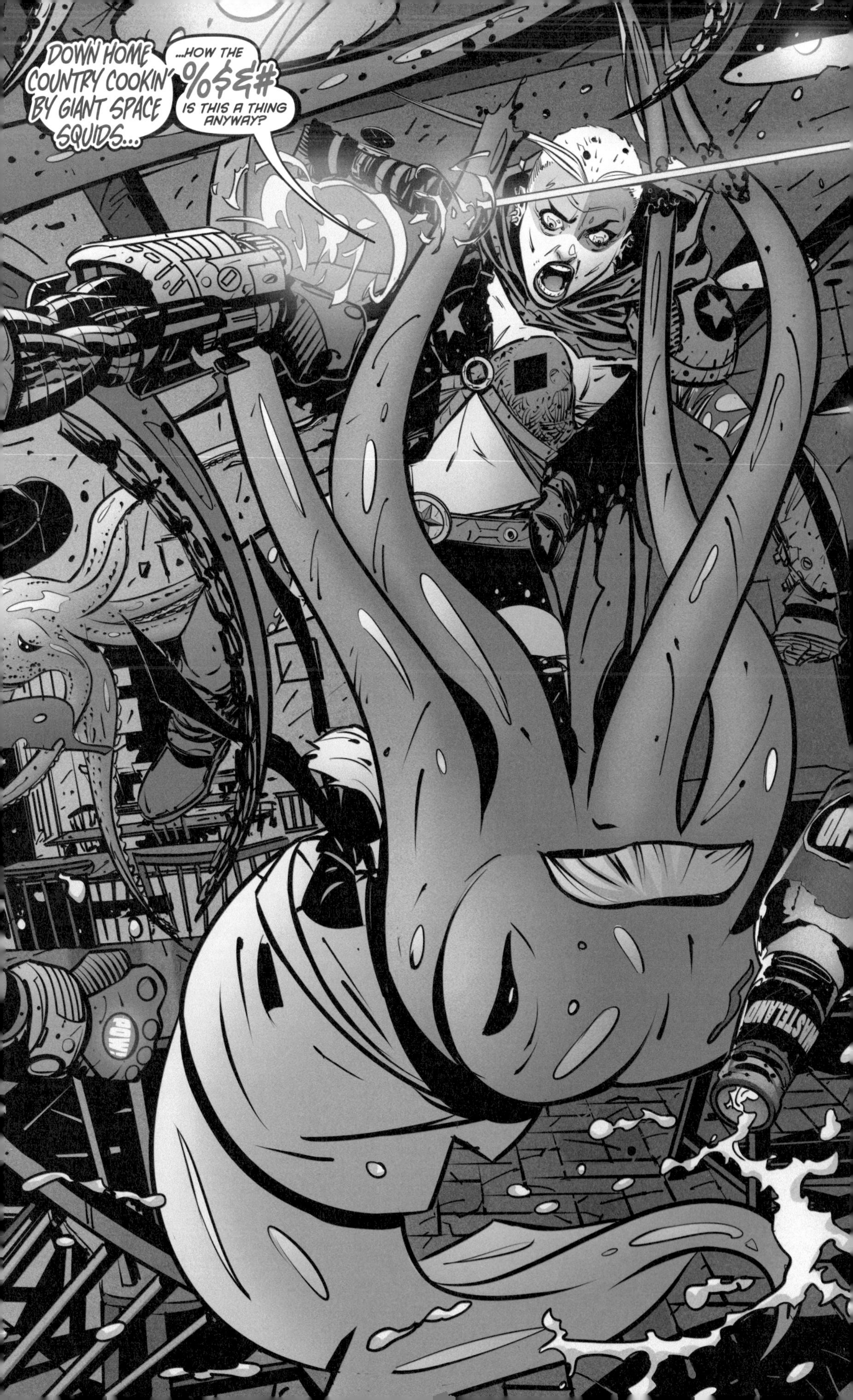
DOWN HOME COUNTRY COOKIN' BY GIANT SPACE SQUIDS...
...HOW THE %$&# IS THIS A THING ANYWAY?
POW!
WASTELAND

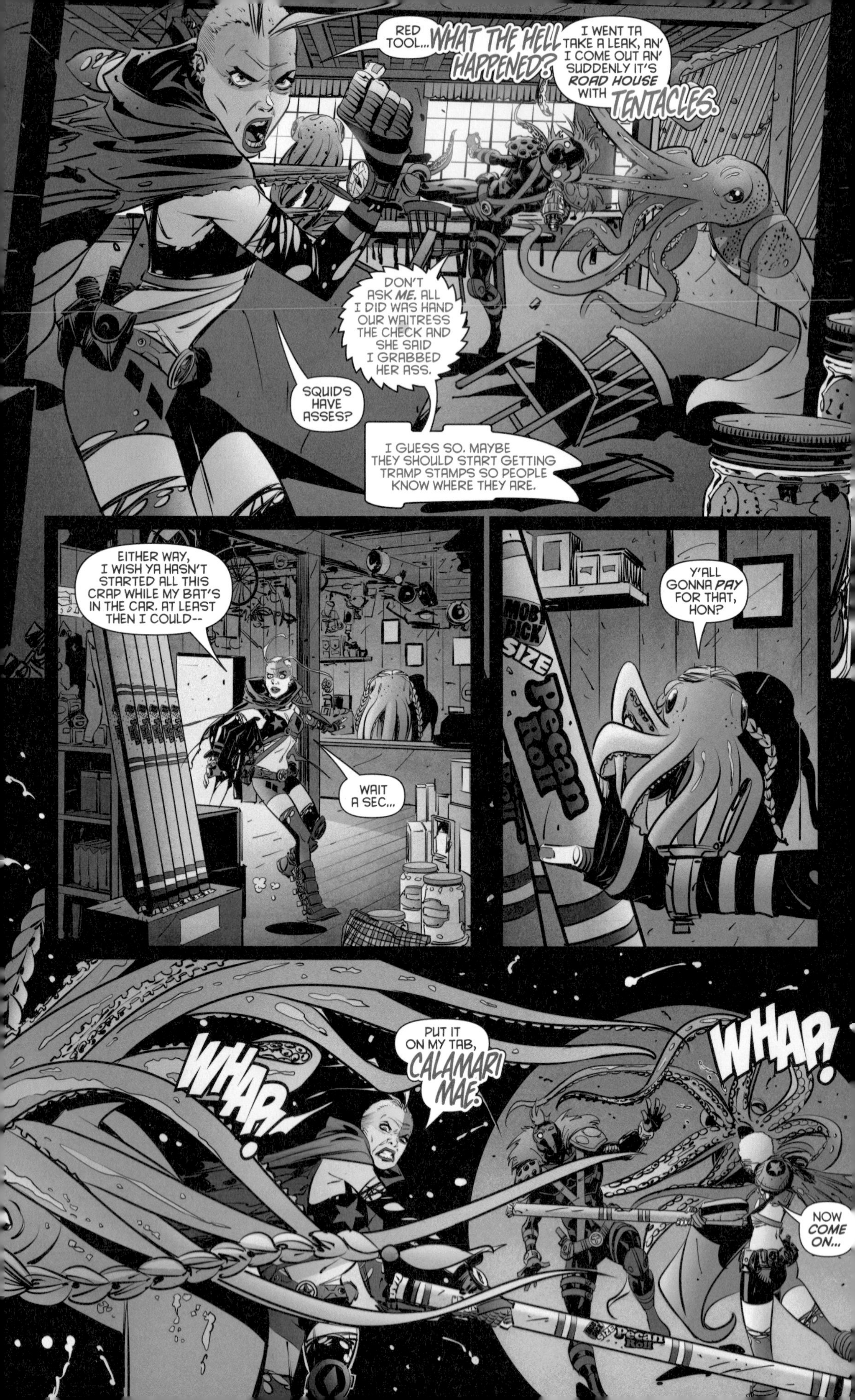

RED TOOL...WHAT THE HELL HAPPENED?
I WENT TA TAKE A LEAK, AN' I COME OUT AN' SUDDENLY IT'S ROAD HOUSE WITH TENTACLES.
DON'T ASK ME. ALL I DID WAS HAND OUR WAITRESS THE CHECK AND SHE SAID I GRABBED HER ASS.
SQUIDS HAVE ASSES?
I GUESS SO. MAYBE THEY SHOULD START GETTING TRAMP STAMPS SO PEOPLE KNOW WHERE THEY ARE.
EITHER WAY, I WISH YA HASN'T STARTED ALL THIS CRAP WHILE MY BAT'S IN THE CAR. AT LEAST THEN I COULD--
WAIT A SEC...
Y'ALL GONNA PAY FOR THAT, HON?
MOBY DICK SIZE Pecan Roll
WHAP!
PUT IT ON MY TAB, CALAMARI MAE.
WHAP!
NOW COME ON...

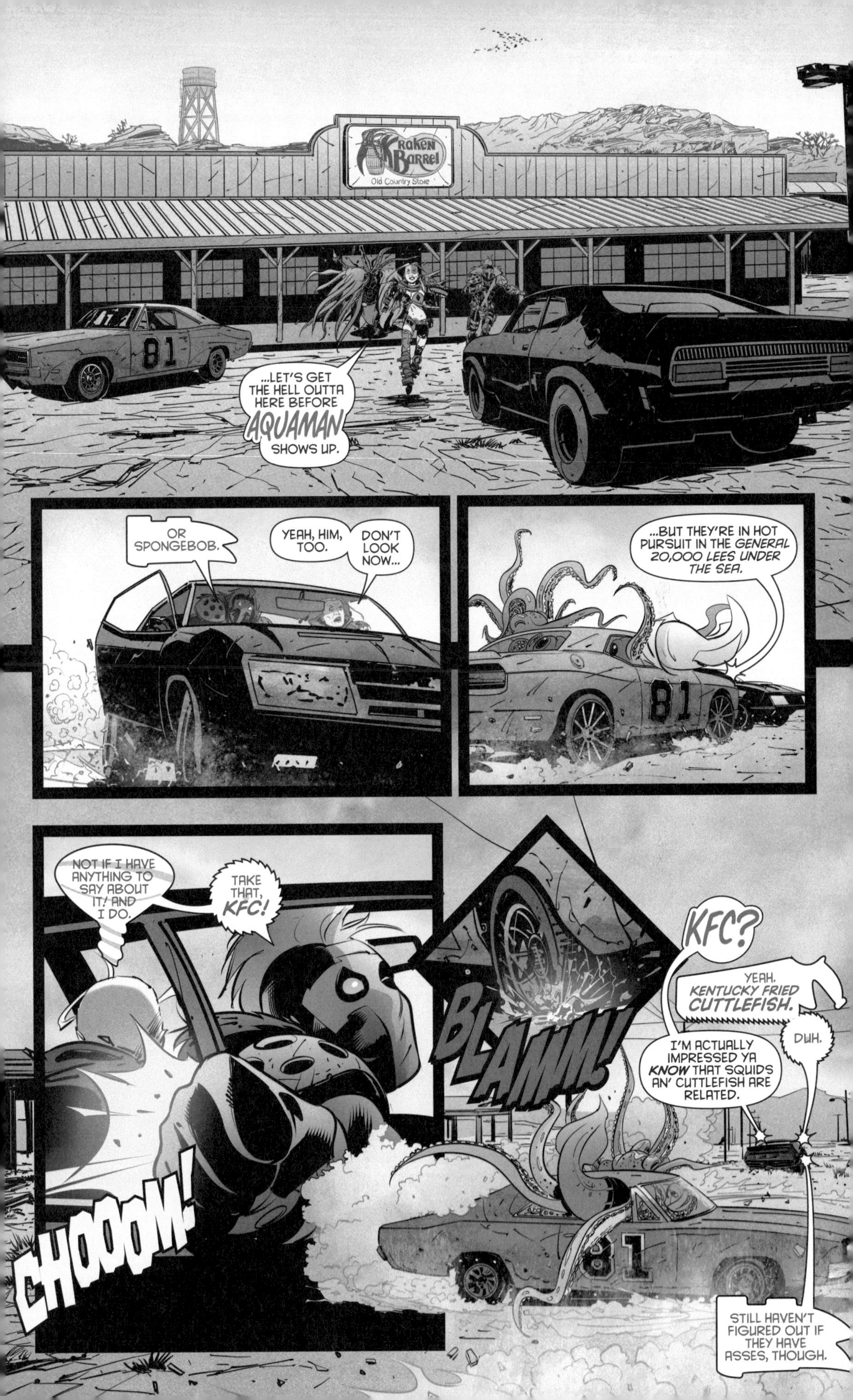

Kraken Barrel
Old Country Store
...LET'S GET THE HELL OUTTA HERE BEFORE AQUAMAN SHOWS UP.
OR SPONGEBOB.
YEAH, HIM, TOO.
DON'T LOOK NOW...
...BUT THEY'RE IN HOT PURSUIT IN THE GENERAL 20,000 LEES UNDER THE SEA.
NOT IF I HAVE ANYTHING TO SAY ABOUT IT! AND I DO.
TAKE THAT, KFC!
BLAMM!
KFC?
YEAH. KENTUCKY FRIED CUTTLEFISH.
DUH.
I'M ACTUALLY IMPRESSED YA KNOW THAT SQUIDS AN' CUTTLEFISH ARE RELATED.
CHOOOM!
STILL HAVEN'T FIGURED OUT IF THEY HAVE ASSES, THOUGH.

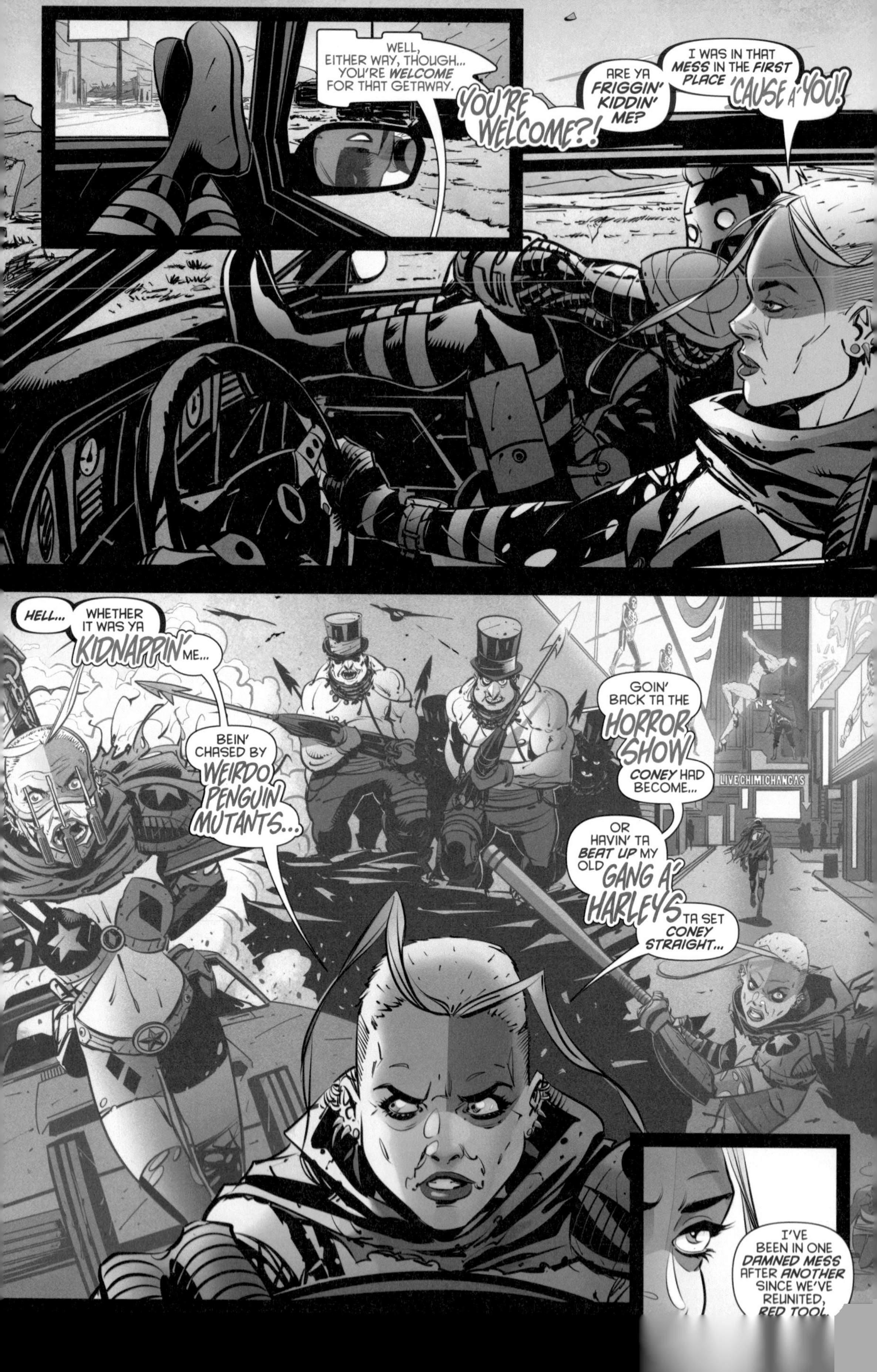

WELL, EITHER WAY, THOUGH... YOU'RE WELCOME FOR THAT GETAWAY.
YOU'RE WELCOME?!
ARE YA FRIGGIN' KIDDIN' ME?
I WAS IN THAT MESS IN THE FIRST PLACE 'CAUSE A' YOU!
HELL... WHETHER IT WAS YA KIDNAPPIN' ME...
BEIN' CHASED BY WEIRDO PENGUIN MUTANTS...
GOIN' BACK TA THE HORROR SHOW CONEY HAD BECOME...
OR HAVIN' TA BEAT UP MY OLD GANG A' HARLEYS TA SET CONEY STRAIGHT...
LIVE CHIMICHANGAS
I'VE BEEN IN ONE DAMNED MESS AFTER ANOTHER SINCE WE'VE REUNITED, RED TOOL.

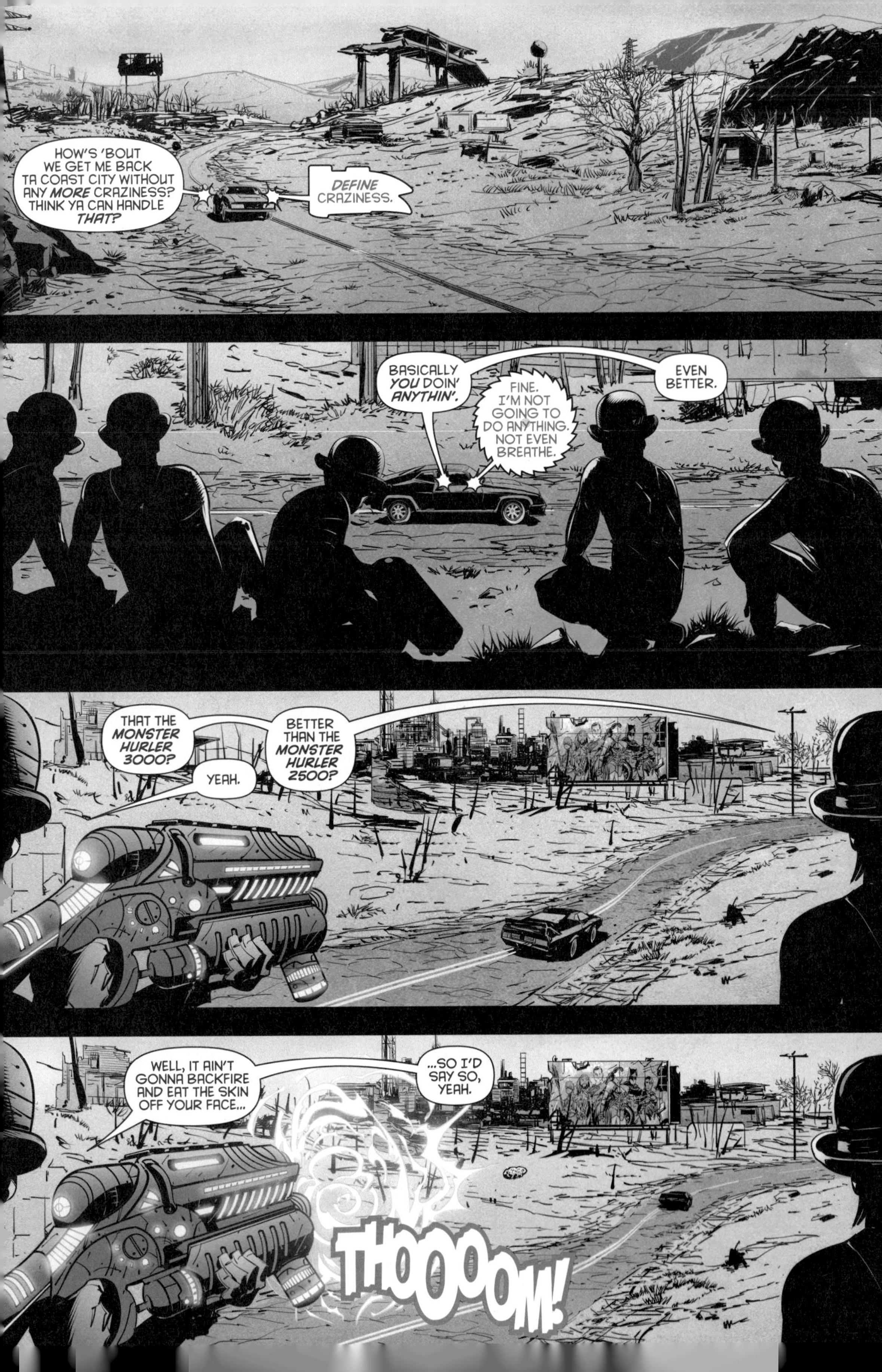
HOW'S 'BOUT WE GET ME BACK TA COAST CITY WITHOUT ANY *MORE* CRAZINESS? THINK YA CAN HANDLE *THAT?*
DEFINE CRAZINESS.
BASICALLY *YOU* DOIN' *ANYTHIN'*.
FINE. I'M NOT GOING TO DO ANYTHING. NOT EVEN BREATHE.
EVEN BETTER.
THAT THE *MONSTER HURLER 3000?*
YEAH.
BETTER THAN THE *MONSTER HURLER 2500?*
WELL, IT AIN'T GONNA BACKFIRE AND EAT THE SKIN OFF YOUR FACE...
...SO I'D SAY SO, YEAH.
THOOOOOM!

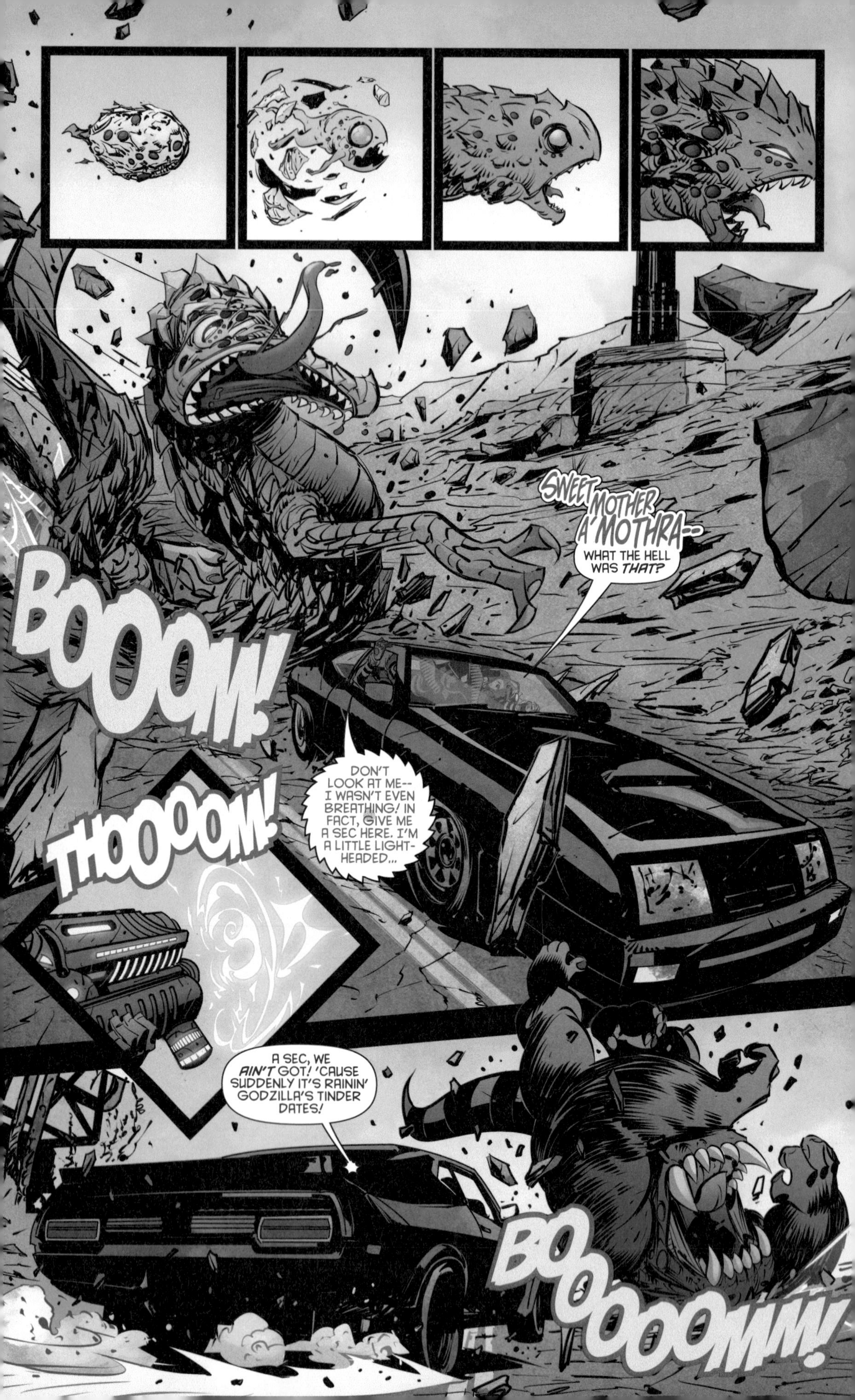
SWEET MOTHER A'MOTHRA--
WHAT THE HELL WAS THAT?
BOOOOM!
DON'T LOOK AT ME-- I WASN'T EVEN BREATHING! IN FACT, GIVE ME A SEC HERE. I'M A LITTLE LIGHT-HEADED...
THOOOOM!
A SEC, WE AIN'T GOT! 'CAUSE SUDDENLY IT'S RAININ' GODZILLA'S TINDER DATES!
BOOOOOOMM!

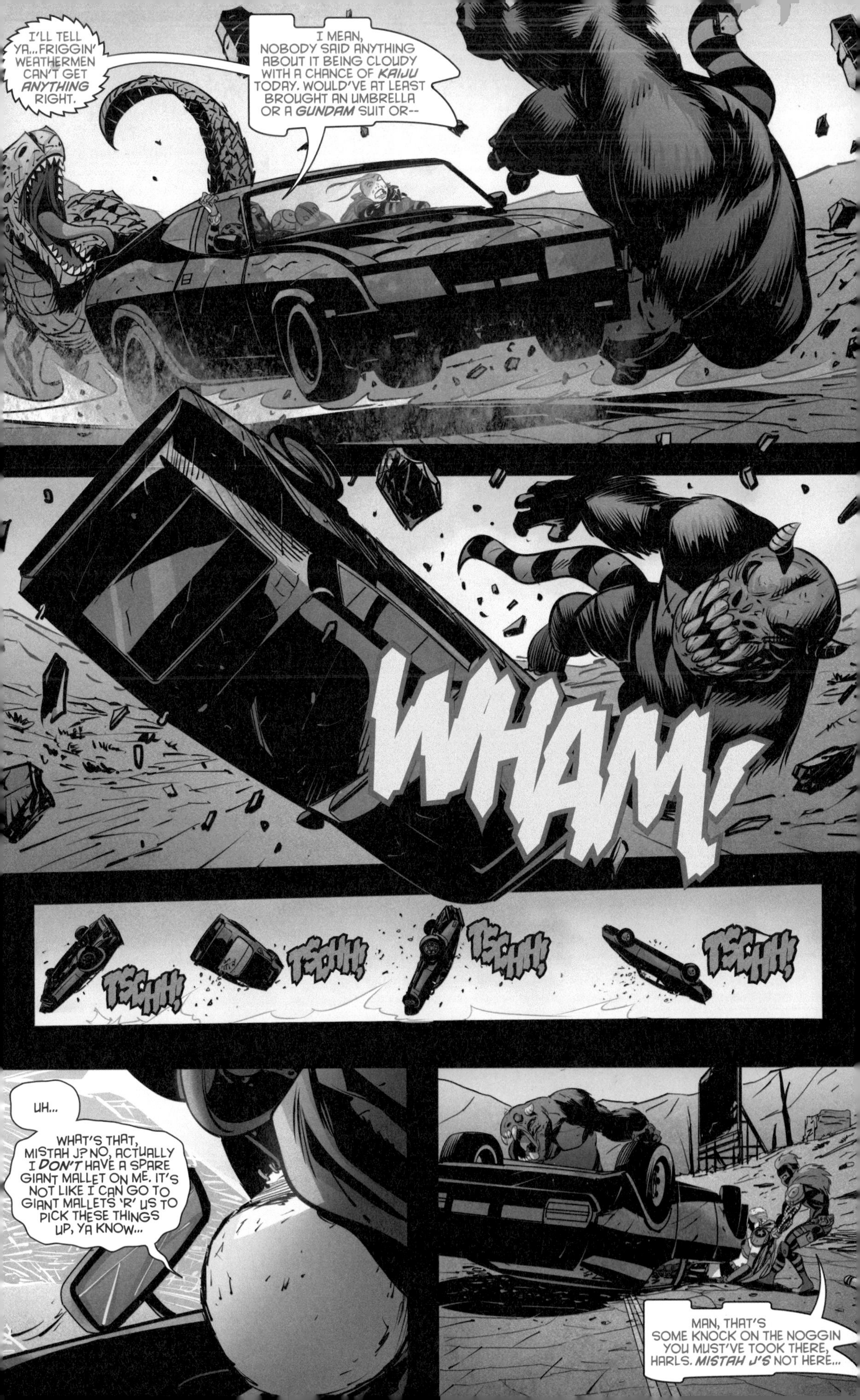
I'LL TELL YA...FRIGGIN' WEATHERMEN CAN'T GET ANYTHING RIGHT.
I MEAN, NOBODY SAID ANYTHING ABOUT IT BEING CLOUDY WITH A CHANCE OF KAIJU TODAY. WOULD'VE AT LEAST BROUGHT AN UMBRELLA OR A GUNDAM SUIT OR--
WHAM!
TSCHH!
TSCHH!
TSCHH!
TSCHH!
UH...
WHAT'S THAT, MISTAH J? NO, ACTUALLY I DON'T HAVE A SPARE GIANT MALLET ON ME. IT'S NOT LIKE I CAN GO TO GIANT MALLETS 'R' US TO PICK THESE THINGS UP, YA KNOW...
MAN, THAT'S SOME KNOCK ON THE NOGGIN YOU MUST'VE TOOK THERE, HARLS. MISTAH J'S NOT HERE...

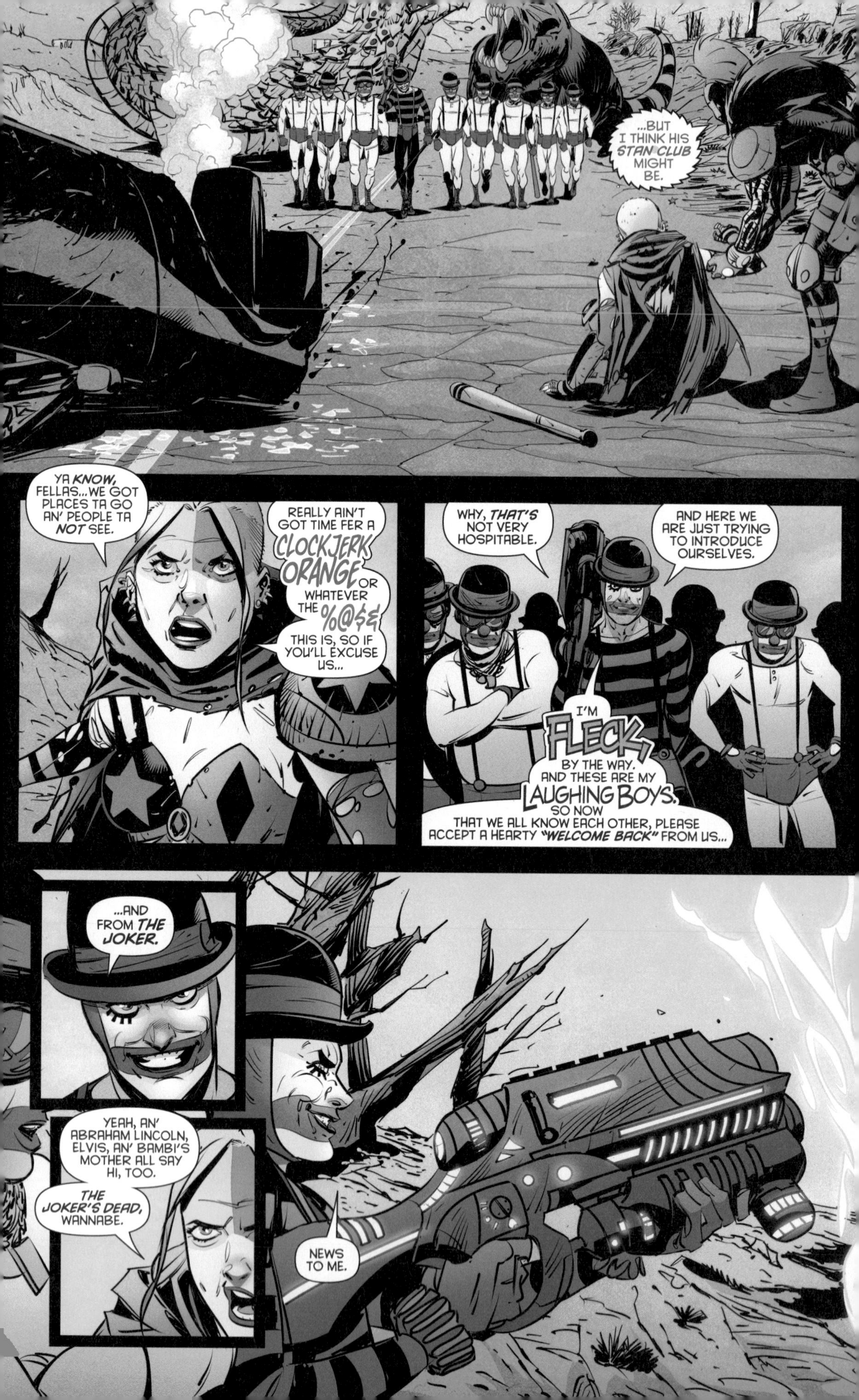
...BUT I THINK HIS STAN CLUB MIGHT BE.
YA KNOW, FELLAS...WE GOT PLACES TA GO AN' PEOPLE TA NOT SEE.
REALLY AIN'T GOT TIME FER A CLOCKJERK ORANGE OR WHATEVER THE %@$& THIS IS, SO IF YOU'LL EXCUSE US...
WHY, THAT'S NOT VERY HOSPITABLE.
AND HERE WE ARE JUST TRYING TO INTRODUCE OURSELVES.
I'M FLECK, BY THE WAY. AND THESE ARE MY LAUGHING BOYS. SO NOW THAT WE ALL KNOW EACH OTHER, PLEASE ACCEPT A HEARTY "WELCOME BACK" FROM US...
...AND FROM THE JOKER.
YEAH, AN' ABRAHAM LINCOLN, ELVIS, AN' BAMBI'S MOTHER ALL SAY HI, TOO.
THE JOKER'S DEAD, WANNABE.
NEWS TO ME.

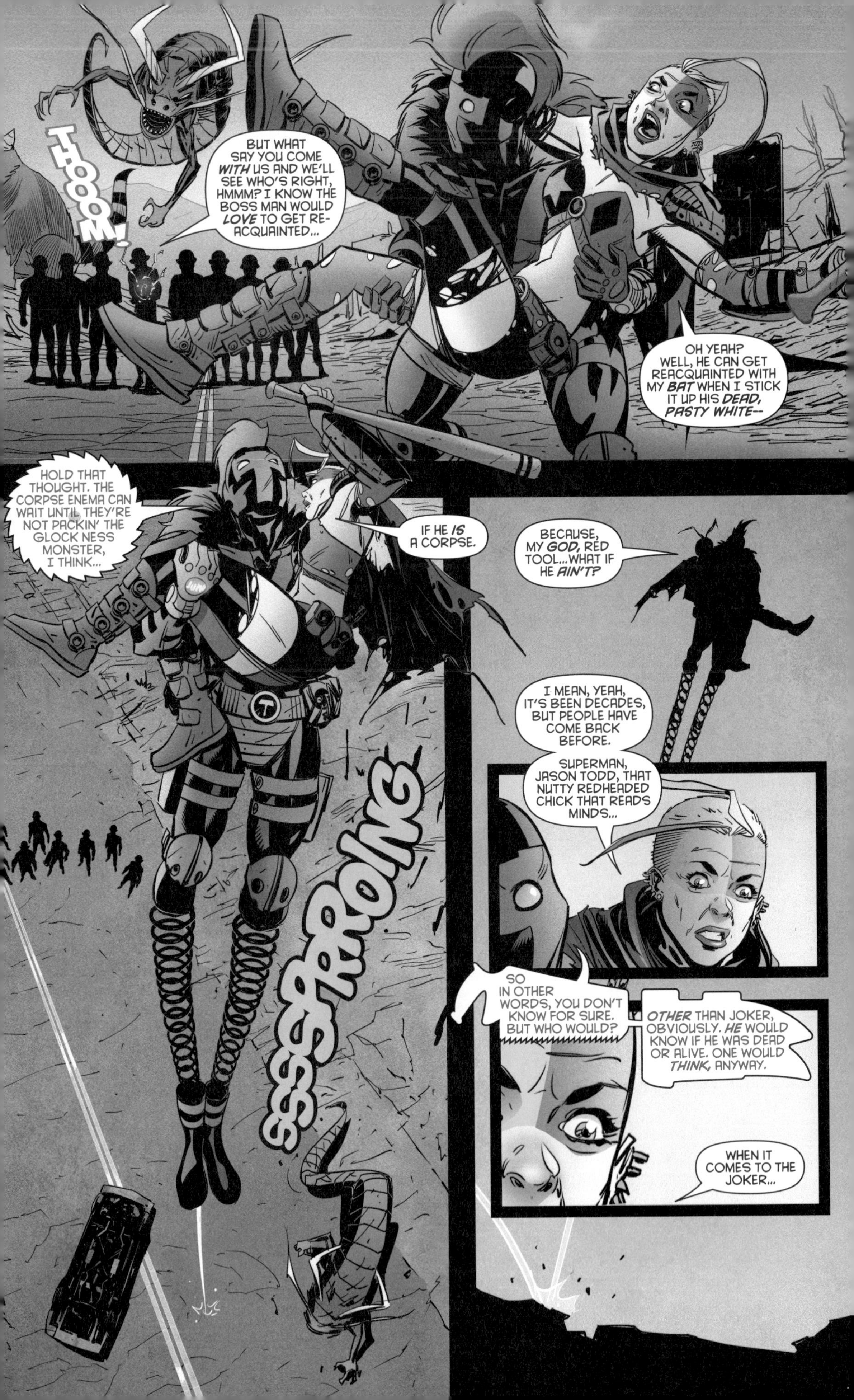
THOOOM!
BUT WHAT SAY YOU COME WITH US AND WE'LL SEE WHO'S RIGHT, HMMM? I KNOW THE BOSS MAN WOULD LOVE TO GET RE-ACQUAINTED...
OH YEAH? WELL, HE CAN GET REACQUAINTED WITH MY BAT WHEN I STICK IT UP HIS DEAD, PASTY WHITE--
HOLD THAT THOUGHT. THE CORPSE ENEMA CAN WAIT UNTIL THEY'RE NOT PACKIN' THE GLOCK NESS MONSTER, I THINK...
IF HE IS A CORPSE.
SSSPROING
BECAUSE, MY GOD, RED TOOL...WHAT IF HE AIN'T?
I MEAN, YEAH, IT'S BEEN DECADES, BUT PEOPLE HAVE COME BACK BEFORE.
SUPERMAN, JASON TODD, THAT NUTTY REDHEADED CHICK THAT READS MINDS...
SO IN OTHER WORDS, YOU DON'T KNOW FOR SURE. BUT WHO WOULD?
OTHER THAN JOKER, OBVIOUSLY. HE WOULD KNOW IF HE WAS DEAD OR ALIVE. ONE WOULD THINK, ANYWAY.
WHEN IT COMES TO THE JOKER...

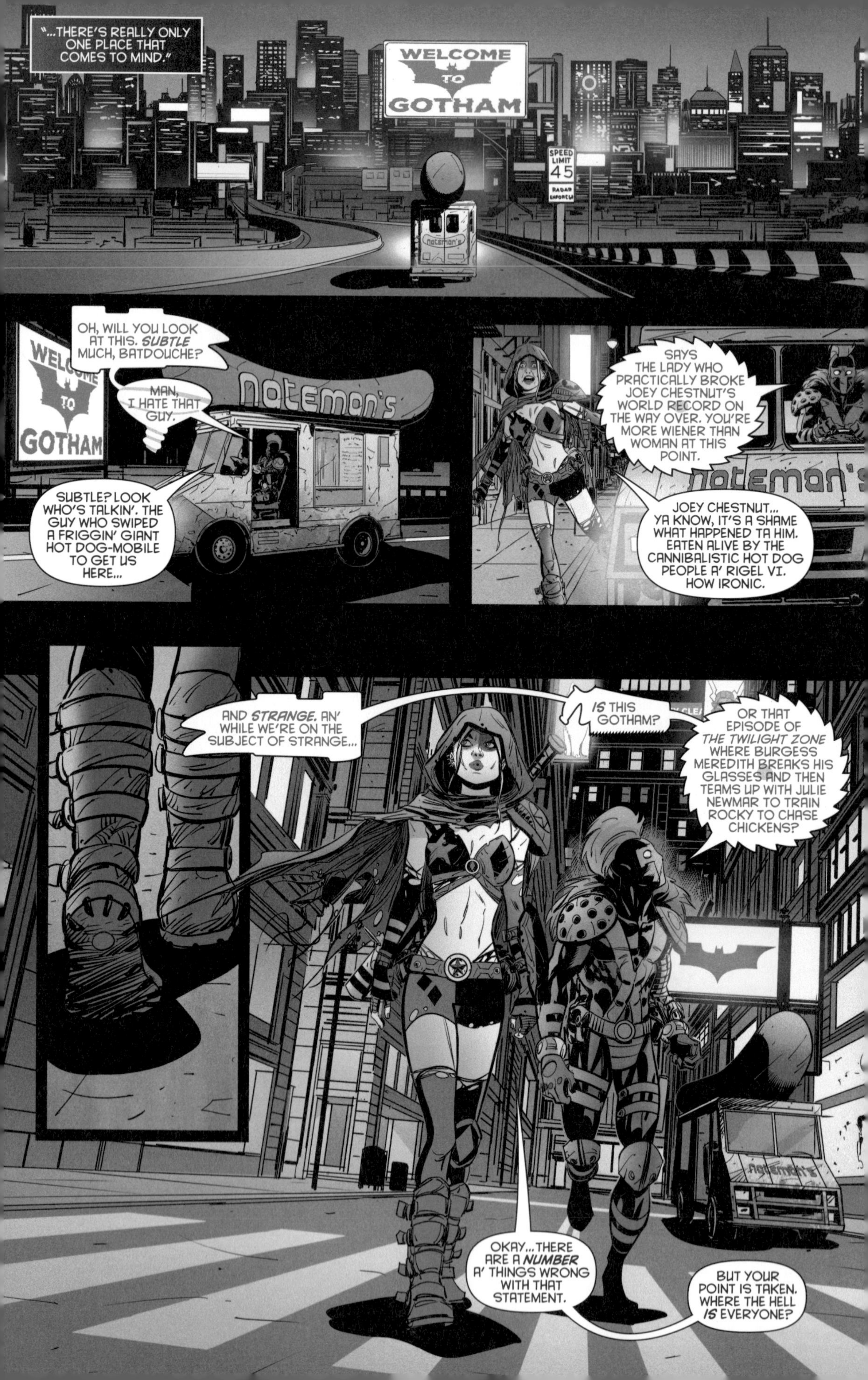
"...THERE'S REALLY ONLY ONE PLACE THAT COMES TO MIND."
WELCOME TO GOTHAM
SPEED LIMIT 45
OH, WILL YOU LOOK AT THIS. SUBTLE MUCH, BATDOUCHE?
MAN, I HATE THAT GUY.
SUBTLE? LOOK WHO'S TALKIN'. THE GUY WHO SWIPED A FRIGGIN' GIANT HOT DOG-MOBILE TO GET US HERE...
SAYS THE LADY WHO PRACTICALLY BROKE JOEY CHESTNUT'S WORLD RECORD ON THE WAY OVER. YOU'RE MORE WIENER THAN WOMAN AT THIS POINT.
JOEY CHESTNUT... YA KNOW, IT'S A SHAME WHAT HAPPENED TA HIM. EATEN ALIVE BY THE CANNIBALISTIC HOT DOG PEOPLE A' RIGEL VI. HOW IRONIC.
AND STRANGE. AN' WHILE WE'RE ON THE SUBJECT OF STRANGE...
IS THIS GOTHAM?
OR THAT EPISODE OF THE TWILIGHT ZONE WHERE BURGESS MEREDITH BREAKS HIS GLASSES AND THEN TEAMS UP WITH JULIE NEWMAR TO TRAIN ROCKY TO CHASE CHICKENS?
OKAY... THERE ARE A NUMBER A' THINGS WRONG WITH THAT STATEMENT.
BUT YOUR POINT IS TAKEN. WHERE THE HELL IS EVERYONE?

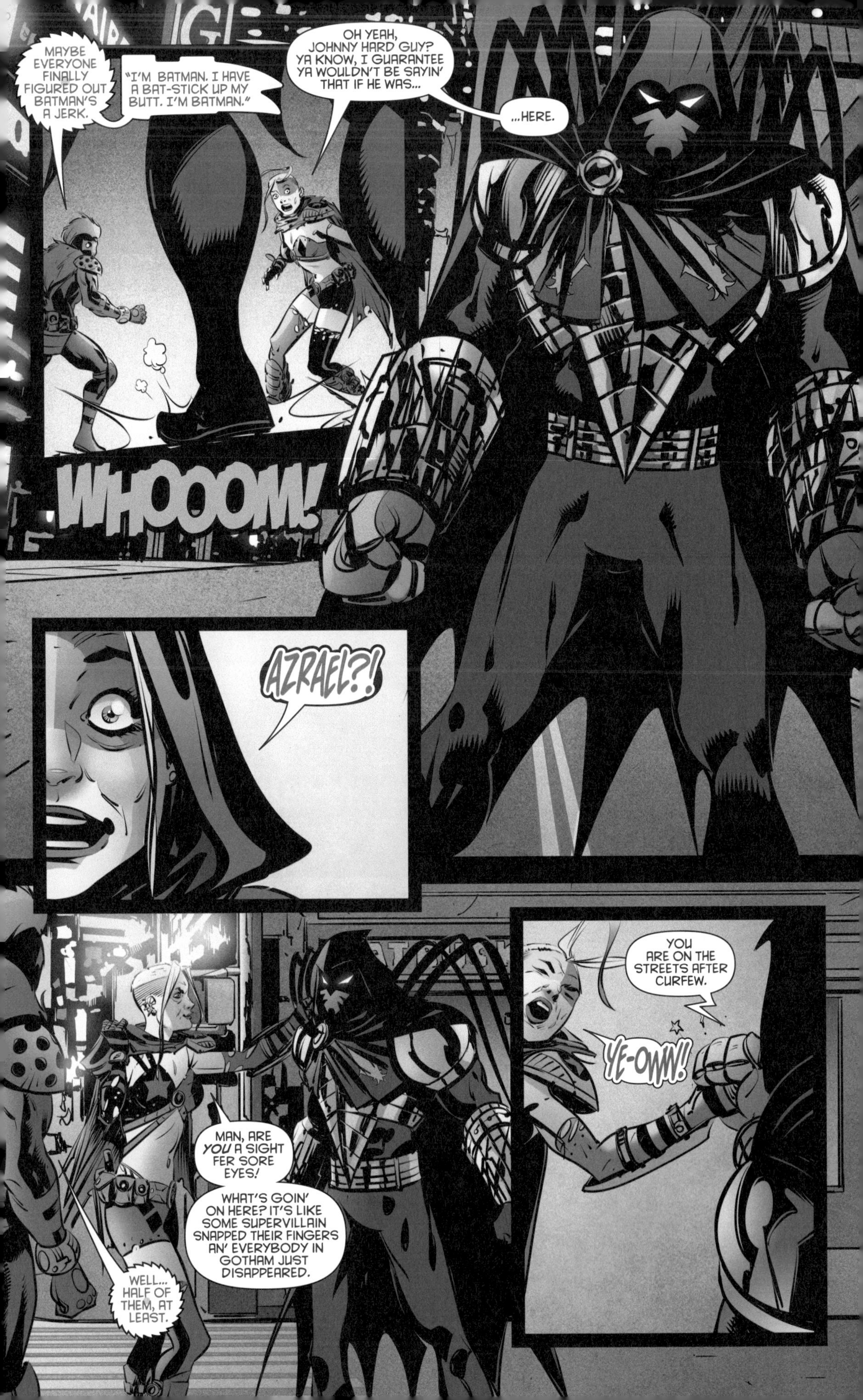
MAYBE EVERYONE FINALLY FIGURED OUT BATMAN'S A JERK.
"I'M BATMAN. I HAVE A BAT-STICK UP MY BUTT. I'M BATMAN."
OH YEAH, JOHNNY HARD GUY? YA KNOW, I GUARANTEE YA WOULDN'T BE SAYIN' THAT IF HE WAS...
...HERE.
WHOOOM!
AZRAEL?!
MAN, ARE YOU A SIGHT FER SORE EYES!
WHAT'S GOIN' ON HERE? IT'S LIKE SOME SUPERVILLAIN SNAPPED THEIR FINGERS AN' EVERYBODY IN GOTHAM JUST DISAPPEARED.
WELL... HALF OF THEM, AT LEAST.
YOU ARE ON THE STREETS AFTER CURFEW.
YE-OWW!

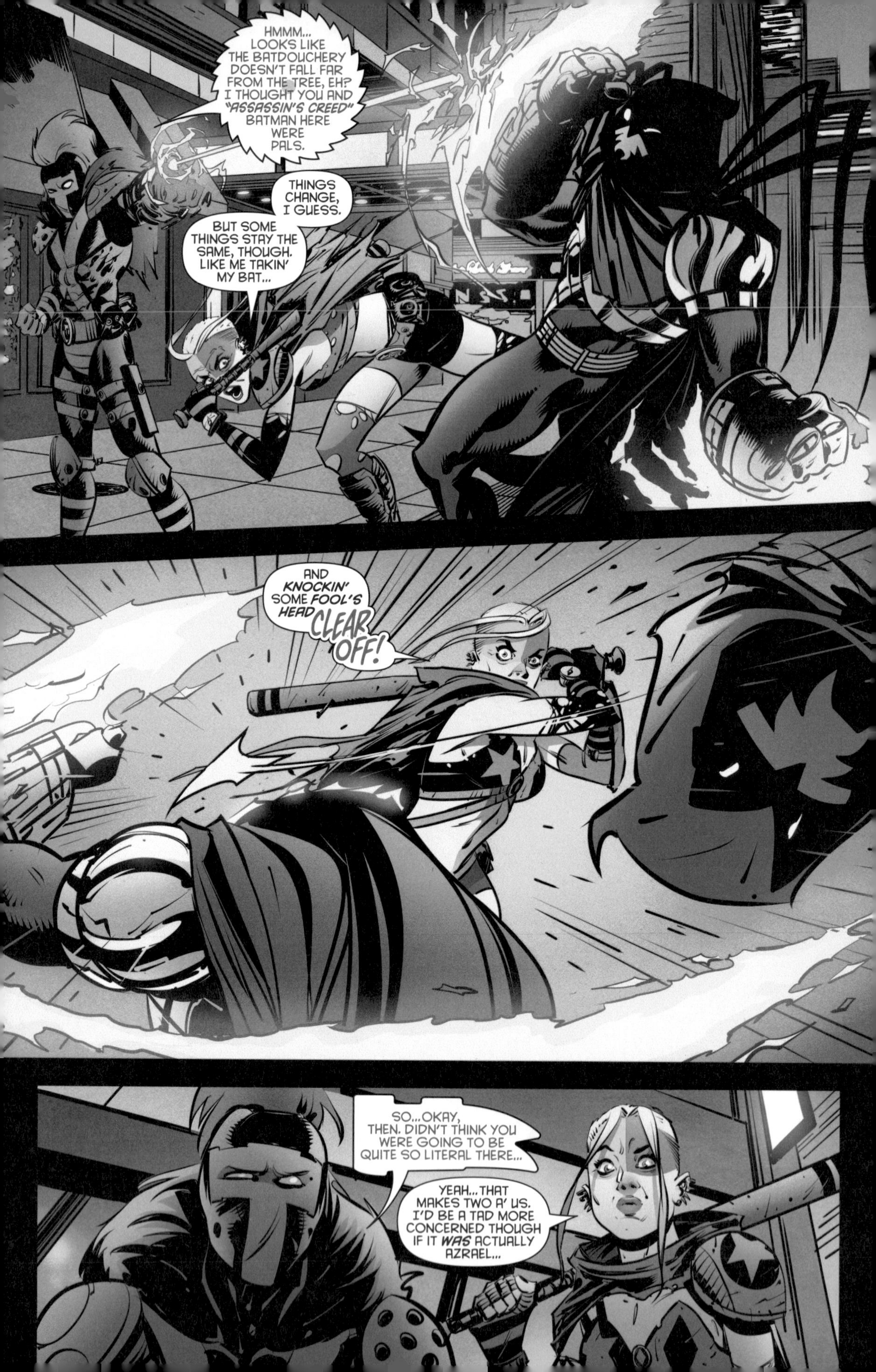
HMMM... LOOKS LIKE THE BATDOUCHERY DOESN'T FALL FAR FROM THE TREE, EH? I THOUGHT YOU AND "ASSASSIN'S CREED" BATMAN HERE WERE PALS.
THINGS CHANGE, I GUESS.
BUT SOME THINGS STAY THE SAME, THOUGH. LIKE ME TAKIN' MY BAT...
AND KNOCKIN' SOME FOOL'S HEAD CLEAR OFF!
SO...OKAY, THEN. DIDN'T THINK YOU WERE GOING TO BE QUITE SO LITERAL THERE...
YEAH... THAT MAKES TWO A' US. I'D BE A TAD MORE CONCERNED THOUGH IF IT WAS ACTUALLY AZRAEL...

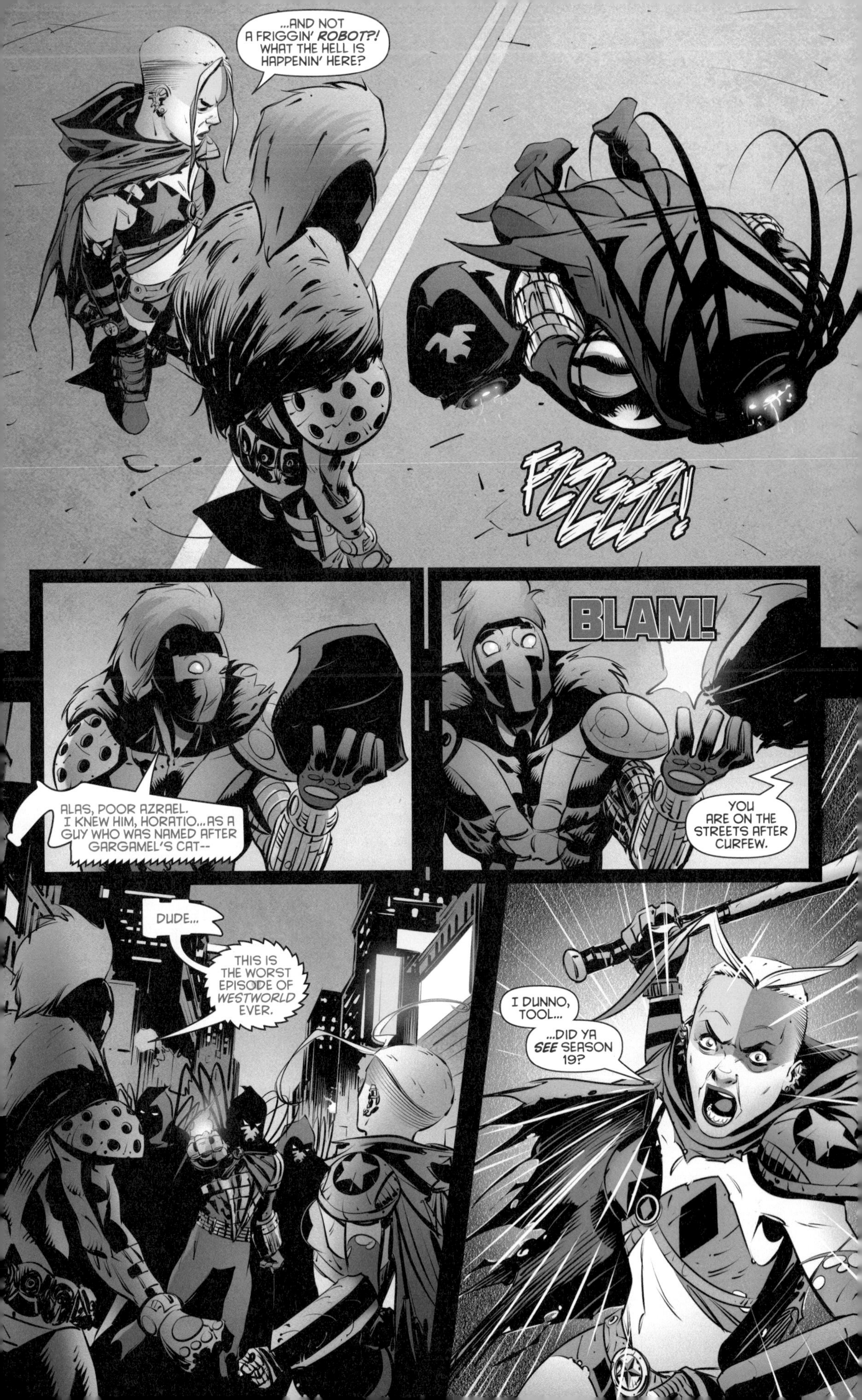
...AND NOT A FRIGGIN' ROBOT?! WHAT THE HELL IS HAPPENIN' HERE?
FZZZZZ!
ALAS, POOR AZRAEL. I KNEW HIM, HORATIO...AS A GUY WHO WAS NAMED AFTER GARGAMEL'S CAT--
BLAM!
YOU ARE ON THE STREETS AFTER CURFEW.
DUDE...
THIS IS THE WORST EPISODE OF WESTWORLD EVER.
I DUNNO, TOOL...
...DID YA SEE SEASON 19?

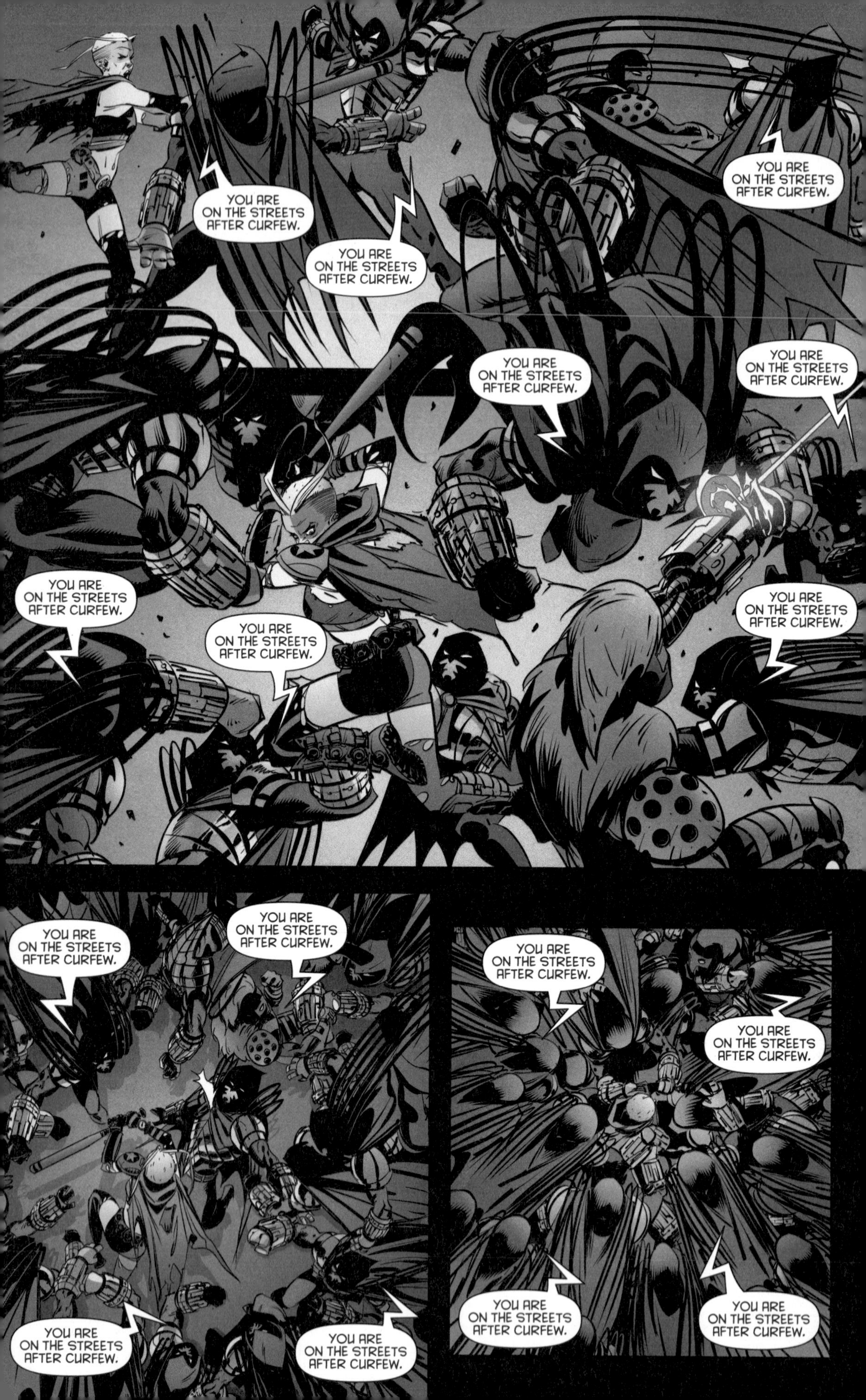
YOU ARE ON THE STREETS AFTER CURFEW.
YOU ARE ON THE STREETS AFTER CURFEW.
YOU ARE ON THE STREETS AFTER CURFEW.
YOU ARE ON THE STREETS AFTER CURFEW.
YOU ARE ON THE STREETS AFTER CURFEW.
YOU ARE ON THE STREETS AFTER CURFEW.
YOU ARE ON THE STREETS AFTER CURFEW.
YOU ARE ON THE STREETS AFTER CURFEW.
YOU ARE ON THE STREETS AFTER CURFEW.
YOU ARE ON THE STREETS AFTER CURFEW.
YOU ARE ON THE STREETS AFTER CURFEW.
YOU ARE ON THE STREETS AFTER CURFEW.
YOU ARE ON THE STREETS AFTER CURFEW.
YOU ARE ON THE STREETS AFTER CURFEW.
YOU ARE ON THE STREETS AFTER CURFEW.
YOU ARE ON THE STREETS AFTER CURFEW.

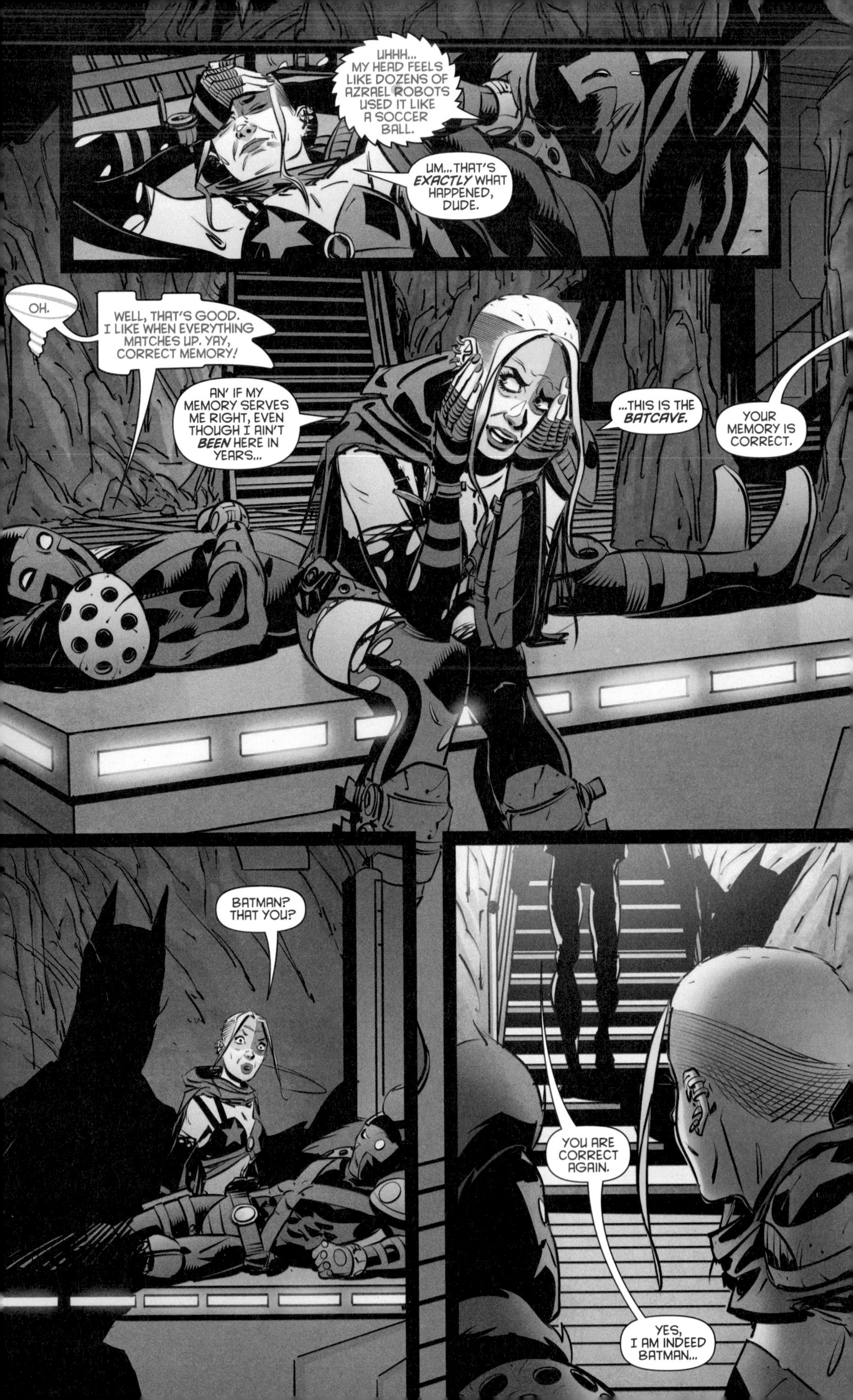
UHHH... MY HEAD FEELS LIKE DOZENS OF AZRAEL ROBOTS USED IT LIKE A SOCCER BALL.
UM...THAT'S *EXACTLY* WHAT HAPPENED, DUDE.
OH.
WELL, THAT'S GOOD. I LIKE WHEN EVERYTHING MATCHES UP. YAY, CORRECT MEMORY!
AN' IF MY MEMORY SERVES ME RIGHT, EVEN THOUGH I AIN'T *BEEN* HERE IN YEARS...
...THIS IS THE *BATCAVE.*
YOUR MEMORY IS CORRECT.
BATMAN? THAT YOU?
YOU ARE CORRECT AGAIN.
YES, I AM INDEED BATMAN...

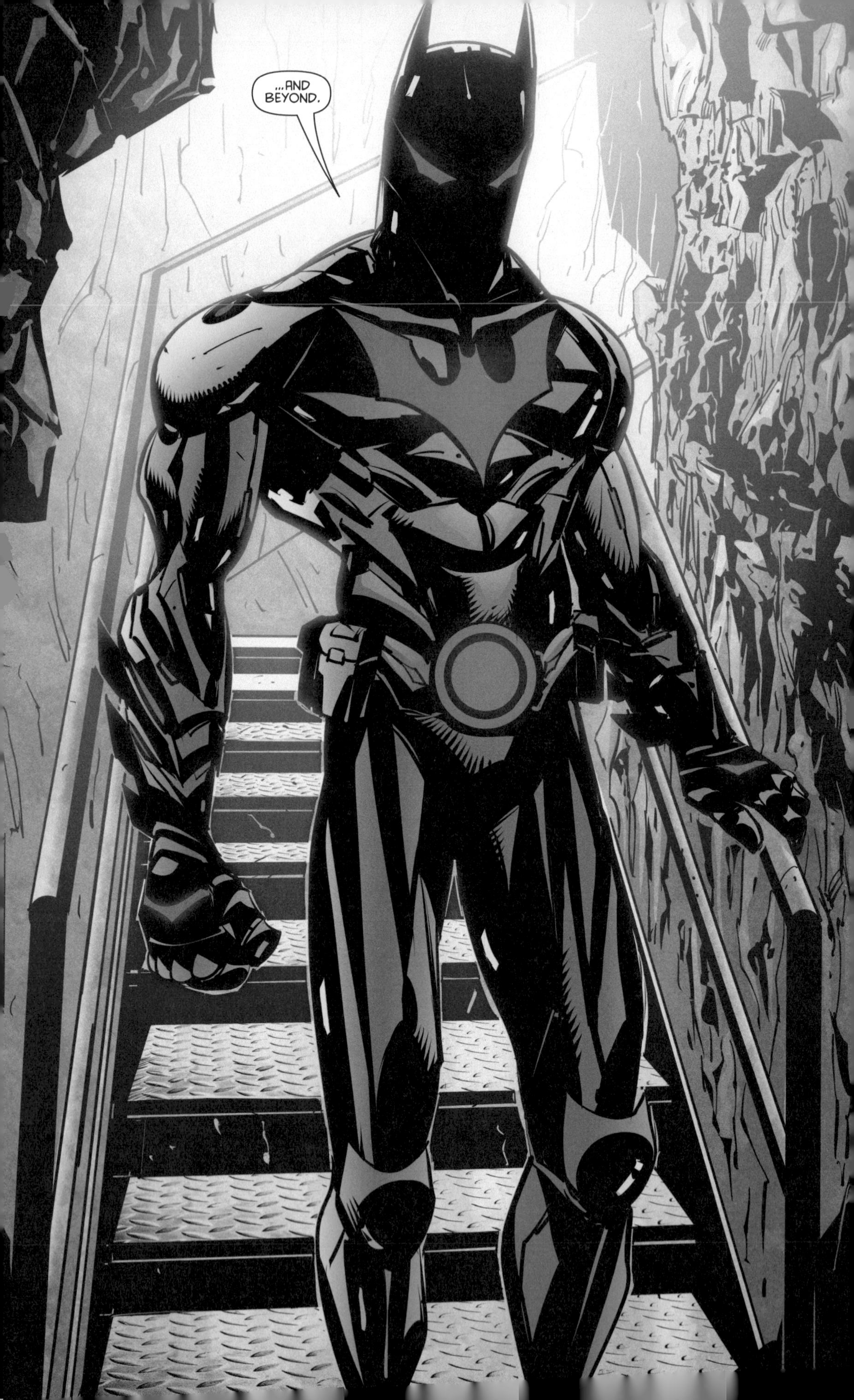
...AND BEYOND.

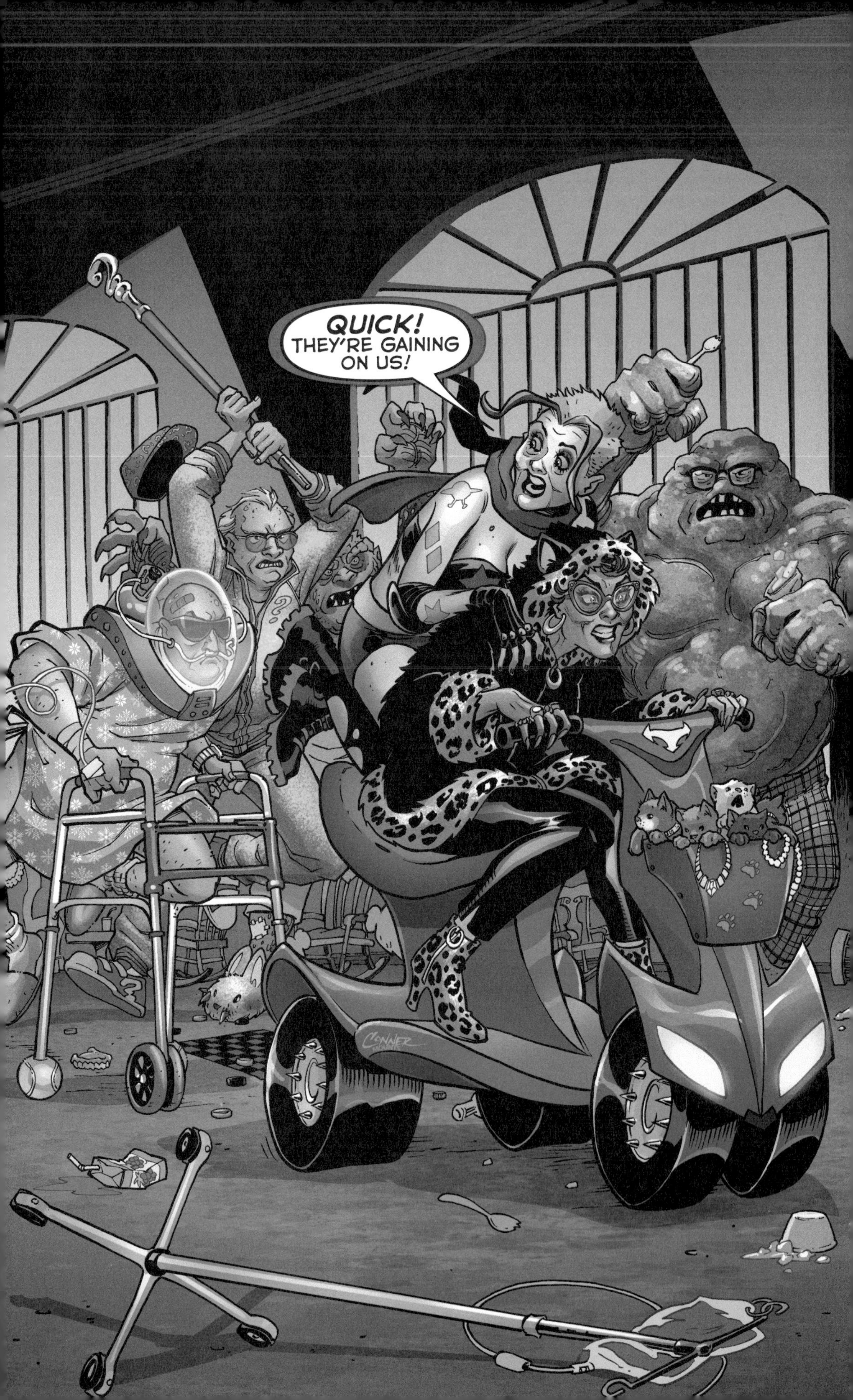
QUICK! THEY'RE GAINING ON US!
CONNER

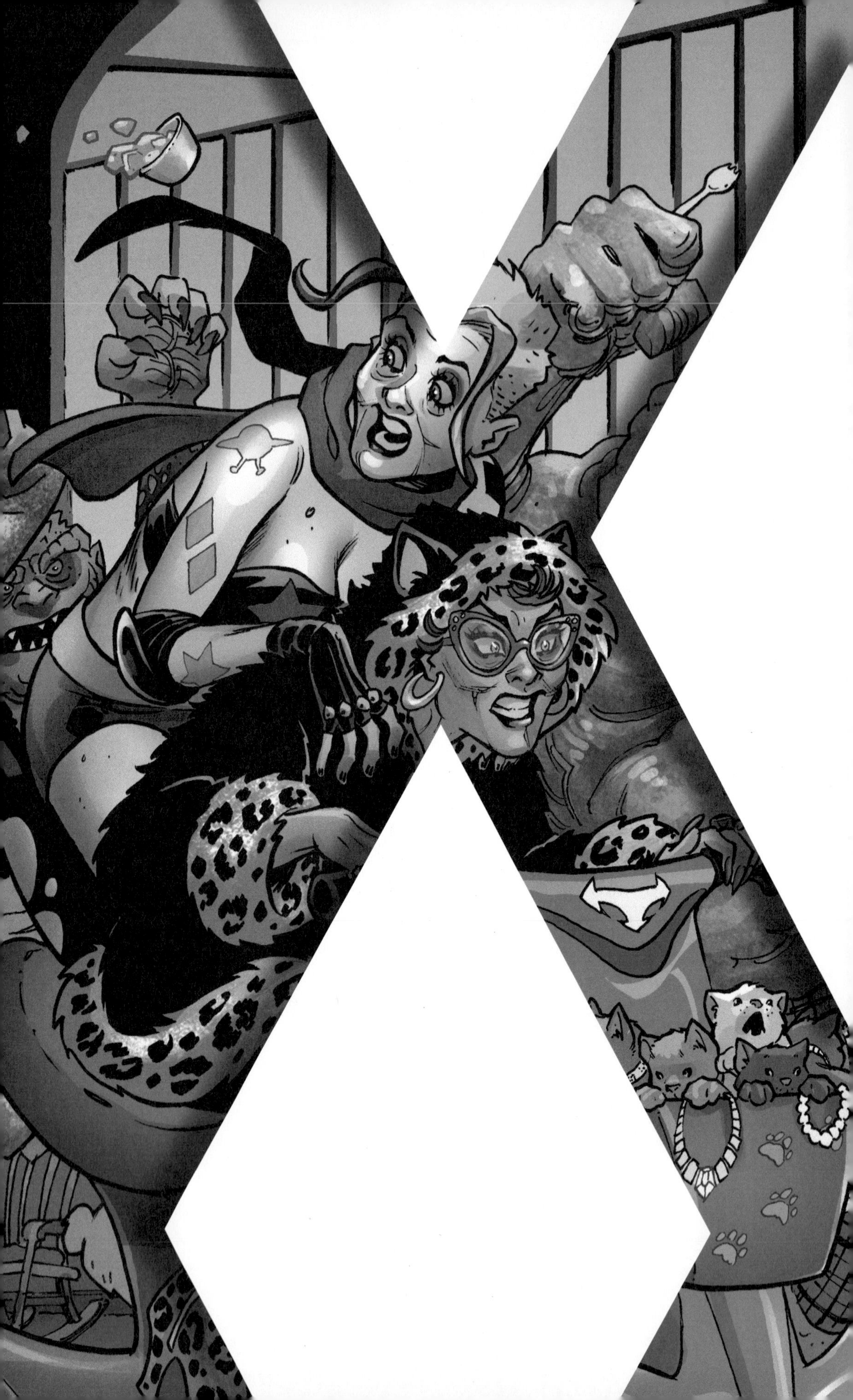

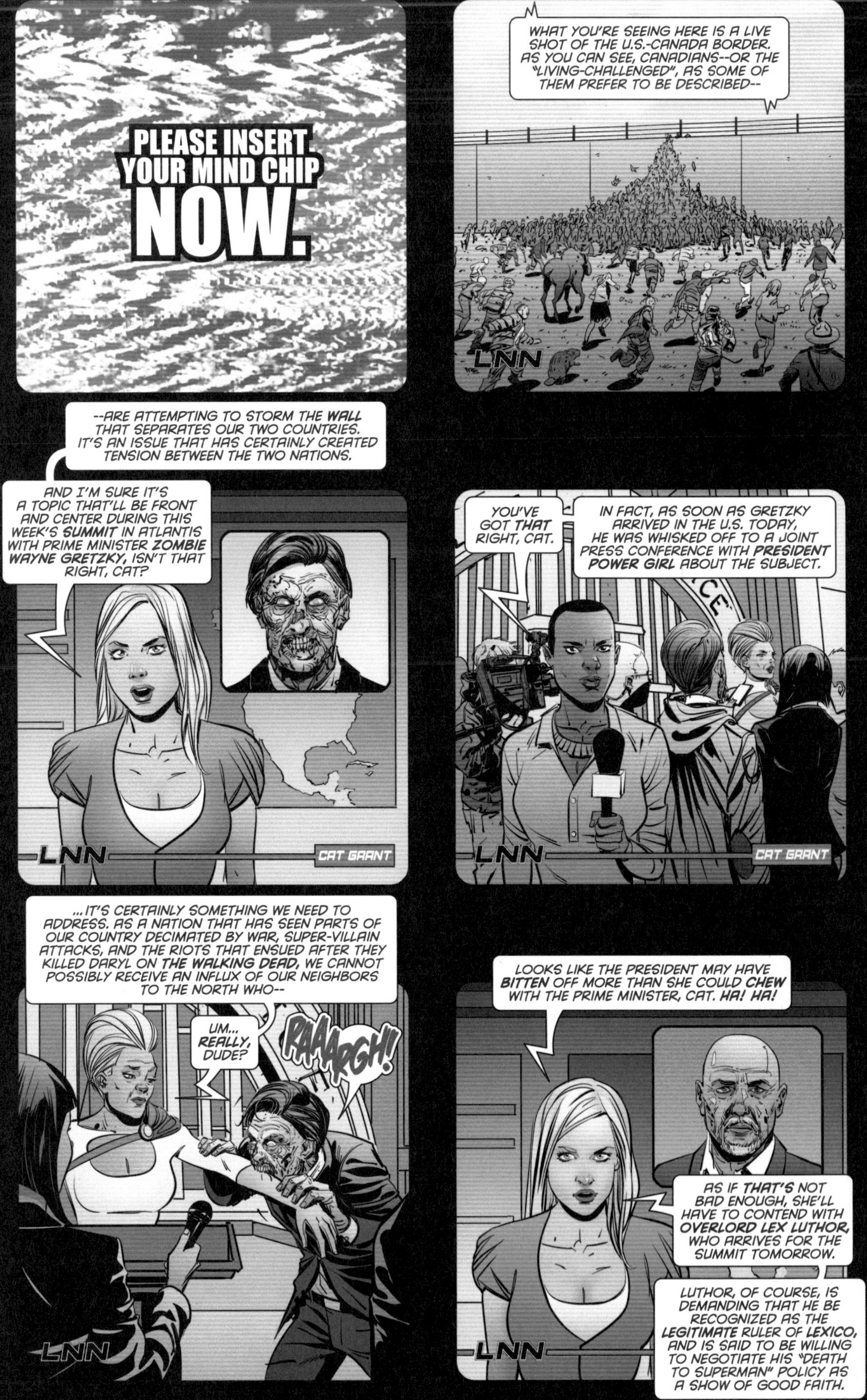
PLEASE INSERT YOUR MIND CHIP NOW.
WHAT YOU'RE SEEING HERE IS A LIVE SHOT OF THE U.S.-CANADA BORDER. AS YOU CAN SEE, CANADIANS--OR THE "LIVING-CHALLENGED", AS SOME OF THEM PREFER TO BE DESCRIBED--
LNN
--ARE ATTEMPTING TO STORM THE WALL THAT SEPARATES OUR TWO COUNTRIES. IT'S AN ISSUE THAT HAS CERTAINLY CREATED TENSION BETWEEN THE TWO NATIONS.
AND I'M SURE IT'S A TOPIC THAT'LL BE FRONT AND CENTER DURING THIS WEEK'S SUMMIT IN ATLANTIS WITH PRIME MINISTER ZOMBIE WAYNE GRETZKY, ISN'T THAT RIGHT, CAT?
LNN
CAT GRANT
YOU'VE GOT THAT RIGHT, CAT.
IN FACT, AS SOON AS GRETZKY ARRIVED IN THE U.S. TODAY, HE WAS WHISKED OFF TO A JOINT PRESS CONFERENCE WITH PRESIDENT POWER GIRL ABOUT THE SUBJECT.
LNN
CAT GRANT
...IT'S CERTAINLY SOMETHING WE NEED TO ADDRESS. AS A NATION THAT HAS SEEN PARTS OF OUR COUNTRY DECIMATED BY WAR, SUPER-VILLAIN ATTACKS, AND THE RIOTS THAT ENSUED AFTER THEY KILLED DARYL ON THE WALKING DEAD, WE CANNOT POSSIBLY RECEIVE AN INFLUX OF OUR NEIGHBORS TO THE NORTH WHO--
UM... REALLY, DUDE?
RAAAARGH!!
LNN
LOOKS LIKE THE PRESIDENT MAY HAVE BITTEN OFF MORE THAN SHE COULD CHEW WITH THE PRIME MINISTER, CAT. HA! HA!
AS IF THAT'S NOT BAD ENOUGH, SHE'LL HAVE TO CONTEND WITH OVERLORD LEX LUTHOR, WHO ARRIVES FOR THE SUMMIT TOMORROW.
LUTHOR, OF COURSE, IS DEMANDING THAT HE BE RECOGNIZED AS THE LEGITIMATE RULER OF LEXICO, AND IS SAID TO BE WILLING TO NEGOTIATE HIS "DEATH TO SUPERMAN" POLICY AS A SHOW OF GOOD FAITH.
LNN

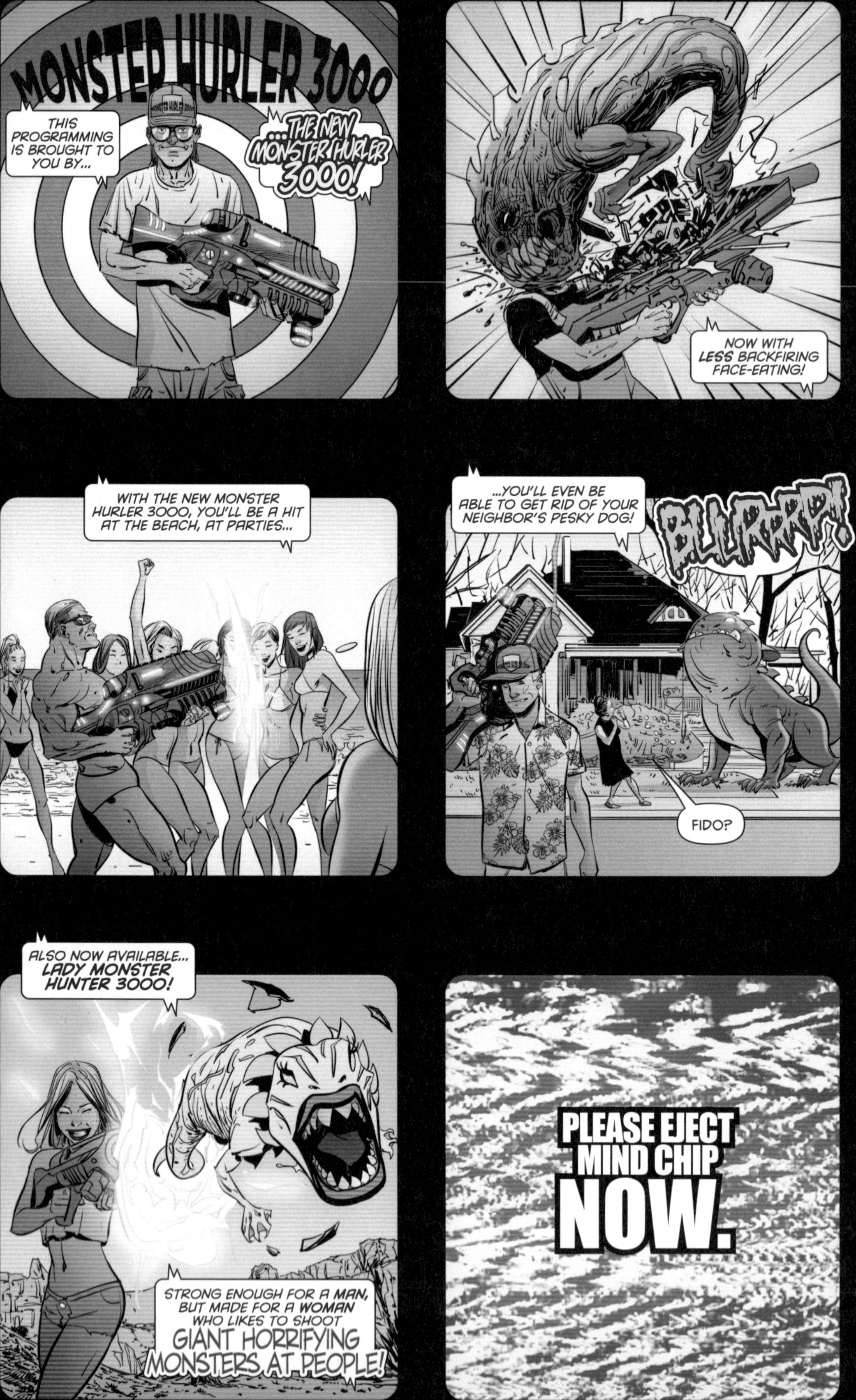
MONSTER HURLER 3000
THIS PROGRAMMING IS BROUGHT TO YOU BY...
...THE NEW MONSTER HURLER 3000!
NOW WITH LESS BACKFIRING FACE-EATING!
WITH THE NEW MONSTER HURLER 3000, YOU'LL BE A HIT AT THE BEACH, AT PARTIES...
...YOU'LL EVEN BE ABLE TO GET RID OF YOUR NEIGHBOR'S PESKY DOG!
BLURRRP!
FIDO?
ALSO NOW AVAILABLE... LADY MONSTER HUNTER 3000!
STRONG ENOUGH FOR A MAN, BUT MADE FOR A WOMAN WHO LIKES TO SHOOT
GIANT HORRIFYING MONSTERS AT PEOPLE!
PLEASE EJECT MIND CHIP NOW.

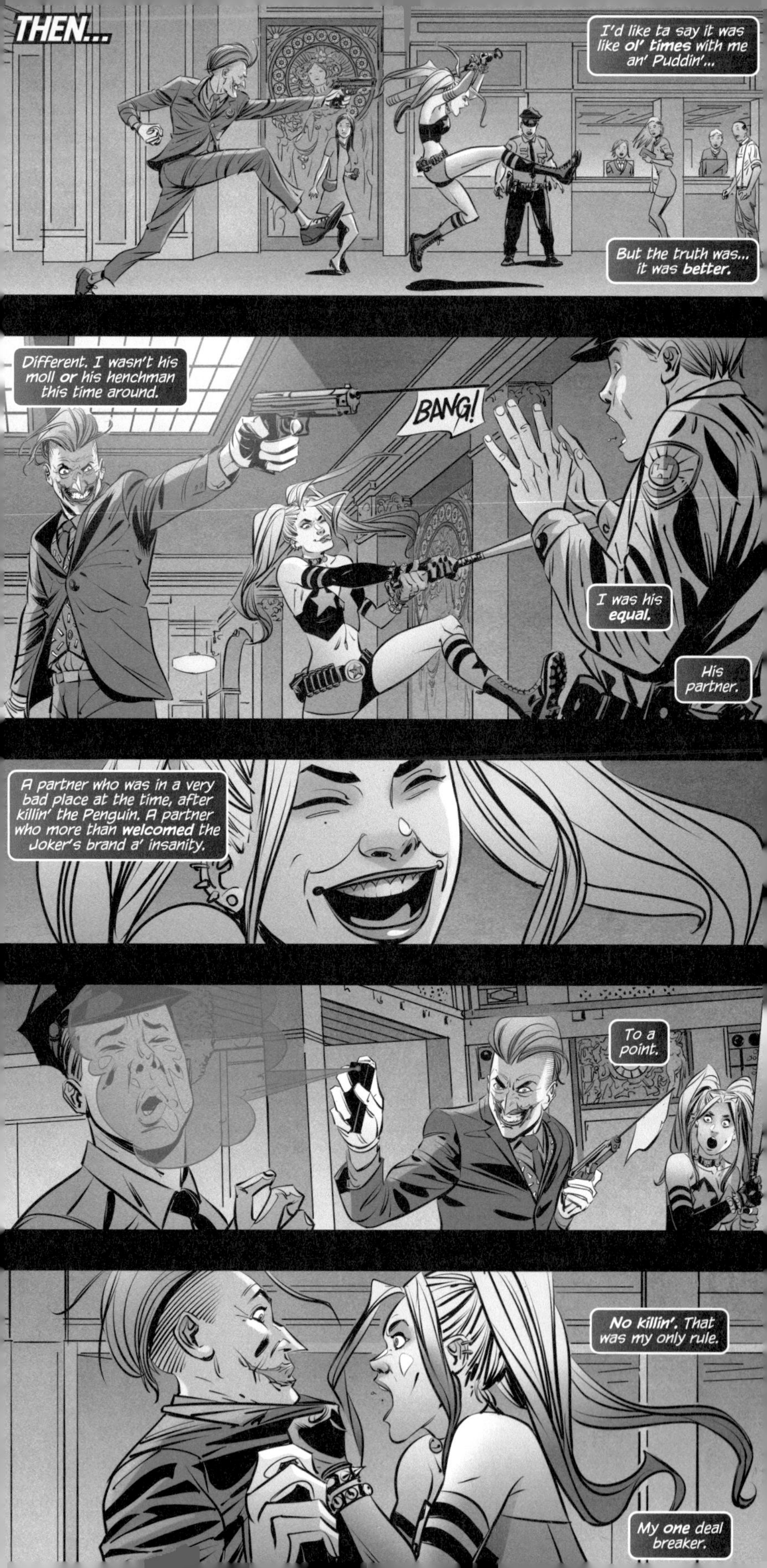
THEN...
I'd like ta say it was like ol' times with me an' Puddin'...
But the truth was... it was better.
Different. I wasn't his moll or his henchman this time around.
BANG!
I was his equal.
His partner.
A partner who was in a very bad place at the time, after killin' the Penguin. A partner who more than welcomed the Joker's brand a' insanity.
To a point.
No killin'. That was my only rule.
My one deal breaker.

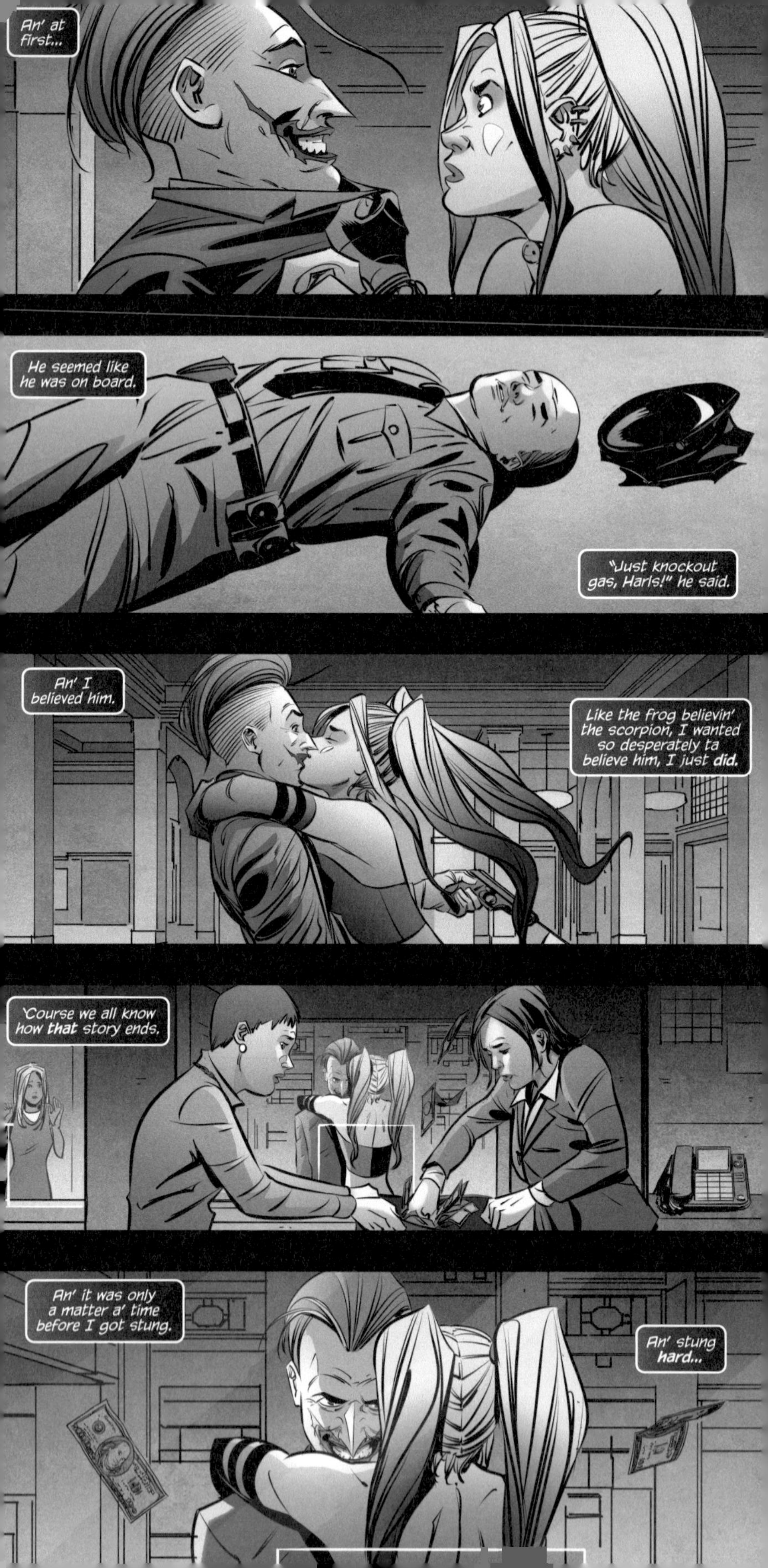
An' at first...
He seemed like he was on board.
"Just knockout gas, Harls!" he said.
An' I believed him.
Like the frog believin' the scorpion, I wanted so desperately ta believe him, I just **did.**
'Course we all know how **that** story ends.
An' it was only a matter a' time before I got stung.
An' stung **hard...**

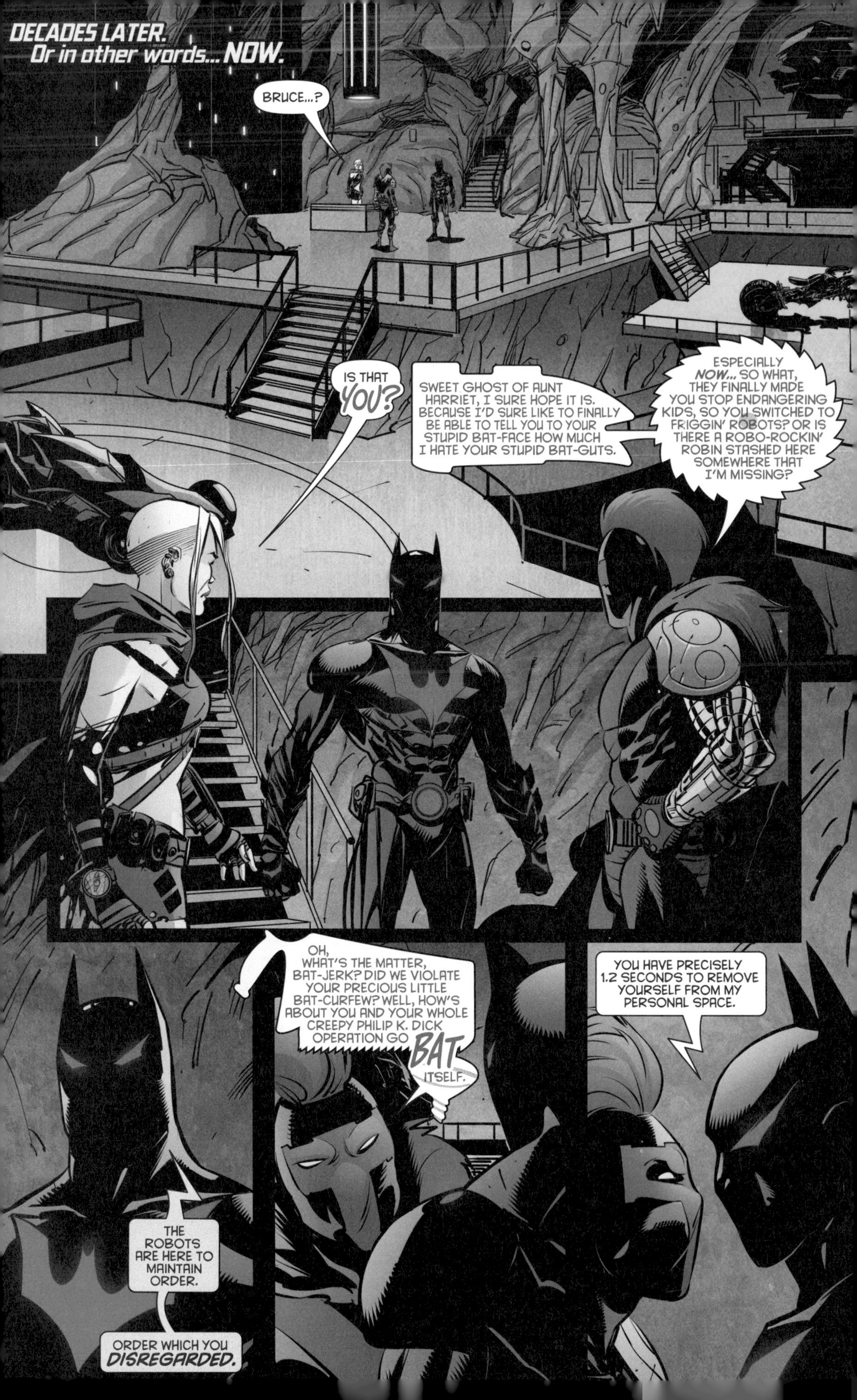
DECADES LATER. Or in other words... NOW.
BRUCE...?
IS THAT YOU?
SWEET GHOST OF AUNT HARRIET, I SURE HOPE IT IS. BECAUSE I'D SURE LIKE TO FINALLY BE ABLE TO TELL YOU TO YOUR STUPID BAT-FACE HOW MUCH I HATE YOUR STUPID BAT-GUTS.
ESPECIALLY NOW... SO WHAT, THEY FINALLY MADE YOU STOP ENDANGERING KIDS, SO YOU SWITCHED TO FRIGGIN' ROBOTS? OR IS THERE A ROBO-ROCKIN' ROBIN STASHED HERE SOMEWHERE THAT I'M MISSING?
THE ROBOTS ARE HERE TO MAINTAIN ORDER.
ORDER WHICH YOU DISREGARDED.
OH, WHAT'S THE MATTER, BAT-JERK? DID WE VIOLATE YOUR PRECIOUS LITTLE BAT-CURFEW? WELL, HOW'S ABOUT YOU AND YOUR WHOLE CREEPY PHILIP K. DICK OPERATION GO BAT ITSELF.
YOU HAVE PRECISELY 1.2 SECONDS TO REMOVE YOURSELF FROM MY PERSONAL SPACE.

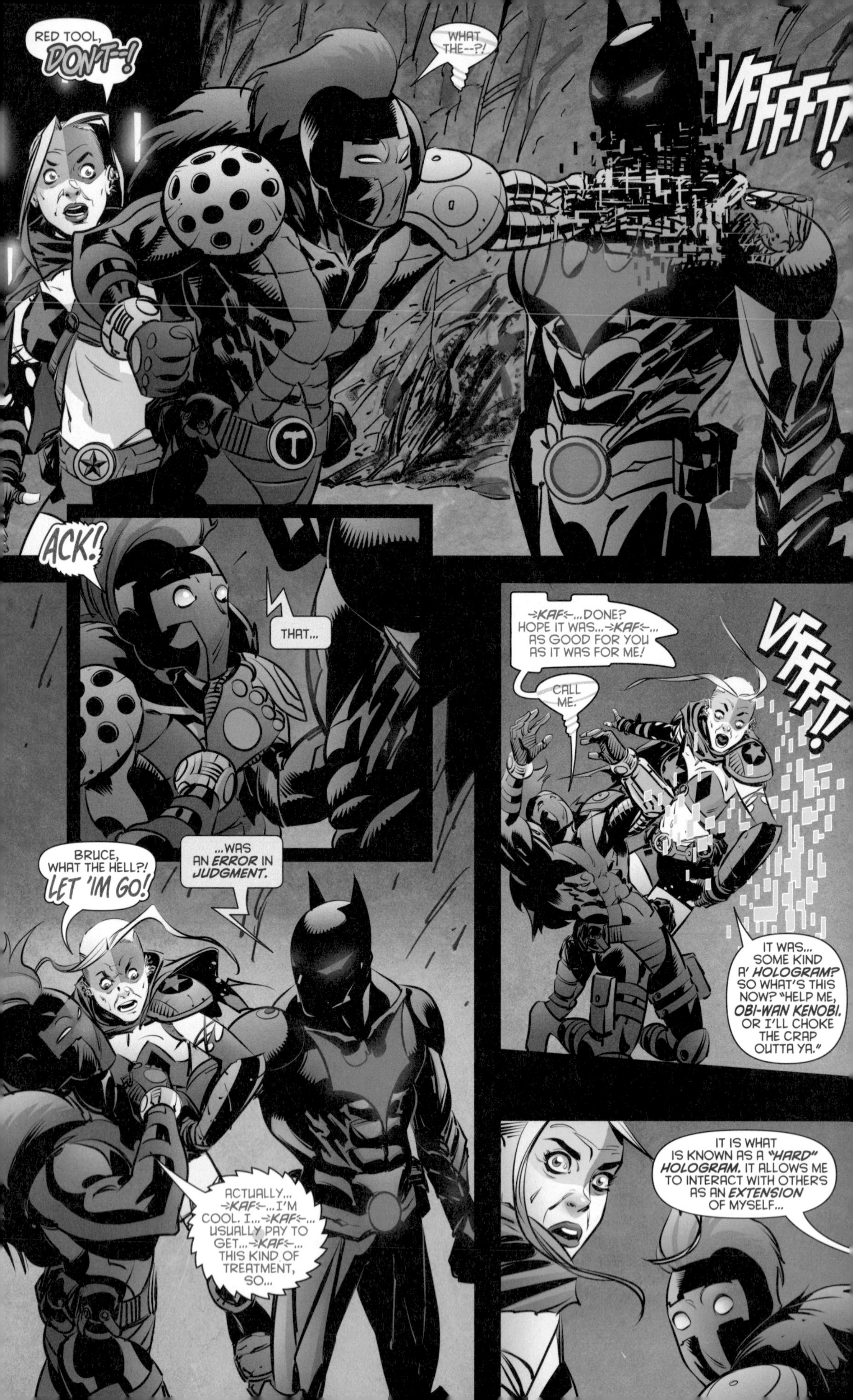
RED TOOL, DON'T-!
WHAT THE--?!
VFFFFT!
ACK!
THAT...
...WAS AN ERROR IN JUDGMENT.
BRUCE, WHAT THE HELL?! LET 'IM GO!
ACTUALLY... ~KAF~...I'M COOL. I...~KAF~... USUALLY PAY TO GET...~KAF~... THIS KIND OF TREATMENT, SO...
~KAF~...DONE? HOPE IT WAS...~KAF~... AS GOOD FOR YOU AS IT WAS FOR ME!
CALL ME.
VFFFT!!
IT WAS... SOME KIND A' HOLOGRAM? SO WHAT'S THIS NOW? "HELP ME, OBI-WAN KENOBI, OR I'LL CHOKE THE CRAP OUTTA YA."
IT IS WHAT IS KNOWN AS A "HARD" HOLOGRAM. IT ALLOWS ME TO INTERACT WITH OTHERS AS AN EXTENSION OF MYSELF...

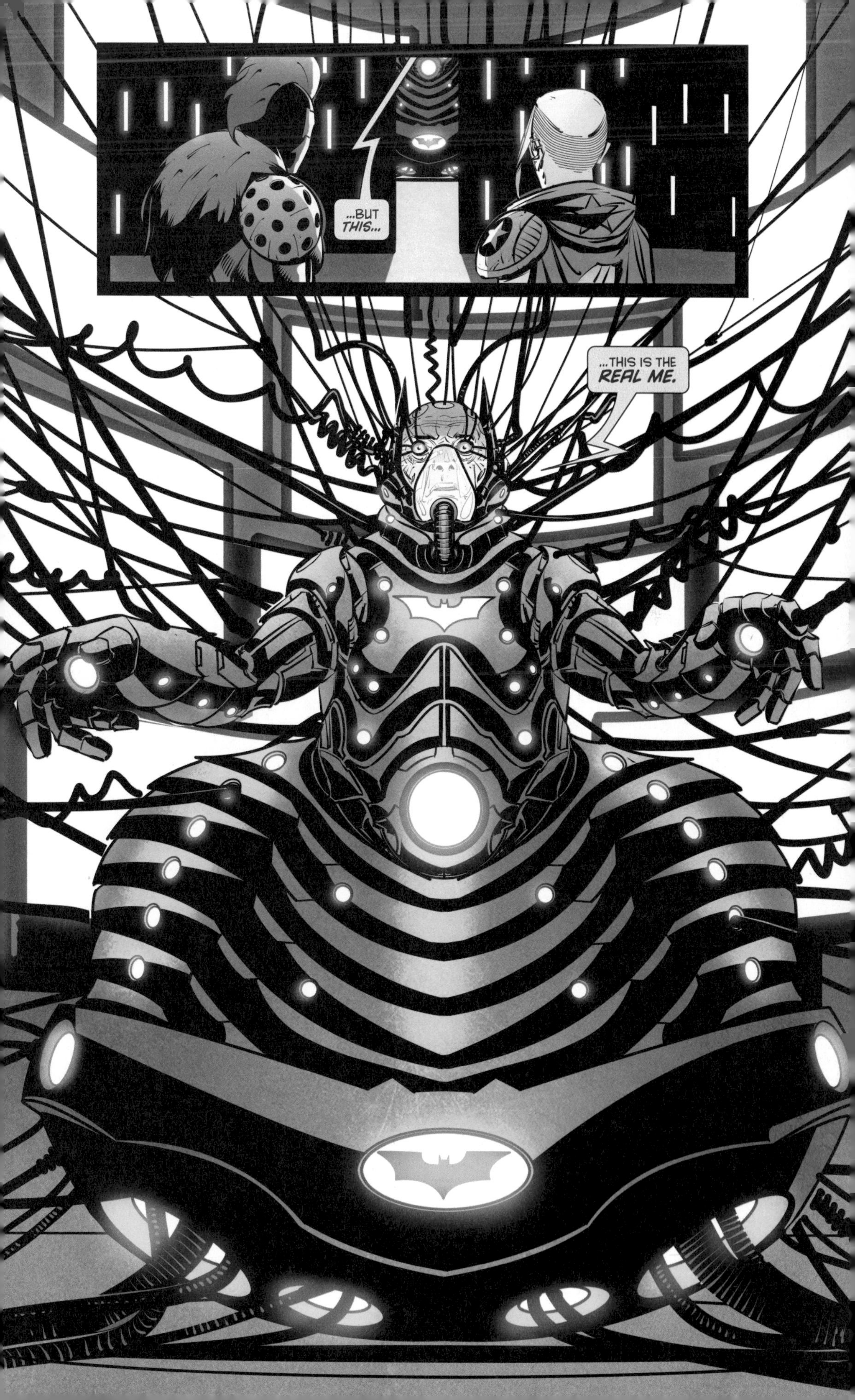
...BUT THIS...
...THIS IS THE REAL ME.

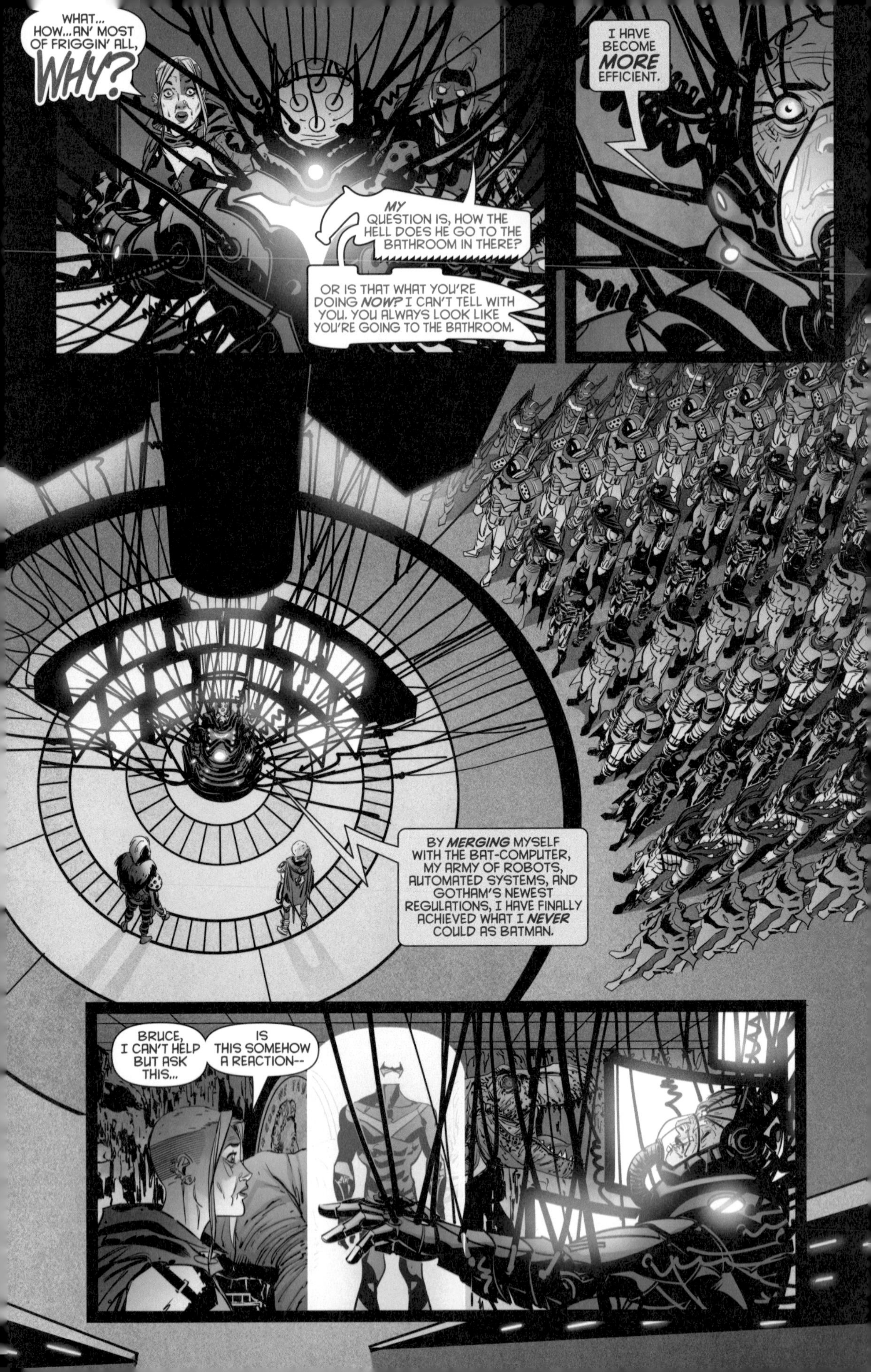
WHAT... HOW...AN' MOST OF FRIGGIN' ALL, WHY?
MY QUESTION IS, HOW THE HELL DOES HE GO TO THE BATHROOM IN THERE?
OR IS THAT WHAT YOU'RE DOING NOW? I CAN'T TELL WITH YOU. YOU ALWAYS LOOK LIKE YOU'RE GOING TO THE BATHROOM.
I HAVE BECOME MORE EFFICIENT.
BY MERGING MYSELF WITH THE BAT-COMPUTER, MY ARMY OF ROBOTS, AUTOMATED SYSTEMS, AND GOTHAM'S NEWEST REGULATIONS, I HAVE FINALLY ACHIEVED WHAT I NEVER COULD AS BATMAN.
BRUCE, I CAN'T HELP BUT ASK THIS...
IS THIS SOMEHOW A REACTION--

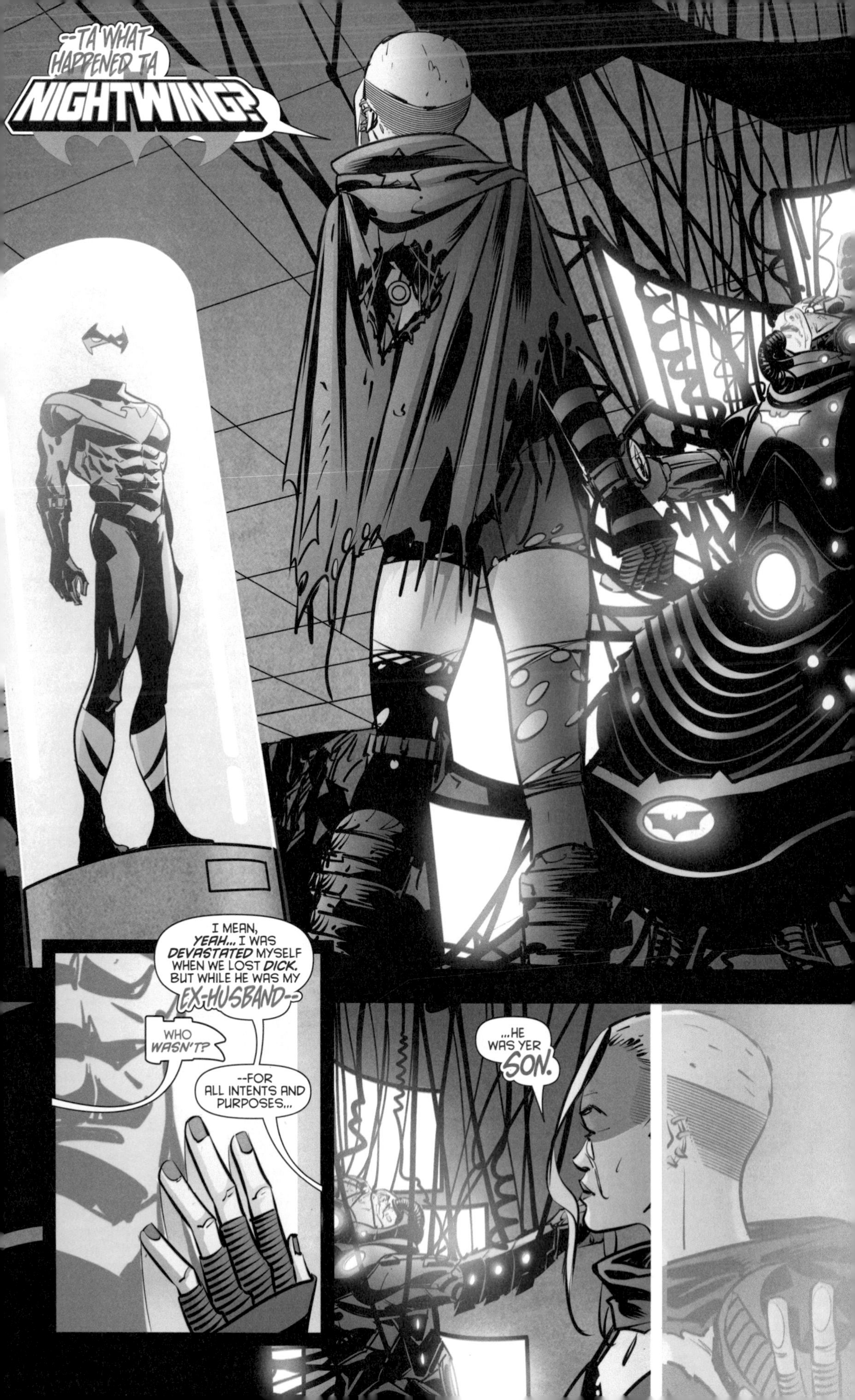
--TA WHAT HAPPENED TA NIGHTWING?
I MEAN, YEAH... I WAS DEVASTATED MYSELF WHEN WE LOST DICK. BUT WHILE HE WAS MY EX-HUSBAND--
WHO WASN'T?
--FOR ALL INTENTS AND PURPOSES...
...HE WAS YER SON.

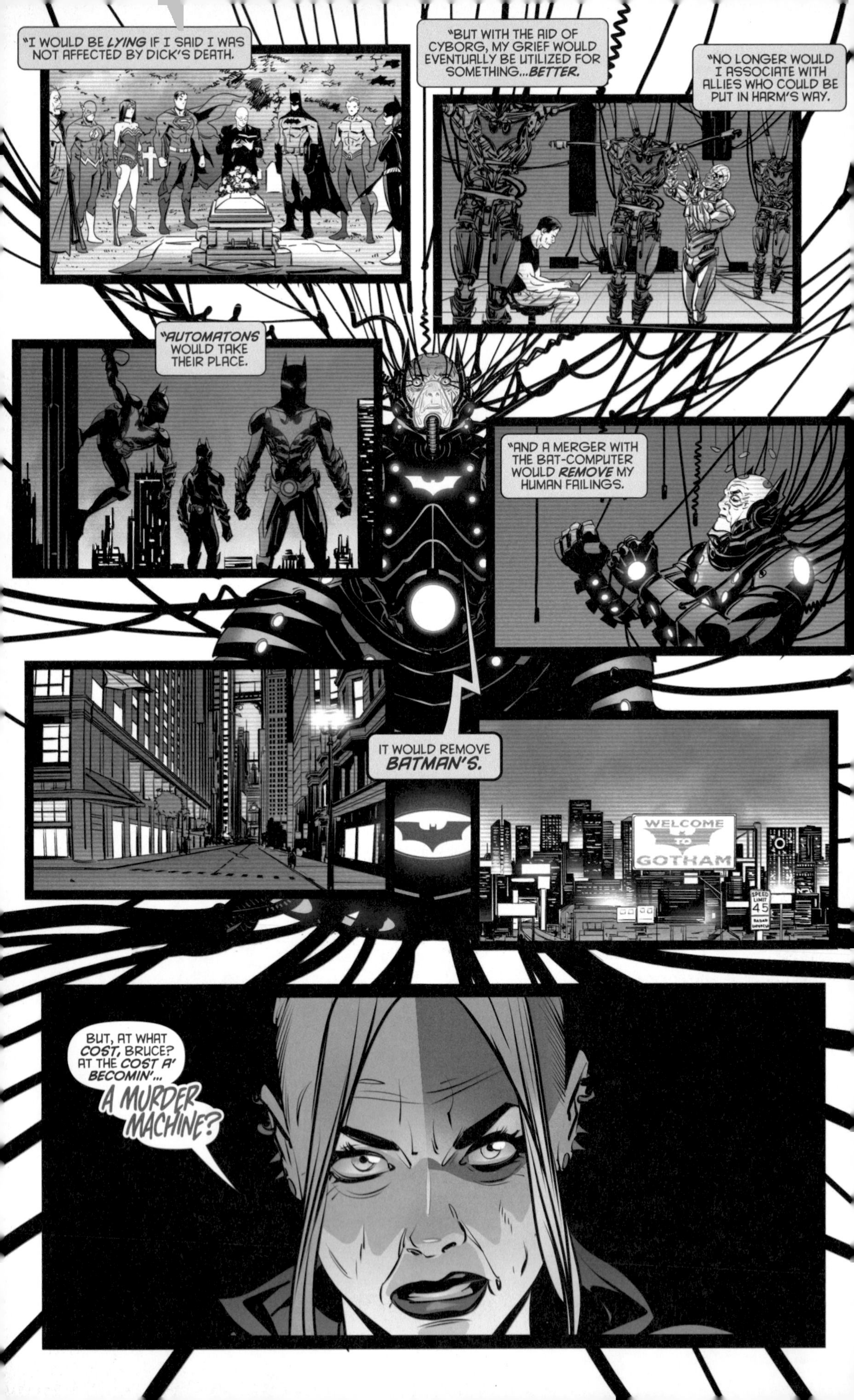
"I WOULD BE LYING IF I SAID I WAS NOT AFFECTED BY DICK'S DEATH.
"BUT WITH THE AID OF CYBORG, MY GRIEF WOULD EVENTUALLY BE UTILIZED FOR SOMETHING...BETTER.
"NO LONGER WOULD I ASSOCIATE WITH ALLIES WHO COULD BE PUT IN HARM'S WAY.
"AUTOMATONS WOULD TAKE THEIR PLACE.
"AND A MERGER WITH THE BAT-COMPUTER WOULD REMOVE MY HUMAN FAILINGS.
IT WOULD REMOVE BATMAN'S.
WELCOME TO GOTHAM
SPEED LIMIT 45
BUT, AT WHAT COST, BRUCE? AT THE COST A' BECOMIN'... A MURDER MACHINE?

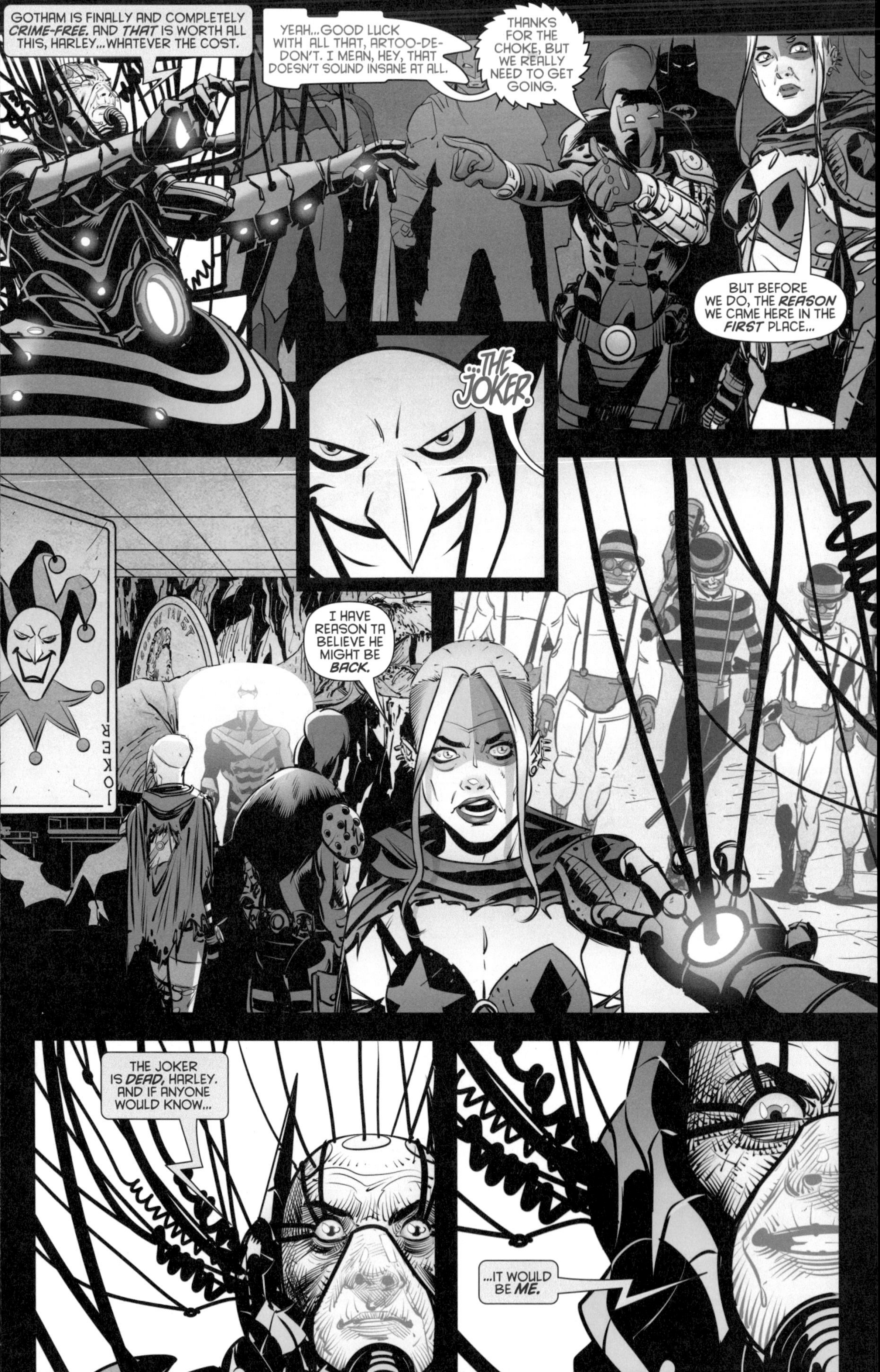

GOTHAM IS FINALLY AND COMPLETELY CRIME-FREE. AND THAT IS WORTH ALL THIS, HARLEY...WHATEVER THE COST.
YEAH...GOOD LUCK WITH ALL THAT, ARTOO-DE-DON'T. I MEAN, HEY, THAT DOESN'T SOUND INSANE AT ALL.
THANKS FOR THE CHOKE, BUT WE REALLY NEED TO GET GOING.
BUT BEFORE WE DO, THE REASON WE CAME HERE IN THE FIRST PLACE...
...THE JOKER.
I HAVE REASON TA BELIEVE HE MIGHT BE BACK.
JOKER
THE JOKER IS DEAD, HARLEY. AND IF ANYONE WOULD KNOW...
...IT WOULD BE ME.

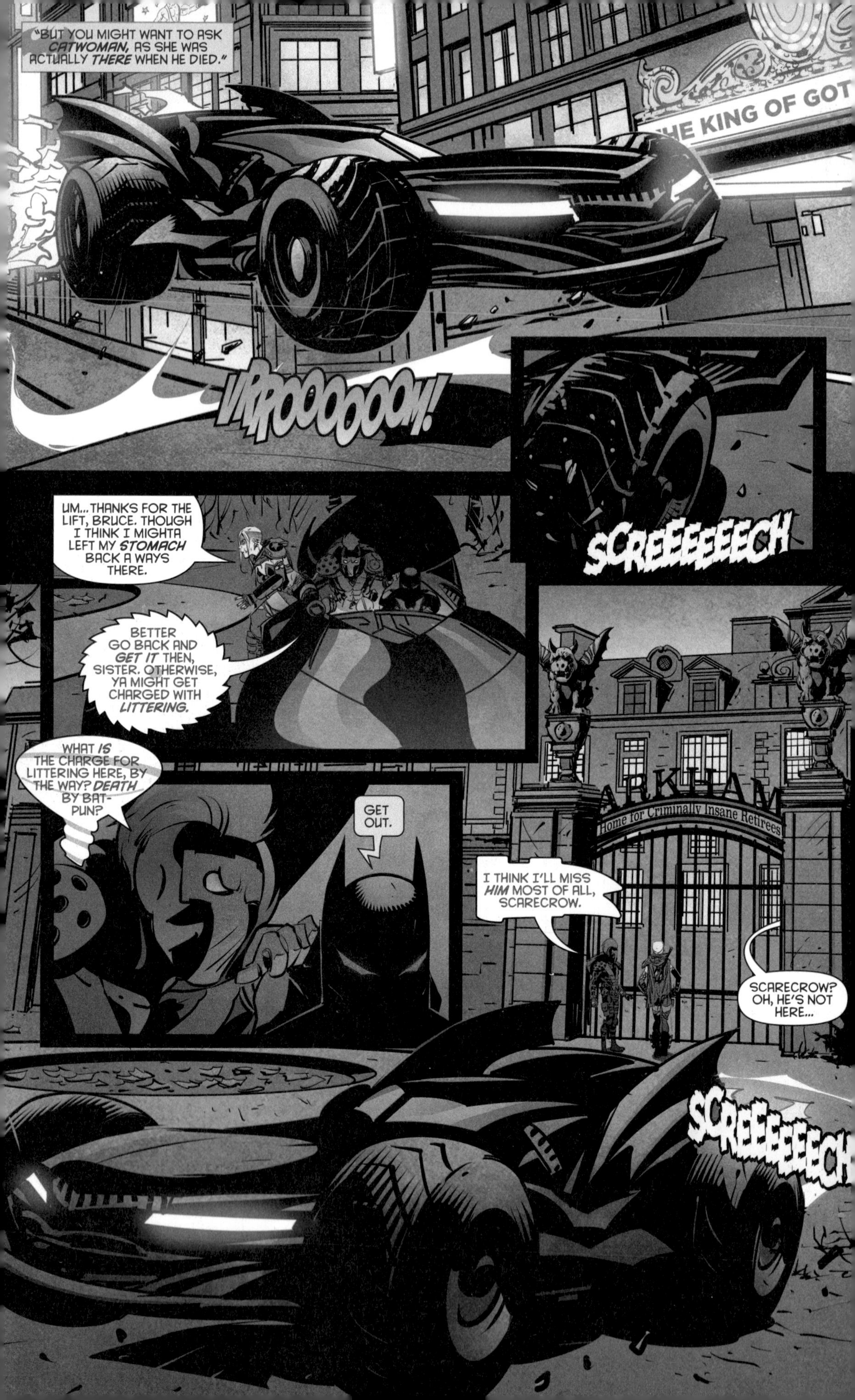
"BUT YOU MIGHT WANT TO ASK CATWOMAN, AS SHE WAS ACTUALLY THERE WHEN HE DIED."
THE KING OF GOT
VRROOOOOOM!
SCREEEEEECH
UM... THANKS FOR THE LIFT, BRUCE. THOUGH I THINK I MIGHTA LEFT MY STOMACH BACK A WAYS THERE.
BETTER GO BACK AND GET IT THEN, SISTER. OTHERWISE, YA MIGHT GET CHARGED WITH LITTERING.
WHAT IS THE CHARGE FOR LITTERING HERE, BY THE WAY? DEATH BY BAT-PUN?
GET OUT.
ARKHAM
Home for Criminally Insane Retirees
I THINK I'LL MISS HIM MOST OF ALL, SCARECROW.
SCARECROW? OH, HE'S NOT HERE...
SCREEEEEECH

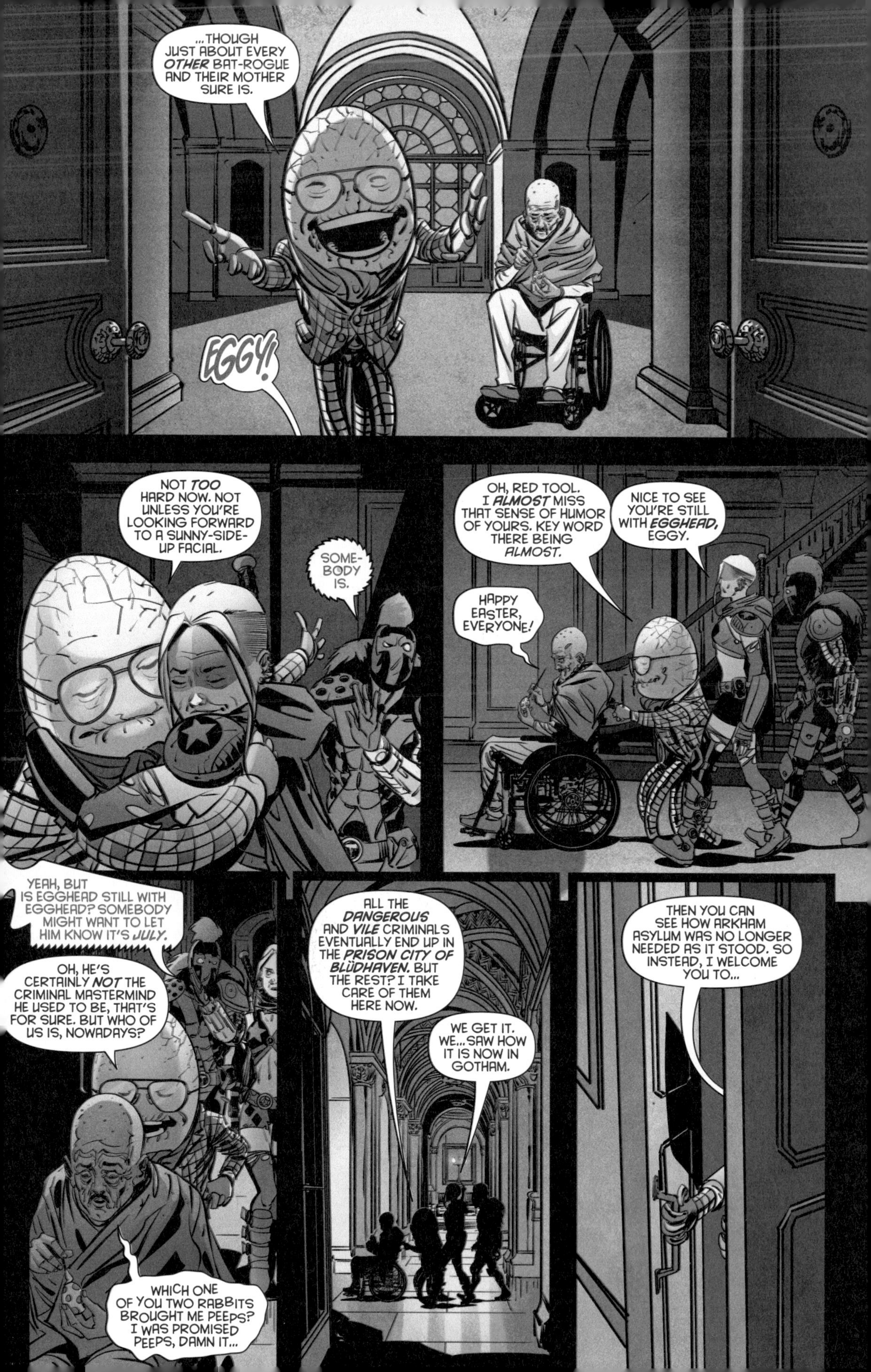
...THOUGH JUST ABOUT EVERY OTHER BAT-ROGUE AND THEIR MOTHER SURE IS.
EGGY!
NOT TOO HARD NOW. NOT UNLESS YOU'RE LOOKING FORWARD TO A SUNNY-SIDE-UP FACIAL.
SOME-BODY IS.
OH, RED TOOL. I ALMOST MISS THAT SENSE OF HUMOR OF YOURS. KEY WORD THERE BEING ALMOST.
NICE TO SEE YOU'RE STILL WITH EGGHEAD, EGGY.
HAPPY EASTER, EVERYONE!
YEAH, BUT IS EGGHEAD STILL WITH EGGHEAD? SOMEBODY MIGHT WANT TO LET HIM KNOW IT'S JULY.
OH, HE'S CERTAINLY NOT THE CRIMINAL MASTERMIND HE USED TO BE, THAT'S FOR SURE. BUT WHO OF US IS, NOWADAYS?
WHICH ONE OF YOU TWO RABBITS BROUGHT ME PEEPS? I WAS PROMISED PEEPS, DAMN IT...
ALL THE DANGEROUS AND VILE CRIMINALS EVENTUALLY END UP IN THE PRISON CITY OF BLÜDHAVEN. BUT THE REST? I TAKE CARE OF THEM HERE NOW.
WE GET IT. WE...SAW HOW IT IS NOW IN GOTHAM.
THEN YOU CAN SEE HOW ARKHAM ASYLUM WAS NO LONGER NEEDED AS IT STOOD. SO INSTEAD, I WELCOME YOU TO...

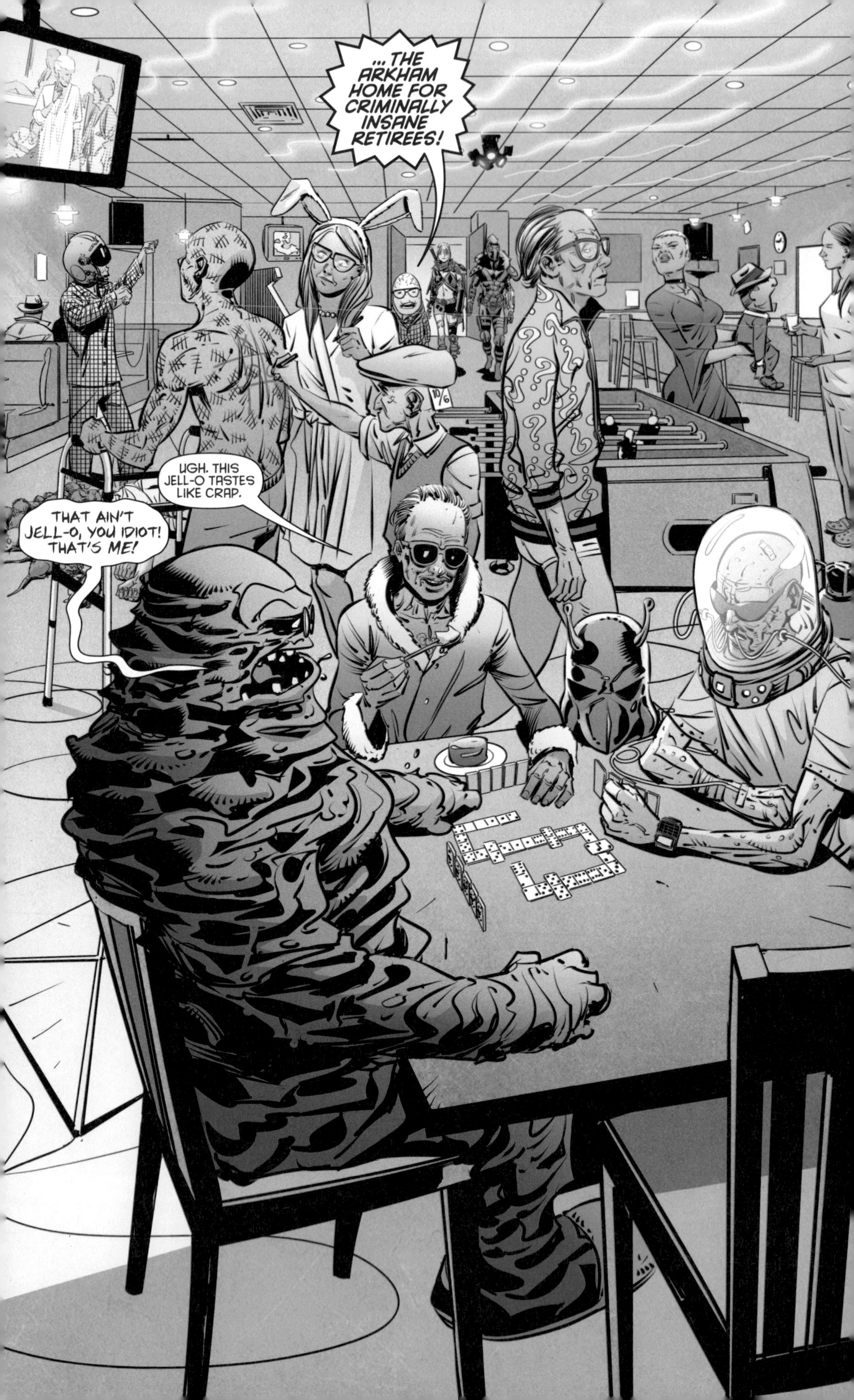
...THE ARKHAM HOME FOR CRIMINALLY INSANE RETIREES!
UGH. THIS JELL-O TASTES LIKE CRAP.
THAT AIN'T JELL-O, YOU IDIOT! THAT'S ME!
10/6

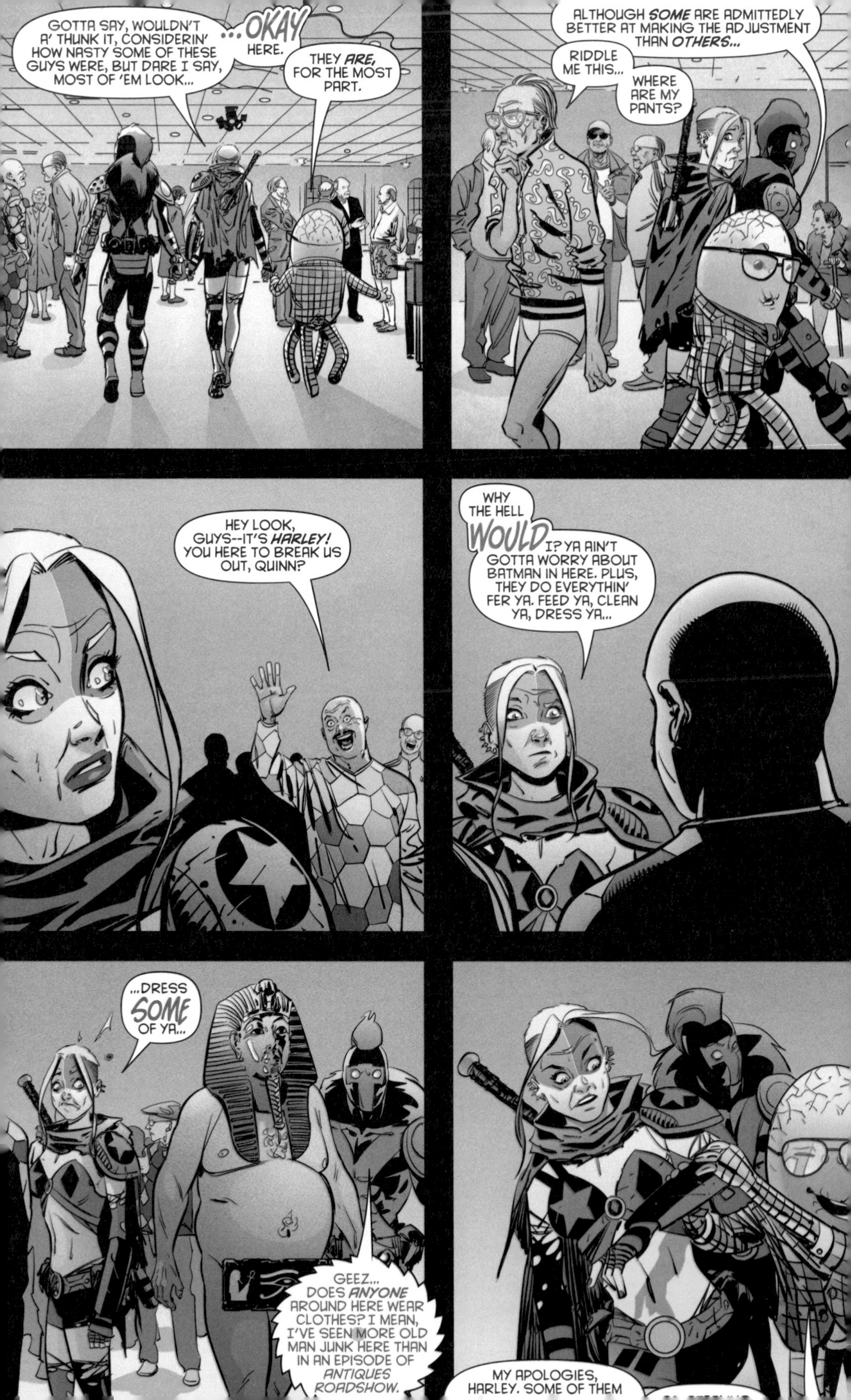
GOTTA SAY, WOULDN'T A' THUNK IT, CONSIDERIN' HOW NASTY SOME OF THESE GUYS WERE, BUT DARE I SAY, MOST OF 'EM LOOK...
...OKAY HERE.
THEY ARE, FOR THE MOST PART.
ALTHOUGH SOME ARE ADMITTEDLY BETTER AT MAKING THE ADJUSTMENT THAN OTHERS...
RIDDLE ME THIS...
WHERE ARE MY PANTS?
HEY LOOK, GUYS--IT'S HARLEY! YOU HERE TO BREAK US OUT, QUINN?
WHY THE HELL WOULD I? YA AIN'T GOTTA WORRY ABOUT BATMAN IN HERE. PLUS, THEY DO EVERYTHIN' FER YA. FEED YA, CLEAN YA, DRESS YA...
...DRESS SOME OF YA...
GEEZ... DOES ANYONE AROUND HERE WEAR CLOTHES? I MEAN, I'VE SEEN MORE OLD MAN JUNK HERE THAN IN AN EPISODE OF ANTIQUES ROADSHOW.
MY APOLOGIES, HARLEY. SOME OF THEM

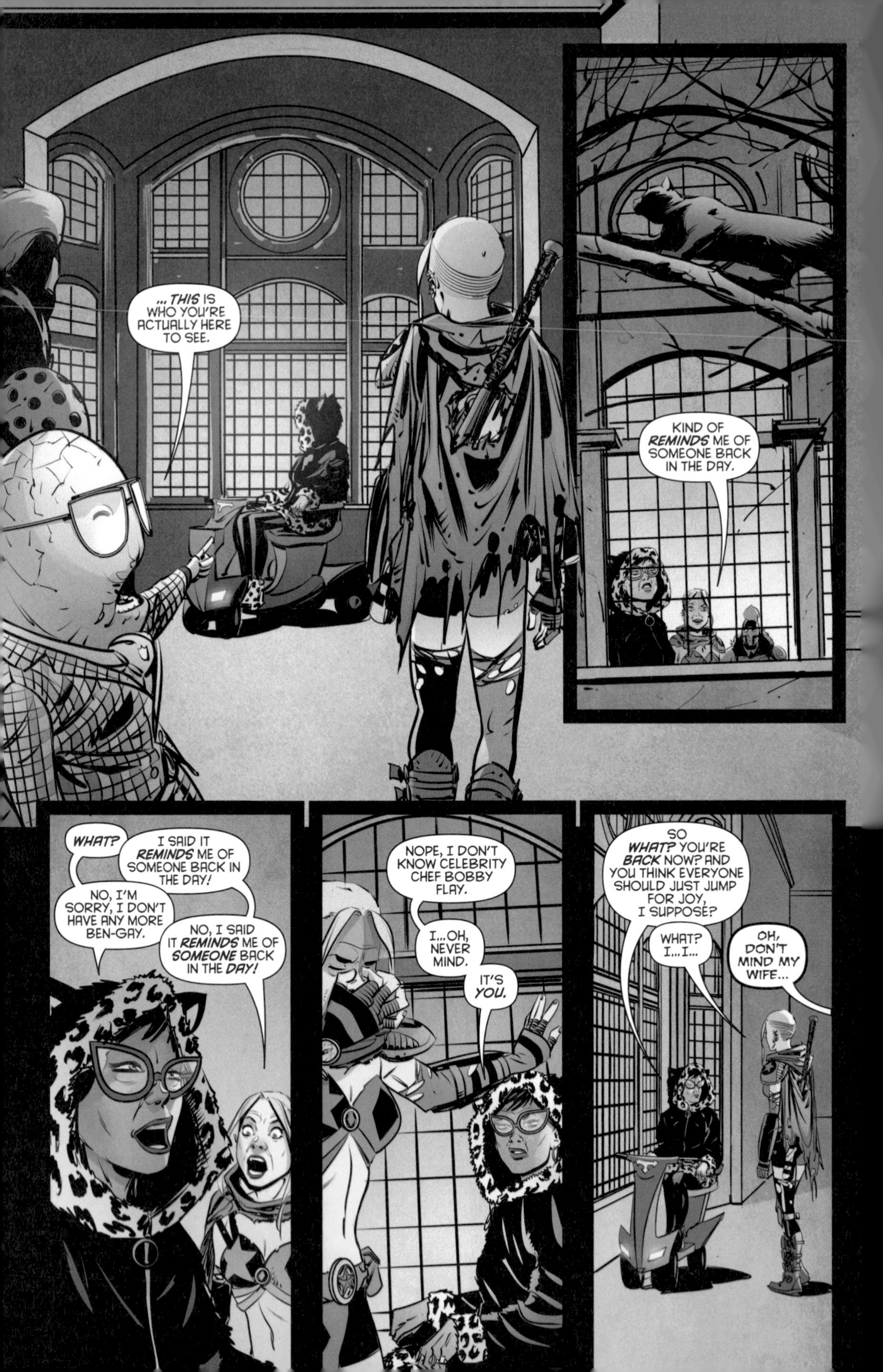
...THIS IS WHO YOU'RE ACTUALLY HERE TO SEE.
KIND OF REMINDS ME OF SOMEONE BACK IN THE DAY.
WHAT?
I SAID IT REMINDS ME OF SOMEONE BACK IN THE DAY!
NO, I'M SORRY, I DON'T HAVE ANY MORE BEN-GAY.
NO, I SAID IT REMINDS ME OF SOMEONE BACK IN THE DAY!
NOPE, I DON'T KNOW CELEBRITY CHEF BOBBY FLAY.
I...OH, NEVER MIND.
IT'S YOU.
SO WHAT? YOU'RE BACK NOW? AND YOU THINK EVERYONE SHOULD JUST JUMP FOR JOY, I SUPPOSE?
WHAT? I...I...
OH, DON'T MIND MY WIFE...

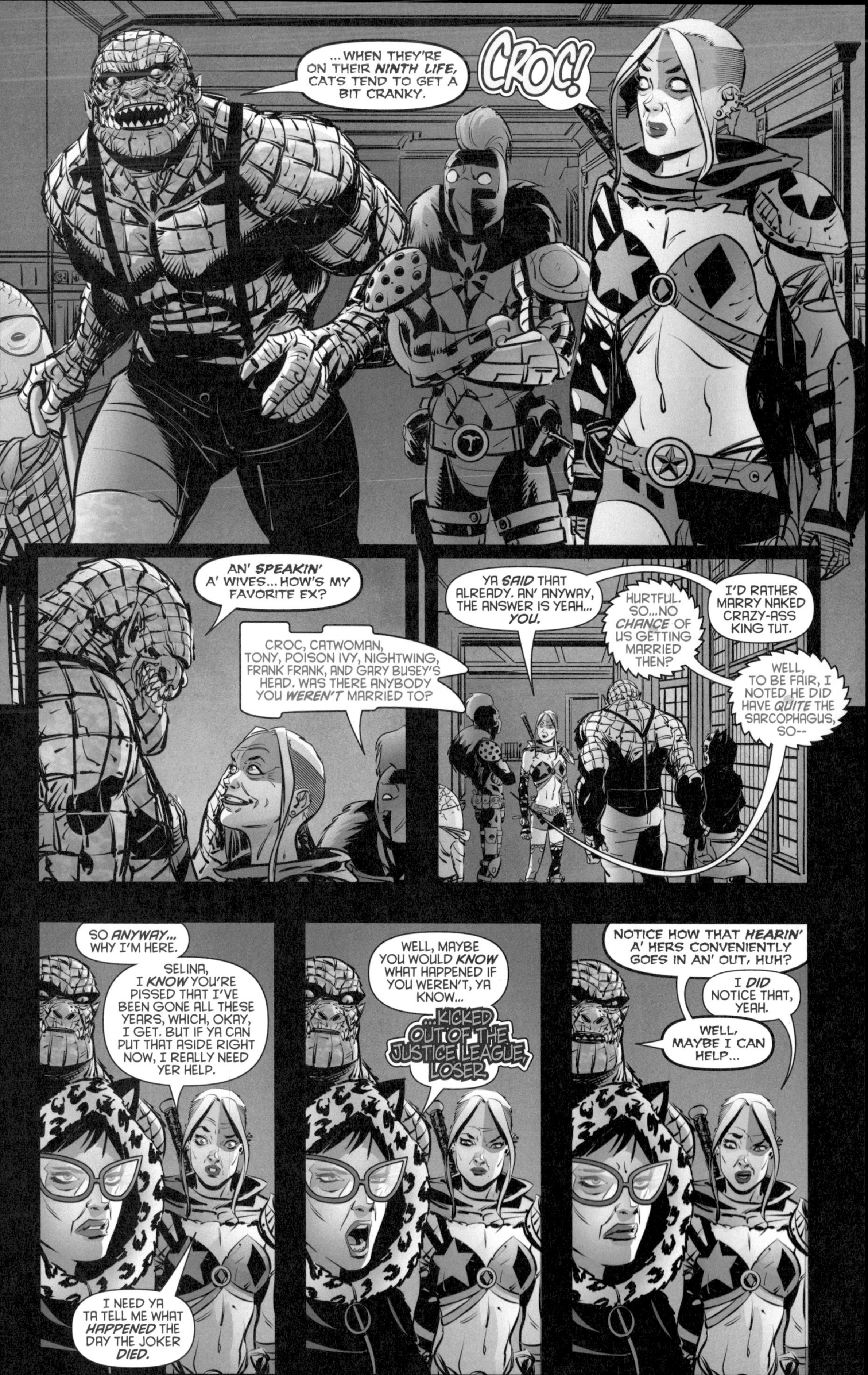
...WHEN THEY'RE ON THEIR *NINTH LIFE,* CATS TEND TO GET A BIT CRANKY.
CROC!
AN' *SPEAKIN'* A' WIVES... HOW'S MY FAVORITE EX?
CROC, CATWOMAN, TONY, POISON IVY, NIGHTWING, FRANK FRANK, AND GARY BUSEY'S HEAD. WAS THERE ANYBODY YOU *WEREN'T* MARRIED TO?
YA *SAID* THAT ALREADY. AN' ANYWAY, THE ANSWER IS YEAH... *YOU.*
HURTFUL. SO...NO *CHANCE* OF US GETTING MARRIED THEN?
I'D RATHER MARRY NAKED CRAZY-ASS KING TUT.
WELL, TO BE FAIR, I NOTED HE DID HAVE *QUITE* THE SARCOPHAGUS, SO--
SO *ANYWAY*... WHY I'M HERE.
SELINA, I *KNOW* YOU'RE PISSED THAT I'VE BEEN GONE ALL THESE YEARS, WHICH, OKAY, I GET. BUT IF YA CAN PUT THAT ASIDE RIGHT NOW, I REALLY NEED YER HELP.
I NEED YA TA TELL ME WHAT *HAPPENED* THE DAY THE JOKER *DIED.*
WELL, MAYBE YOU WOULD *KNOW* WHAT HAPPENED IF YOU WEREN'T, YA KNOW...
...KICKED OUT OF THE JUSTICE LEAGUE, LOSER
NOTICE HOW THAT *HEARIN'* A' HERS CONVENIENTLY GOES IN AN' OUT, HUH?
I *DID* NOTICE THAT, YEAH.
WELL, MAYBE I CAN HELP...

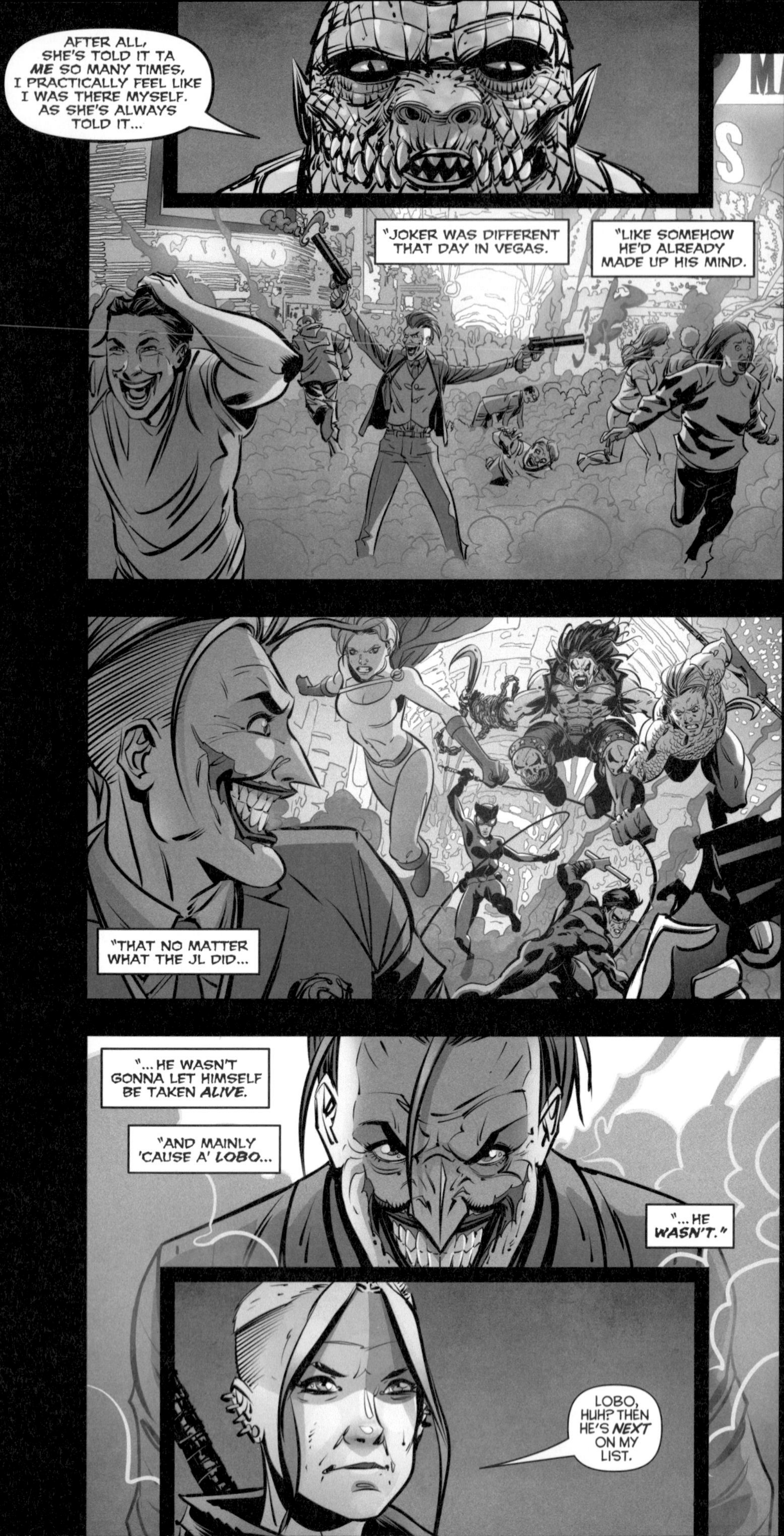
AFTER ALL, SHE'S TOLD IT TA *ME* SO MANY TIMES, I PRACTICALLY FEEL LIKE I WAS THERE MYSELF. AS SHE'S ALWAYS TOLD IT...
"JOKER WAS DIFFERENT THAT DAY IN VEGAS.
"LIKE SOMEHOW HE'D ALREADY MADE UP HIS MIND.
"THAT NO MATTER WHAT THE JL DID...
"...HE WASN'T GONNA LET HIMSELF BE TAKEN *ALIVE*.
"AND MAINLY 'CAUSE A' *LOBO*...
"...HE *WASN'T*."
LOBO, HUH? THEN HE'S *NEXT* ON MY LIST.

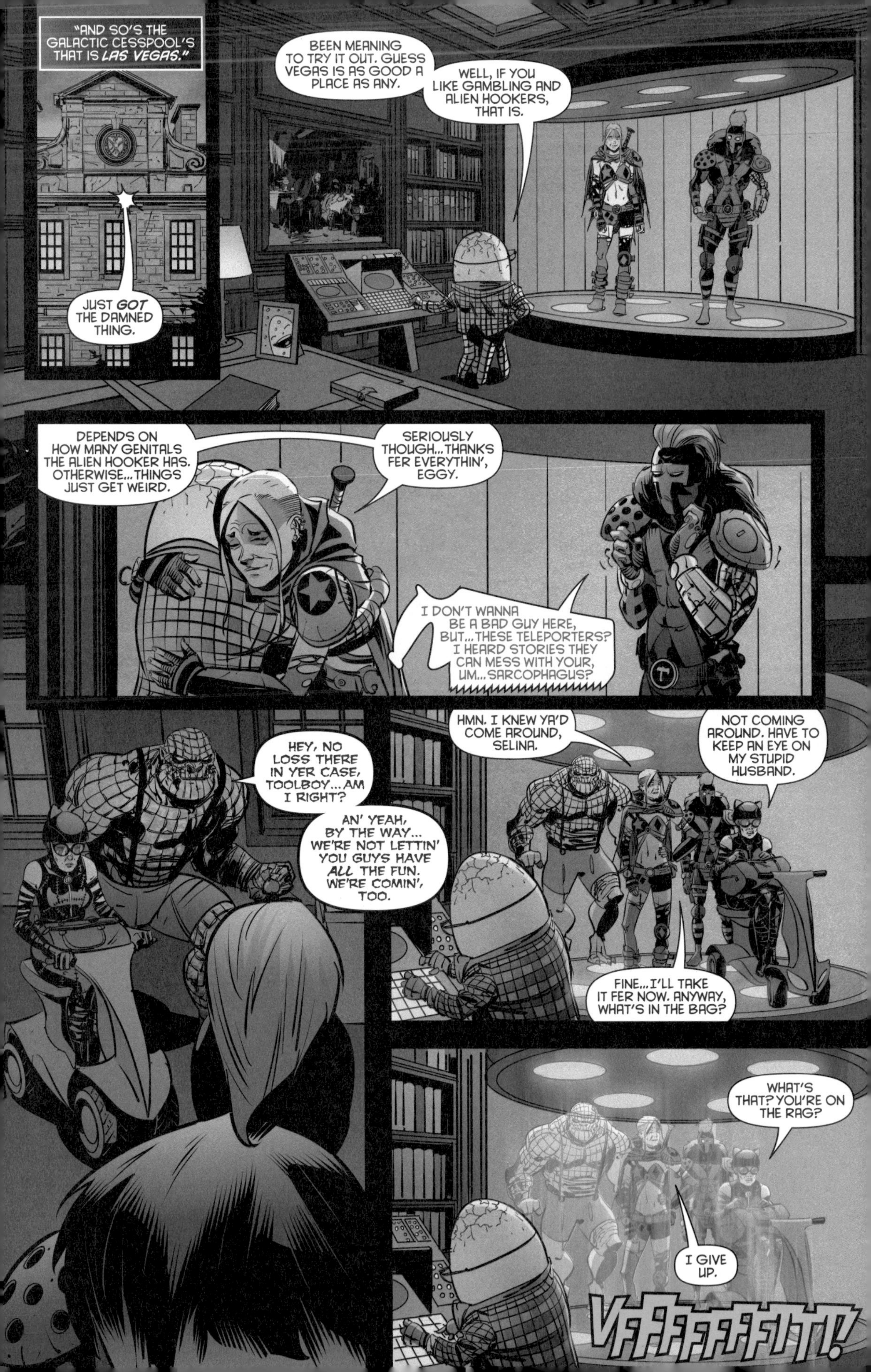
"AND SO'S THE GALACTIC CESSPOOL'S THAT IS LAS VEGAS."
JUST GOT THE DAMNED THING.
BEEN MEANING TO TRY IT OUT. GUESS VEGAS IS AS GOOD A PLACE AS ANY.
WELL, IF YOU LIKE GAMBLING AND ALIEN HOOKERS, THAT IS.
DEPENDS ON HOW MANY GENITALS THE ALIEN HOOKER HAS. OTHERWISE...THINGS JUST GET WEIRD.
SERIOUSLY THOUGH...THANKS FER EVERYTHIN', EGGY.
I DON'T WANNA BE A BAD GUY HERE, BUT...THESE TELEPORTERS? I HEARD STORIES THEY CAN MESS WITH YOUR, UM...SARCOPHAGUS?
HEY, NO LOSS THERE IN YER CASE, TOOLBOY...AM I RIGHT?
AN' YEAH, BY THE WAY... WE'RE NOT LETTIN' YOU GUYS HAVE ALL THE FUN. WE'RE COMIN', TOO.
HMN. I KNEW YA'D COME AROUND, SELINA.
NOT COMING AROUND. HAVE TO KEEP AN EYE ON MY STUPID HUSBAND.
FINE...I'LL TAKE IT FER NOW. ANYWAY, WHAT'S IN THE BAG?
WHAT'S THAT? YOU'RE ON THE RAG?
I GIVE UP.
VFFFFFFFTT!

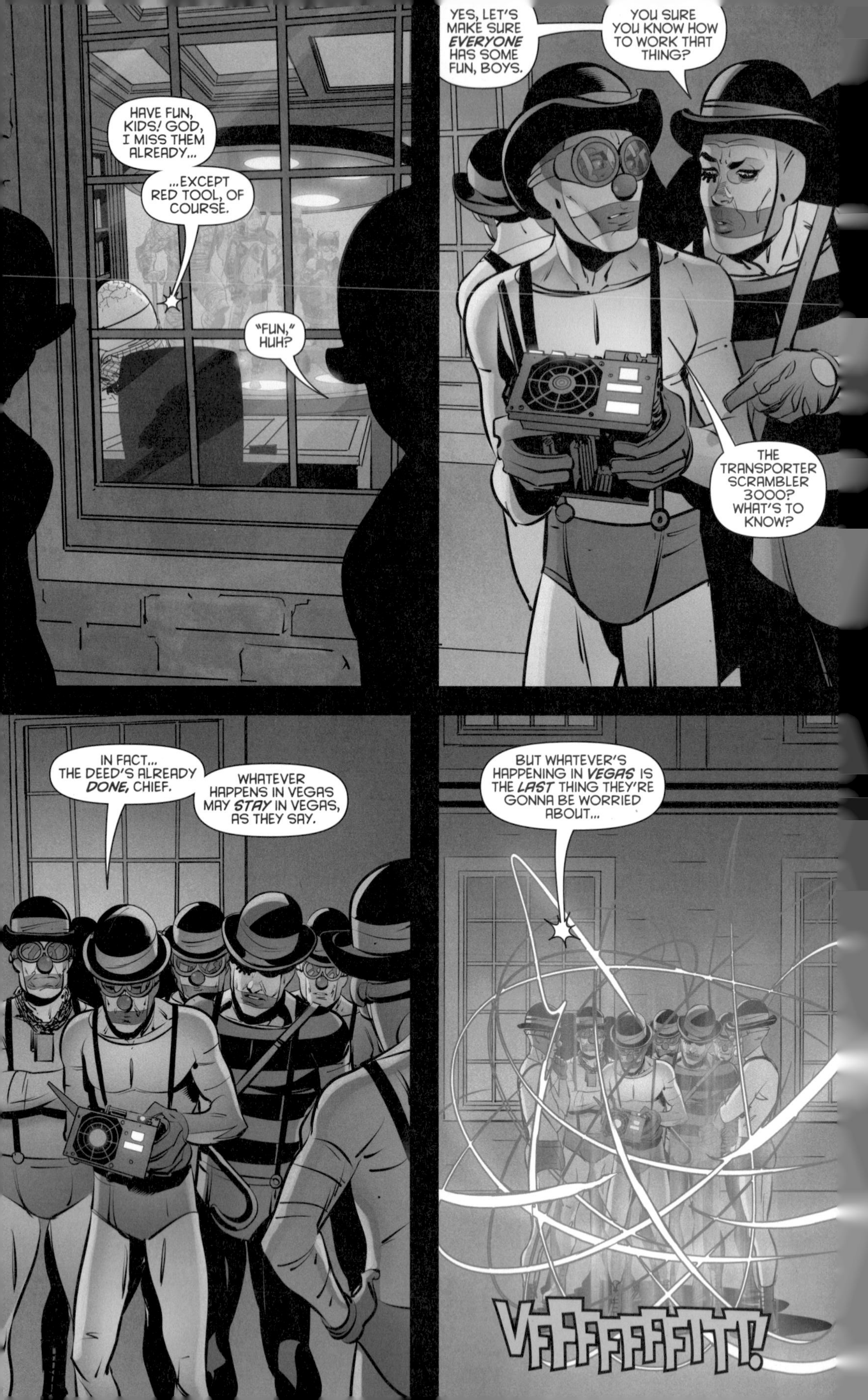
HAVE FUN, KIDS! GOD, I MISS THEM ALREADY...
...EXCEPT RED TOOL, OF COURSE.
"FUN," HUH?
YES, LET'S MAKE SURE EVERYONE HAS SOME FUN, BOYS.
YOU SURE YOU KNOW HOW TO WORK THAT THING?
THE TRANSPORTER SCRAMBLER 3000? WHAT'S TO KNOW?
IN FACT... THE DEED'S ALREADY DONE, CHIEF.
WHATEVER HAPPENS IN VEGAS MAY STAY IN VEGAS, AS THEY SAY.
BUT WHATEVER'S HAPPENING IN VEGAS IS THE LAST THING THEY'RE GONNA BE WORRIED ABOUT...
VFFFFFFFTTT!

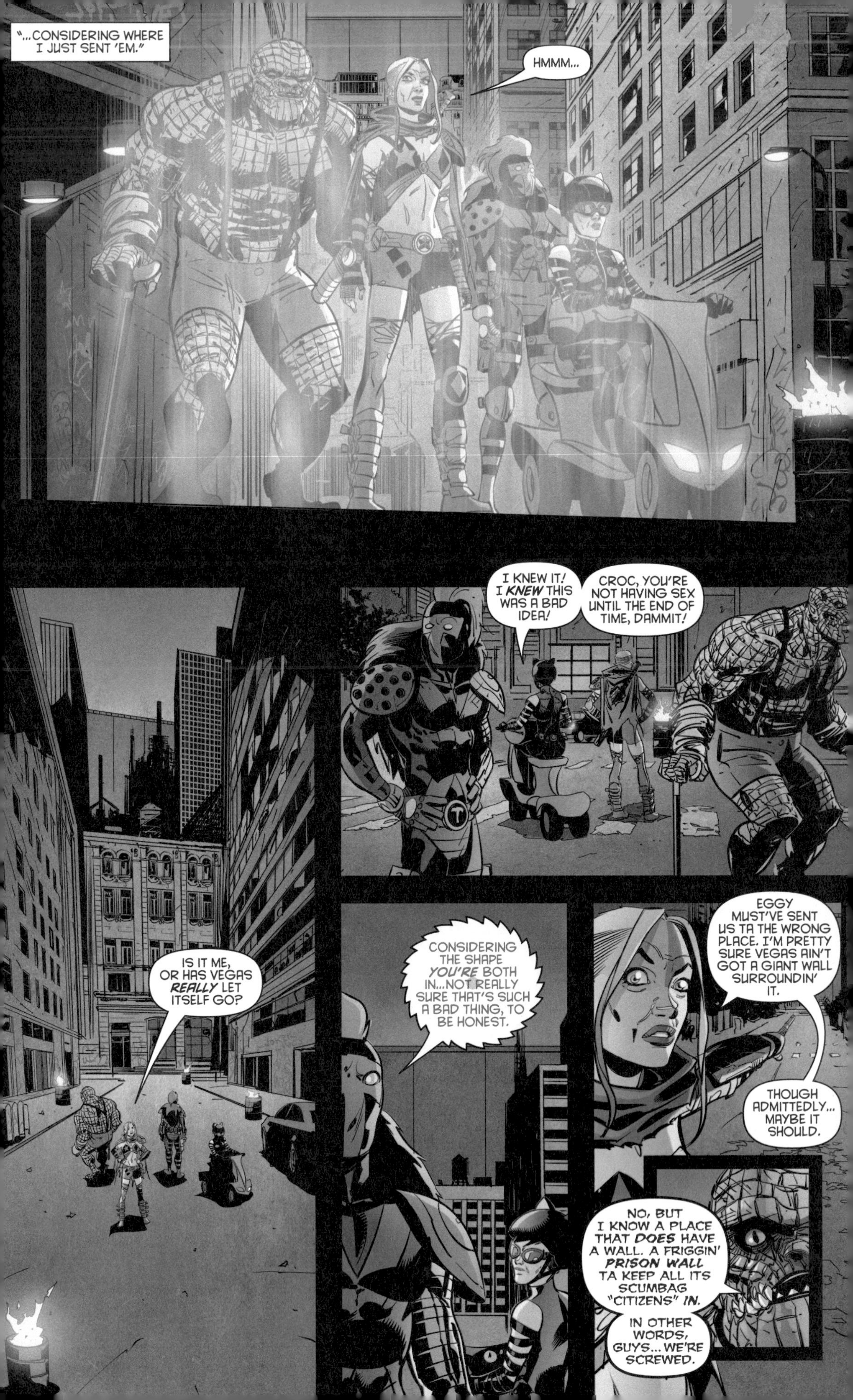
"...CONSIDERING WHERE I JUST SENT 'EM."
HMMM...
IS IT ME, OR HAS VEGAS *REALLY* LET ITSELF GO?
I KNEW IT! I *KNEW* THIS WAS A BAD IDEA!
CROC, YOU'RE NOT HAVING SEX UNTIL THE END OF TIME, DAMMIT!
CONSIDERING THE SHAPE *YOU'RE* BOTH IN...NOT REALLY SURE THAT'S SUCH A BAD THING, TO BE HONEST.
EGGY MUST'VE SENT US TA THE WRONG PLACE. I'M PRETTY SURE VEGAS AIN'T GOT A GIANT WALL SURROUNDIN' IT.
THOUGH ADMITTEDLY... MAYBE IT SHOULD.
NO, BUT I KNOW A PLACE THAT *DOES* HAVE A WALL. A FRIGGIN' *PRISON WALL* TA KEEP ALL ITS SCUMBAG "CITIZENS" *IN*.
IN OTHER WORDS, GUYS... WE'RE SCREWED.

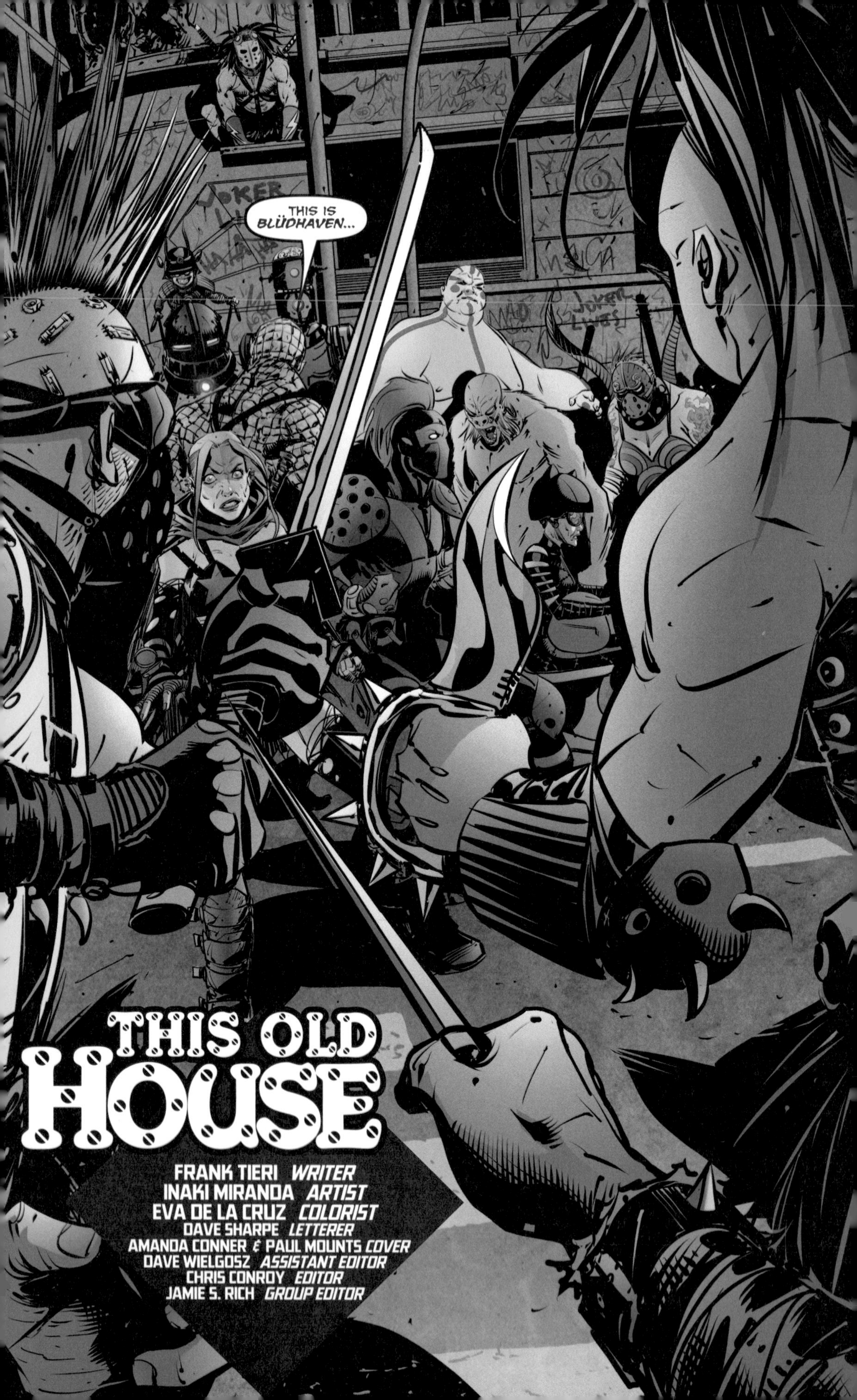
...THIS IS BLÜDHAVEN...
THIS OLD HOUSE
FRANK TIERI WRITER
INAKI MIRANDA ARTIST
EVA DE LA CRUZ COLORIST
DAVE SHARPE LETTERER
AMANDA CONNER & PAUL MOUNTS COVER
DAVE WIELGOSZ ASSISTANT EDITOR
CHRIS CONROY EDITOR
JAMIE S. RICH GROUP EDITOR

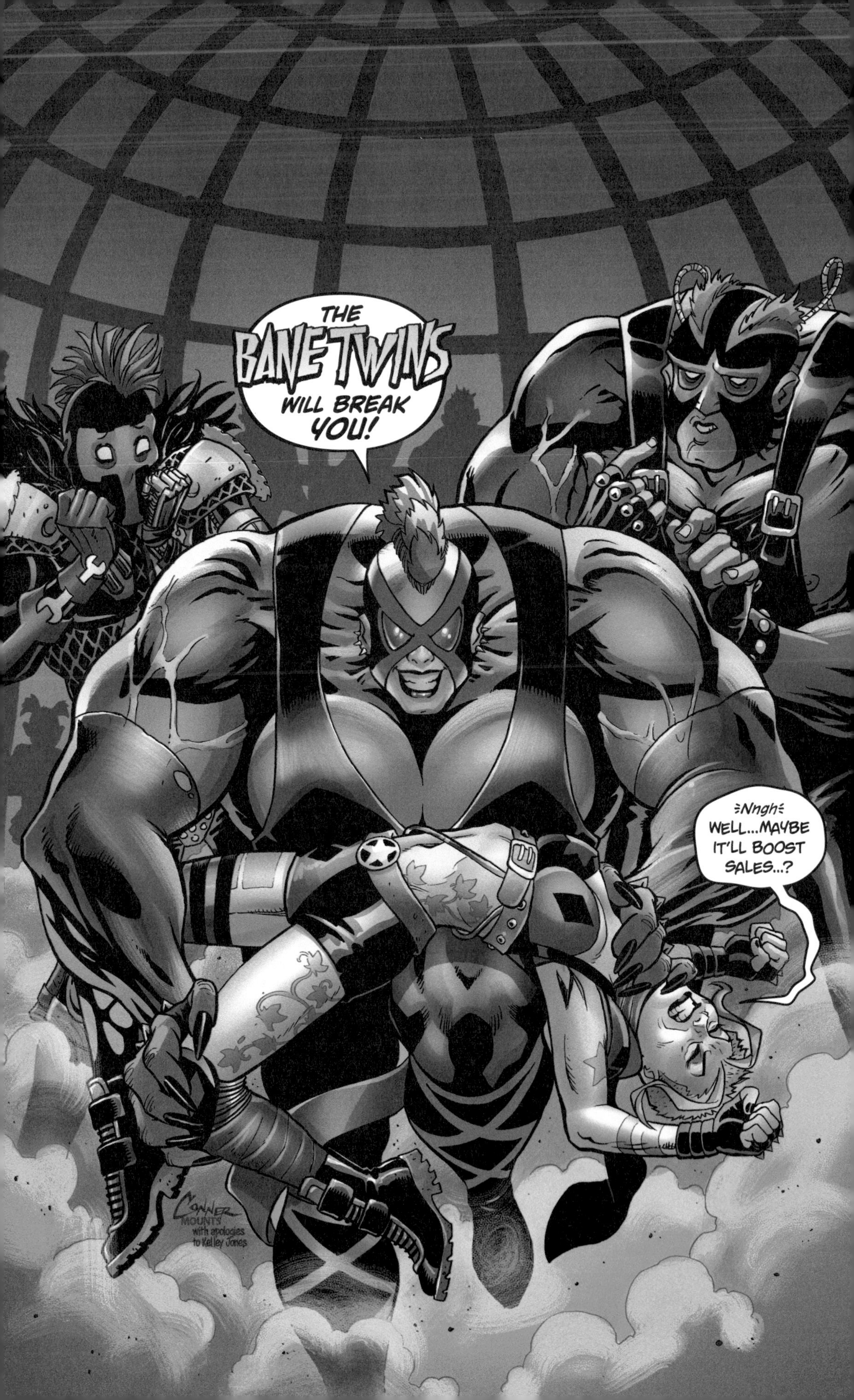
THE BANE TWINS WILL BREAK YOU!
Nngh WELL...MAYBE IT'LL BOOST SALES...?
CONNER MOUNTS with apologies to Kelley Jones

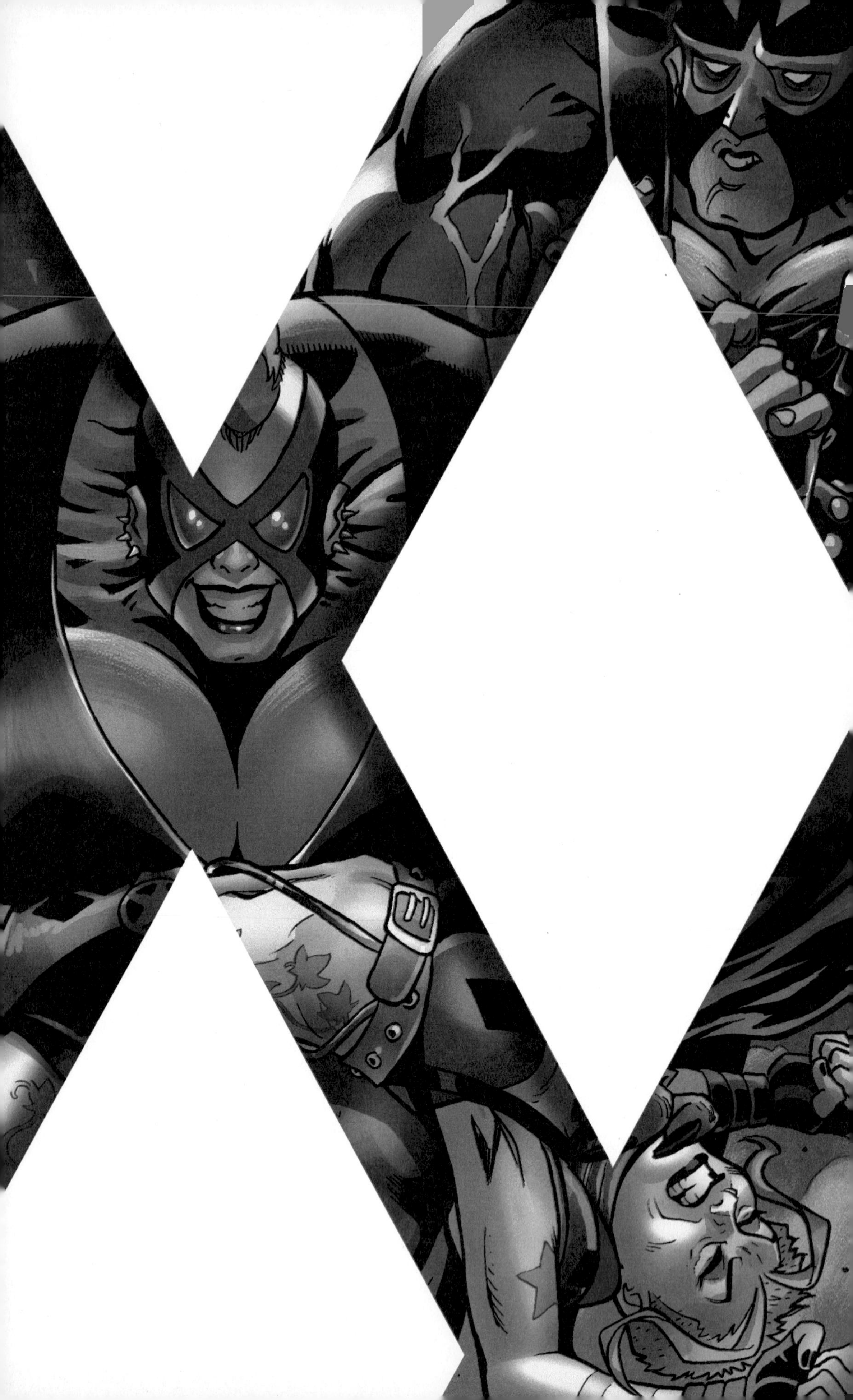

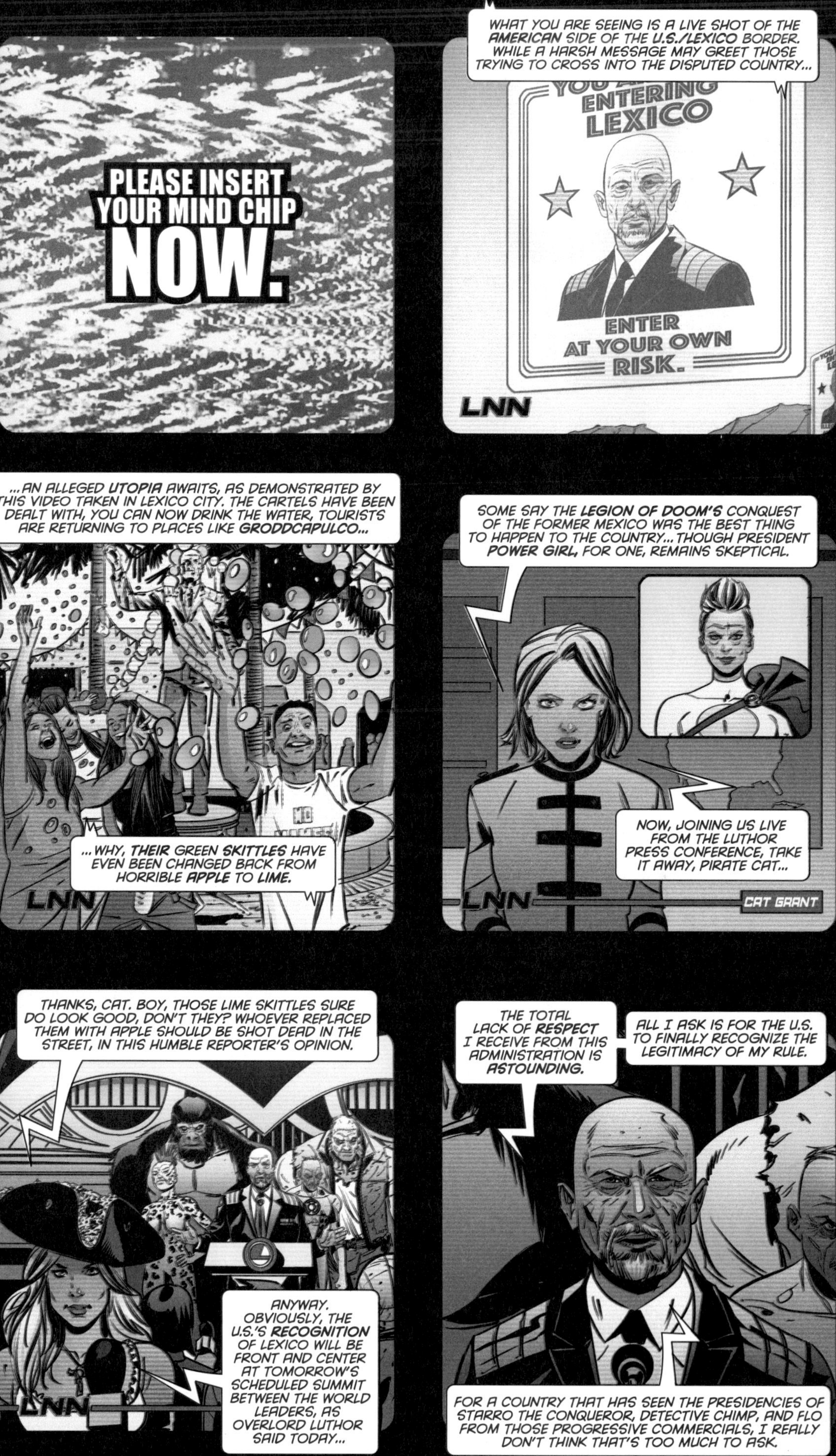
PLEASE INSERT YOUR MIND CHIP NOW.
WHAT YOU ARE SEEING IS A LIVE SHOT OF THE AMERICAN SIDE OF THE U.S./LEXICO BORDER. WHILE A HARSH MESSAGE MAY GREET THOSE TRYING TO CROSS INTO THE DISPUTED COUNTRY...
ENTERING LEXICO
ENTER AT YOUR OWN RISK.
LNN
...AN ALLEGED UTOPIA AWAITS, AS DEMONSTRATED BY THIS VIDEO TAKEN IN LEXICO CITY. THE CARTELS HAVE BEEN DEALT WITH, YOU CAN NOW DRINK THE WATER, TOURISTS ARE RETURNING TO PLACES LIKE GRODDCAPULCO...
...WHY, THEIR GREEN SKITTLES HAVE EVEN BEEN CHANGED BACK FROM HORRIBLE APPLE TO LIME.
LNN
SOME SAY THE LEGION OF DOOM'S CONQUEST OF THE FORMER MEXICO WAS THE BEST THING TO HAPPEN TO THE COUNTRY...THOUGH PRESIDENT POWER GIRL, FOR ONE, REMAINS SKEPTICAL.
NOW, JOINING US LIVE FROM THE LUTHOR PRESS CONFERENCE, TAKE IT AWAY, PIRATE CAT...
LNN
CAT GRANT
THANKS, CAT. BOY, THOSE LIME SKITTLES SURE DO LOOK GOOD, DON'T THEY? WHOEVER REPLACED THEM WITH APPLE SHOULD BE SHOT DEAD IN THE STREET, IN THIS HUMBLE REPORTER'S OPINION.
ANYWAY. OBVIOUSLY, THE U.S.'S RECOGNITION OF LEXICO WILL BE FRONT AND CENTER AT TOMORROW'S SCHEDULED SUMMIT BETWEEN THE WORLD LEADERS, AS OVERLORD LUTHOR SAID TODAY...
LNN
THE TOTAL LACK OF RESPECT I RECEIVE FROM THIS ADMINISTRATION IS ASTOUNDING.
ALL I ASK IS FOR THE U.S. TO FINALLY RECOGNIZE THE LEGITIMACY OF MY RULE.
FOR A COUNTRY THAT HAS SEEN THE PRESIDENCIES OF STARRO THE CONQUEROR, DETECTIVE CHIMP, AND FLO FROM THOSE PROGRESSIVE COMMERCIALS, I REALLY DON'T THINK THAT'S TOO MUCH TO ASK.

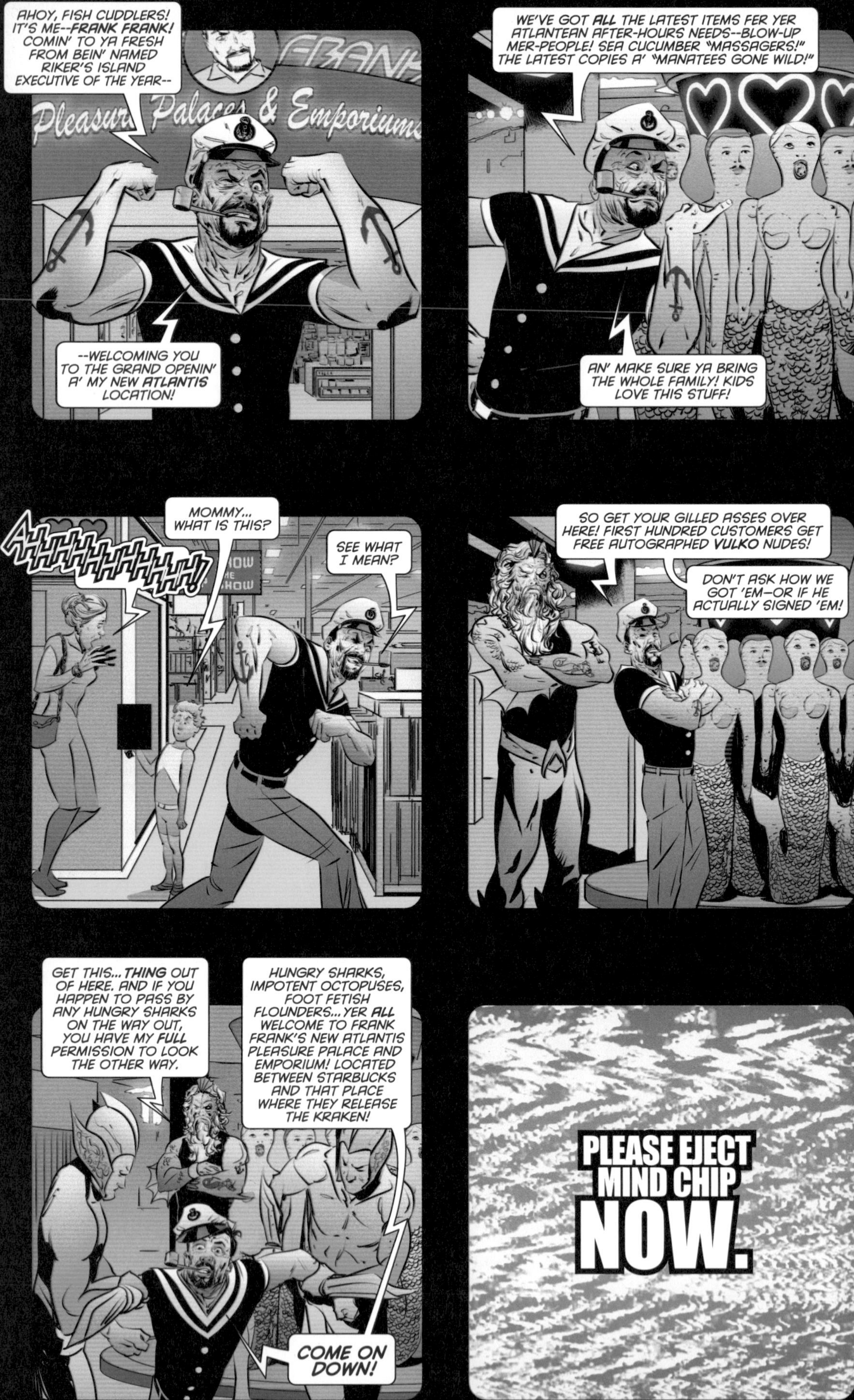
AHOY, FISH CUDDLERS! IT'S ME--FRANK FRANK! COMIN' TO YA FRESH FROM BEIN' NAMED RIKER'S ISLAND EXECUTIVE OF THE YEAR--
FRANK
Pleasure Palaces & Emporiums
--WELCOMING YOU TO THE GRAND OPENIN' A' MY NEW ATLANTIS LOCATION!
WE'VE GOT ALL THE LATEST ITEMS FER YER ATLANTEAN AFTER-HOURS NEEDS--BLOW-UP MER-PEOPLE! SEA CUCUMBER "MASSAGERS!" THE LATEST COPIES A' "MANATEES GONE WILD!"
AN' MAKE SURE YA BRING THE WHOLE FAMILY! KIDS LOVE THIS STUFF!
AHHHHHHHHHH!
MOMMY... WHAT IS THIS?
SEE WHAT I MEAN?
SO GET YOUR GILLED ASSES OVER HERE! FIRST HUNDRED CUSTOMERS GET FREE AUTOGRAPHED VULKO NUDES!
DON'T ASK HOW WE GOT 'EM—OR IF HE ACTUALLY SIGNED 'EM!
GET THIS... THING OUT OF HERE. AND IF YOU HAPPEN TO PASS BY ANY HUNGRY SHARKS ON THE WAY OUT, YOU HAVE MY FULL PERMISSION TO LOOK THE OTHER WAY.
HUNGRY SHARKS, IMPOTENT OCTOPUSES, FOOT FETISH FLOUNDERS... YER ALL WELCOME TO FRANK FRANK'S NEW ATLANTIS PLEASURE PALACE AND EMPORIUM! LOCATED BETWEEN STARBUCKS AND THAT PLACE WHERE THEY RELEASE THE KRAKEN!
COME ON DOWN!
PLEASE EJECT MIND CHIP NOW.

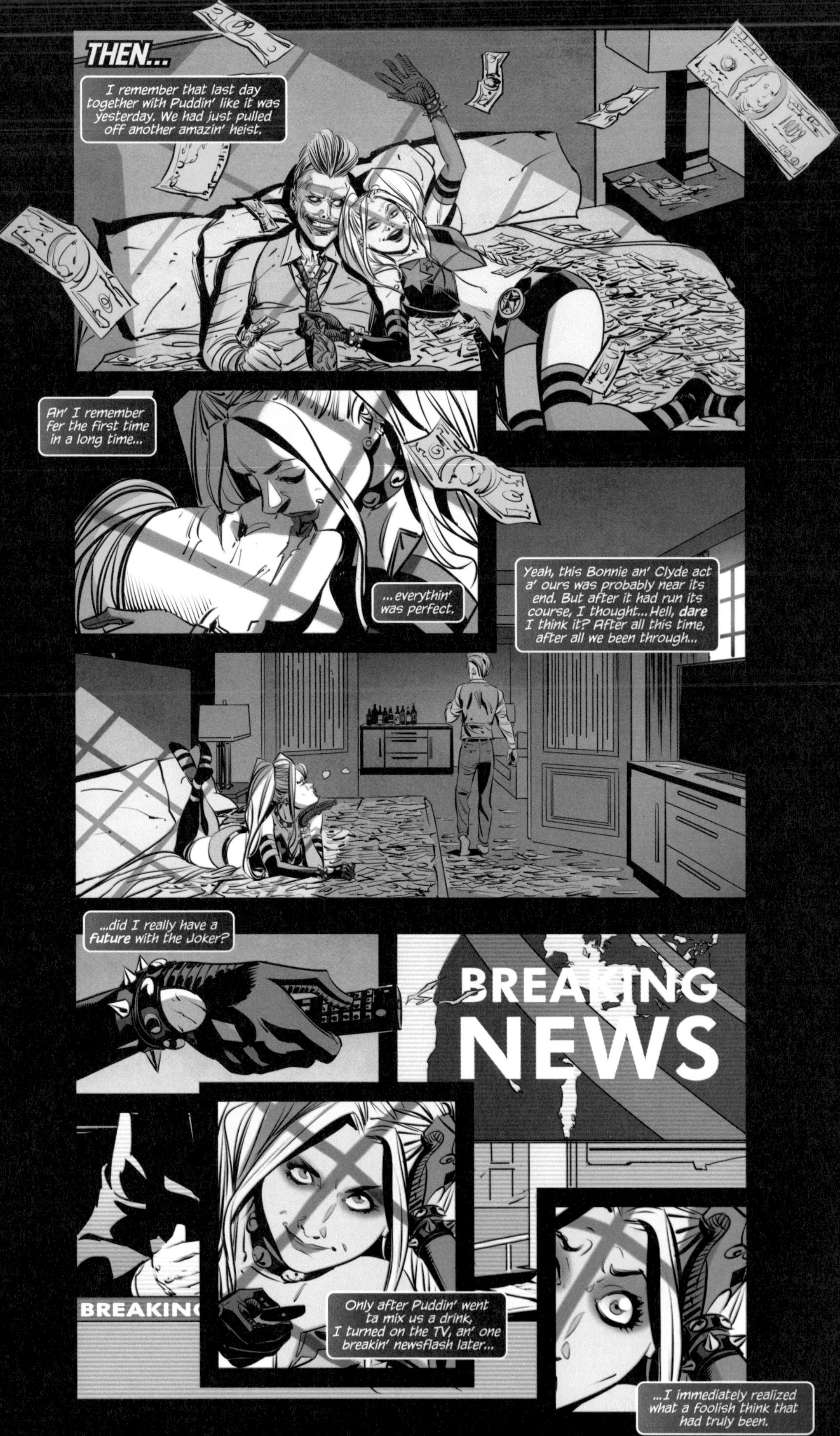
THEN...
I remember that last day together with Puddin' like it was yesterday. We had just pulled off another amazin' heist.
An' I remember fer the first time in a long time...
...everythin' was perfect.
Yeah, this Bonnie an' Clyde act a' ours was probably near its end. But after it had run its course, I thought... Hell, dare I think it? After all this time, after all we been through...
...did I really have a future with the Joker?
BREAKING NEWS
BREAKING
Only after Puddin' went ta mix us a drink, I turned on the TV, an' one breakin' newsflash later...
...I immediately realized what a foolish think that had truly been.

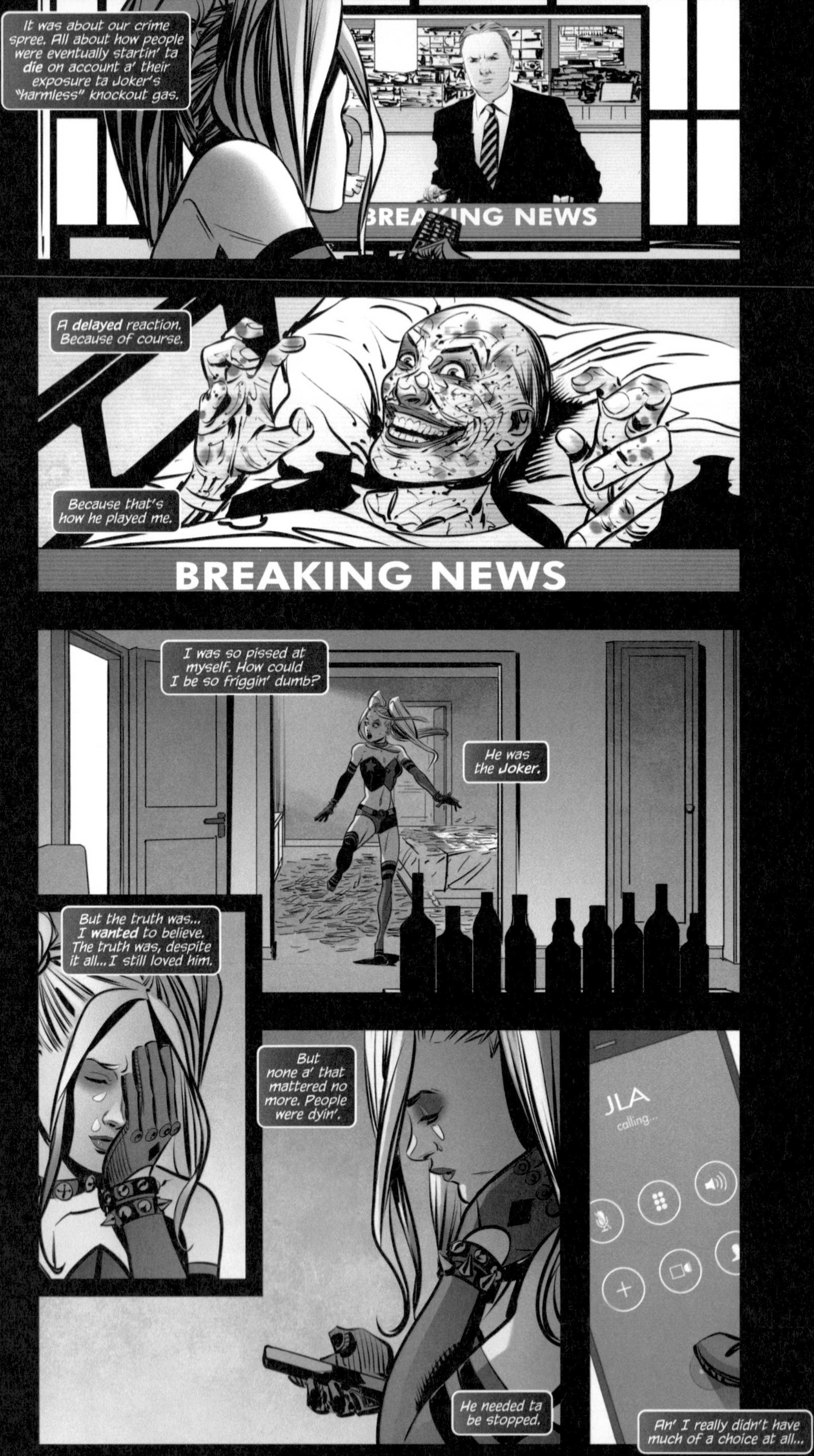
It was about our crime spree. All about how people were eventually startin' ta die on account a' their exposure ta Joker's "harmless" knockout gas.
BREAKING NEWS
A delayed reaction. Because of course.
Because that's how he played me.
BREAKING NEWS
I was so pissed at myself. How could I be so friggin' dumb?
He was the Joker.
But the truth was... I wanted to believe. The truth was, despite it all...I still loved him.
But none a' that mattered no more. People were dyin'.
JLA
calling...
He needed ta be stopped.
An' I really didn't have much of a choice at all...

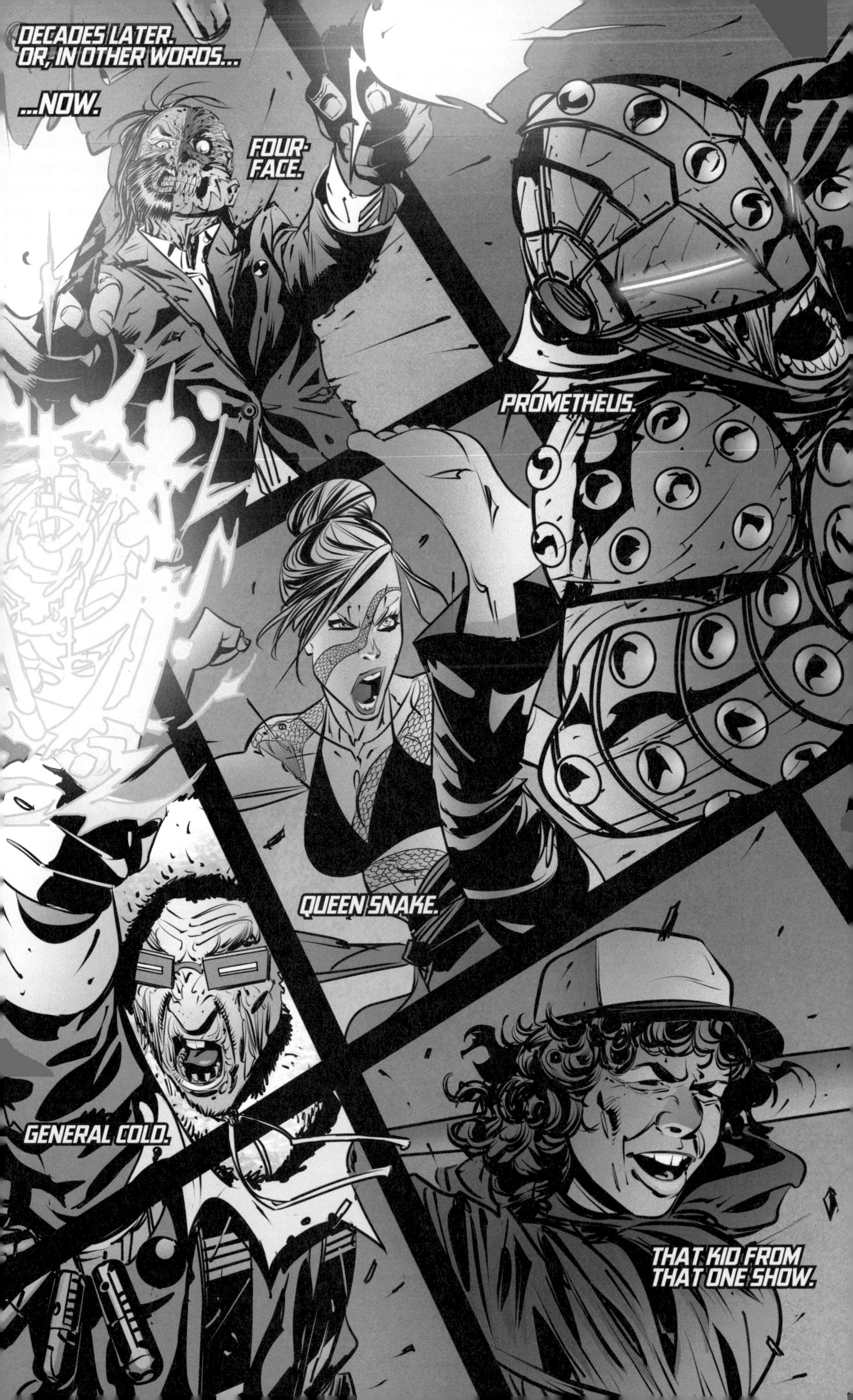
DECADES LATER.
OR, IN OTHER WORDS...
...NOW.
FOUR-FACE.
PROMETHEUS.
QUEEN SNAKE.
GENERAL COLD.
THAT KID FROM THAT ONE SHOW.

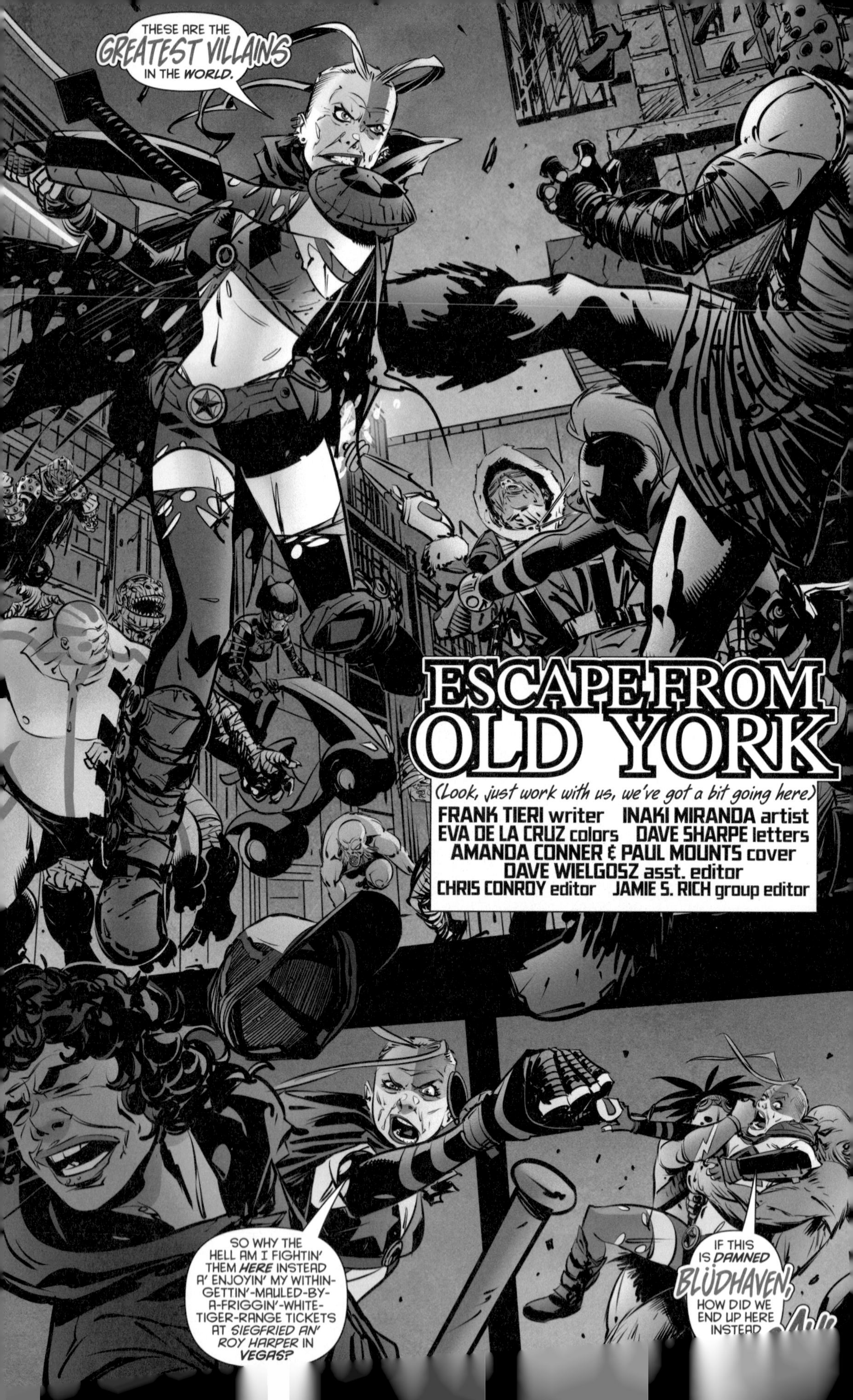
THESE ARE THE GREATEST VILLAINS IN THE WORLD.
ESCAPE FROM OLD YORK
(Look, just work with us, we've got a bit going here)
FRANK TIERI writer INAKI MIRANDA artist
EVA DE LA CRUZ colors DAVE SHARPE letters
AMANDA CONNER & PAUL MOUNTS cover
DAVE WIELGOSZ asst. editor
CHRIS CONROY editor JAMIE S. RICH group editor
SO WHY THE HELL AM I FIGHTIN' THEM HERE INSTEAD A' ENJOYIN' MY WITHIN-GETTIN'-MAULED-BY-A-FRIGGIN'-WHITE-TIGER-RANGE TICKETS AT SIEGFRIED AN' ROY HARPER IN VEGAS?
IF THIS IS DAMNED BLÜDHAVEN, HOW DID WE END UP HERE INSTEAD

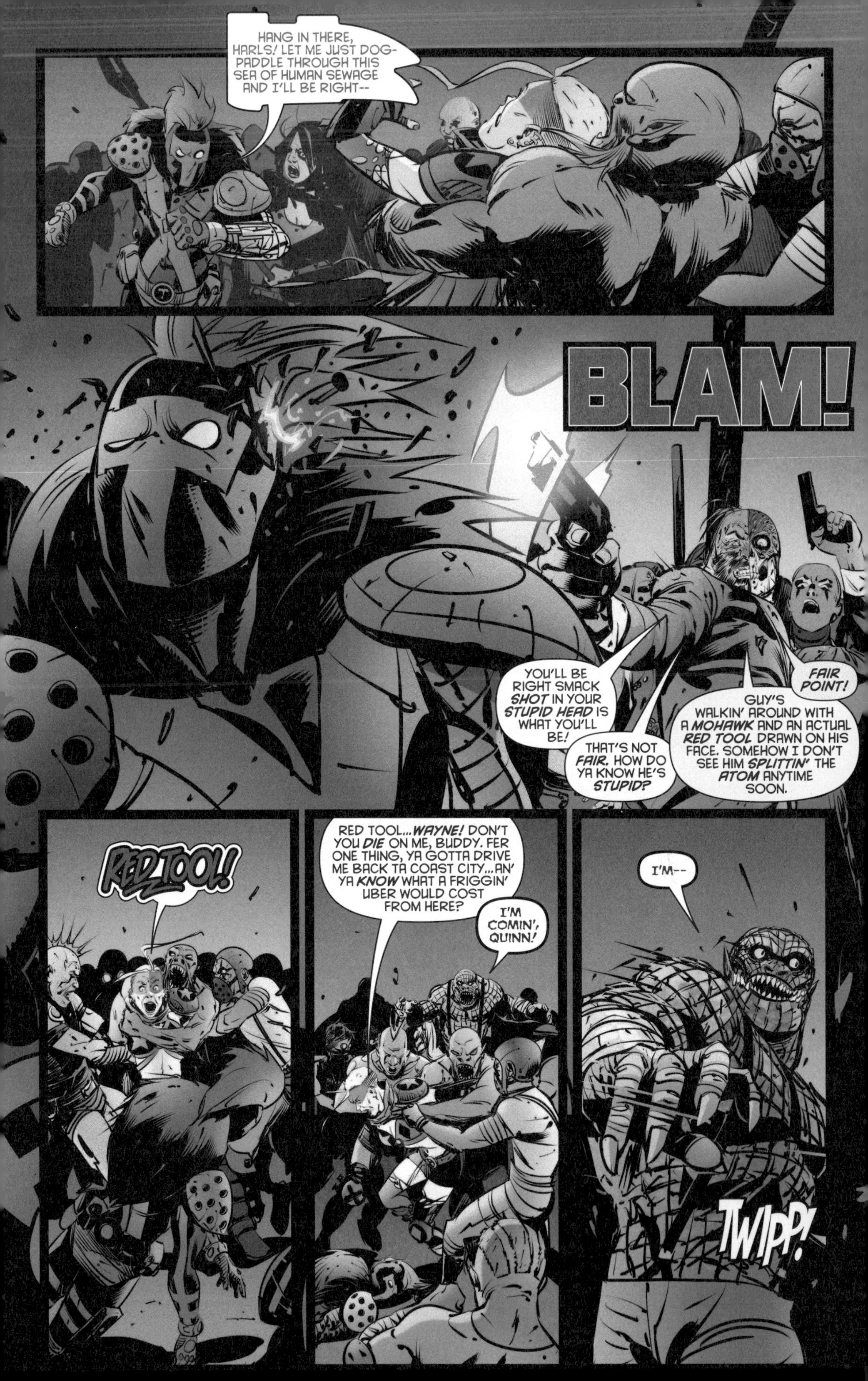
HANG IN THERE, HARLS! LET ME JUST DOG-PADDLE THROUGH THIS SEA OF HUMAN SEWAGE AND I'LL BE RIGHT--
BLAM!
YOU'LL BE RIGHT SMACK SHOT IN YOUR STUPID HEAD IS WHAT YOU'LL BE!
THAT'S NOT FAIR. HOW DO YA KNOW HE'S STUPID?
FAIR POINT!
GUY'S WALKIN' AROUND WITH A MOHAWK AND AN ACTUAL RED TOOL DRAWN ON HIS FACE. SOMEHOW I DON'T SEE HIM SPLITTIN' THE ATOM ANYTIME SOON.
RED TOOL!
RED TOOL...WAYNE! DON'T YOU DIE ON ME, BUDDY. FER ONE THING, YA GOTTA DRIVE ME BACK TA COAST CITY...AN' YA KNOW WHAT A FRIGGIN' UBER WOULD COST FROM HERE?
I'M COMIN', QUINN!
I'M--
TWIPP!

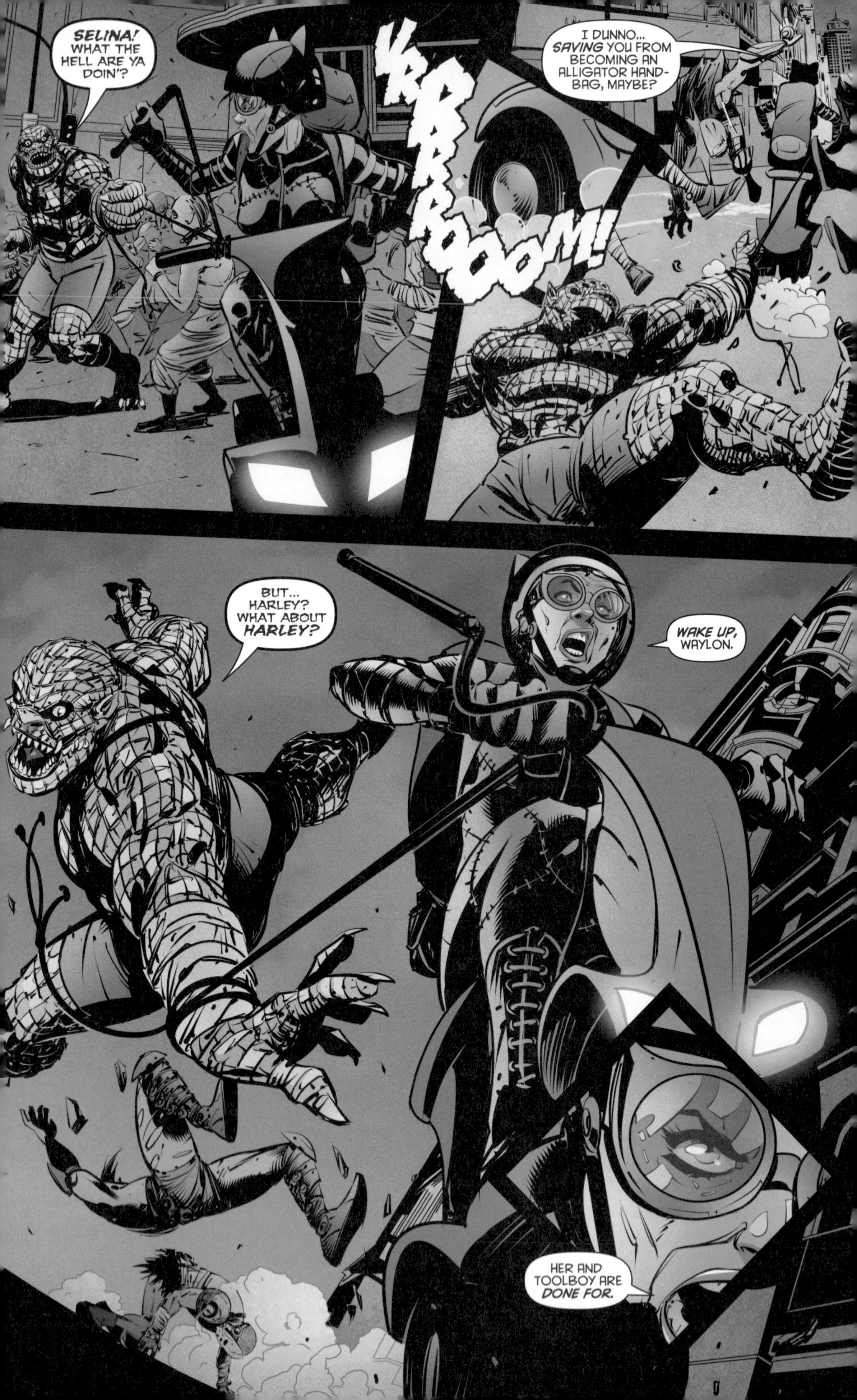
SELINA! WHAT THE HELL ARE YA DOIN'?
VRRRROOOOM!
I DUNNO... SAVING YOU FROM BECOMING AN ALLIGATOR HAND-BAG, MAYBE?
BUT... HARLEY? WHAT ABOUT HARLEY?
WAKE UP, WAYLON.
HER AND TOOLBOY ARE DONE FOR.

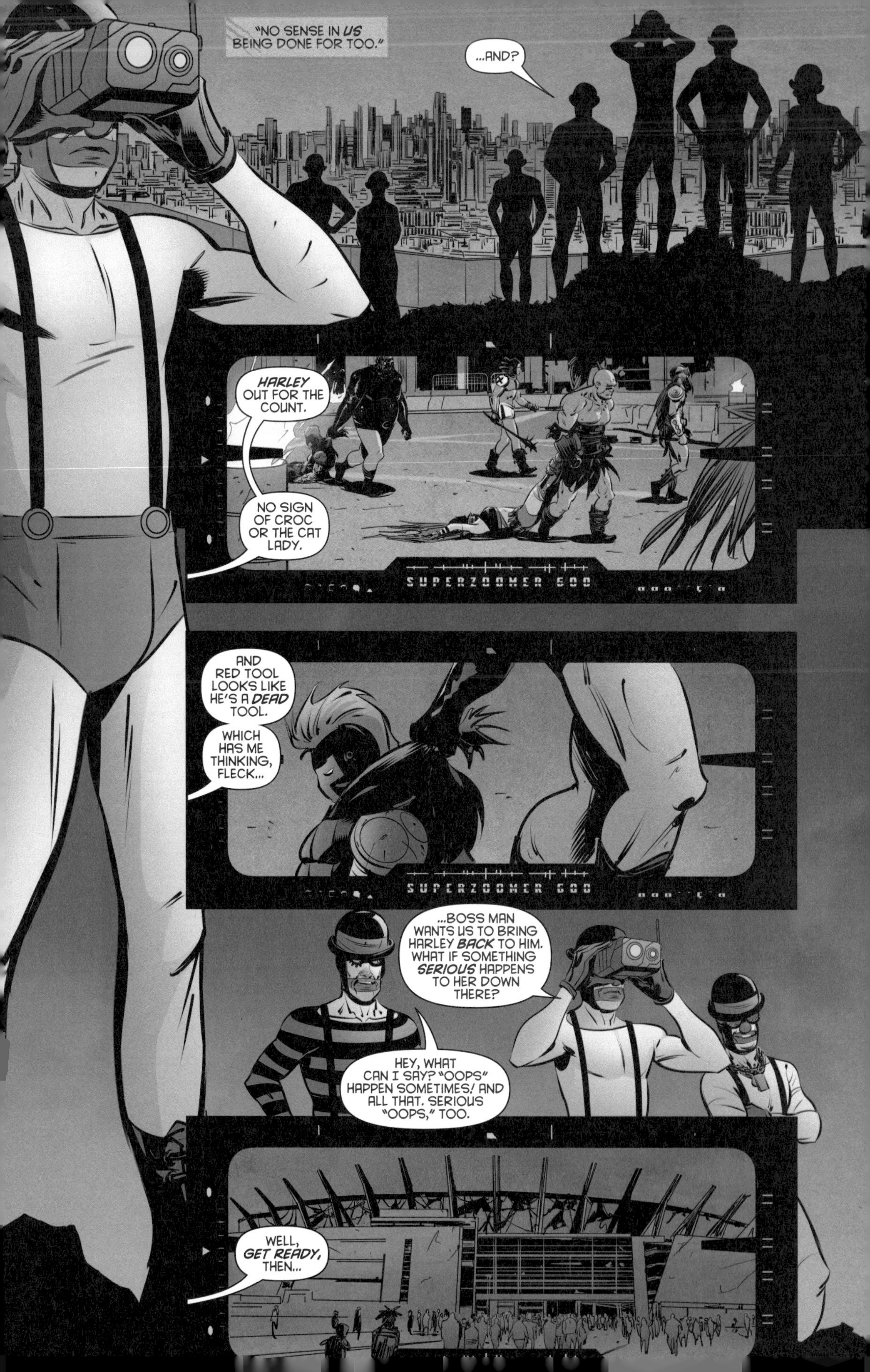
"NO SENSE IN US BEING DONE FOR TOO."
...AND?
HARLEY OUT FOR THE COUNT.
NO SIGN OF CROC OR THE CAT LADY.
SUPERZOOMER 600
AND RED TOOL LOOKS LIKE HE'S A DEAD TOOL.
WHICH HAS ME THINKING, FLECK...
SUPERZOOMER 600
...BOSS MAN WANTS US TO BRING HARLEY BACK TO HIM. WHAT IF SOMETHING SERIOUS HAPPENS TO HER DOWN THERE?
HEY, WHAT CAN I SAY? "OOPS" HAPPEN SOMETIMES! AND ALL THAT. SERIOUS "OOPS," TOO.
WELL, GET READY, THEN...

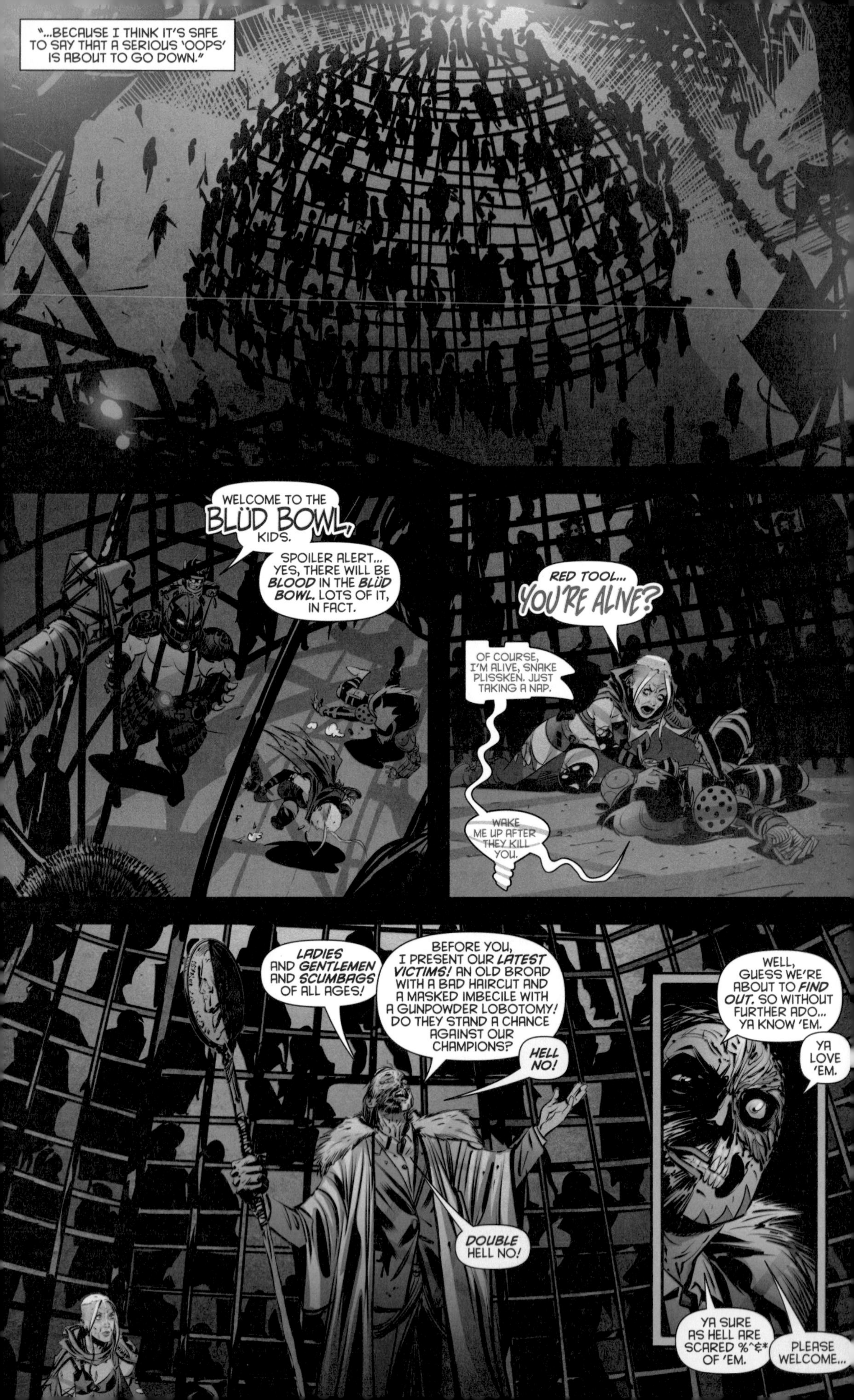
"...BECAUSE I THINK IT'S SAFE TO SAY THAT A SERIOUS 'OOPS' IS ABOUT TO GO DOWN."
WELCOME TO THE BLÜD BOWL, KIDS.
SPOILER ALERT... YES, THERE WILL BE BLOOD IN THE BLÜD BOWL. LOTS OF IT, IN FACT.
RED TOOL... YOU'RE ALIVE?
OF COURSE, I'M ALIVE, SNAKE PLISSKEN. JUST TAKING A NAP.
WAKE ME UP AFTER THEY KILL YOU.
LADIES AND GENTLEMEN AND SCUMBAGS OF ALL AGES!
BEFORE YOU, I PRESENT OUR LATEST VICTIMS! AN OLD BROAD WITH A BAD HAIRCUT AND A MASKED IMBECILE WITH A GUNPOWDER LOBOTOMY! DO THEY STAND A CHANCE AGAINST OUR CHAMPIONS?
HELL NO!
DOUBLE HELL NO!
WELL, GUESS WE'RE ABOUT TO FIND OUT. SO WITHOUT FURTHER ADO... YA KNOW 'EM.
YA LOVE 'EM.
YA SURE AS HELL ARE SCARED %^&* OF 'EM.
PLEASE WELCOME...

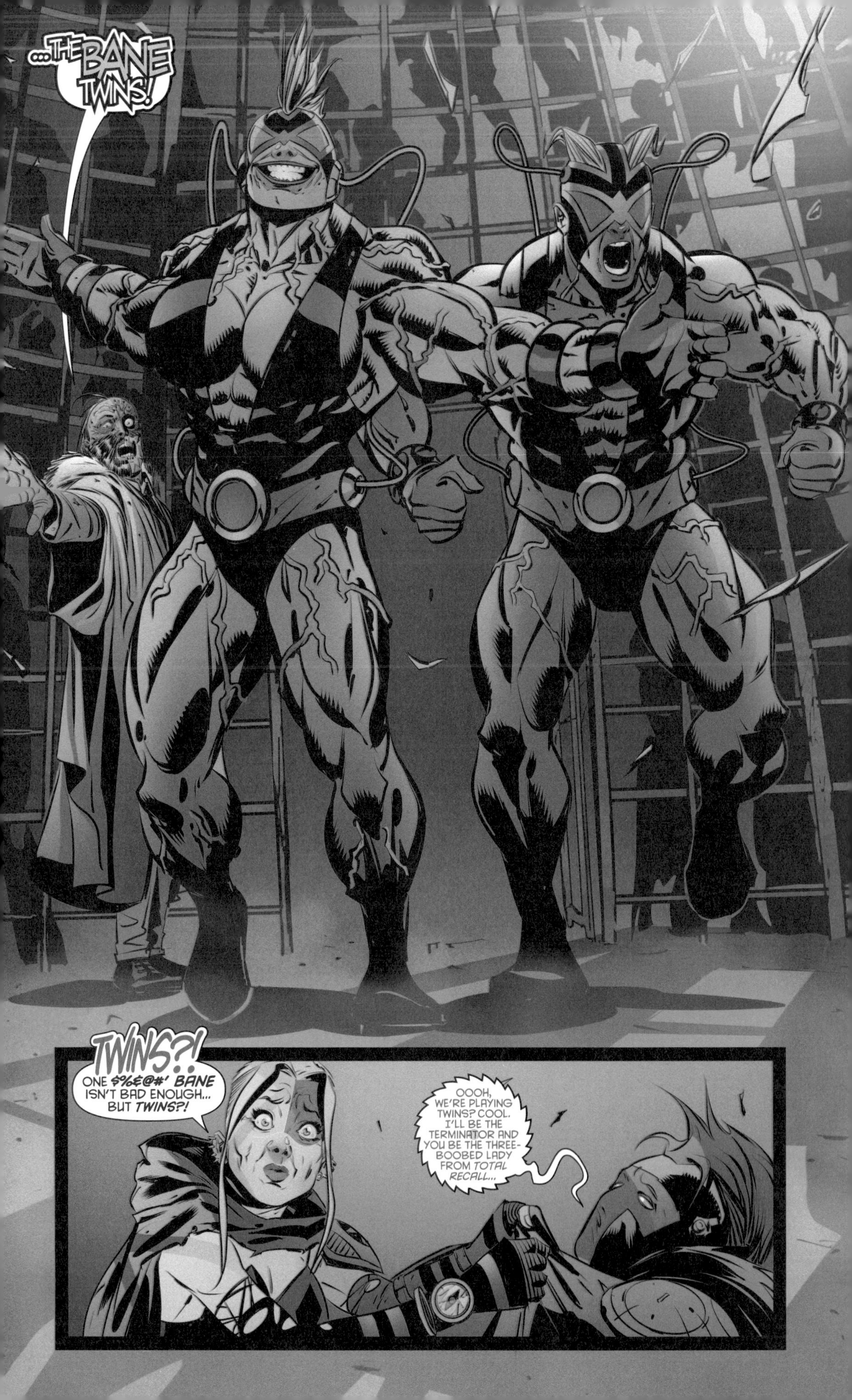
...THE BANE TWINS!
TWINS?!
ONE $%&@#' BANE ISN'T BAD ENOUGH... BUT TWINS?!
OOOH, WE'RE PLAYING TWINS? COOL. I'LL BE THE TERMINATOR AND YOU BE THE THREE-BOOBED LADY FROM TOTAL RECALL...

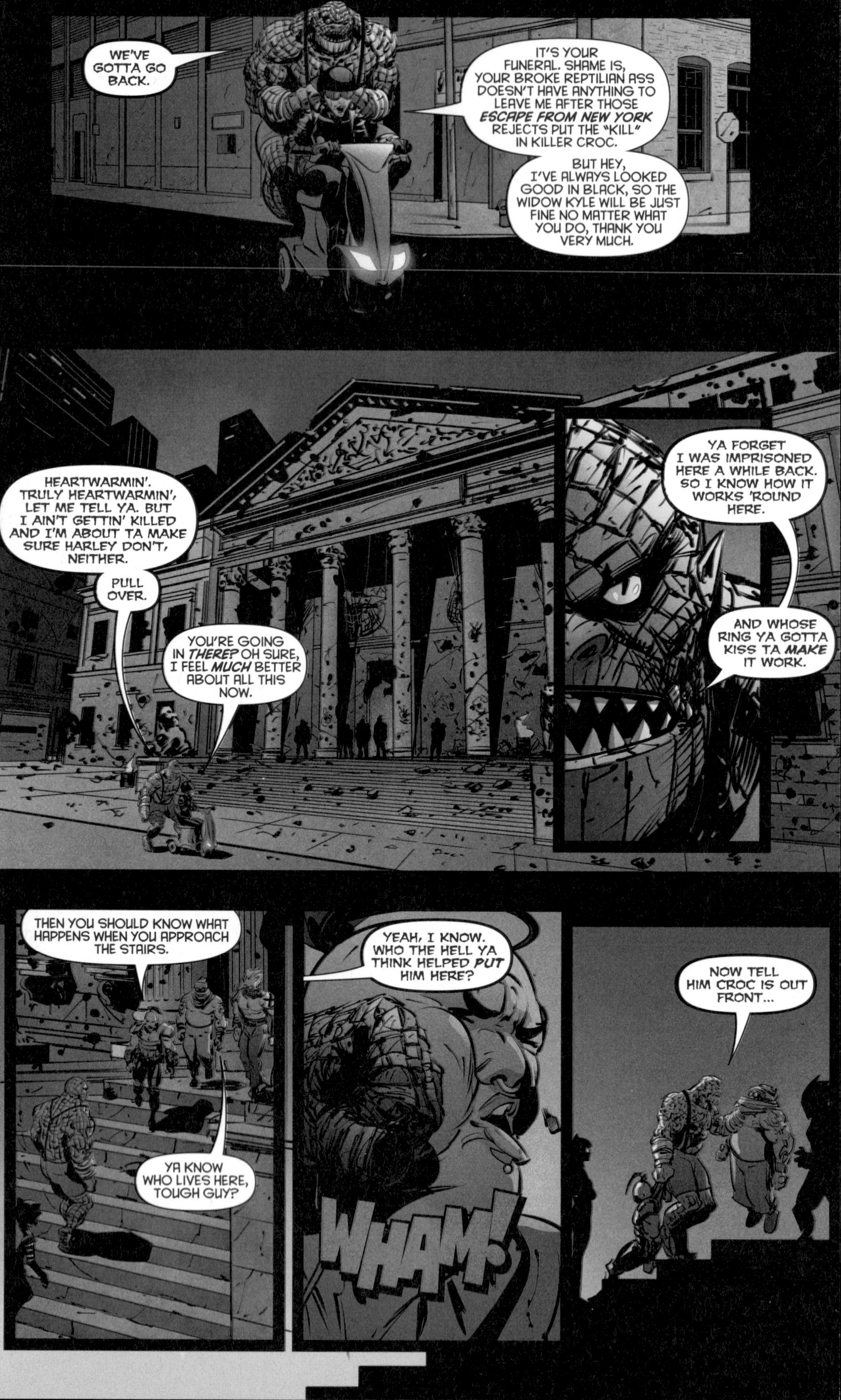
WE'VE GOTTA GO BACK.
IT'S YOUR FUNERAL. SHAME IS, YOUR BROKE REPTILIAN ASS DOESN'T HAVE ANYTHING TO LEAVE ME AFTER THOSE ESCAPE FROM NEW YORK REJECTS PUT THE "KILL" IN KILLER CROC.
BUT HEY, I'VE ALWAYS LOOKED GOOD IN BLACK, SO THE WIDOW KYLE WILL BE JUST FINE NO MATTER WHAT YOU DO, THANK YOU VERY MUCH.
HEARTWARMIN'. TRULY HEARTWARMIN', LET ME TELL YA. BUT I AIN'T GETTIN' KILLED AND I'M ABOUT TA MAKE SURE HARLEY DON'T, NEITHER.
PULL OVER.
YOU'RE GOING IN THERE? OH SURE, I FEEL MUCH BETTER ABOUT ALL THIS NOW.
YA FORGET I WAS IMPRISONED HERE A WHILE BACK. SO I KNOW HOW IT WORKS 'ROUND HERE.
AND WHOSE RING YA GOTTA KISS TA MAKE IT WORK.
THEN YOU SHOULD KNOW WHAT HAPPENS WHEN YOU APPROACH THE STAIRS.
YA KNOW WHO LIVES HERE, TOUGH GUY?
YEAH, I KNOW. WHO THE HELL YA THINK HELPED PUT HIM HERE?
WHAM!
NOW TELL HIM CROC IS OUT FRONT...

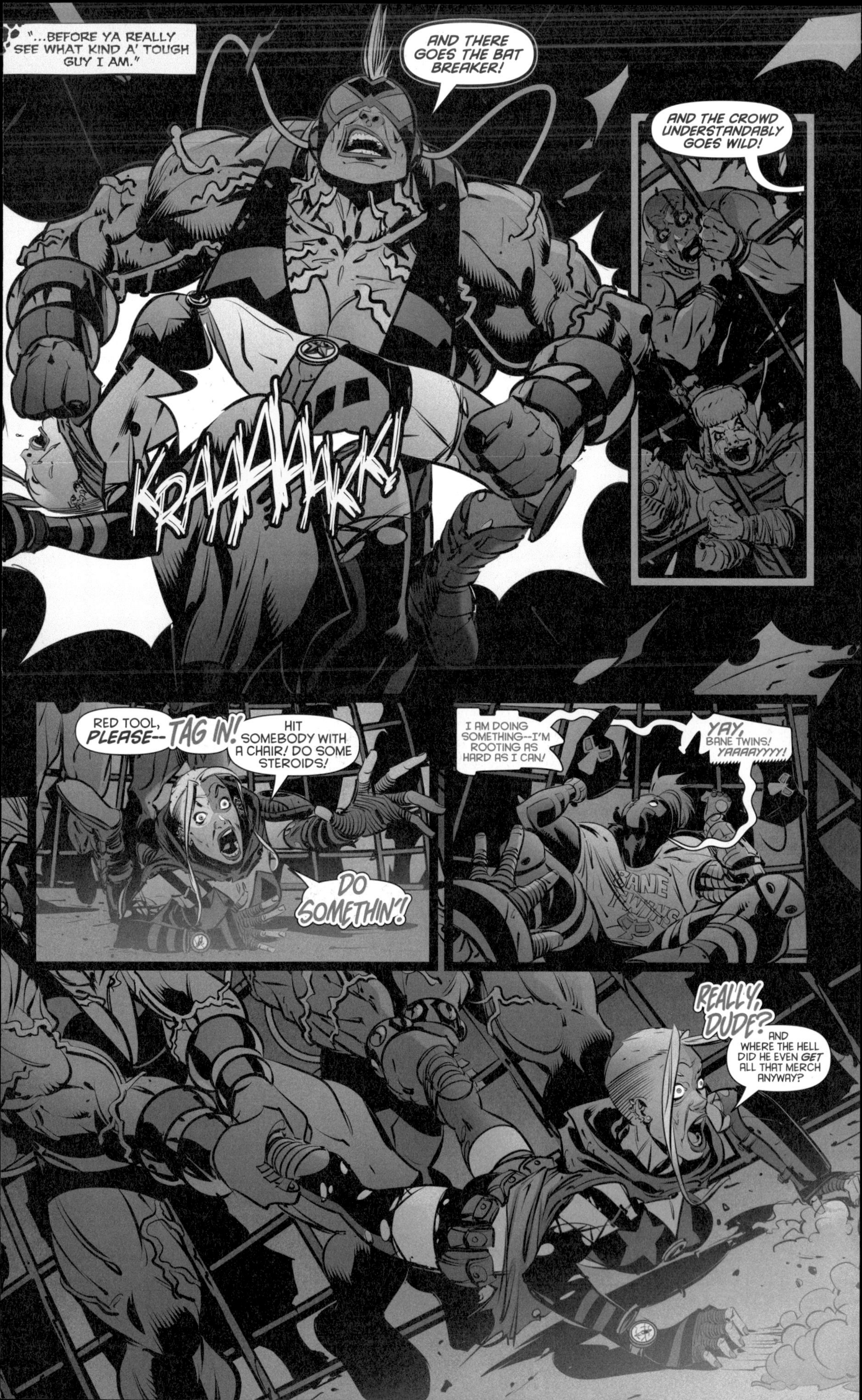
"...BEFORE YA REALLY SEE WHAT KIND A' TOUGH GUY I AM."
AND THERE GOES THE BAT BREAKER!
KRAAAAAAKK!
AND THE CROWD UNDERSTANDABLY GOES WILD!
RED TOOL, PLEASE-- TAG IN!
HIT SOMEBODY WITH A CHAIR! DO SOME STEROIDS!
DO SOMETHIN'!
I AM DOING SOMETHING--I'M ROOTING AS HARD AS I CAN!
YAY, BANE TWINS! YAAAAAYYYY!
REALLY, DUDE?
AND WHERE THE HELL DID HE EVEN GET ALL THAT MERCH ANYWAY?

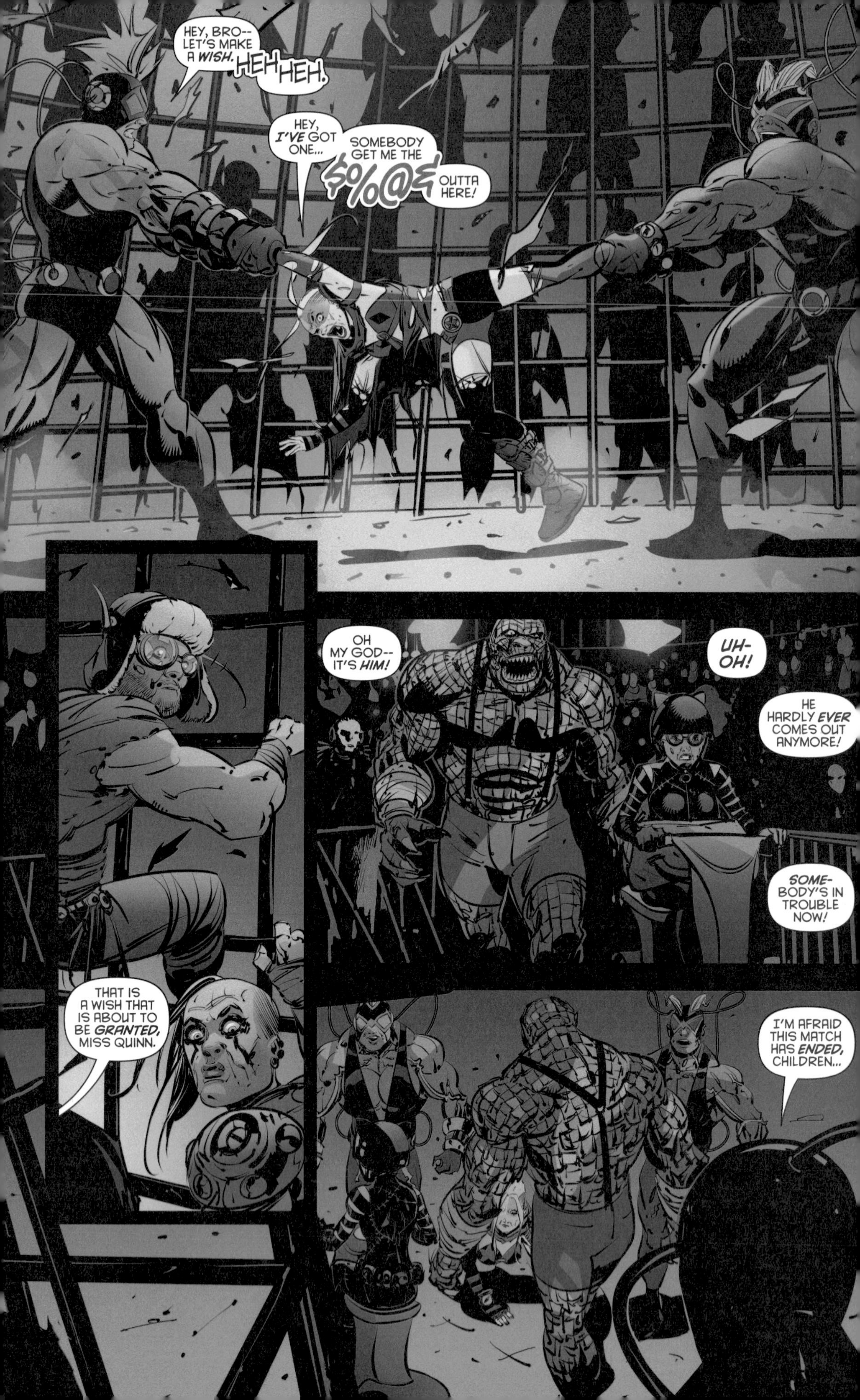

HEY, BRO--
LET'S MAKE A *WISH.* HEH HEH.
HEY, *I'VE* GOT ONE...
SOMEBODY GET ME THE $%@& OUTTA HERE!
OH MY GOD-- IT'S *HIM!*
UH-OH!
HE HARDLY *EVER* COMES OUT ANYMORE!
SOME-BODY'S IN TROUBLE NOW!
THAT IS A WISH THAT IS ABOUT TO BE *GRANTED,* MISS QUINN.
I'M AFRAID THIS MATCH HAS *ENDED,* CHILDREN...

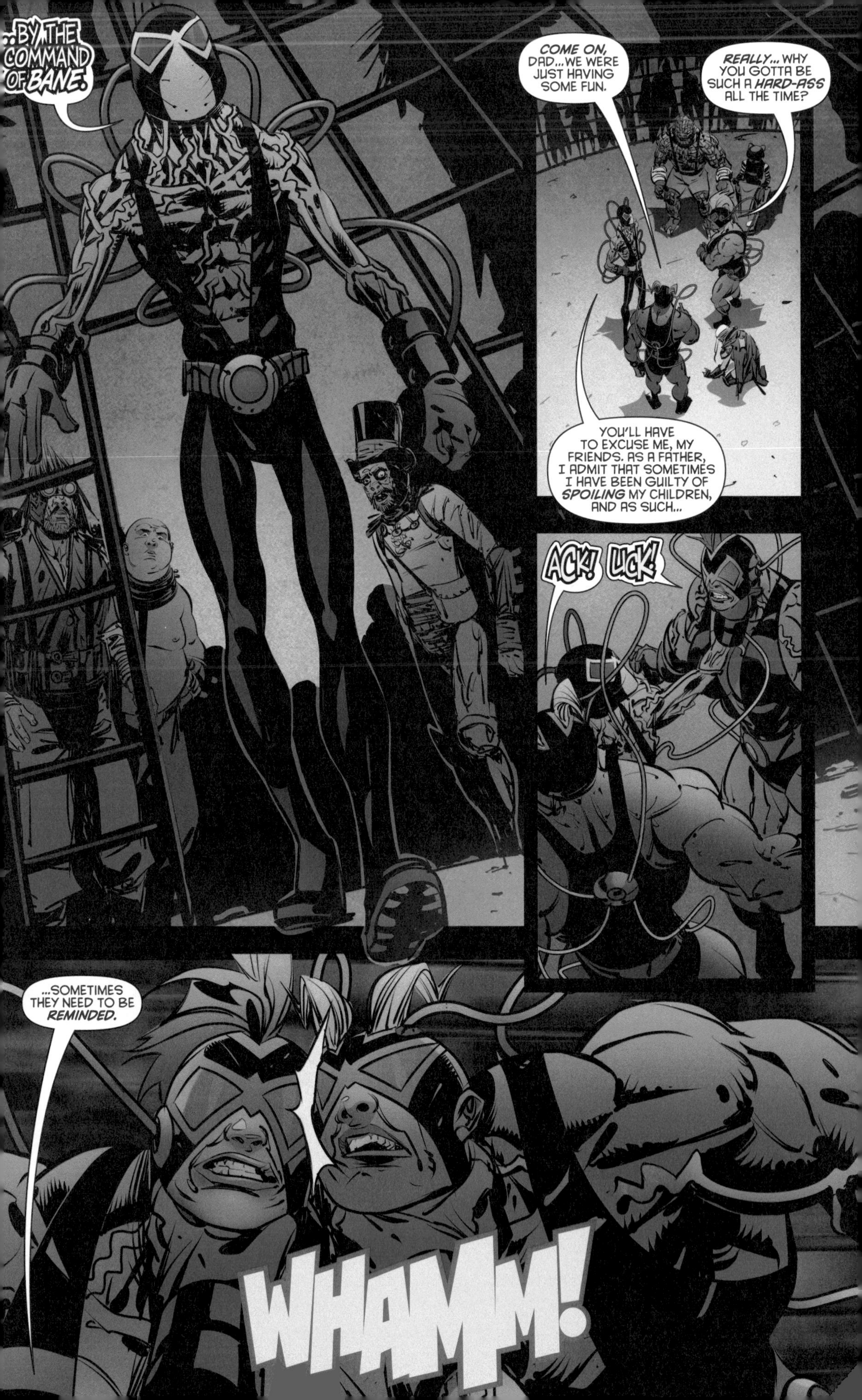
...BY THE COMMAND OF BANE.
COME ON, DAD...WE WERE JUST HAVING SOME FUN.
REALLY... WHY YOU GOTTA BE SUCH A HARD-ASS ALL THE TIME?
YOU'LL HAVE TO EXCUSE ME, MY FRIENDS. AS A FATHER, I ADMIT THAT SOMETIMES I HAVE BEEN GUILTY OF SPOILING MY CHILDREN, AND AS SUCH...
ACK! UCK!
...SOMETIMES THEY NEED TO BE REMINDED.
WHAMM!

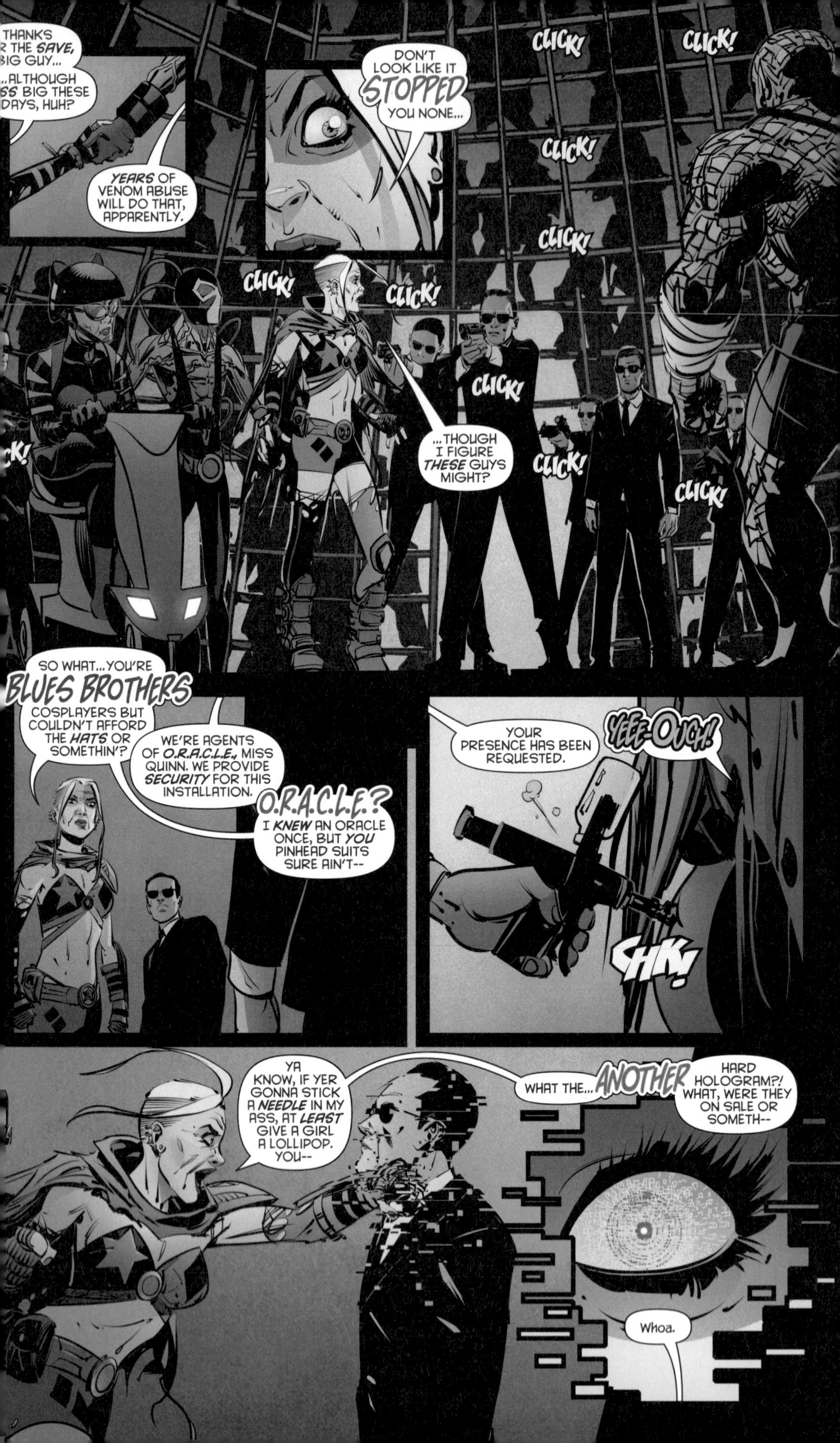

THANKS R THE SAVE, BIG GUY...
...ALTHOUGH SS BIG THESE DAYS, HUH?
YEARS OF VENOM ABUSE WILL DO THAT, APPARENTLY.
DON'T LOOK LIKE IT STOPPED YOU NONE...
CLICK!
CLICK!
CLICK!
CLICK!
CLICK!
CLICK!
CLICK!
...THOUGH I FIGURE THESE GUYS MIGHT?
CLICK!
CLICK!
SO WHAT...YOU'RE BLUES BROTHERS COSPLAYERS BUT COULDN'T AFFORD THE HATS OR SOMETHIN'?
WE'RE AGENTS OF O.R.A.C.L.E., MISS QUINN. WE PROVIDE SECURITY FOR THIS INSTALLATION.
O.R.A.C.L.E.? I KNEW AN ORACLE ONCE, BUT YOU PINHEAD SUITS SURE AIN'T--
YOUR PRESENCE HAS BEEN REQUESTED.
YEEE-OUCH!
CHK!
YA KNOW, IF YER GONNA STICK A NEEDLE IN MY ASS, AT LEAST GIVE A GIRL A LOLLIPOP. YOU--
WHAT THE... ANOTHER HARD HOLOGRAM?! WHAT, WERE THEY ON SALE OR SOMETH--
Whoa.

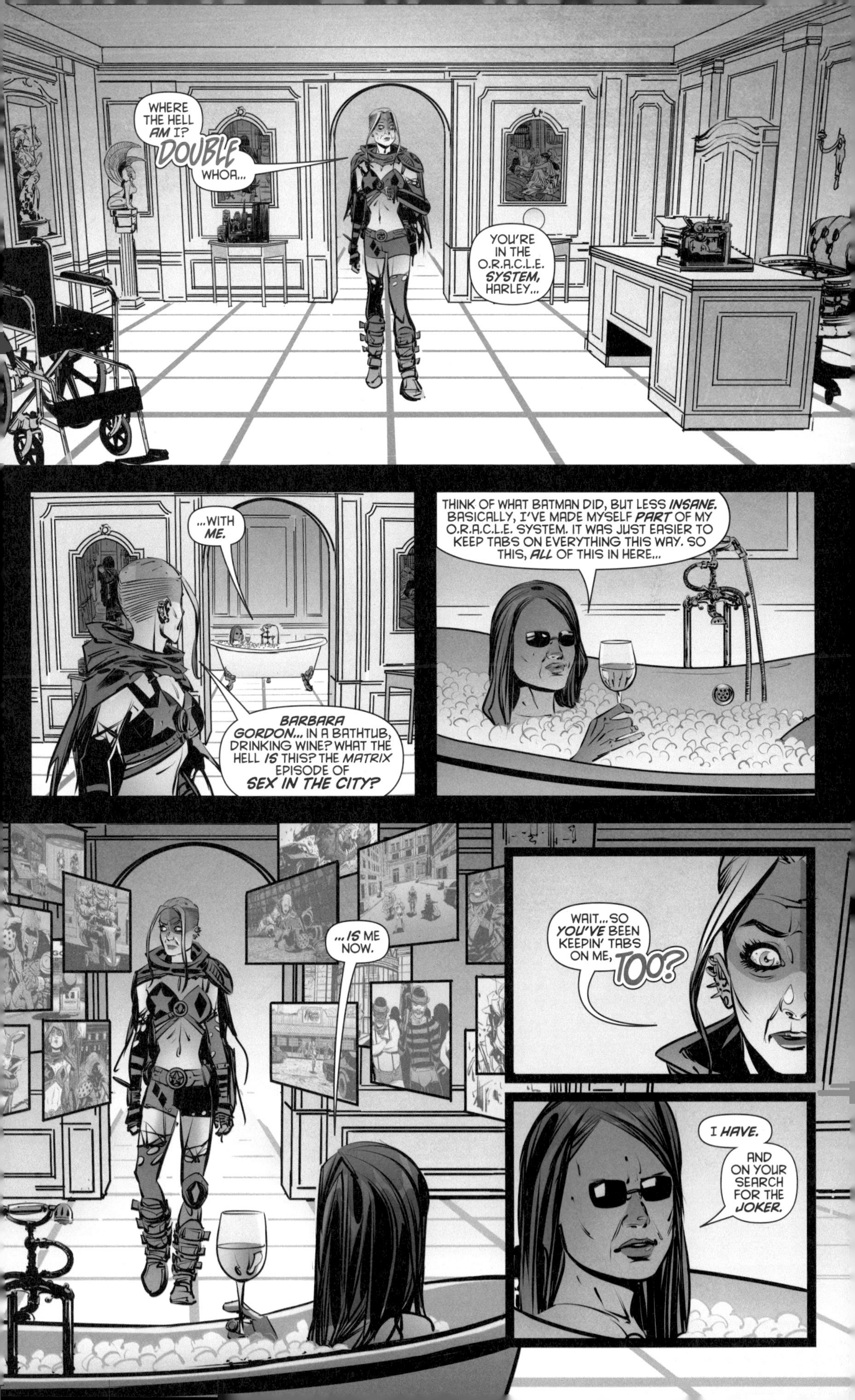
WHERE THE HELL AM I? DOUBLE WHOA...
YOU'RE IN THE O.R.A.C.L.E. SYSTEM, HARLEY...
...WITH ME.
BARBARA GORDON... IN A BATHTUB, DRINKING WINE? WHAT THE HELL IS THIS? THE MATRIX EPISODE OF SEX IN THE CITY?
THINK OF WHAT BATMAN DID, BUT LESS INSANE. BASICALLY, I'VE MADE MYSELF PART OF MY O.R.A.C.L.E. SYSTEM. IT WAS JUST EASIER TO KEEP TABS ON EVERYTHING THIS WAY. SO THIS, ALL OF THIS IN HERE...
...IS ME NOW.
WAIT... SO YOU'VE BEEN KEEPIN' TABS ON ME, TOO?
I HAVE.
AND ON YOUR SEARCH FOR THE JOKER.

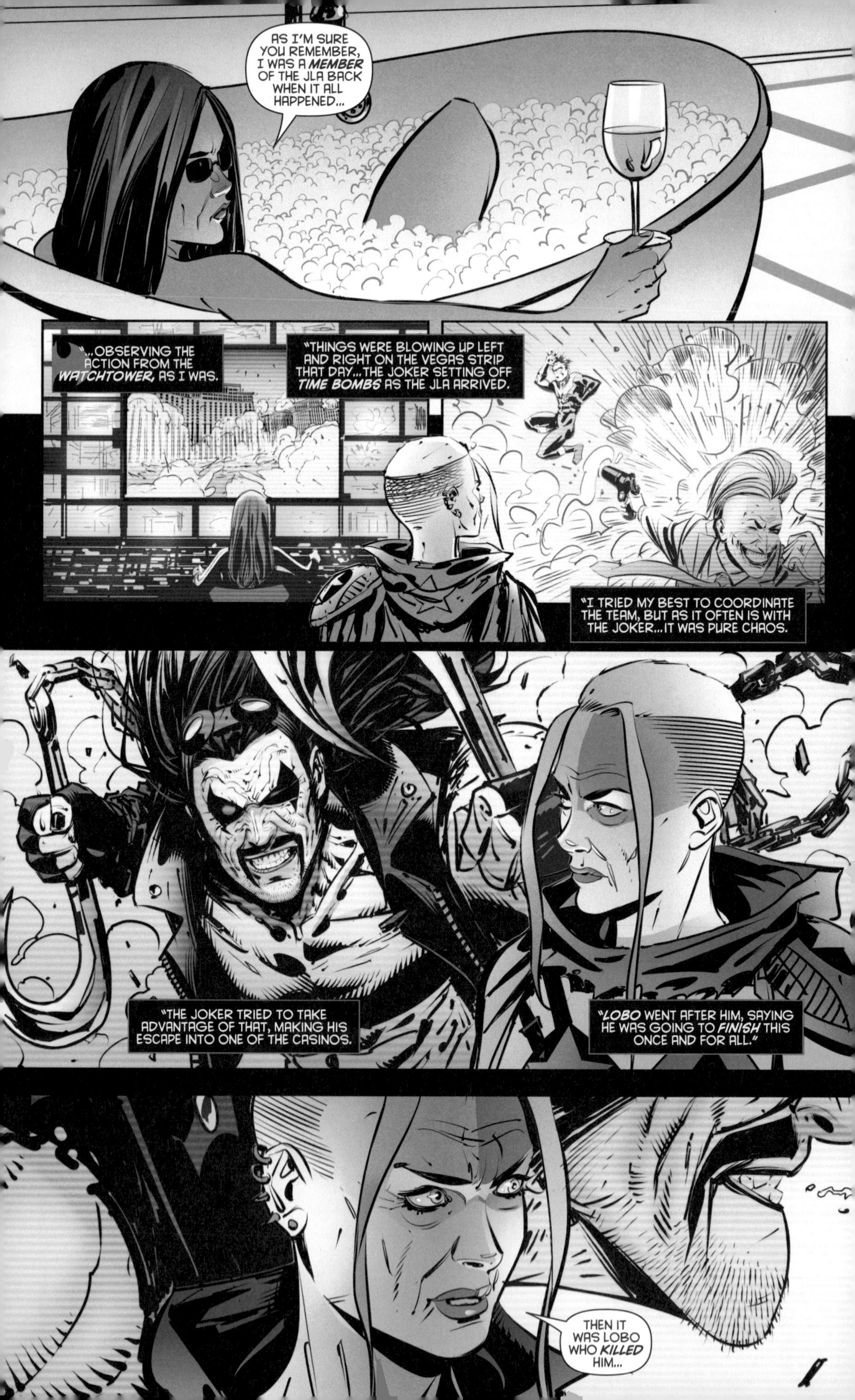
AS I'M SURE YOU REMEMBER, I WAS A MEMBER OF THE JLA BACK WHEN IT ALL HAPPENED...
"...OBSERVING THE ACTION FROM THE WATCHTOWER, AS I WAS.
"THINGS WERE BLOWING UP LEFT AND RIGHT ON THE VEGAS STRIP THAT DAY...THE JOKER SETTING OFF TIME BOMBS AS THE JLA ARRIVED.
"I TRIED MY BEST TO COORDINATE THE TEAM, BUT AS IT OFTEN IS WITH THE JOKER...IT WAS PURE CHAOS.
"THE JOKER TRIED TO TAKE ADVANTAGE OF THAT, MAKING HIS ESCAPE INTO ONE OF THE CASINOS.
"LOBO WENT AFTER HIM, SAYING HE WAS GOING TO FINISH THIS ONCE AND FOR ALL."
THEN IT WAS LOBO WHO KILLED HIM...

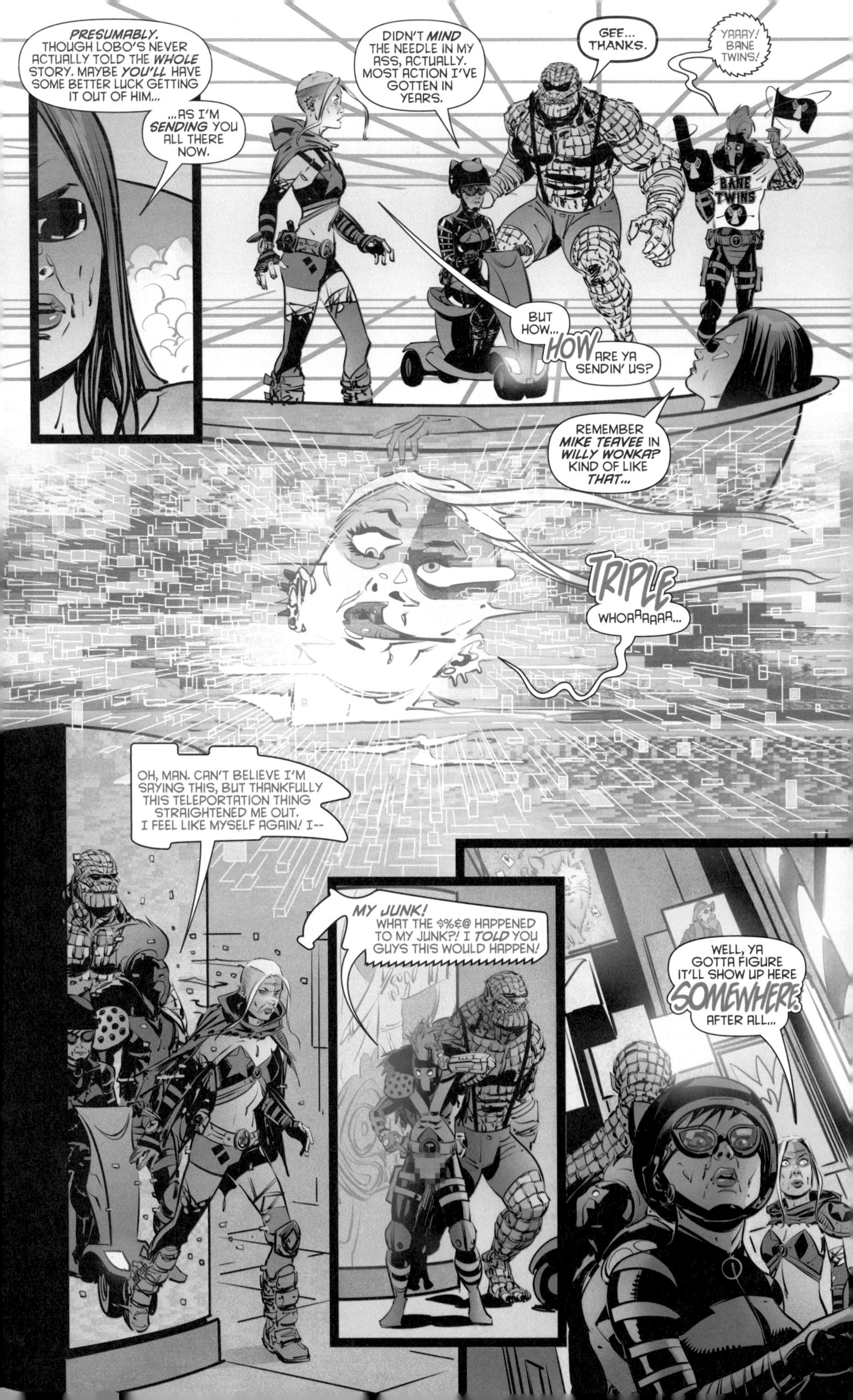
PRESUMABLY. THOUGH LOBO'S NEVER ACTUALLY TOLD THE WHOLE STORY. MAYBE YOU'LL HAVE SOME BETTER LUCK GETTING IT OUT OF HIM...
...AS I'M SENDING YOU ALL THERE NOW.
DIDN'T MIND THE NEEDLE IN MY ASS, ACTUALLY. MOST ACTION I'VE GOTTEN IN YEARS.
GEE... THANKS.
YAAAY! BANE TWINS!
BANE TWINS
BUT HOW... HOW ARE YA SENDIN' US?
REMEMBER MIKE TEAVEE IN WILLY WONKA? KIND OF LIKE THAT...
TRIPLE
WHOAAAAAA...
OH, MAN. CAN'T BELIEVE I'M SAYING THIS, BUT THANKFULLY THIS TELEPORTATION THING STRAIGHTENED ME OUT. I FEEL LIKE MYSELF AGAIN! I--
MY JUNK! WHAT THE $%&@ HAPPENED TO MY JUNK?! I TOLD YOU GUYS THIS WOULD HAPPEN!
WELL, YA GOTTA FIGURE IT'LL SHOW UP HERE SOMEWHERE AFTER ALL...

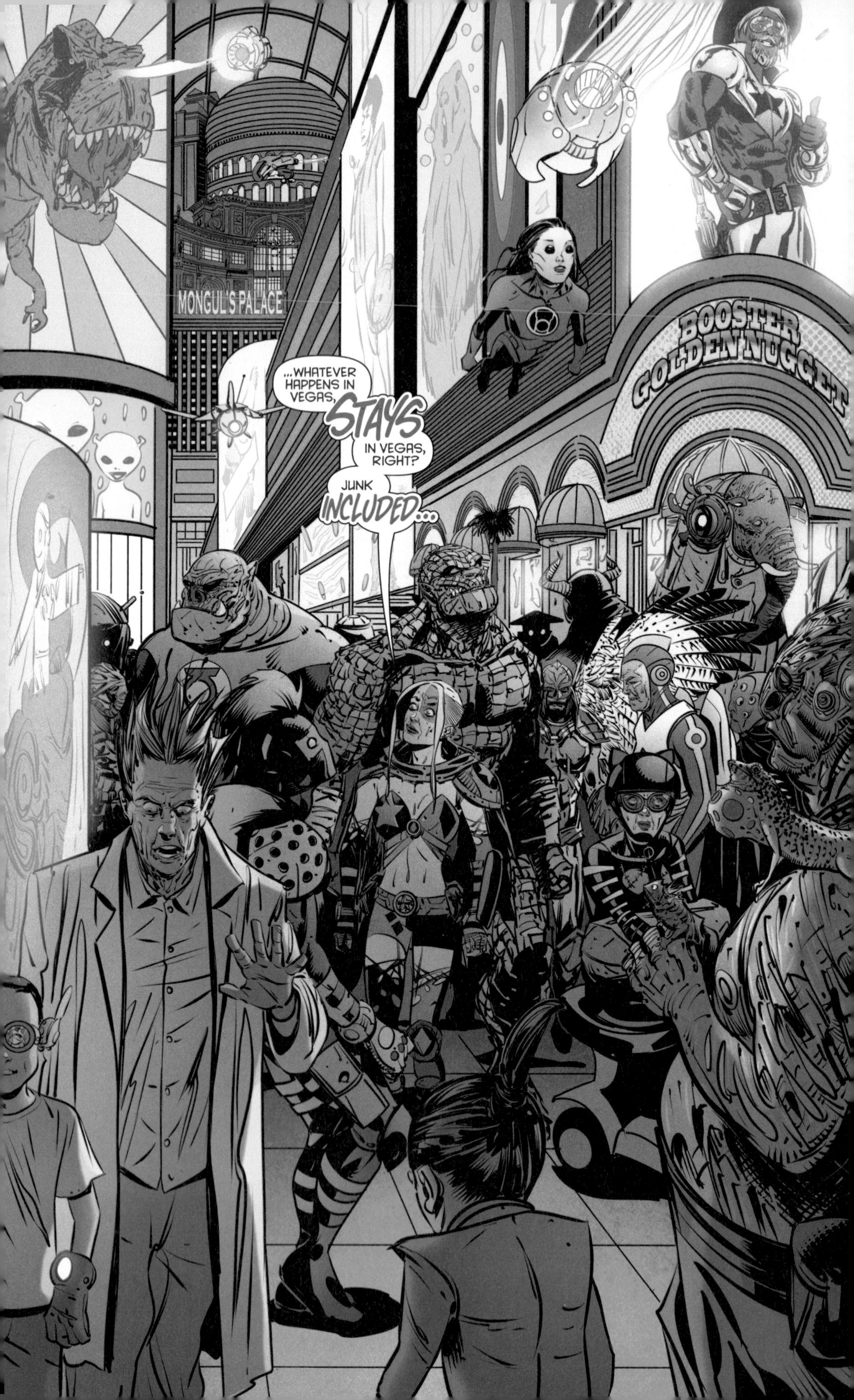
MONGUL'S PALACE
BOOSTER GOLDEN NUGGET
...WHATEVER HAPPENS IN VEGAS, STAYS IN VEGAS, RIGHT?
JUNK INCLUDED...

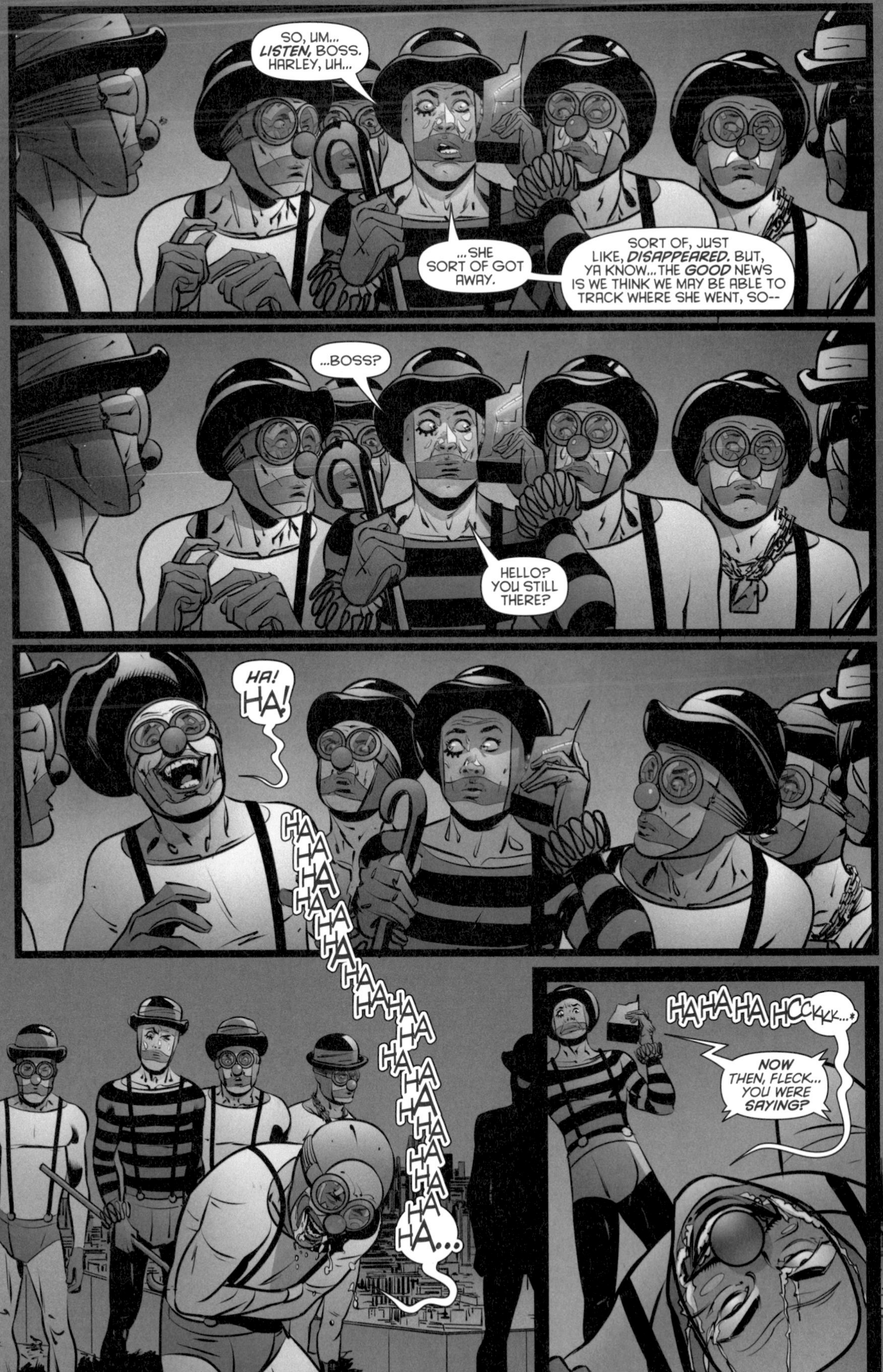
SO, UM... LISTEN, BOSS. HARLEY, UH...
...SHE SORT OF GOT AWAY.
SORT OF, JUST LIKE, DISAPPEARED. BUT, YA KNOW... THE GOOD NEWS IS WE THINK WE MAY BE ABLE TO TRACK WHERE SHE WENT, SO--
...BOSS?
HELLO? YOU STILL THERE?
HA! HA!
HAHAHAHAHAHAHAHAHAHAHAHAHAHAHAHA...
HAHAHA HCCKKK...*
NOW THEN, FLECK... YOU WERE SAYING?

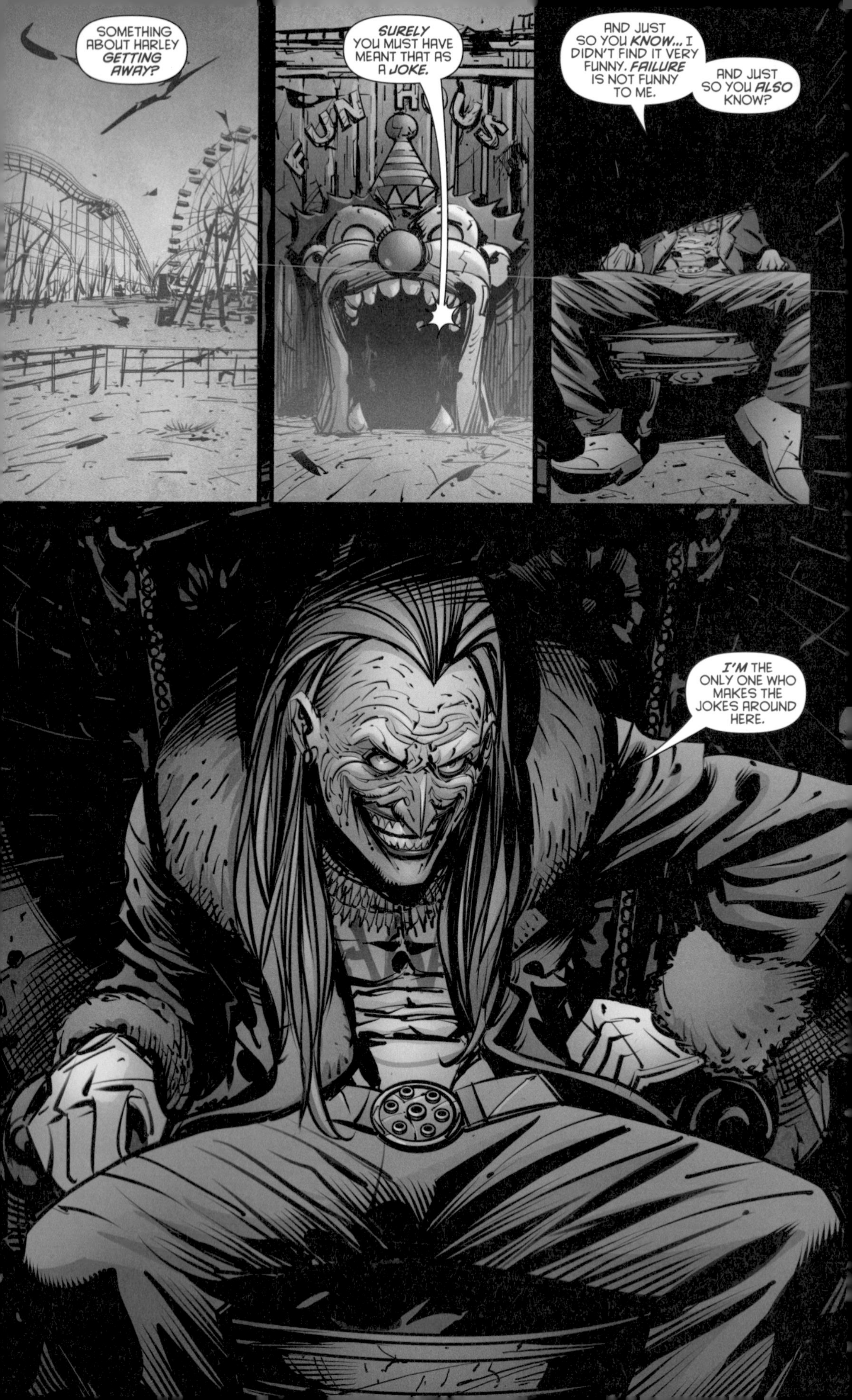
SOMETHING ABOUT HARLEY GETTING AWAY?
SURELY YOU MUST HAVE MEANT THAT AS A JOKE.
FUN HOUSE
AND JUST SO YOU KNOW... I DIDN'T FIND IT VERY FUNNY. FAILURE IS NOT FUNNY TO ME.
AND JUST SO YOU ALSO KNOW?
I'M THE ONLY ONE WHO MAKES THE JOKES AROUND HERE.

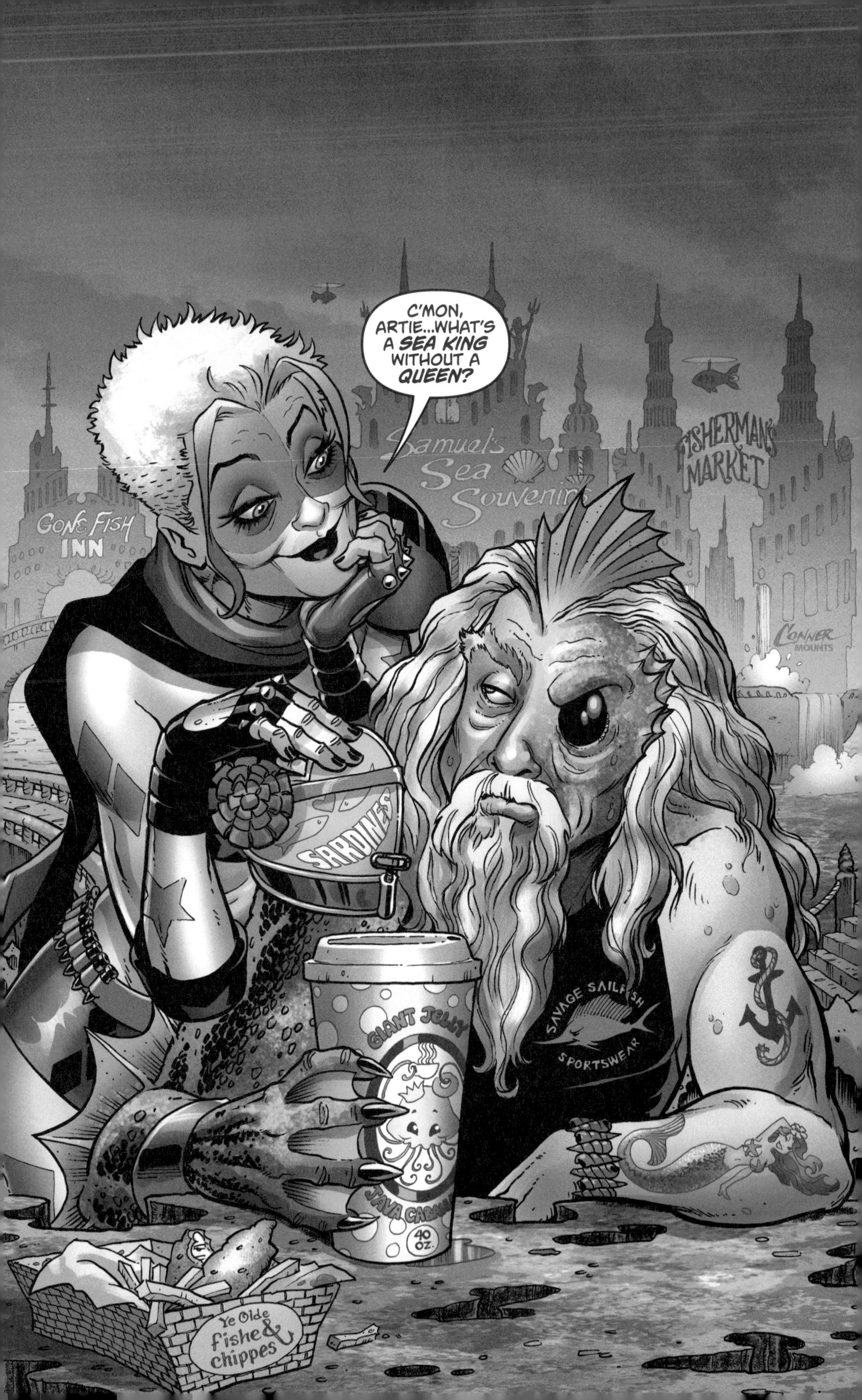
C'MON, ARTIE...WHAT'S A SEA KING WITHOUT A QUEEN?
Samuel's Sea Souvenirs
FISHERMAN'S MARKET
GONE FISH INN
CONNER MOUNTS
SARDINES
GIANT JELLY
JAVA CABANA
40 OZ.
SAVAGE SAILFISH SPORTSWEAR
Ye Olde fishe & chippes

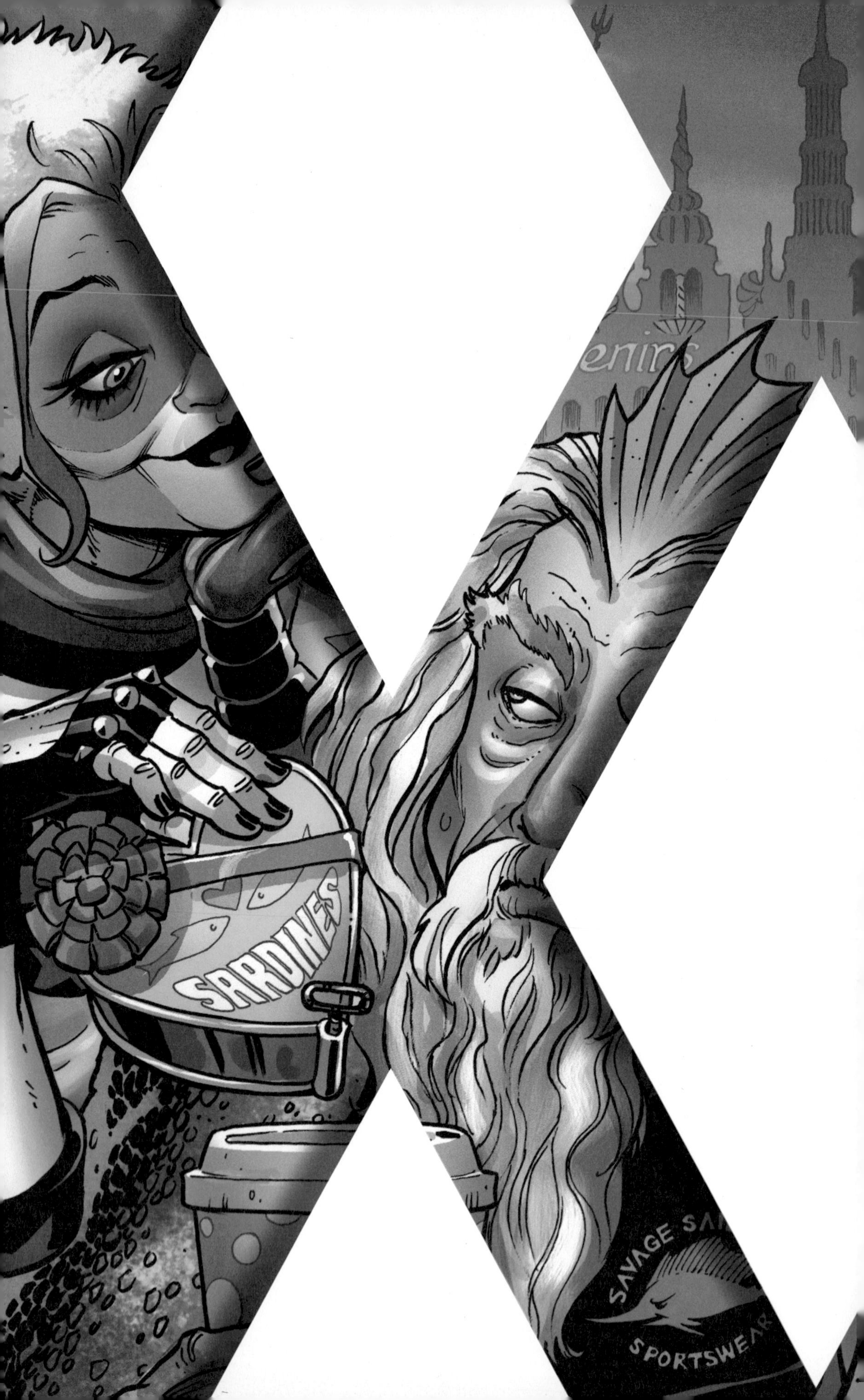
SARDINES

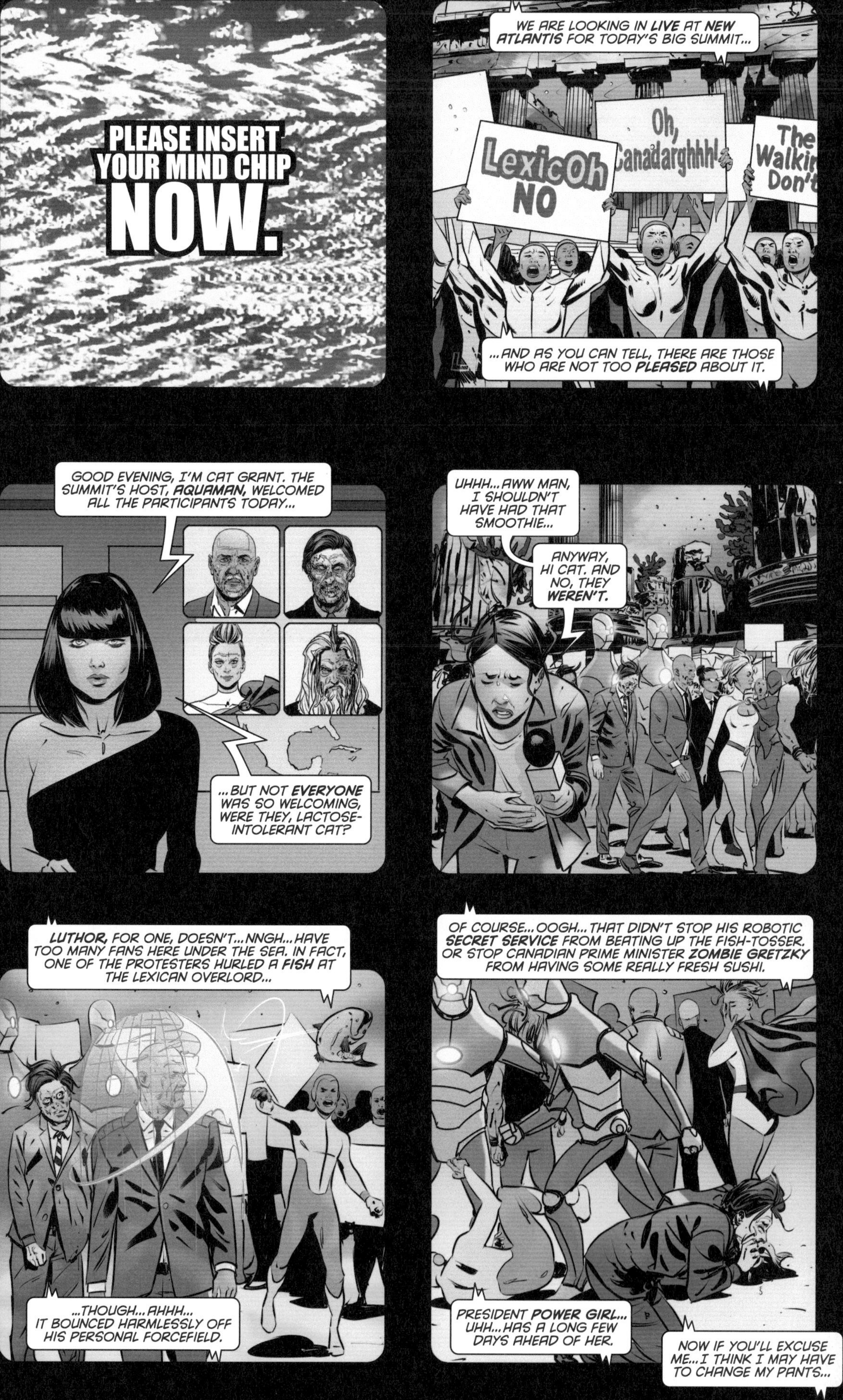
PLEASE INSERT YOUR MIND CHIP NOW.
WE ARE LOOKING IN LIVE AT NEW ATLANTIS FOR TODAY'S BIG SUMMIT...
LexicOh NO
Oh, Canadarghhh!
The Walkin Don't
...AND AS YOU CAN TELL, THERE ARE THOSE WHO ARE NOT TOO PLEASED ABOUT IT.
GOOD EVENING, I'M CAT GRANT. THE SUMMIT'S HOST, AQUAMAN, WELCOMED ALL THE PARTICIPANTS TODAY...
...BUT NOT EVERYONE WAS SO WELCOMING, WERE THEY, LACTOSE-INTOLERANT CAT?
UHHH...AWW MAN, I SHOULDN'T HAVE HAD THAT SMOOTHIE...
ANYWAY, HI CAT. AND NO, THEY WEREN'T.
LUTHOR, FOR ONE, DOESN'T...NNGH...HAVE TOO MANY FANS HERE UNDER THE SEA. IN FACT, ONE OF THE PROTESTERS HURLED A FISH AT THE LEXICAN OVERLORD...
...THOUGH...AHHH... IT BOUNCED HARMLESSLY OFF HIS PERSONAL FORCEFIELD.
OF COURSE...OOGH...THAT DIDN'T STOP HIS ROBOTIC SECRET SERVICE FROM BEATING UP THE FISH-TOSSER. OR STOP CANADIAN PRIME MINISTER ZOMBIE GRETZKY FROM HAVING SOME REALLY FRESH SUSHI.
PRESIDENT POWER GIRL... UHH...HAS A LONG FEW DAYS AHEAD OF HER.
NOW IF YOU'LL EXCUSE ME...I THINK I MAY HAVE TO CHANGE MY PANTS...

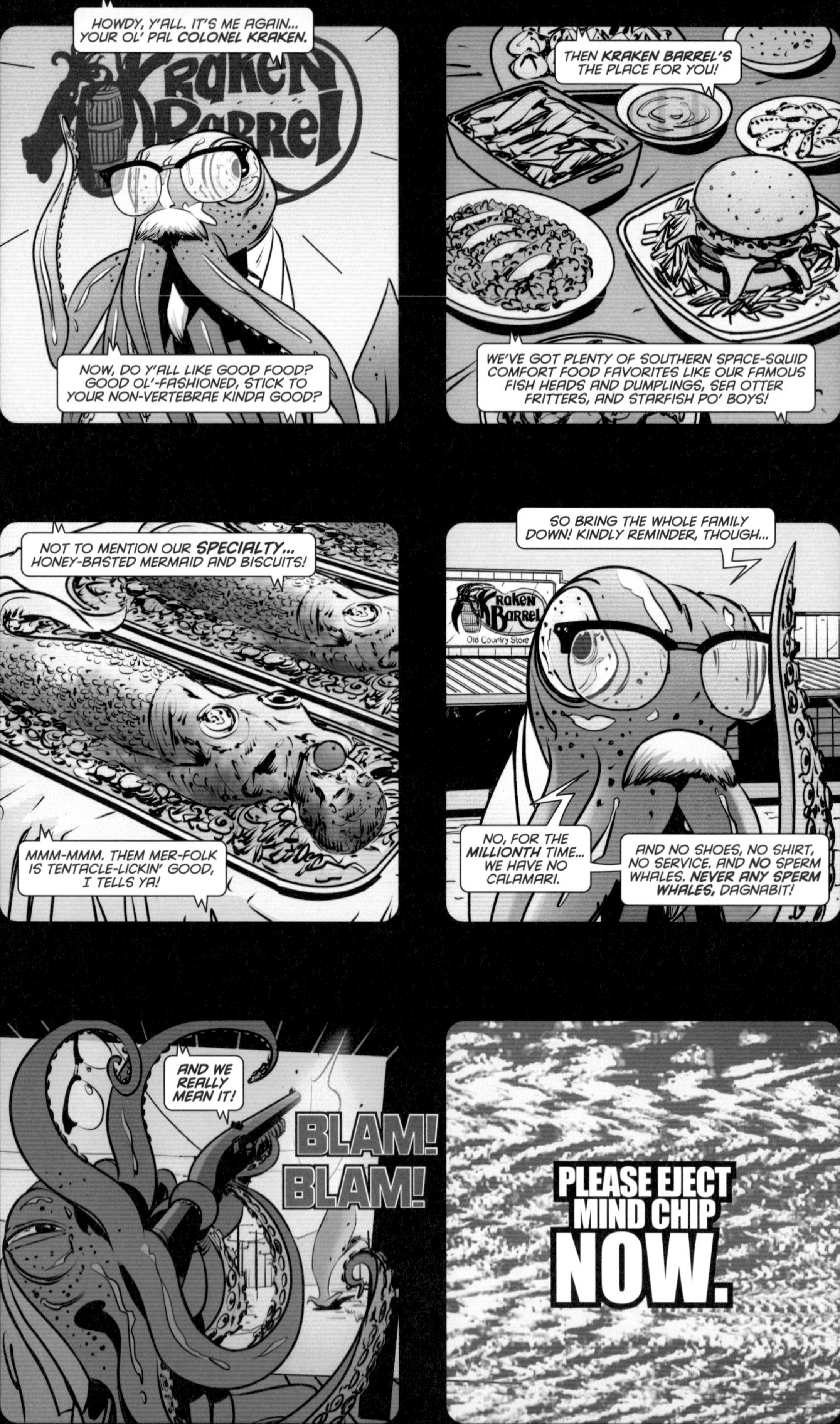
HOWDY, Y'ALL. IT'S ME AGAIN... YOUR OL' PAL COLONEL KRAKEN.
KRAKEN BARREL
NOW, DO Y'ALL LIKE GOOD FOOD? GOOD OL'-FASHIONED, STICK TO YOUR NON-VERTEBRAE KINDA GOOD?
THEN KRAKEN BARREL'S THE PLACE FOR YOU!
WE'VE GOT PLENTY OF SOUTHERN SPACE-SQUID COMFORT FOOD FAVORITES LIKE OUR FAMOUS FISH HEADS AND DUMPLINGS, SEA OTTER FRITTERS, AND STARFISH PO' BOYS!
NOT TO MENTION OUR SPECIALTY... HONEY-BASTED MERMAID AND BISCUITS!
MMM-MMM. THEM MER-FOLK IS TENTACLE-LICKIN' GOOD, I TELLS YA!
SO BRING THE WHOLE FAMILY DOWN! KINDLY REMINDER, THOUGH...
KRAKEN BARREL
Old Country Store
NO, FOR THE MILLIONTH TIME... WE HAVE NO CALAMARI.
AND NO SHOES, NO SHIRT, NO SERVICE. AND NO SPERM WHALES. NEVER ANY SPERM WHALES, DAGNABIT!
AND WE REALLY MEAN IT!
BLAM! BLAM!
PLEASE EJECT MIND CHIP NOW.

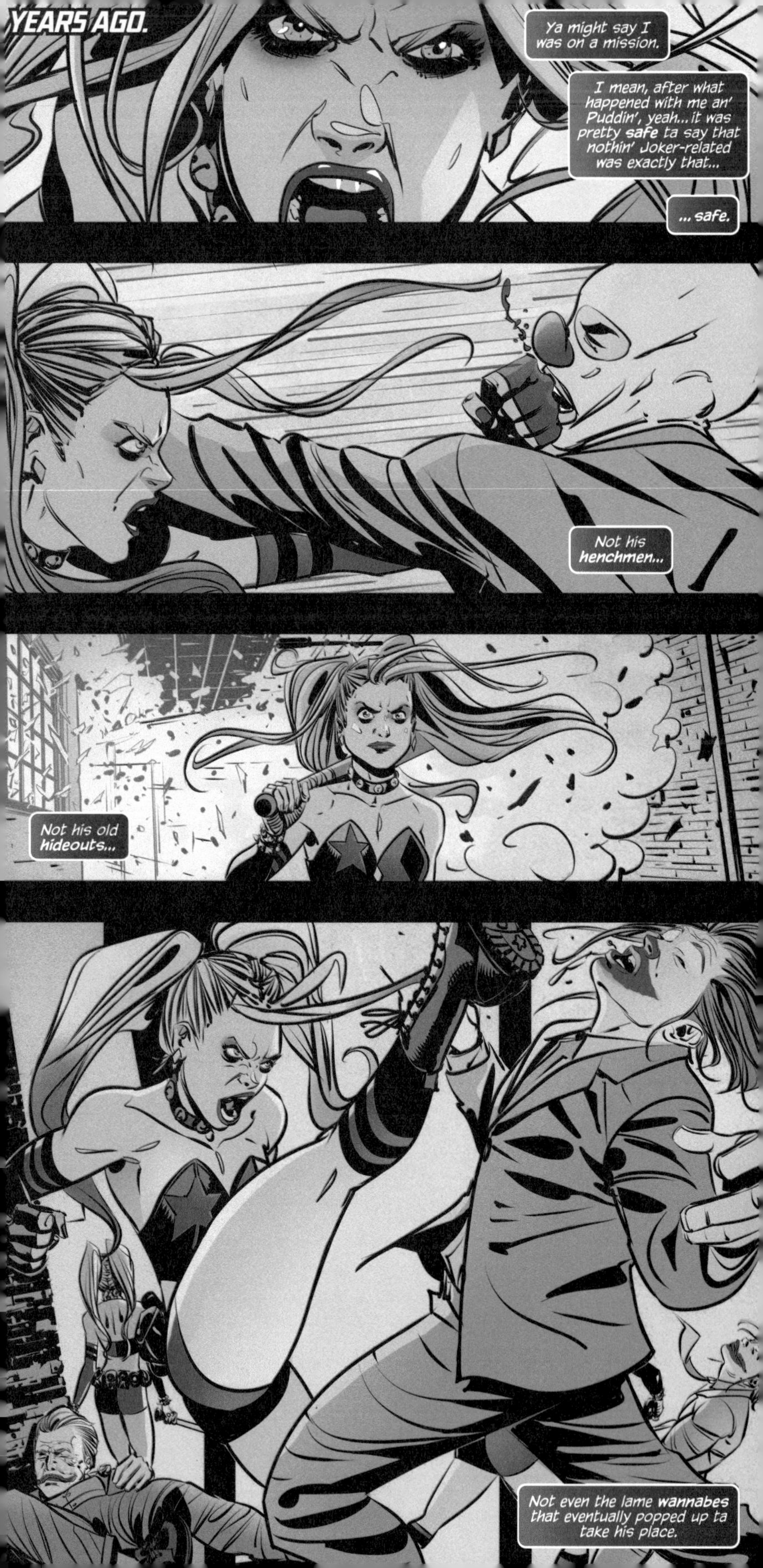
YEARS AGO.
Ya might say I was on a mission.
I mean, after what happened with me an' Puddin', yeah... it was pretty **safe** ta say that nothin' Joker-related was exactly that...
... safe.
Not his **henchmen**...
Not his old **hideouts**...
Not even the lame **wannabes** that eventually popped up ta take his place.

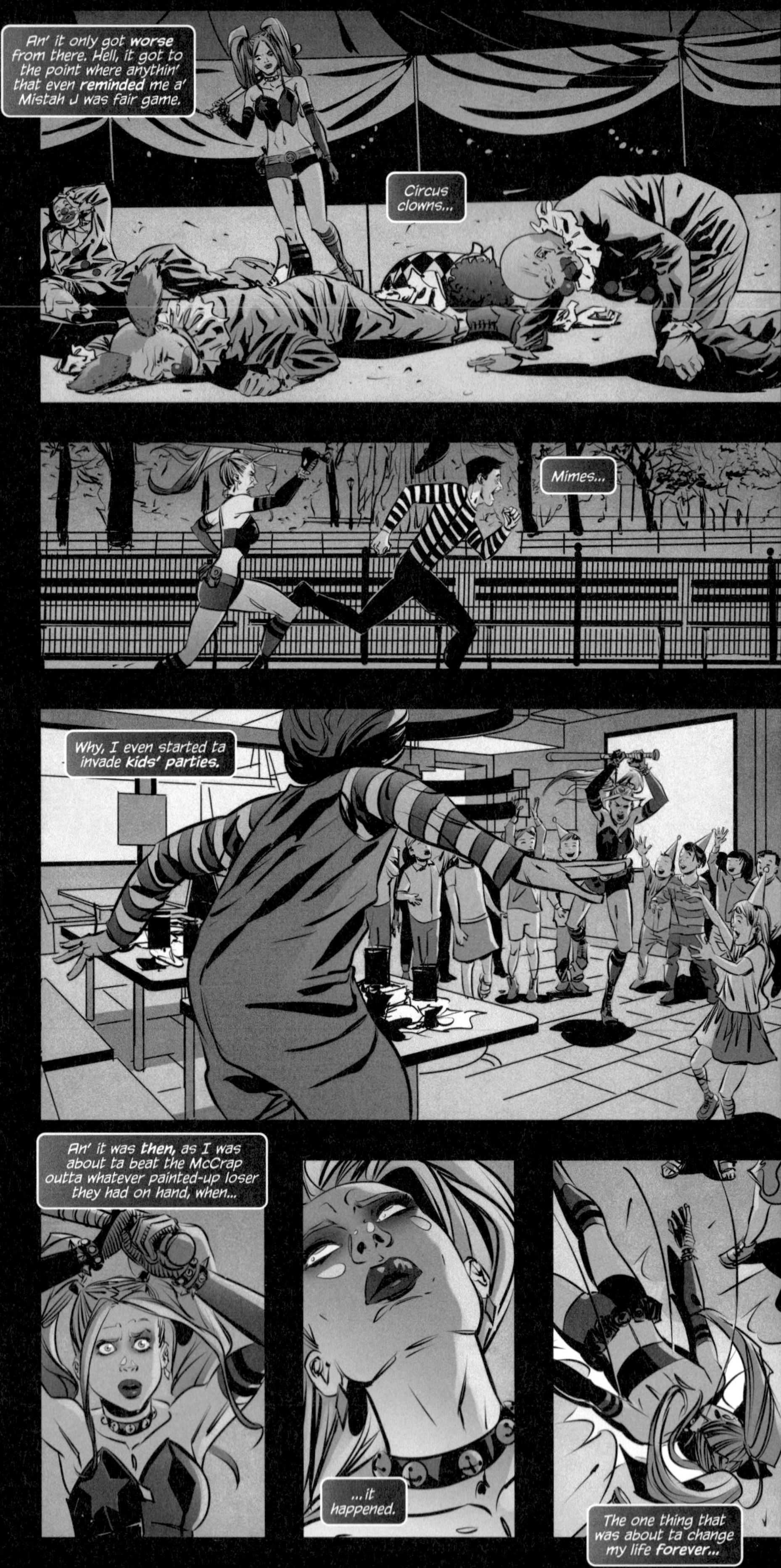
An' it only got worse from there. Hell, it got to the point where anythin' that even reminded me a' Mistah J was fair game.
Circus clowns...
Mimes...
Why, I even started ta invade kids' parties.
An' it was then, as I was about ta beat the McCrap outta whatever painted-up loser they had on hand, when...
...it happened.
The one thing that was about ta change my life forever...

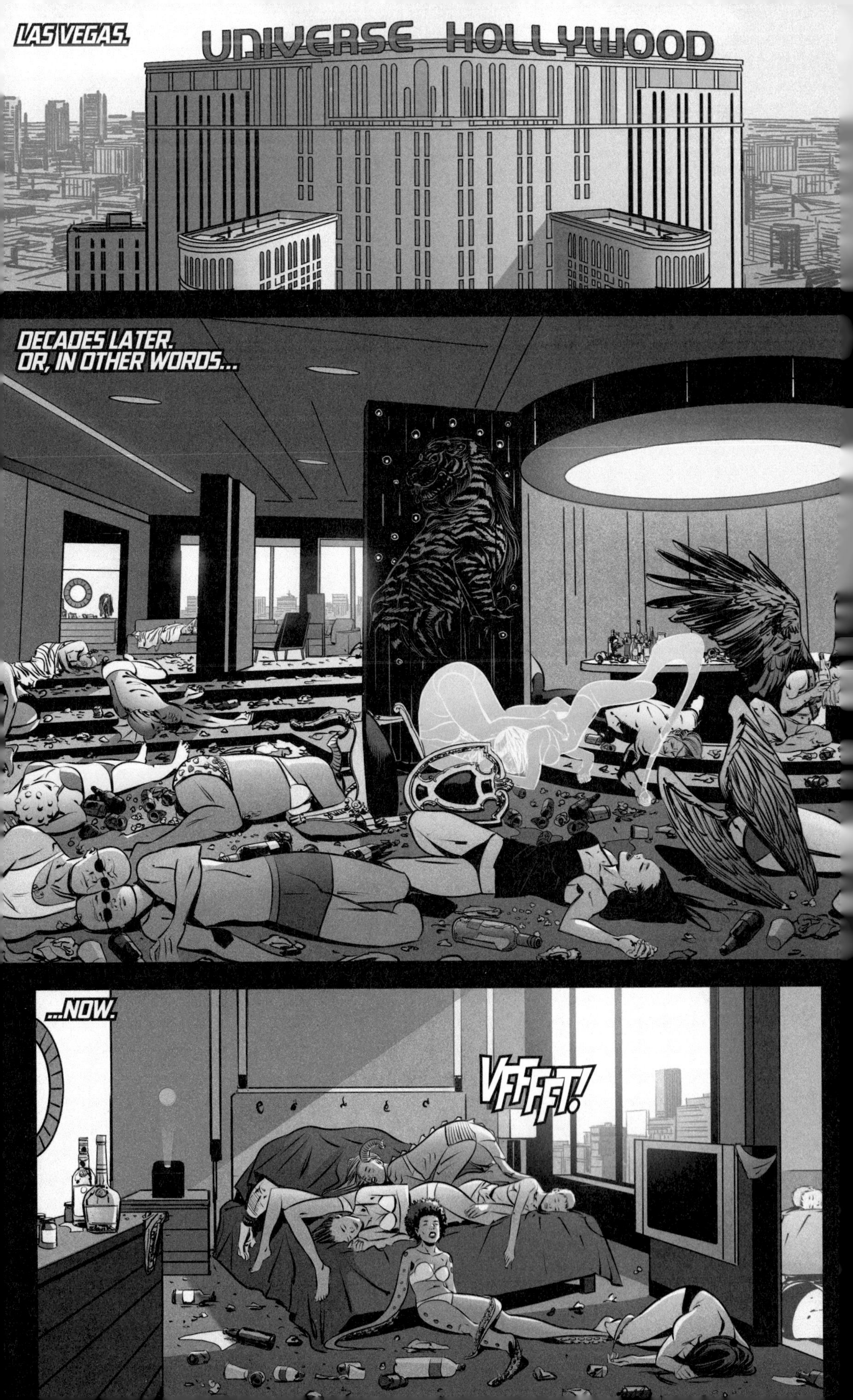
LAS VEGAS.
UNIVERSE HOLLYWOOD
DECADES LATER.
OR, IN OTHER WORDS...
...NOW.
VFFFFT!

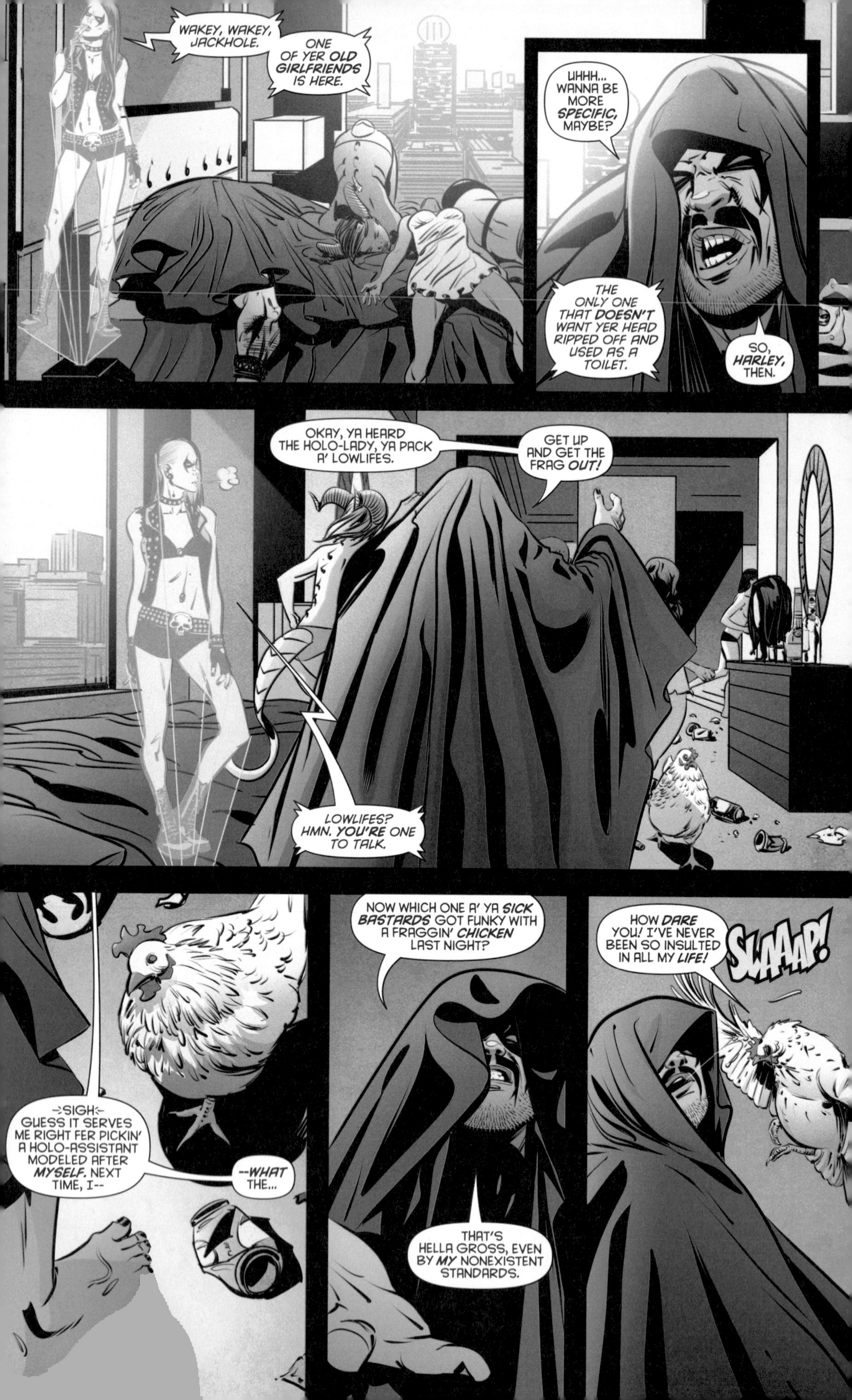

WAKEY, WAKEY, JACKHOLE.
ONE OF YER OLD GIRLFRIENDS IS HERE.
UHHH... WANNA BE MORE SPECIFIC, MAYBE?
THE ONLY ONE THAT DOESN'T WANT YER HEAD RIPPED OFF AND USED AS A TOILET.
SO, HARLEY, THEN.
OKAY, YA HEARD THE HOLO-LADY, YA PACK A' LOWLIFES.
GET UP AND GET THE FRAG OUT!
LOWLIFES? HMN. YOU'RE ONE TO TALK.
>SIGH< GUESS IT SERVES ME RIGHT FER PICKIN' A HOLO-ASSISTANT MODELED AFTER MYSELF. NEXT TIME, I--
--WHAT THE...
NOW WHICH ONE A' YA SICK BASTARDS GOT FUNKY WITH A FRAGGIN' CHICKEN LAST NIGHT?
THAT'S HELLA GROSS, EVEN BY MY NONEXISTENT STANDARDS.
HOW DARE YOU! I'VE NEVER BEEN SO INSULTED IN ALL MY LIFE!
SLAAAP!

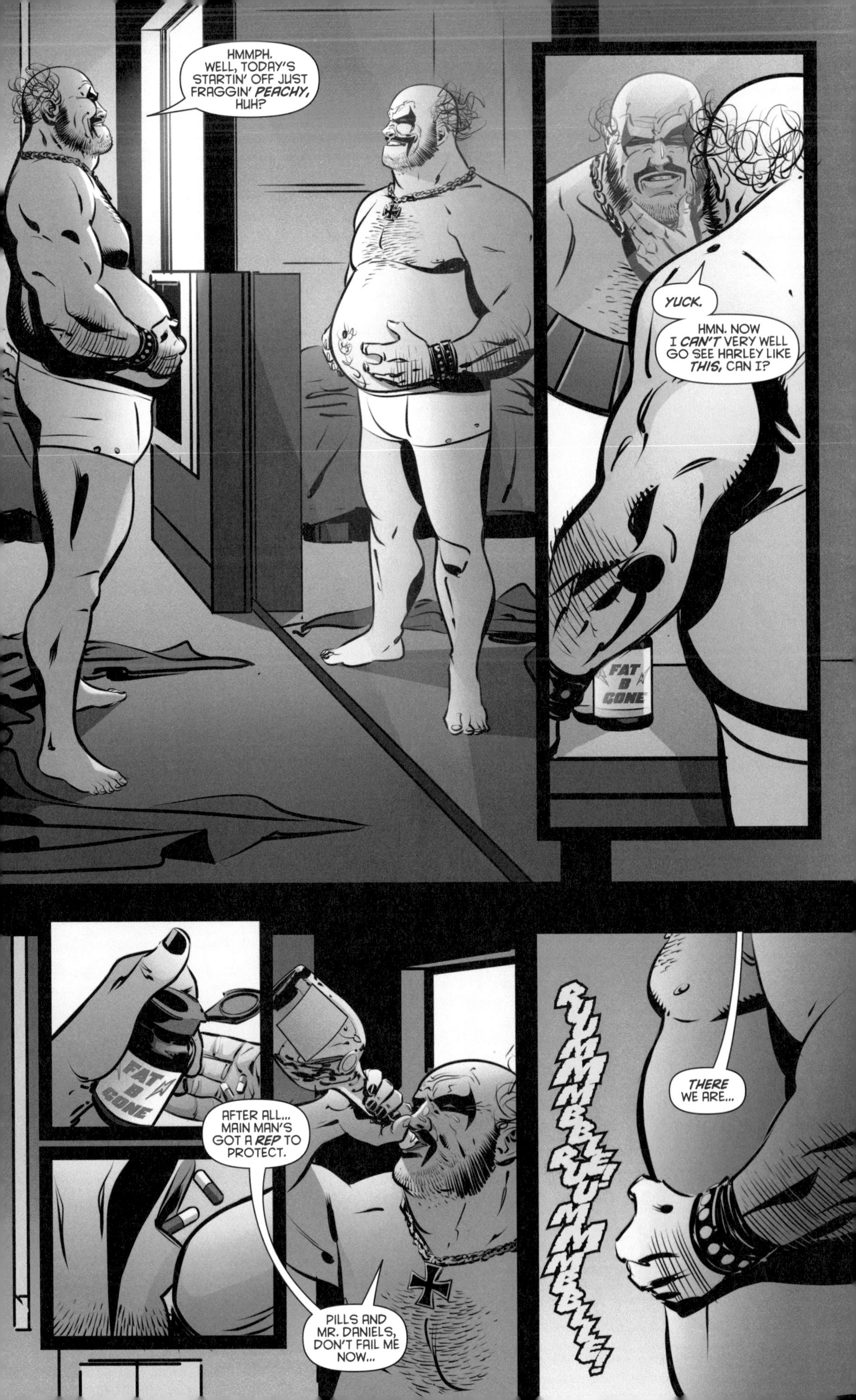
HMMPH. WELL, TODAY'S STARTIN' OFF JUST FRAGGIN' *PEACHY,* HUH?
YUCK.
HMN. NOW I *CAN'T* VERY WELL GO SEE HARLEY LIKE *THIS,* CAN I?
FAT B GONE
FAT B GONE
AFTER ALL... MAIN MAN'S GOT A *REP* TO PROTECT.
PILLS AND MR. DANIELS, DON'T FAIL ME NOW...
RUMMMBBLE! RUMMMBBLE!
THERE WE ARE...

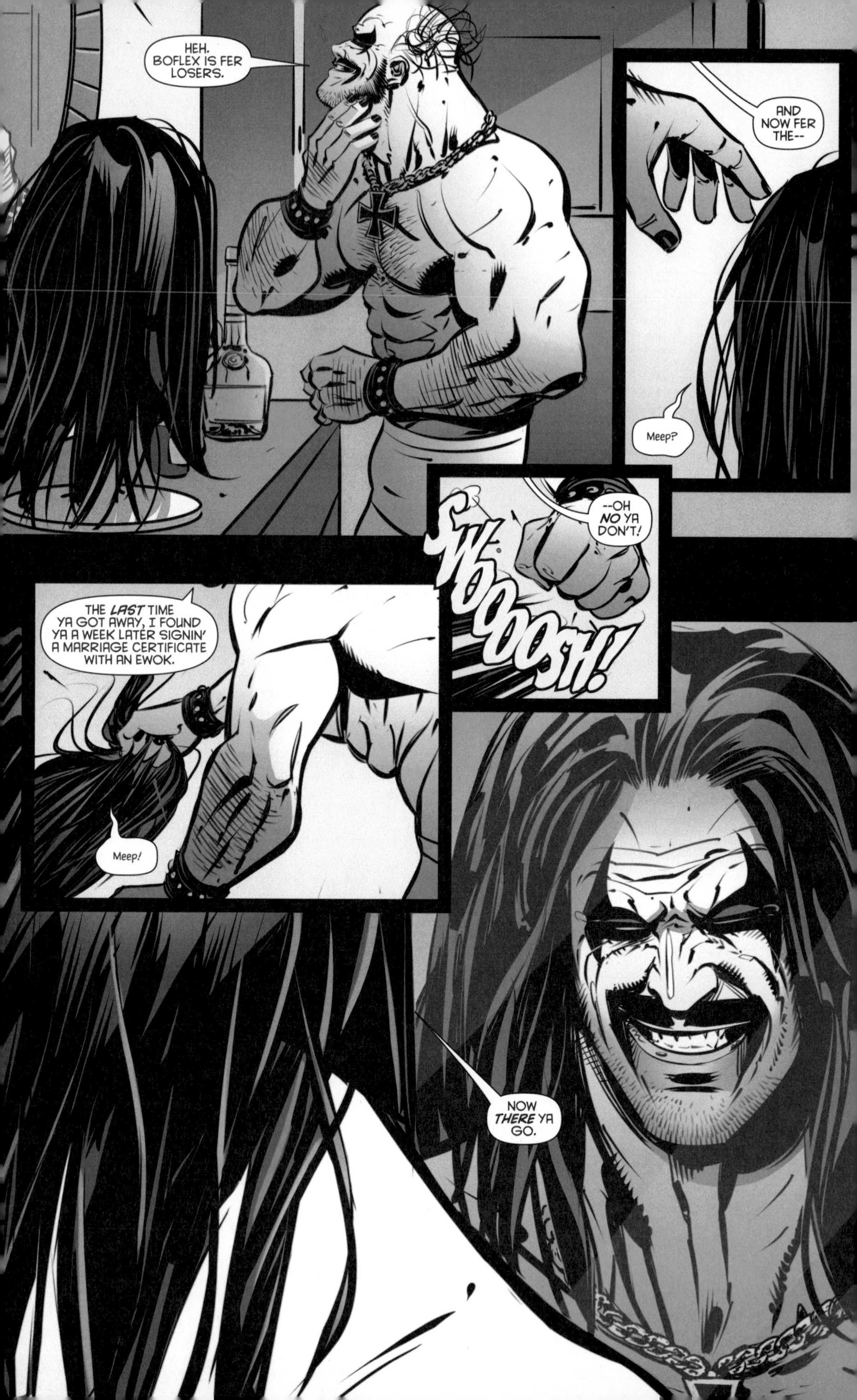
HEH. BOFLEX IS FER LOSERS.
AND NOW FER THE--
Meep?
SWOOOOSH!
--OH *NO* YA DON'T!
THE *LAST* TIME YA GOT AWAY, I FOUND YA A WEEK LATER SIGNIN' A MARRIAGE CERTIFICATE WITH AN EWOK.
Meep!
NOW *THERE* YA GO.

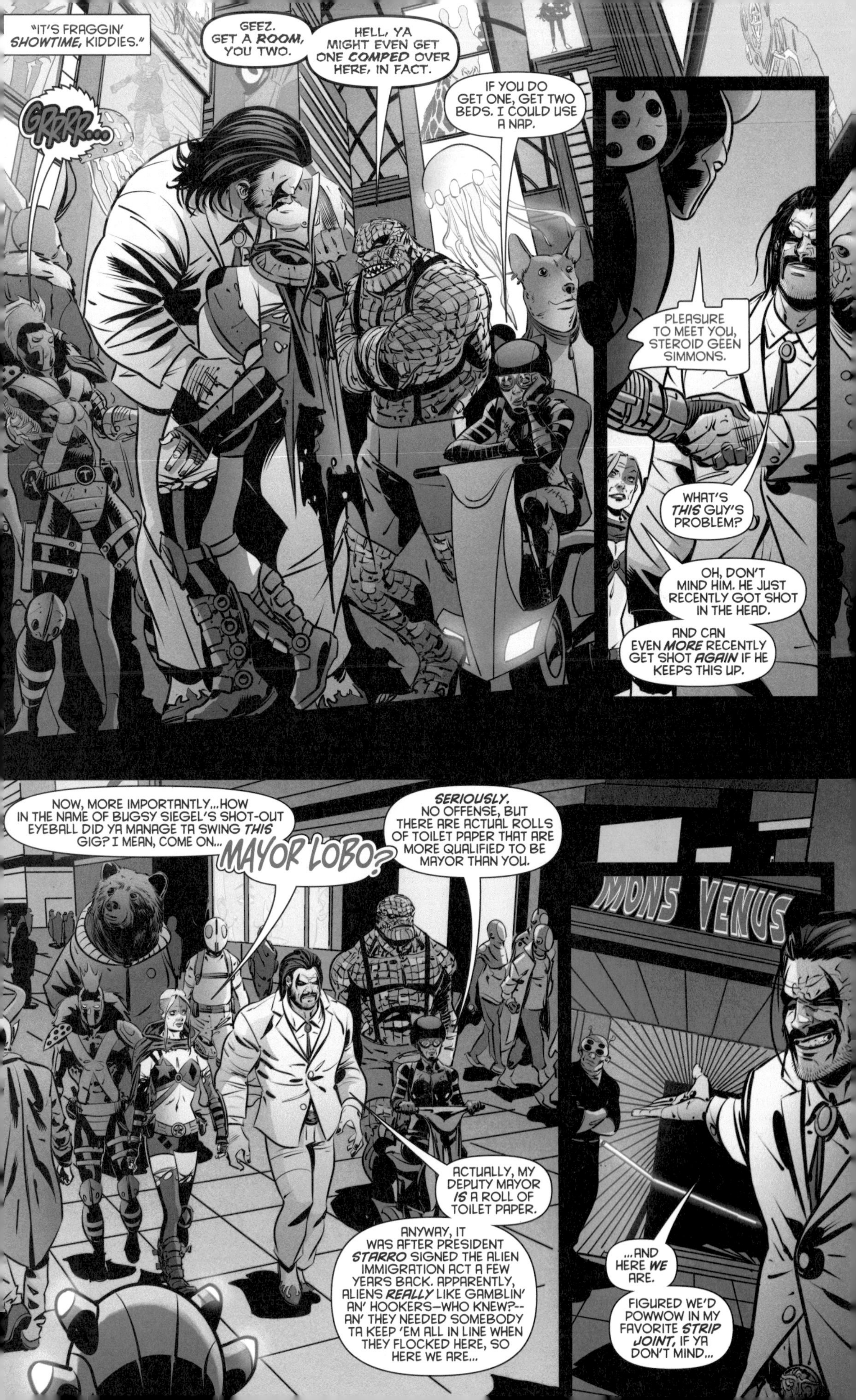
"IT'S FRAGGIN' SHOWTIME, KIDDIES."
GRRRR...
GEEZ. GET A ROOM, YOU TWO.
HELL, YA MIGHT EVEN GET ONE COMPED OVER HERE, IN FACT.
IF YOU DO GET ONE, GET TWO BEDS. I COULD USE A NAP.
PLEASURE TO MEET YOU, STEROID GEEN SIMMONS.
WHAT'S THIS GUY'S PROBLEM?
OH, DON'T MIND HIM. HE JUST RECENTLY GOT SHOT IN THE HEAD.
AND CAN EVEN MORE RECENTLY GET SHOT AGAIN IF HE KEEPS THIS UP.
NOW, MORE IMPORTANTLY...HOW IN THE NAME OF BUGSY SIEGEL'S SHOT-OUT EYEBALL DID YA MANAGE TA SWING THIS GIG? I MEAN, COME ON... MAYOR LOBO?
SERIOUSLY. NO OFFENSE, BUT THERE ARE ACTUAL ROLLS OF TOILET PAPER THAT ARE MORE QUALIFIED TO BE MAYOR THAN YOU.
ACTUALLY, MY DEPUTY MAYOR IS A ROLL OF TOILET PAPER.
ANYWAY, IT WAS AFTER PRESIDENT STARRO SIGNED THE ALIEN IMMIGRATION ACT A FEW YEARS BACK. APPARENTLY, ALIENS REALLY LIKE GAMBLIN' AN' HOOKERS—WHO KNEW?--AN' THEY NEEDED SOMEBODY TA KEEP 'EM ALL IN LINE WHEN THEY FLOCKED HERE, SO HERE WE ARE...
MONS VENUS
...AND HERE WE ARE.
FIGURED WE'D POWWOW IN MY FAVORITE STRIP JOINT, IF YA DON'T MIND...

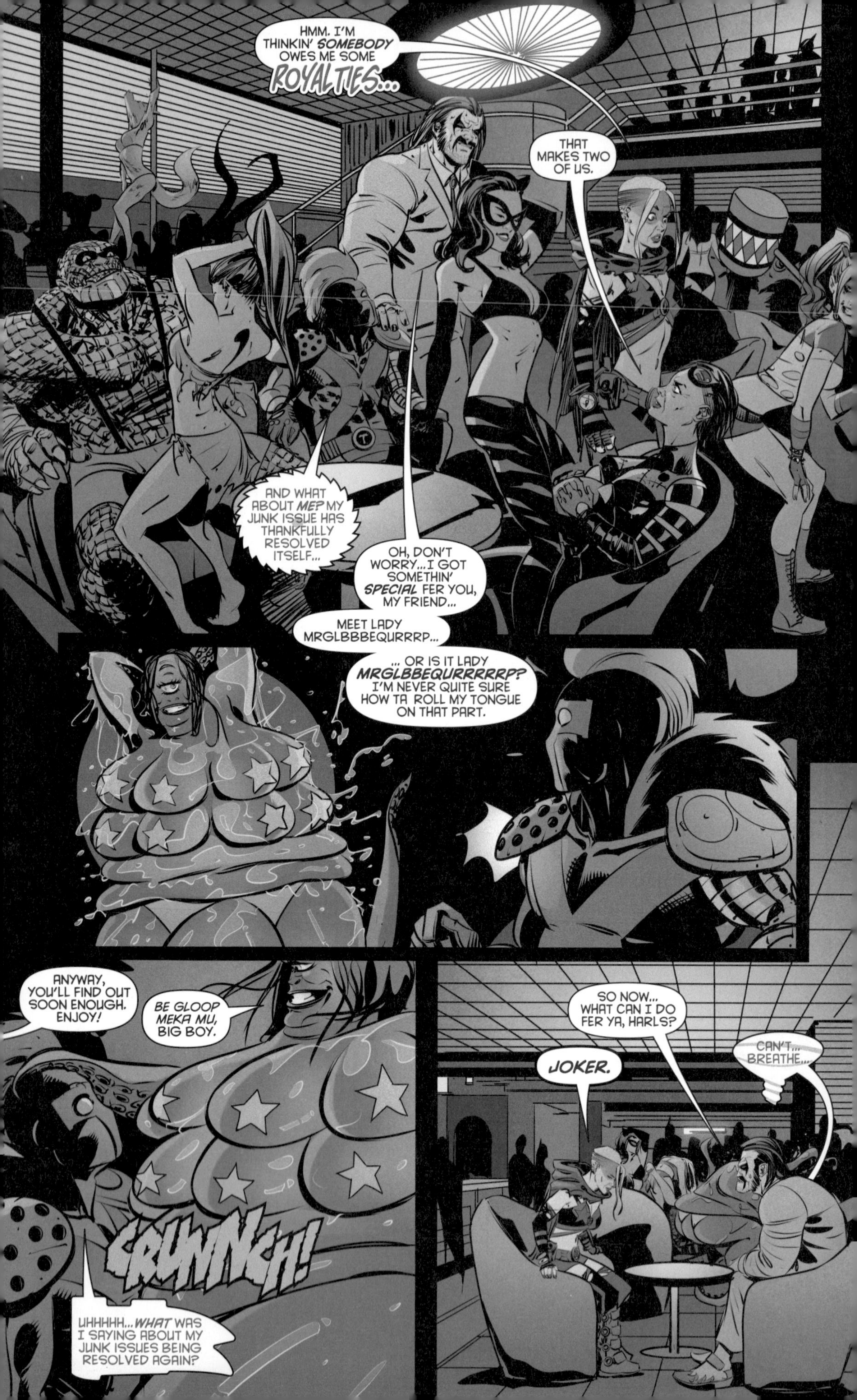
HMM. I'M THINKIN' SOMEBODY OWES ME SOME ROYALTIES...
THAT MAKES TWO OF US.
AND WHAT ABOUT ME? MY JUNK ISSUE HAS THANKFULLY RESOLVED ITSELF...
OH, DON'T WORRY...I GOT SOMETHIN' SPECIAL FER YOU, MY FRIEND...
MEET LADY MRGLBBBEQURRRP...
... OR IS IT LADY MRGLBBEQURRRRRRP? I'M NEVER QUITE SURE HOW TA ROLL MY TONGUE ON THAT PART.
ANYWAY, YOU'LL FIND OUT SOON ENOUGH. ENJOY!
BE GLOOP MEKA MU, BIG BOY.
CRUNNCH!
UHHHHH...WHAT WAS I SAYING ABOUT MY JUNK ISSUES BEING RESOLVED AGAIN?
SO NOW... WHAT CAN I DO FER YA, HARLS?
JOKER.
CAN'T... BREATHE...

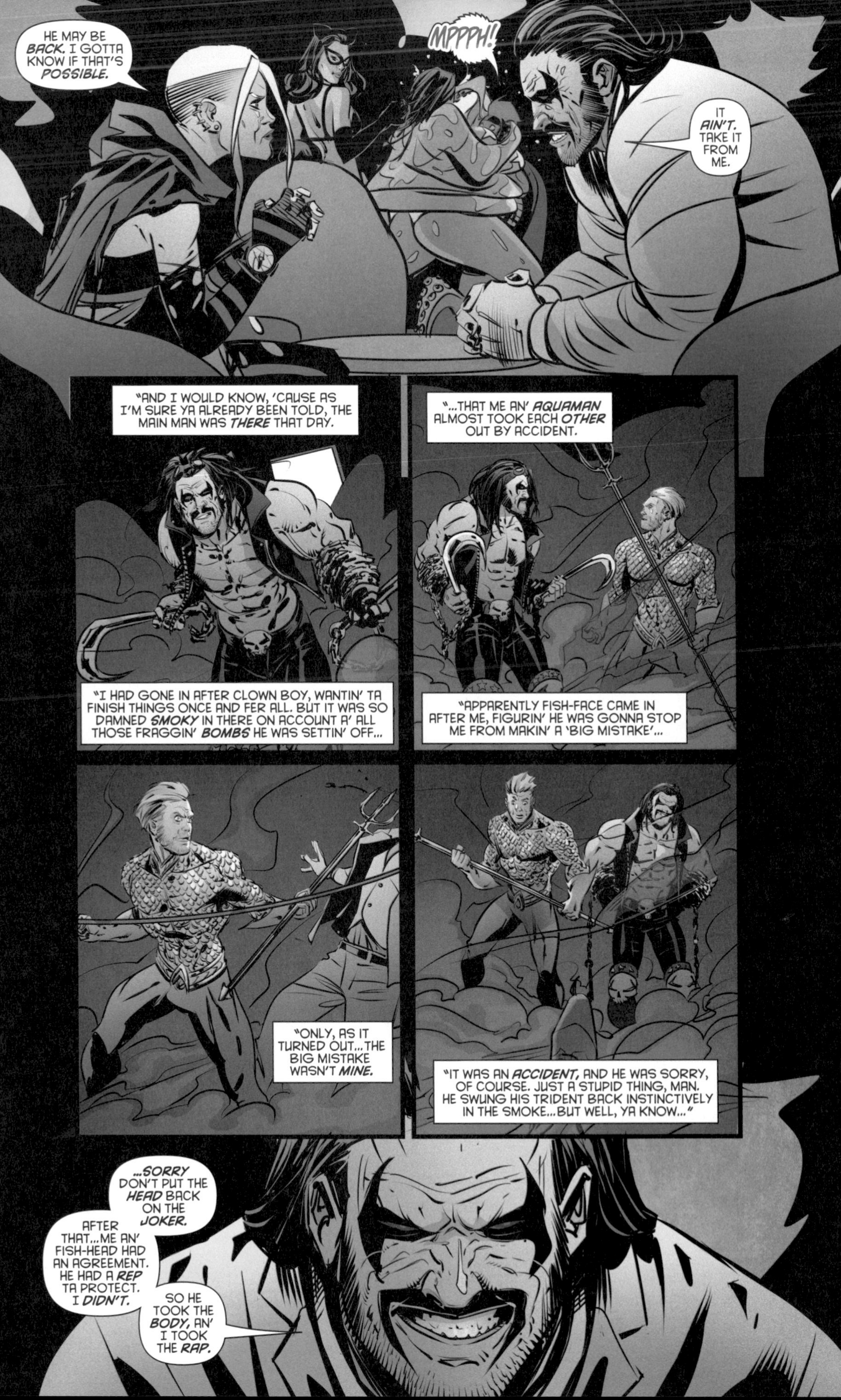

HE MAY BE BACK. I GOTTA KNOW IF THAT'S POSSIBLE.
MPPPH!
IT AIN'T. TAKE IT FROM ME.
"AND I WOULD KNOW, 'CAUSE AS I'M SURE YA ALREADY BEEN TOLD, THE MAIN MAN WAS THERE THAT DAY.
"I HAD GONE IN AFTER CLOWN BOY, WANTIN' TA FINISH THINGS ONCE AND FER ALL. BUT IT WAS SO DAMNED SMOKY IN THERE ON ACCOUNT A' ALL THOSE FRAGGIN' BOMBS HE WAS SETTIN' OFF...
"...THAT ME AN' AQUAMAN ALMOST TOOK EACH OTHER OUT BY ACCIDENT.
"APPARENTLY FISH-FACE CAME IN AFTER ME, FIGURIN' HE WAS GONNA STOP ME FROM MAKIN' A 'BIG MISTAKE'...
"ONLY, AS IT TURNED OUT...THE BIG MISTAKE WASN'T MINE.
"IT WAS AN ACCIDENT, AND HE WAS SORRY, OF COURSE. JUST A STUPID THING, MAN. HE SWUNG HIS TRIDENT BACK INSTINCTIVELY IN THE SMOKE...BUT WELL, YA KNOW..."
...SORRY DON'T PUT THE HEAD BACK ON THE JOKER.
AFTER THAT...ME AN' FISH-HEAD HAD AN AGREEMENT. HE HAD A REP TA PROTECT. I DIDN'T.
SO HE TOOK THE BODY, AN' I TOOK THE RAP.

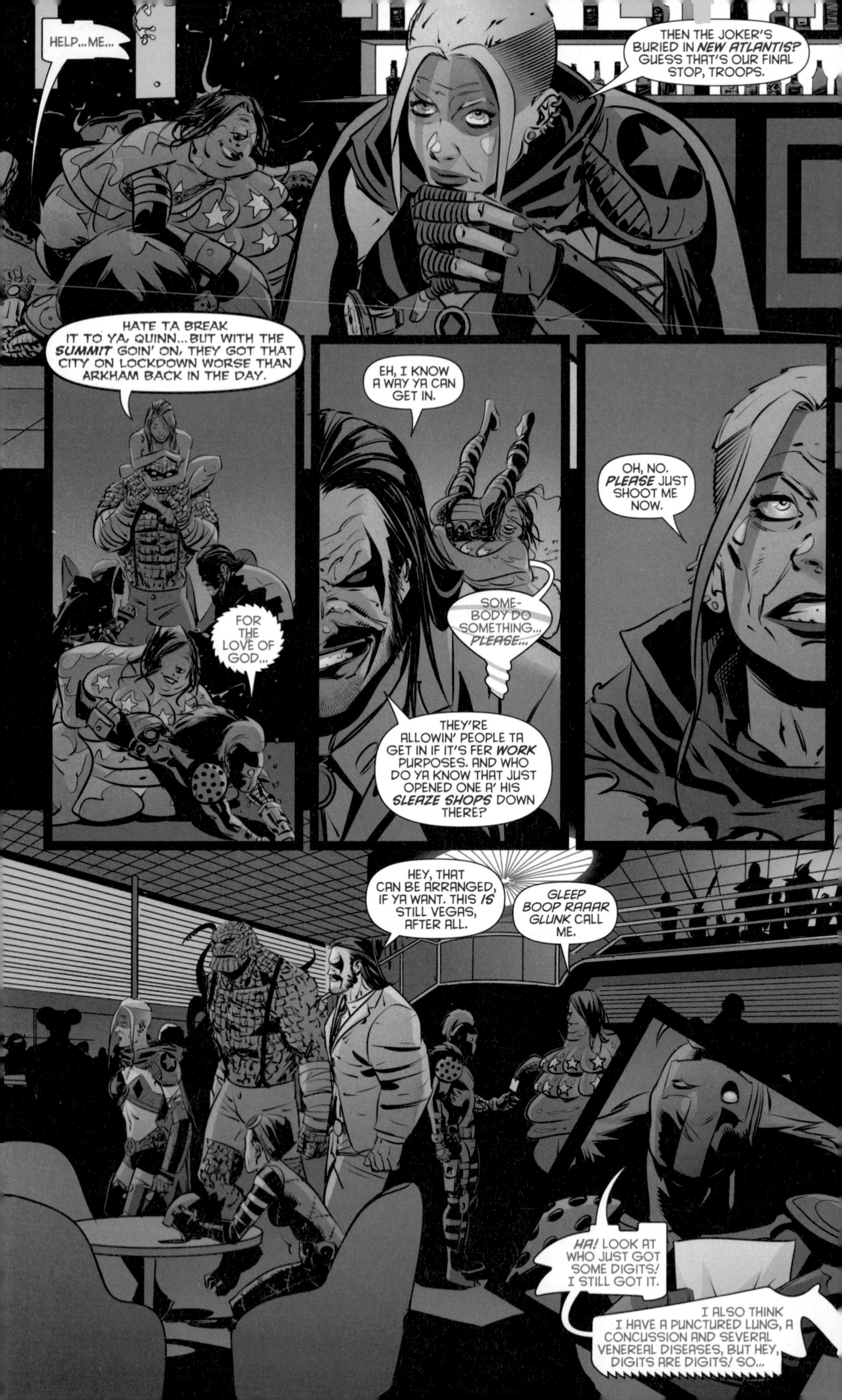
HELP...ME...
THEN THE JOKER'S BURIED IN NEW ATLANTIS? GUESS THAT'S OUR FINAL STOP, TROOPS.
HATE TA BREAK IT TO YA, QUINN...BUT WITH THE SUMMIT GOIN' ON, THEY GOT THAT CITY ON LOCKDOWN WORSE THAN ARKHAM BACK IN THE DAY.
FOR THE LOVE OF GOD...
EH, I KNOW A WAY YA CAN GET IN.
SOME-BODY DO SOMETHING... PLEASE...
THEY'RE ALLOWIN' PEOPLE TA GET IN IF IT'S FER WORK PURPOSES. AND WHO DO YA KNOW THAT JUST OPENED ONE A' HIS SLEAZE SHOPS DOWN THERE?
OH, NO. PLEASE JUST SHOOT ME NOW.
HEY, THAT CAN BE ARRANGED, IF YA WANT. THIS IS STILL VEGAS, AFTER ALL.
GLEEP BOOP RAAAR GLUNK CALL ME.
HA! LOOK AT WHO JUST GOT SOME DIGITS! I STILL GOT IT.
I ALSO THINK I HAVE A PUNCTURED LUNG, A CONCUSSION AND SEVERAL VENEREAL DISEASES, BUT HEY, DIGITS ARE DIGITS! SO...

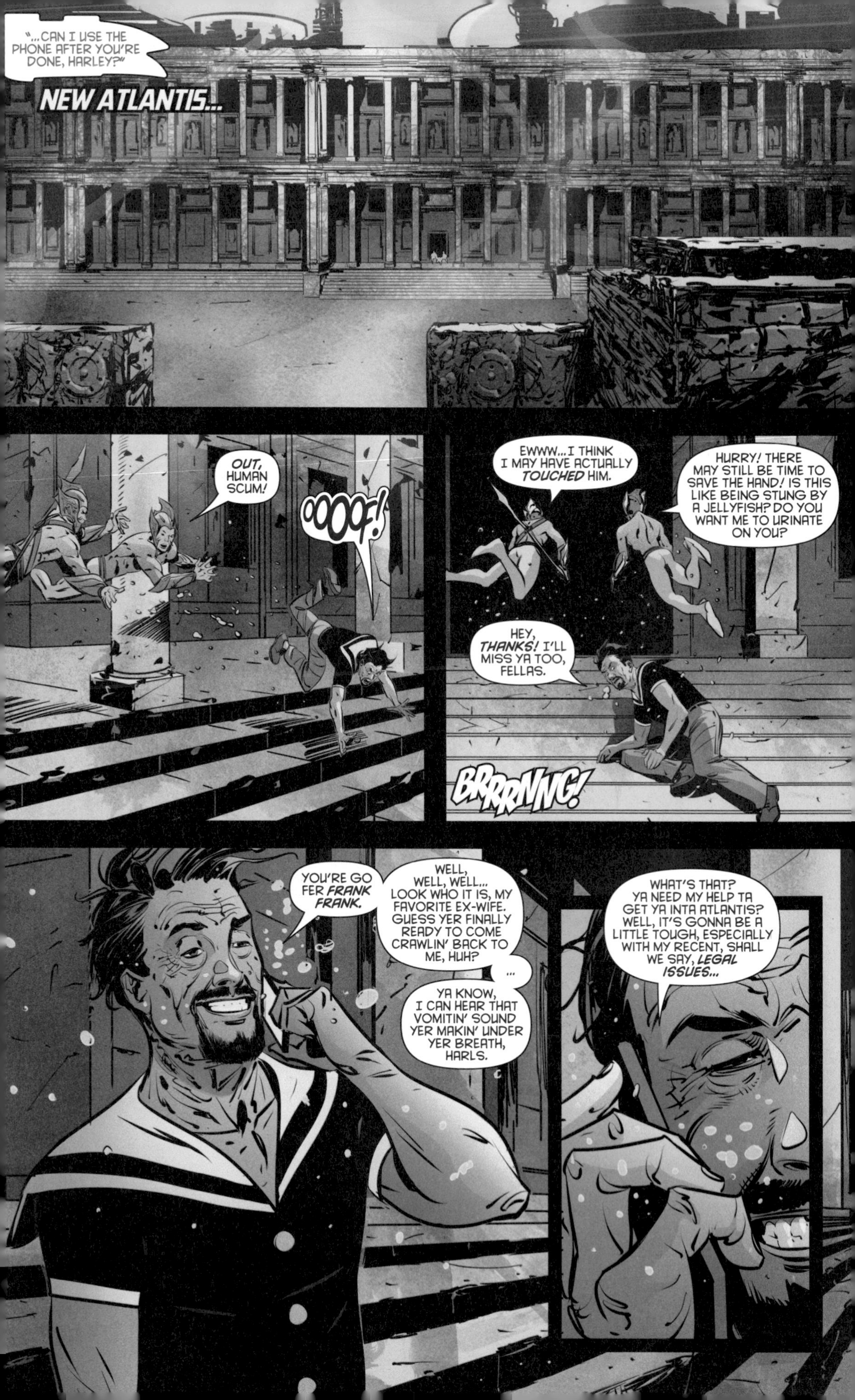
"...CAN I USE THE PHONE AFTER YOU'RE DONE, HARLEY?"
NEW ATLANTIS...
OUT, HUMAN SCUM!
OOOOF!
EWWW...I THINK I MAY HAVE ACTUALLY TOUCHED HIM.
HURRY! THERE MAY STILL BE TIME TO SAVE THE HAND! IS THIS LIKE BEING STUNG BY A JELLYFISH? DO YOU WANT ME TO URINATE ON YOU?
HEY, THANKS! I'LL MISS YA TOO, FELLAS.
BRRRING!
YOU'RE GO FER FRANK FRANK.
WELL, WELL, WELL... LOOK WHO IT IS, MY FAVORITE EX-WIFE. GUESS YER FINALLY READY TO COME CRAWLIN' BACK TO ME, HUH?
...
YA KNOW, I CAN HEAR THAT VOMITIN' SOUND YER MAKIN' UNDER YER BREATH, HARLS.
WHAT'S THAT? YA NEED MY HELP TA GET YA INTA ATLANTIS? WELL, IT'S GONNA BE A LITTLE TOUGH, ESPECIALLY WITH MY RECENT, SHALL WE SAY, LEGAL ISSUES...

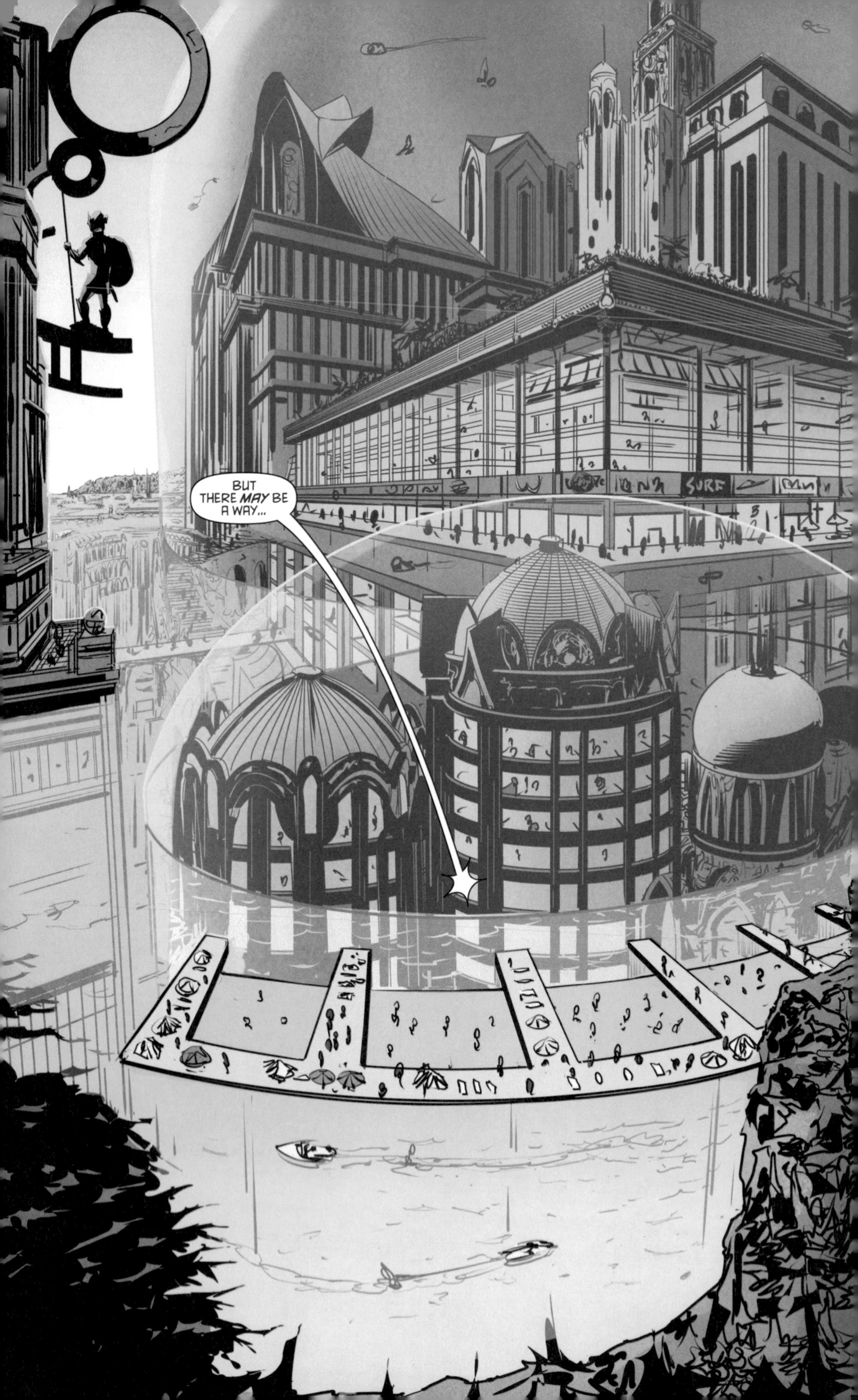
BUT THERE MAY BE A WAY...
SURF

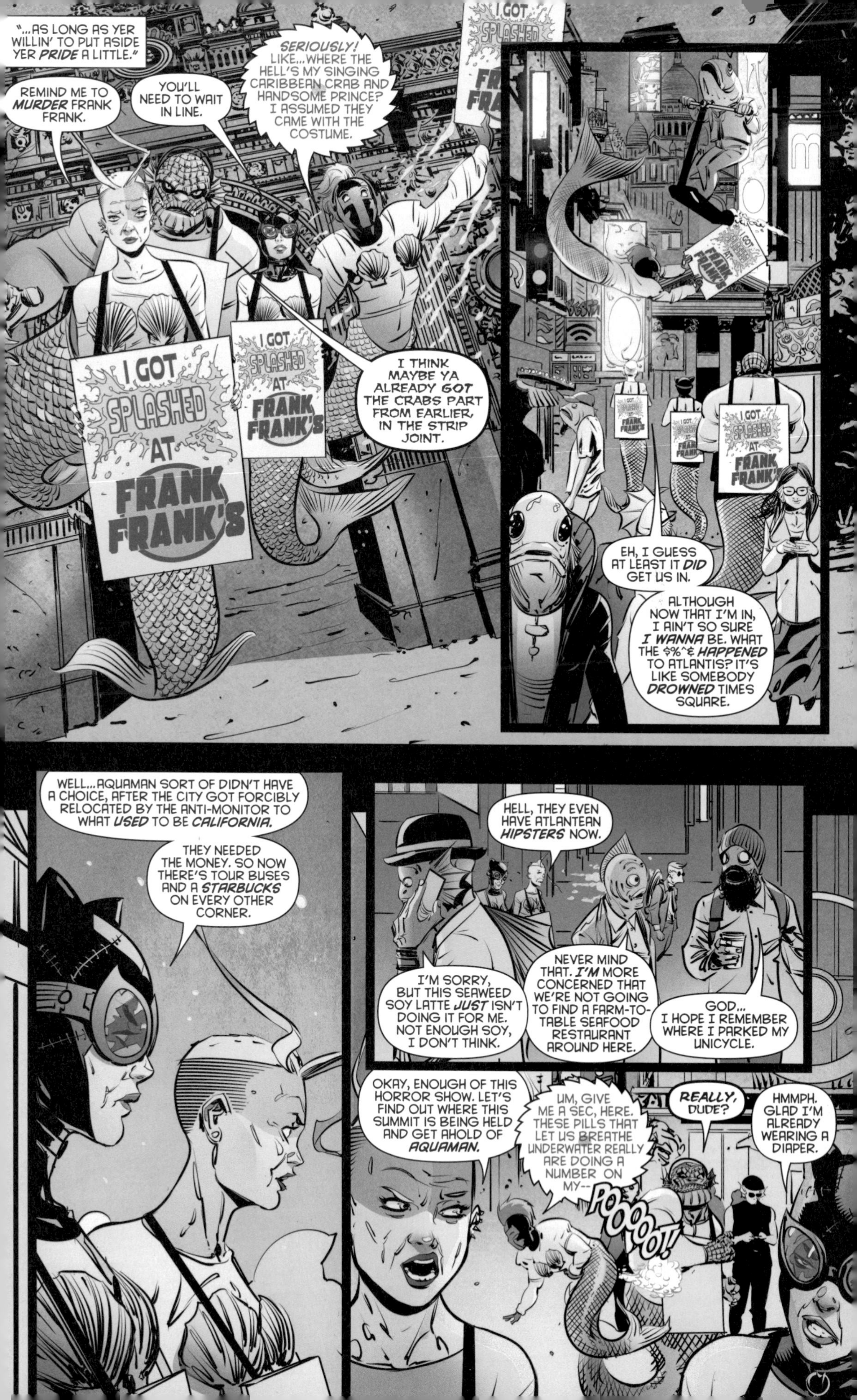

"...AS LONG AS YER WILLIN' TO PUT ASIDE YER PRIDE A LITTLE."
REMIND ME TO MURDER FRANK FRANK.
YOU'LL NEED TO WAIT IN LINE.
SERIOUSLY! LIKE...WHERE THE HELL'S MY SINGING CARIBBEAN CRAB AND HANDSOME PRINCE? I ASSUMED THEY CAME WITH THE COSTUME.
I GOT SPLASHED AT FRANK FRANK'S
I THINK MAYBE YA ALREADY GOT THE CRABS PART FROM EARLIER, IN THE STRIP JOINT.
EH, I GUESS AT LEAST IT DID GET US IN.
ALTHOUGH NOW THAT I'M IN, I AIN'T SO SURE I WANNA BE. WHAT THE $%^& HAPPENED TO ATLANTIS? IT'S LIKE SOMEBODY DROWNED TIMES SQUARE.
WELL...AQUAMAN SORT OF DIDN'T HAVE A CHOICE, AFTER THE CITY GOT FORCIBLY RELOCATED BY THE ANTI-MONITOR TO WHAT USED TO BE CALIFORNIA.
THEY NEEDED THE MONEY. SO NOW THERE'S TOUR BUSES AND A STARBUCKS ON EVERY OTHER CORNER.
HELL, THEY EVEN HAVE ATLANTEAN HIPSTERS NOW.
I'M SORRY, BUT THIS SEAWEED SOY LATTE JUST ISN'T DOING IT FOR ME. NOT ENOUGH SOY, I DON'T THINK.
NEVER MIND THAT. I'M MORE CONCERNED THAT WE'RE NOT GOING TO FIND A FARM-TO-TABLE SEAFOOD RESTAURANT AROUND HERE.
GOD... I HOPE I REMEMBER WHERE I PARKED MY UNICYCLE.
OKAY, ENOUGH OF THIS HORROR SHOW. LET'S FIND OUT WHERE THIS SUMMIT IS BEING HELD AND GET AHOLD OF AQUAMAN.
UM, GIVE ME A SEC, HERE. THESE PILLS THAT LET US BREATHE UNDERWATER REALLY ARE DOING A NUMBER ON MY--
POOOOOT!
REALLY, DUDE?
HMMPH. GLAD I'M ALREADY WEARING A DIAPER.

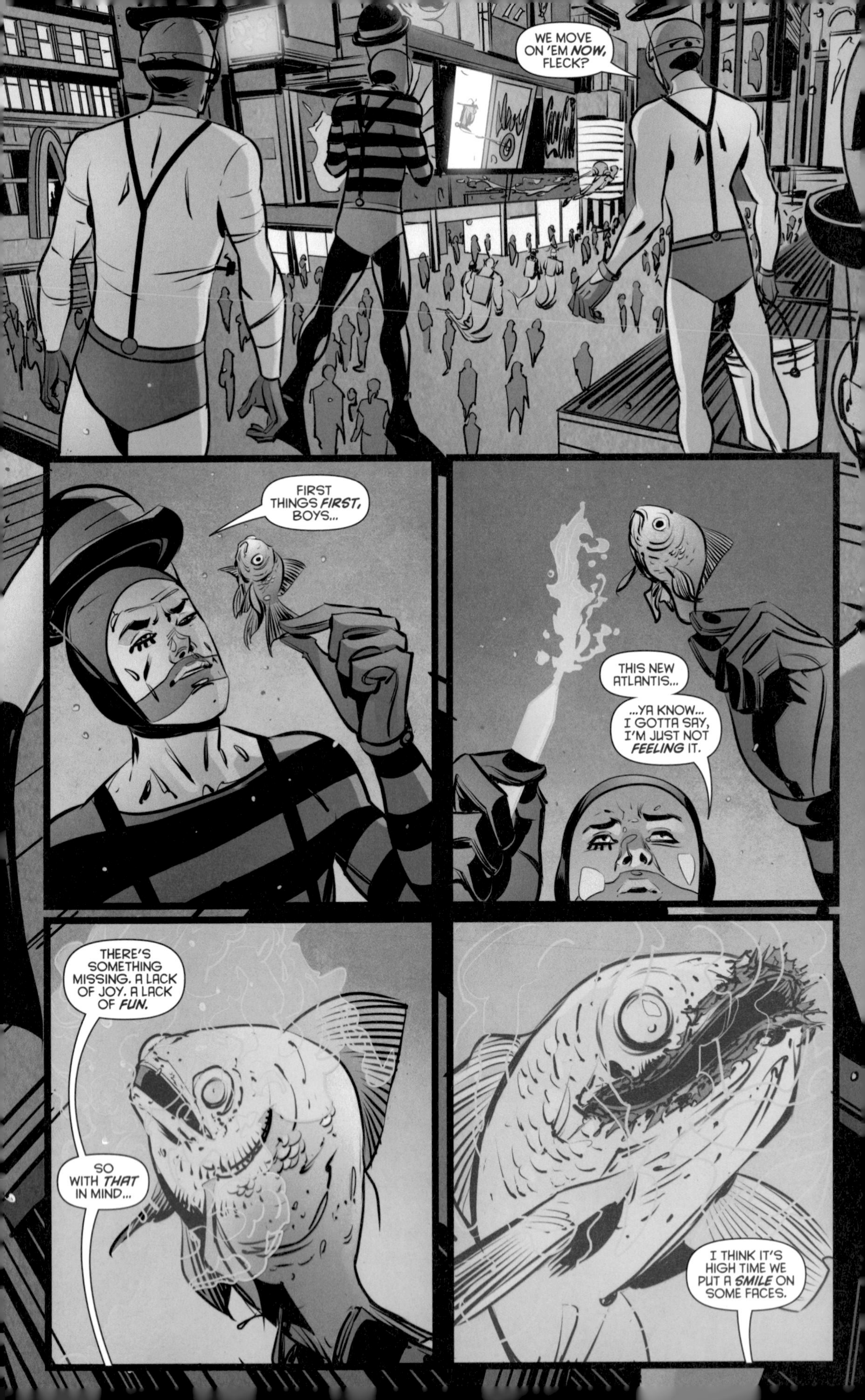
WE MOVE ON 'EM NOW, FLECK?
FIRST THINGS FIRST, BOYS...
THIS NEW ATLANTIS...
...YA KNOW... I GOTTA SAY, I'M JUST NOT FEELING IT.
THERE'S SOMETHING MISSING. A LACK OF JOY. A LACK OF FUN.
SO WITH THAT IN MIND...
I THINK IT'S HIGH TIME WE PUT A SMILE ON SOME FACES.

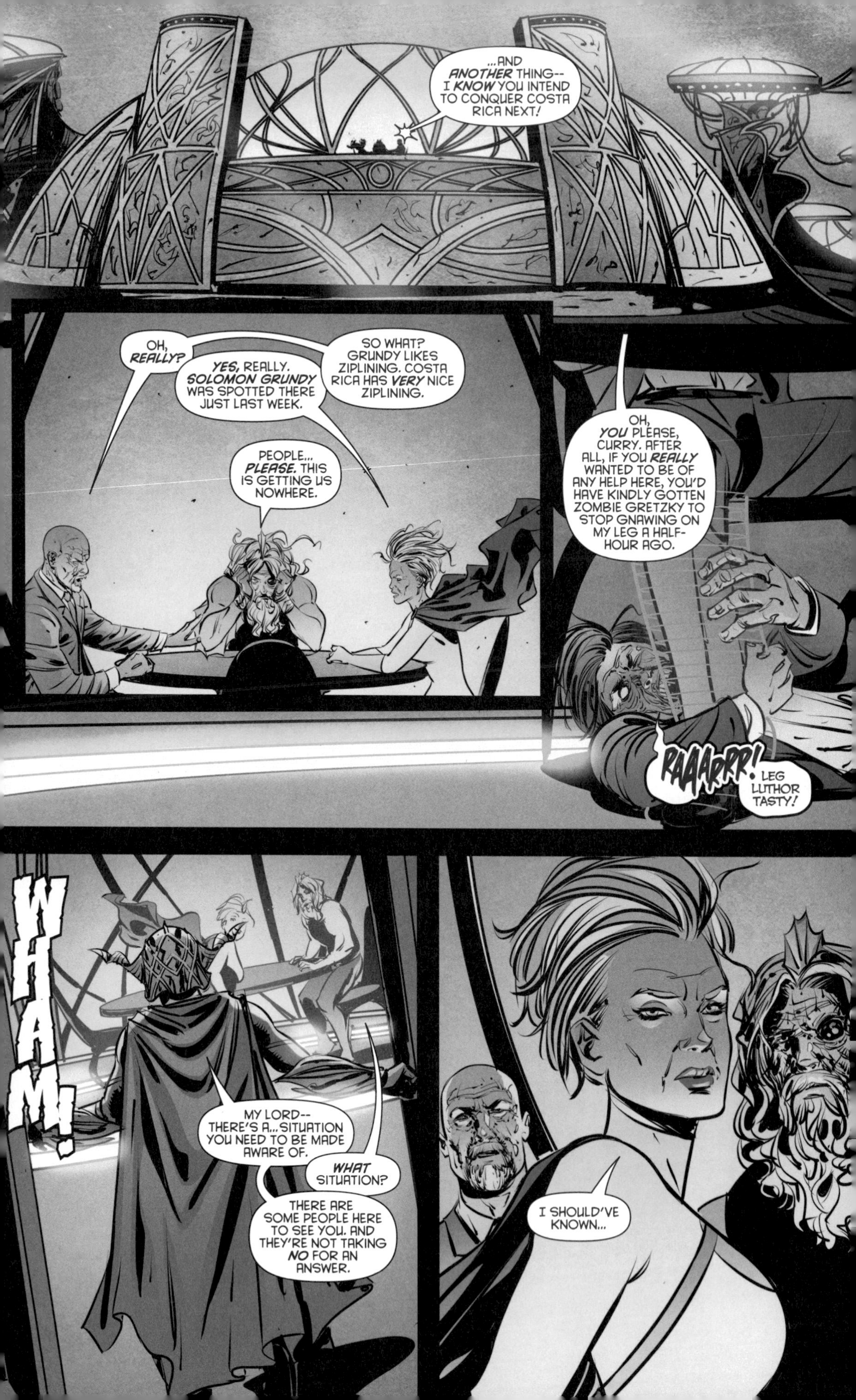

...AND ANOTHER THING-- I KNOW YOU INTEND TO CONQUER COSTA RICA NEXT!
OH, REALLY?
YES, REALLY. SOLOMON GRUNDY WAS SPOTTED THERE JUST LAST WEEK.
SO WHAT? GRUNDY LIKES ZIPLINING. COSTA RICA HAS VERY NICE ZIPLINING.
PEOPLE... PLEASE. THIS IS GETTING US NOWHERE.
OH, YOU PLEASE, CURRY. AFTER ALL, IF YOU REALLY WANTED TO BE OF ANY HELP HERE, YOU'D HAVE KINDLY GOTTEN ZOMBIE GRETZKY TO STOP GNAWING ON MY LEG A HALF-HOUR AGO.
RAAAARRR! LEG LUTHOR TASTY!
WHAM!
MY LORD-- THERE'S A... SITUATION YOU NEED TO BE MADE AWARE OF.
WHAT SITUATION?
THERE ARE SOME PEOPLE HERE TO SEE YOU. AND THEY'RE NOT TAKING NO FOR AN ANSWER.
I SHOULD'VE KNOWN...

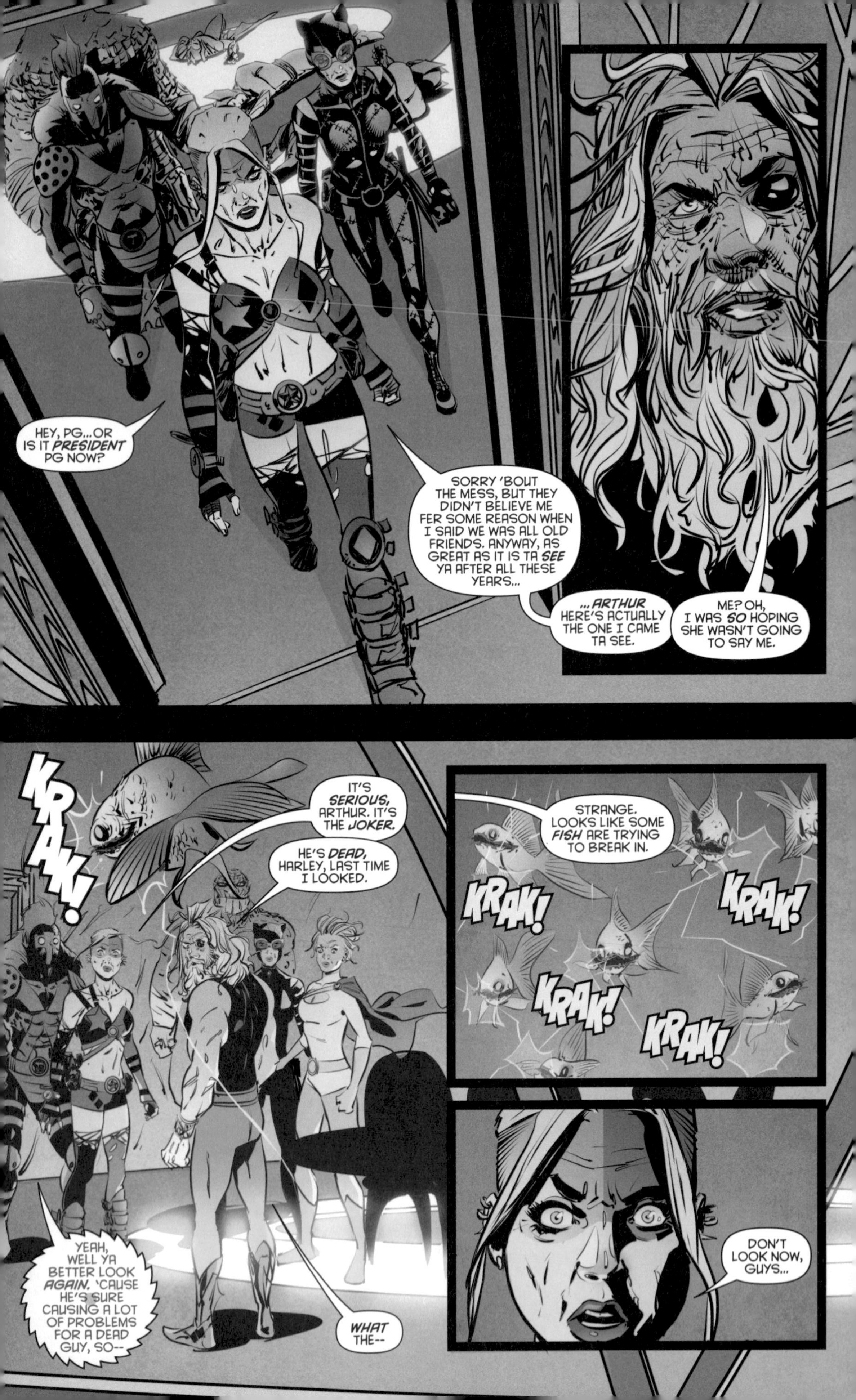
HEY, PG...OR IS IT PRESIDENT PG NOW?
SORRY 'BOUT THE MESS, BUT THEY DIDN'T BELIEVE ME FER SOME REASON WHEN I SAID WE WAS ALL OLD FRIENDS. ANYWAY, AS GREAT AS IT IS TA SEE YA AFTER ALL THESE YEARS...
...ARTHUR HERE'S ACTUALLY THE ONE I CAME TA SEE.
ME? OH, I WAS SO HOPING SHE WASN'T GOING TO SAY ME.
KRAK!
IT'S SERIOUS, ARTHUR. IT'S THE JOKER.
HE'S DEAD, HARLEY, LAST TIME I LOOKED.
YEAH, WELL YA BETTER LOOK AGAIN. 'CAUSE HE'S SURE CAUSING A LOT OF PROBLEMS FOR A DEAD GUY, SO--
WHAT THE--
STRANGE. LOOKS LIKE SOME FISH ARE TRYING TO BREAK IN.
KRAK!
KRAK!
KRAK!
KRAK!
DON'T LOOK NOW, GUYS...

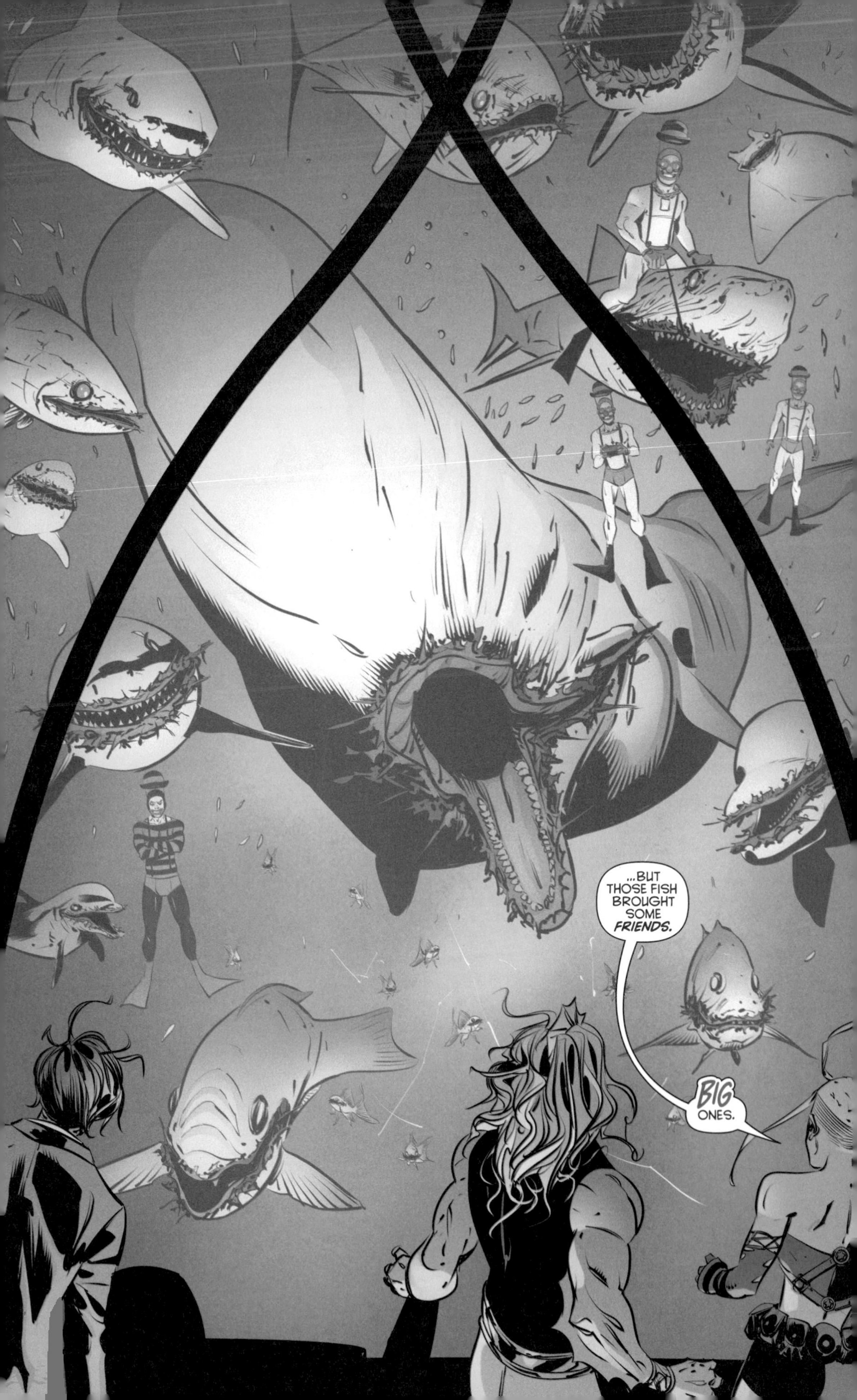
...BUT THOSE FISH BROUGHT SOME FRIENDS.
BIG ONES.

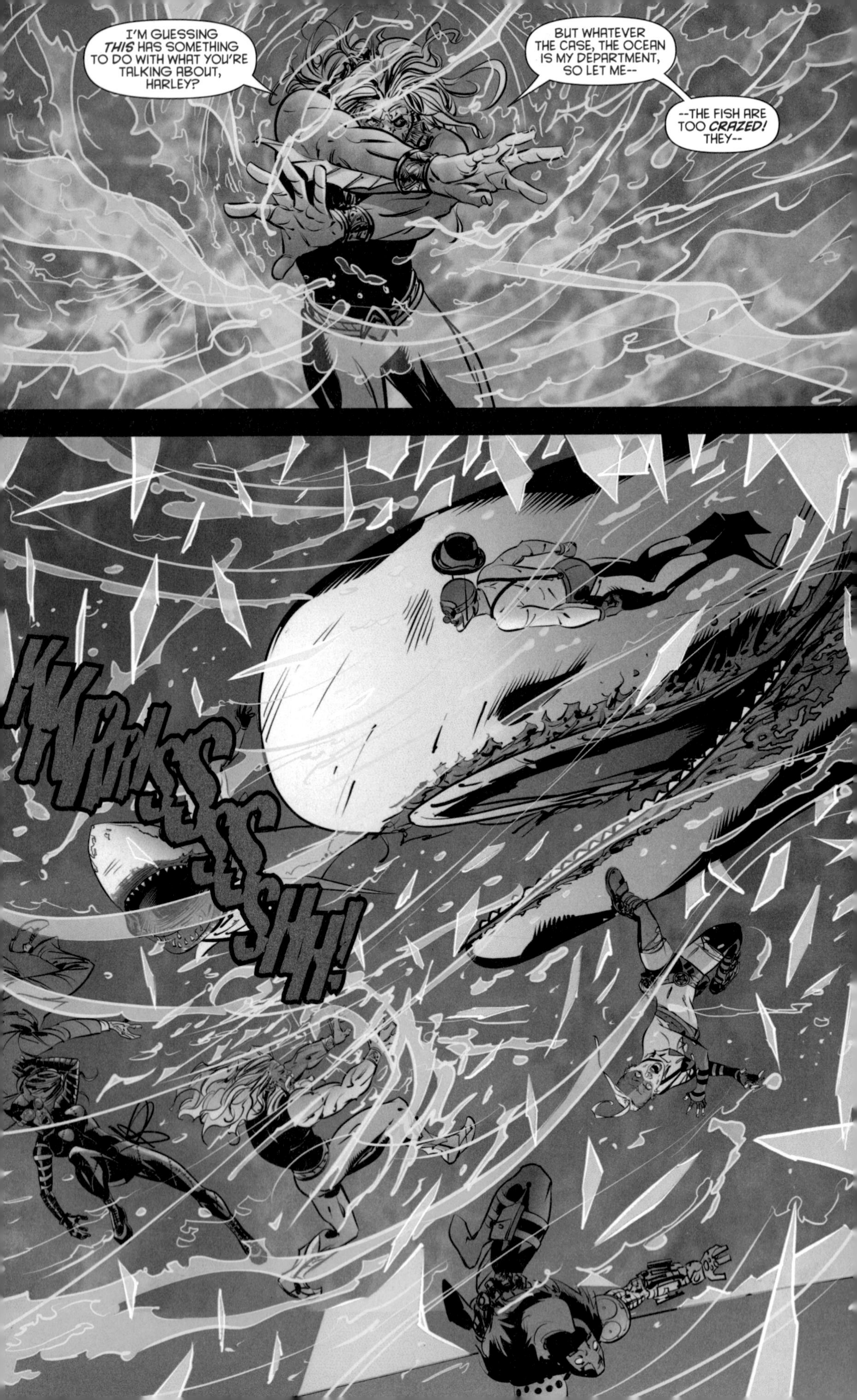
I'M GUESSING THIS HAS SOMETHING TO DO WITH WHAT YOU'RE TALKING ABOUT, HARLEY?
BUT WHATEVER THE CASE, THE OCEAN IS MY DEPARTMENT, SO LET ME--
--THE FISH ARE TOO CRAZED! THEY--

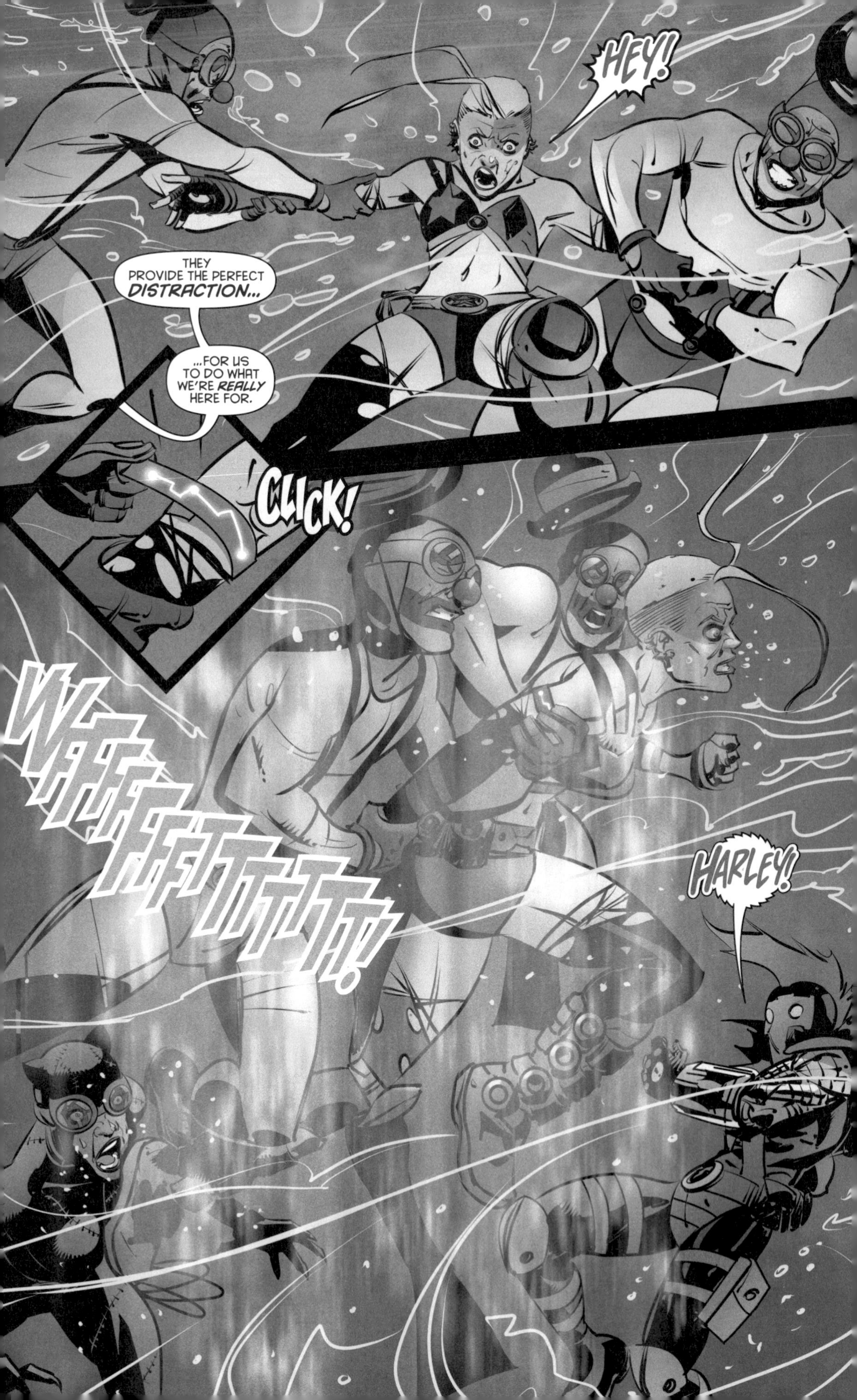
HEY!
THEY PROVIDE THE PERFECT DISTRACTION...
...FOR US TO DO WHAT WE'RE REALLY HERE FOR.
CLICK!
WFFFFFTTTTTT!!
HARLEY!

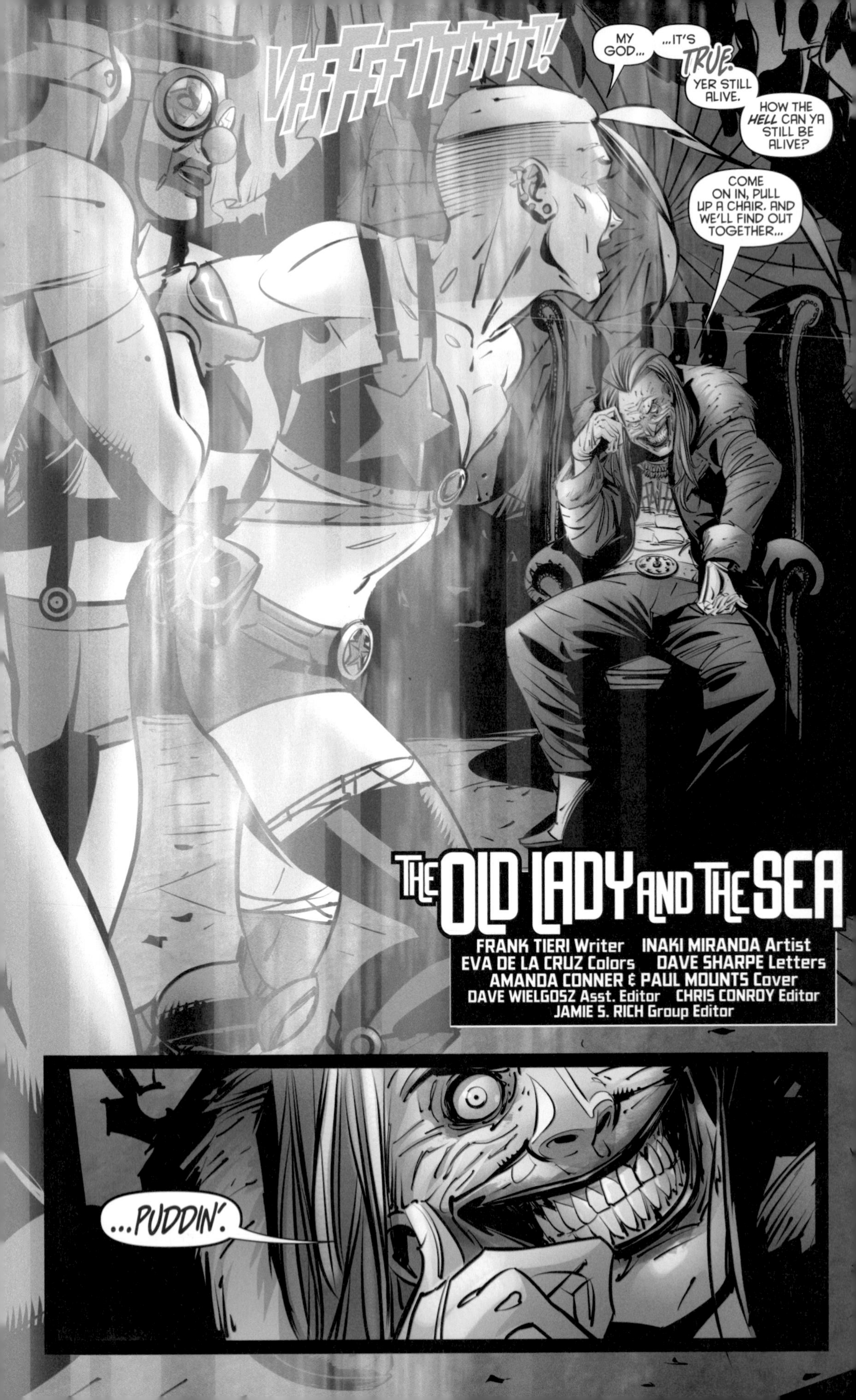
VFFFFTTTTT!
MY GOD...
...IT'S TRUE. YER STILL ALIVE.
HOW THE HELL CAN YA STILL BE ALIVE?
COME ON IN, PULL UP A CHAIR. AND WE'LL FIND OUT TOGETHER...
THE OLD LADY AND THE SEA
FRANK TIERI Writer INAKI MIRANDA Artist
EVA DE LA CRUZ Colors DAVE SHARPE Letters
AMANDA CONNER & PAUL MOUNTS Cover
DAVE WIELGOSZ Asst. Editor CHRIS CONROY Editor
JAMIE S. RICH Group Editor
...PUDDIN'.

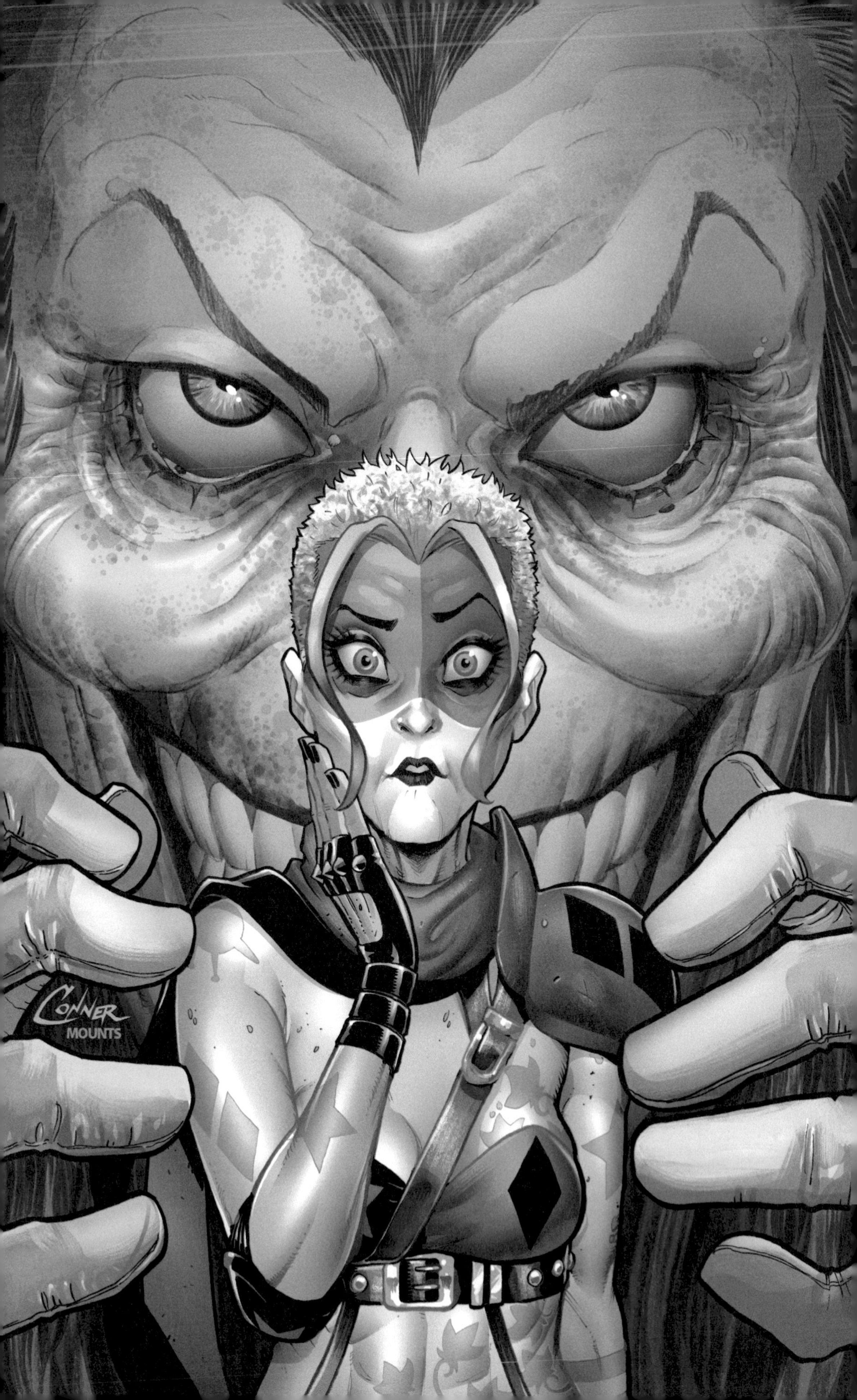
CONNER
MOUNTS

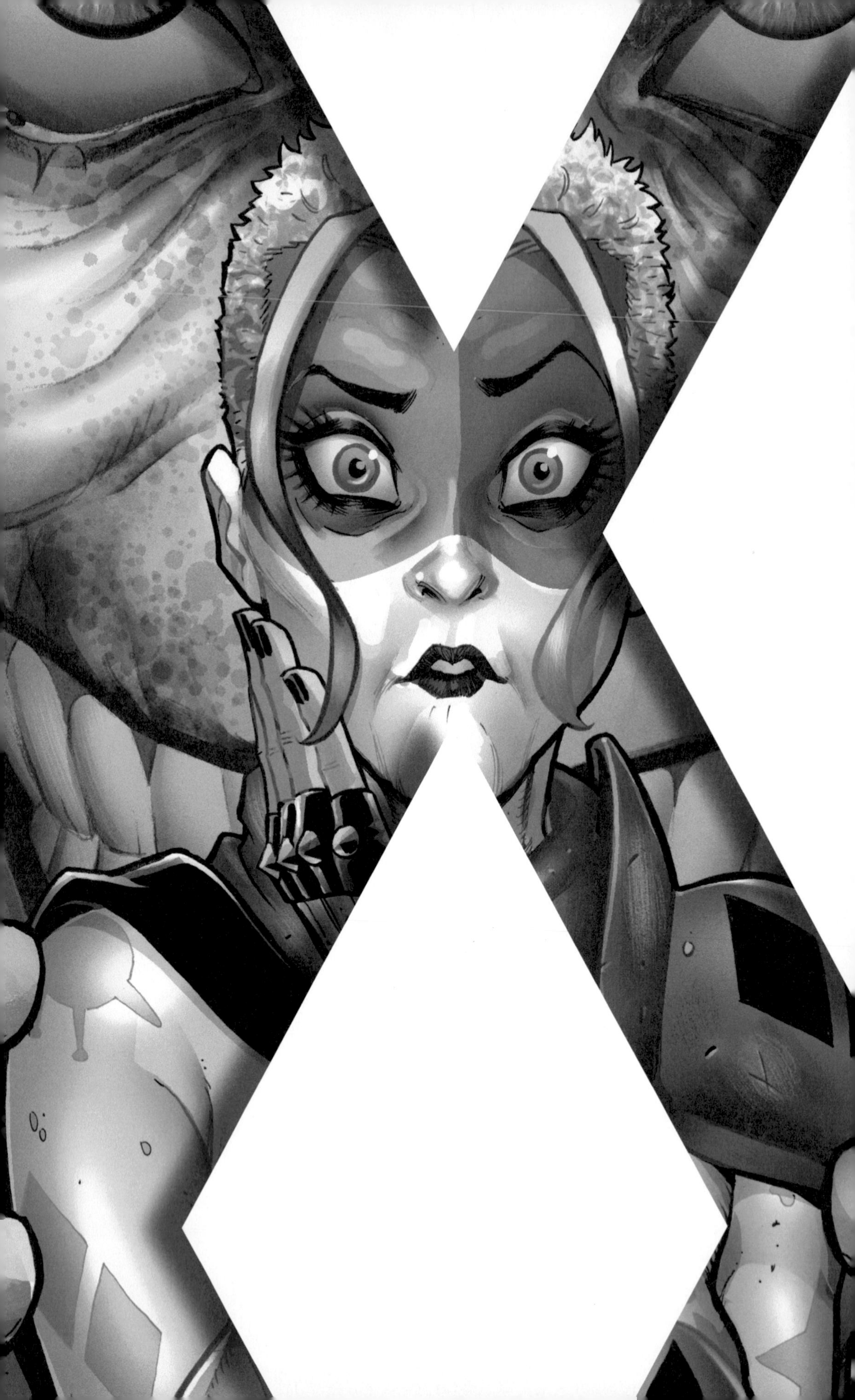

PLEASE INSERT YOUR MIND CHIP **NOW.**

THEY ARE YOUR FRIENDS. YOUR NEIGHBORS.

THEY ARE THE FAMILY NEXT DOOR.

LNN

AND NOW THEY ARE **LAUGHING BOYS.**

LNN

THE JOKER, WHO WAS LONG CONSIDERED TO BE **DECEASED...**

JOKER
JOKER

...IS APPARENTLY NOT.

LNN

CAT GRANT

CITY TO CITY, STATE TO STATE, **SCORES** OF THE CLOWN PRINCE OF CRIME'S LAUGHING BOY **SLEEPER CELLS** WERE ACTIVATED YESTERDAY. THE RESULT IS PRODUCING MAYHEM, MURDER...

OKER
JOKER

AND... HA. **HA...**

HAHAHAHAHAHAHAHAHAHAHAHAHA

LNN

CAT GRANT

JOKER
R

HAHAHA-ACCKK!

THUD!

LNN

CAT GRA

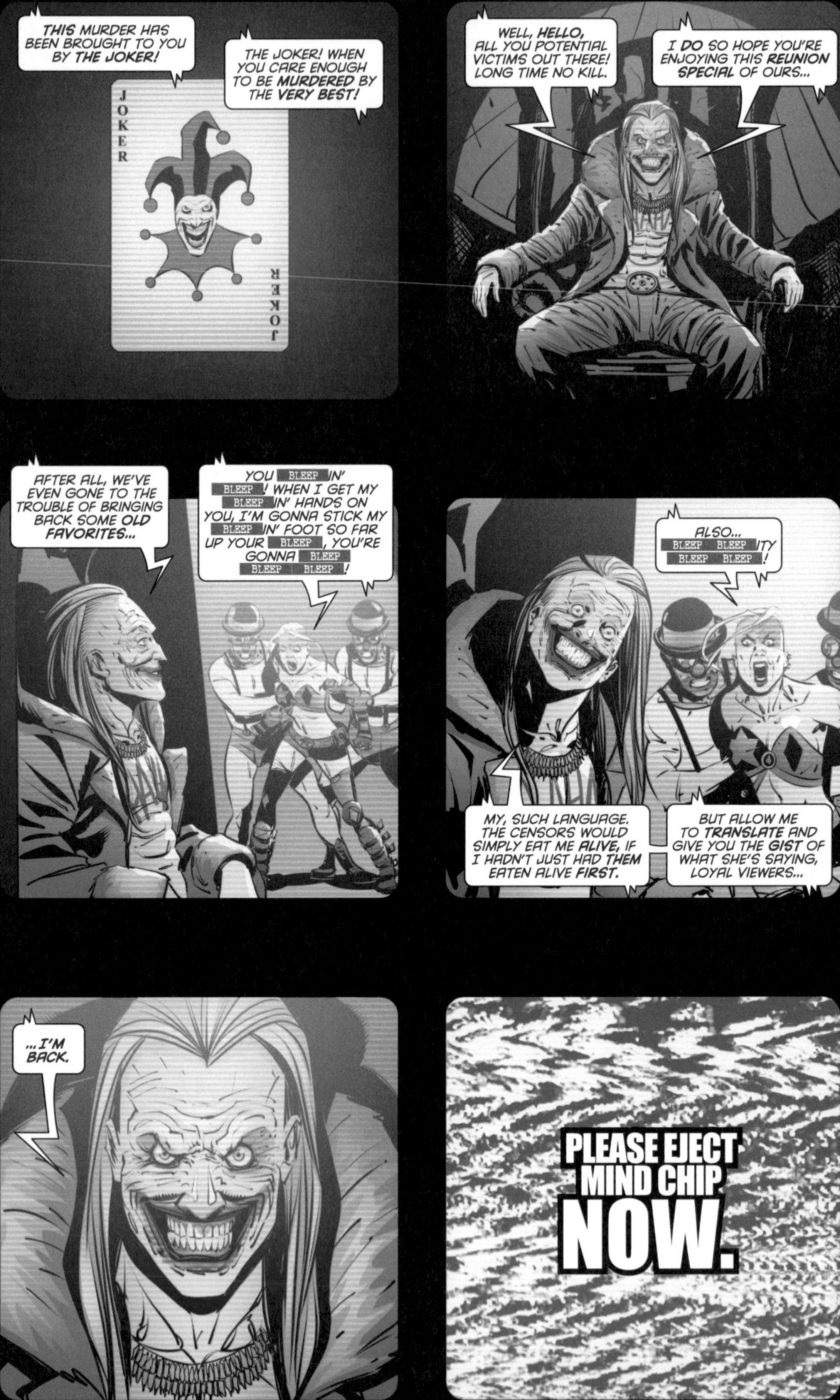
THIS MURDER HAS BEEN BROUGHT TO YOU BY THE JOKER!
THE JOKER! WHEN YOU CARE ENOUGH TO BE MURDERED BY THE VERY BEST!
JOKER
JOKER
WELL, HELLO, ALL YOU POTENTIAL VICTIMS OUT THERE! LONG TIME NO KILL.
I DO SO HOPE YOU'RE ENJOYING THIS REUNION SPECIAL OF OURS...
AFTER ALL, WE'VE EVEN GONE TO THE TROUBLE OF BRINGING BACK SOME OLD FAVORITES...
YOU BLEEP IN' BLEEP! WHEN I GET MY BLEEP IN' HANDS ON YOU, I'M GONNA STICK MY BLEEP IN' FOOT SO FAR UP YOUR BLEEP, YOU'RE GONNA BLEEP BLEEP BLEEP!
ALSO... BLEEP BLEEP ITY BLEEP BLEEP!
MY, SUCH LANGUAGE. THE CENSORS WOULD SIMPLY EAT ME ALIVE, IF I HADN'T JUST HAD THEM EATEN ALIVE FIRST.
BUT ALLOW ME TO TRANSLATE AND GIVE YOU THE GIST OF WHAT SHE'S SAYING, LOYAL VIEWERS...
...I'M BACK.
PLEASE EJECT MIND CHIP NOW.

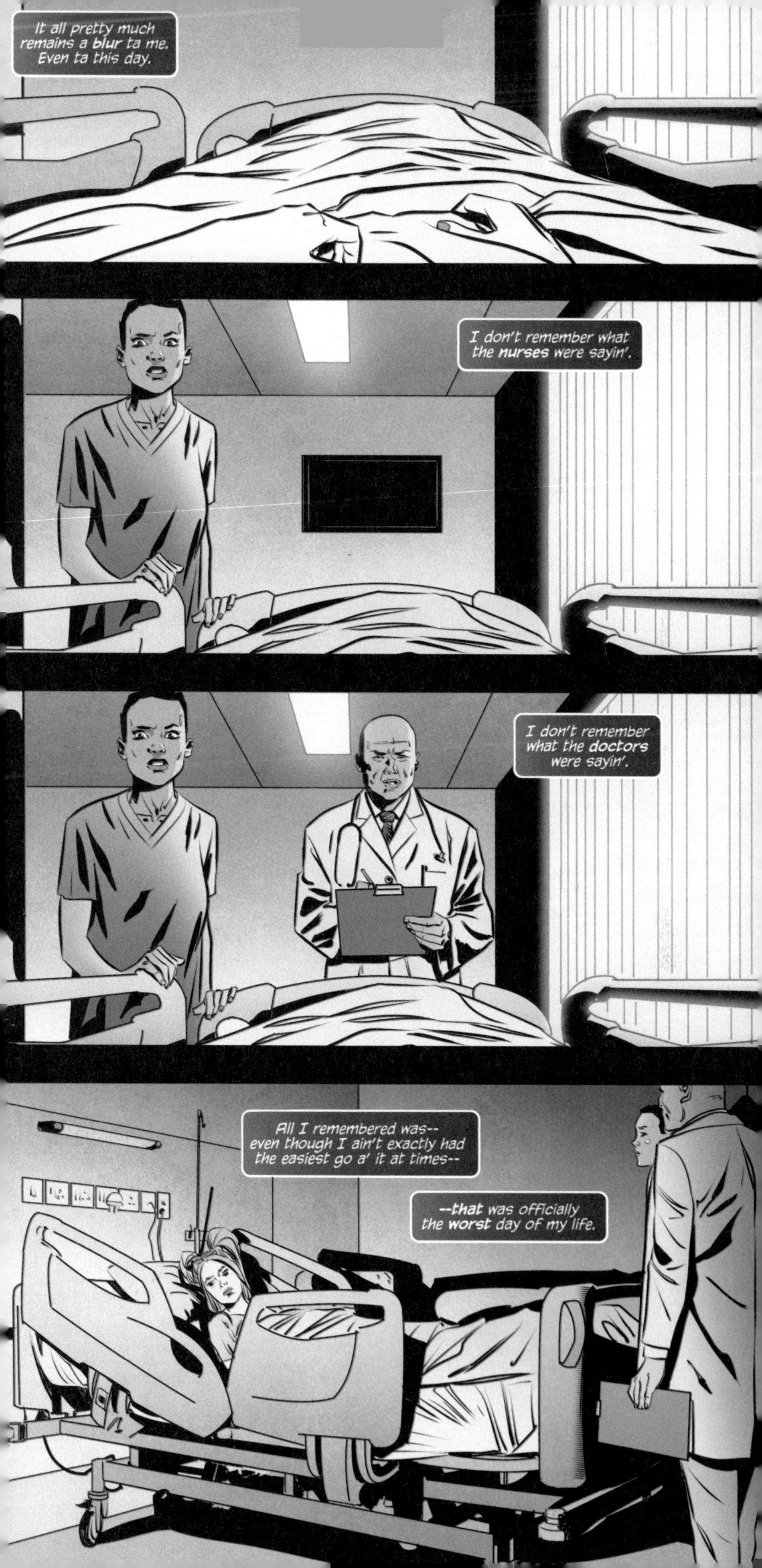
It all pretty much remains a blur ta me. Even ta this day.
I don't remember what the nurses were sayin'.
I don't remember what the doctors were sayin'.
All I remembered was-- even though I ain't exactly had the easiest go a' it at times--
--that was officially the worst day of my life.

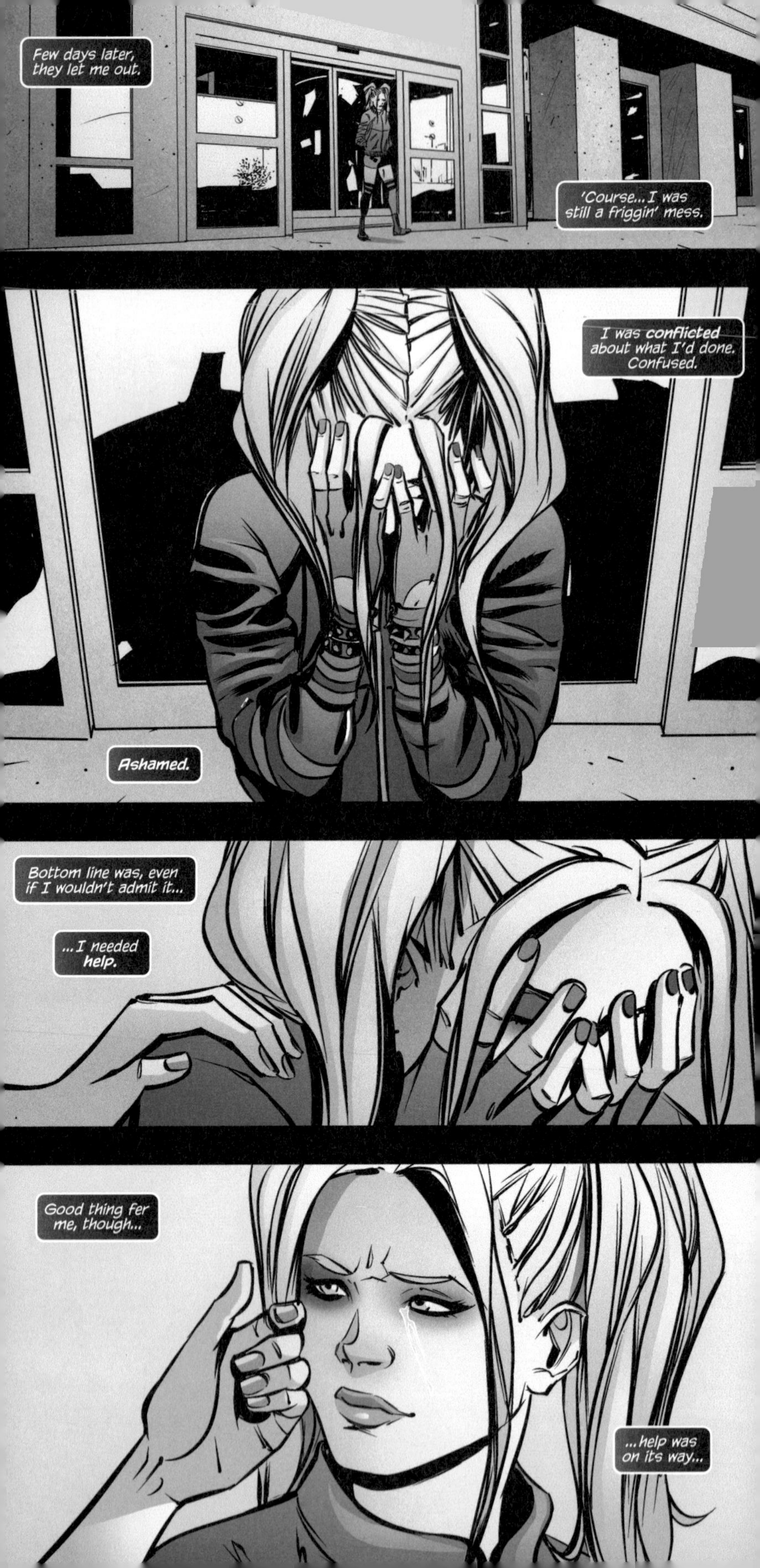
Few days later, they let me out.
'Course... I was still a friggin' mess.
I was **conflicted** about what I'd done. Confused.
Ashamed.
Bottom line was, even if I wouldn't admit it...
...I needed **help.**
Good thing fer me, though...
...help was on its way...

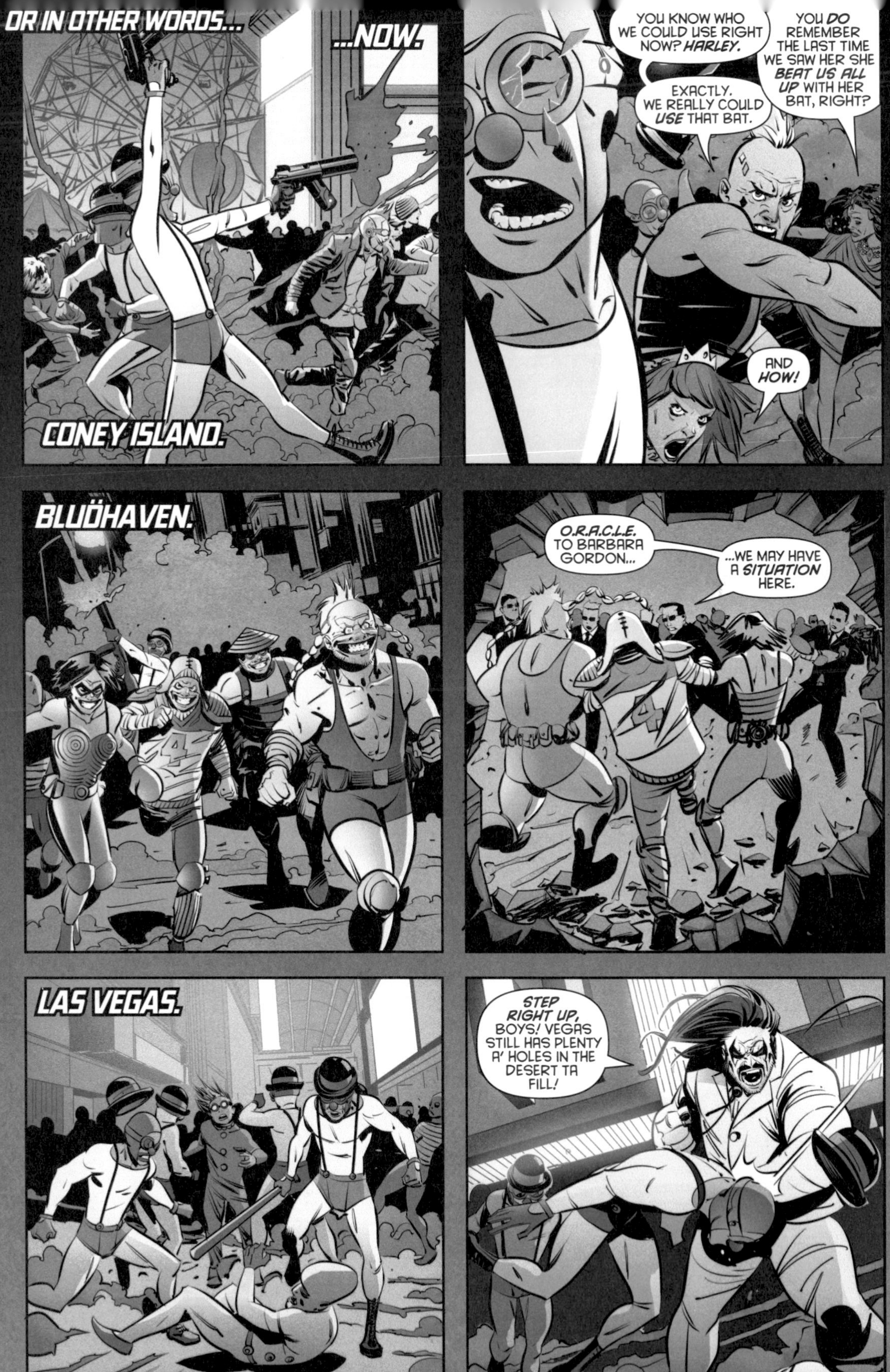
OR IN OTHER WORDS...
...NOW.
CONEY ISLAND.
YOU KNOW WHO WE COULD USE RIGHT NOW? HARLEY.
YOU DO REMEMBER THE LAST TIME WE SAW HER SHE BEAT US ALL UP WITH HER BAT, RIGHT?
EXACTLY. WE REALLY COULD USE THAT BAT.
AND HOW!
BLÜDHAVEN.
O.R.A.C.L.E. TO BARBARA GORDON...
...WE MAY HAVE A SITUATION HERE.
LAS VEGAS.
STEP RIGHT UP, BOYS! VEGAS STILL HAS PLENTY A' HOLES IN THE DESERT TA FILL!

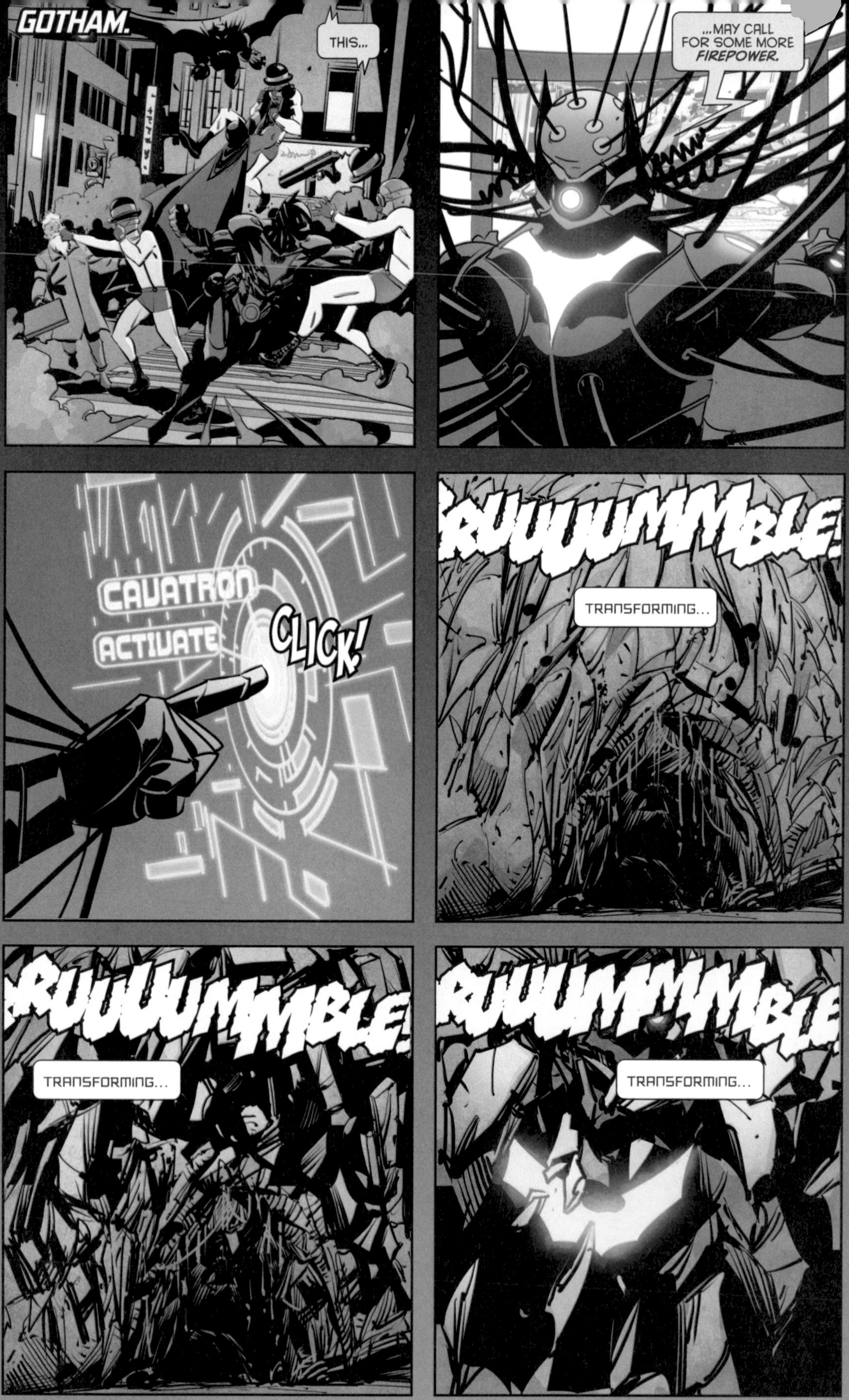
GOTHAM.
THIS...
...MAY CALL FOR SOME MORE FIREPOWER.
CAVATRON
ACTIVATE
CLICK!
RUUUUMMMBLE
TRANSFORMING...
RUUUUMMMBLE
TRANSFORMING...
RUUUMMMBLE
TRANSFORMING...

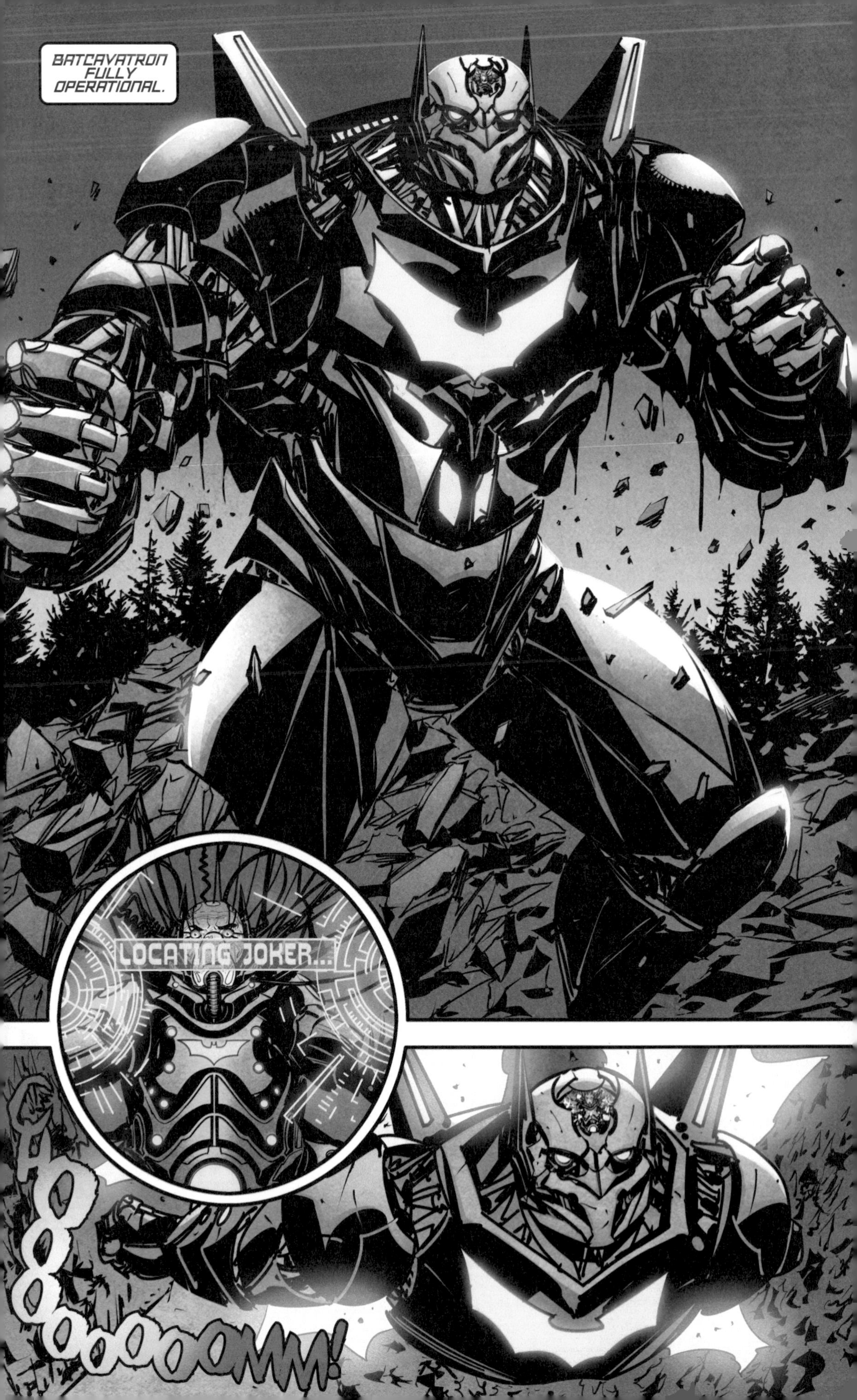

BATCAVATRON FULLY OPERATIONAL.
LOCATING JOKER...
BOOOOOOOOMM!

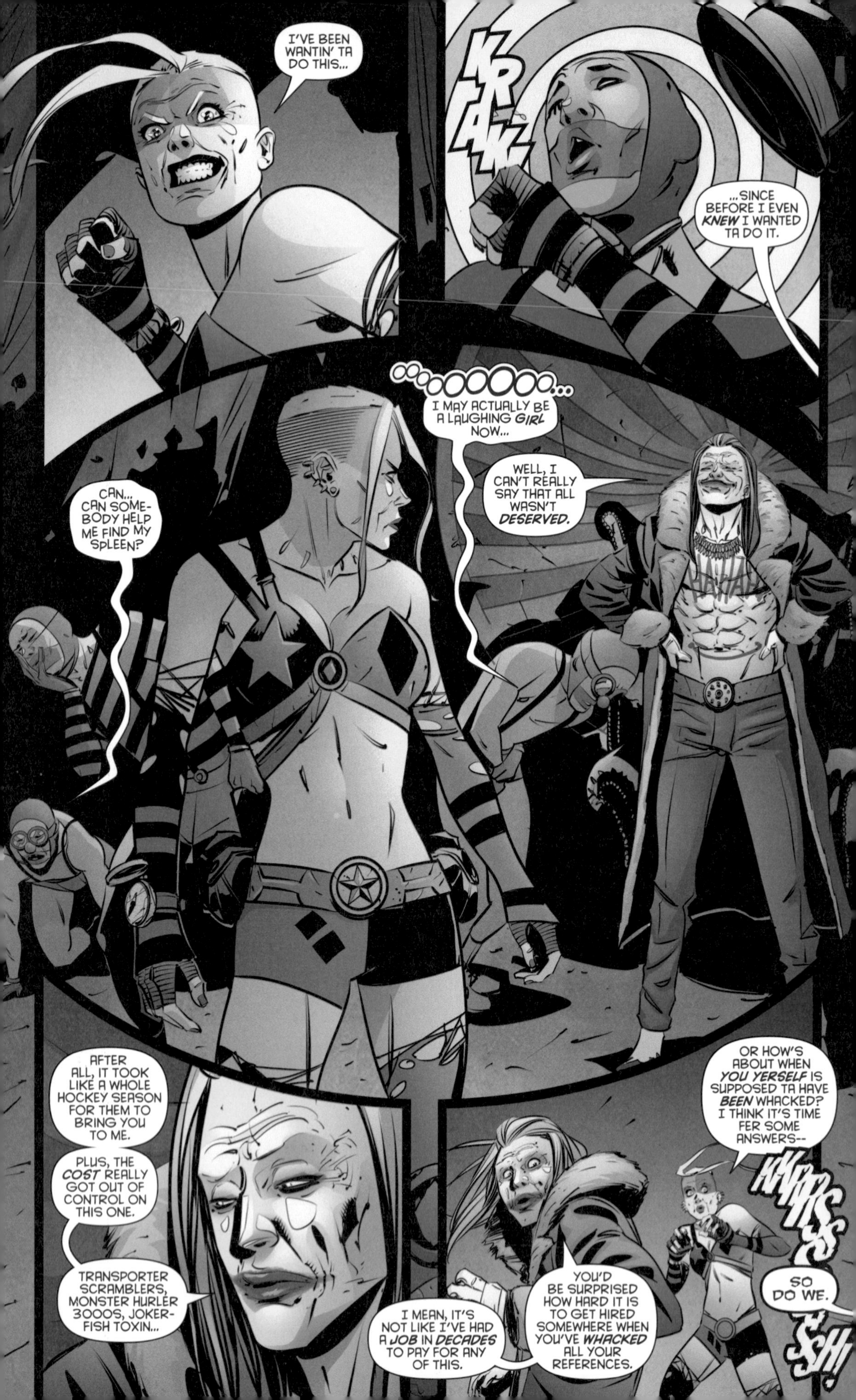
I'VE BEEN WANTIN' TA DO THIS...
KRAK
...SINCE BEFORE I EVEN KNEW I WANTED TA DO IT.
OOOOOOOOOO...
I MAY ACTUALLY BE A LAUGHING GIRL NOW...
CAN... CAN SOME-BODY HELP ME FIND MY SPLEEN?
WELL, I CAN'T REALLY SAY THAT ALL WASN'T DESERVED.
AFTER ALL, IT TOOK LIKE A WHOLE HOCKEY SEASON FOR THEM TO BRING YOU TO ME.
PLUS, THE COST REALLY GOT OUT OF CONTROL ON THIS ONE.
TRANSPORTER SCRAMBLERS, MONSTER HURLER 3000S, JOKER-FISH TOXIN...
I MEAN, IT'S NOT LIKE I'VE HAD A JOB IN DECADES TO PAY FOR ANY OF THIS.
YOU'D BE SURPRISED HOW HARD IT IS TO GET HIRED SOMEWHERE WHEN YOU'VE WHACKED ALL YOUR REFERENCES.
OR HOW'S ABOUT WHEN YOU YERSELF IS SUPPOSED TA HAVE BEEN WHACKED? I THINK IT'S TIME FER SOME ANSWERS--
SO DO WE.

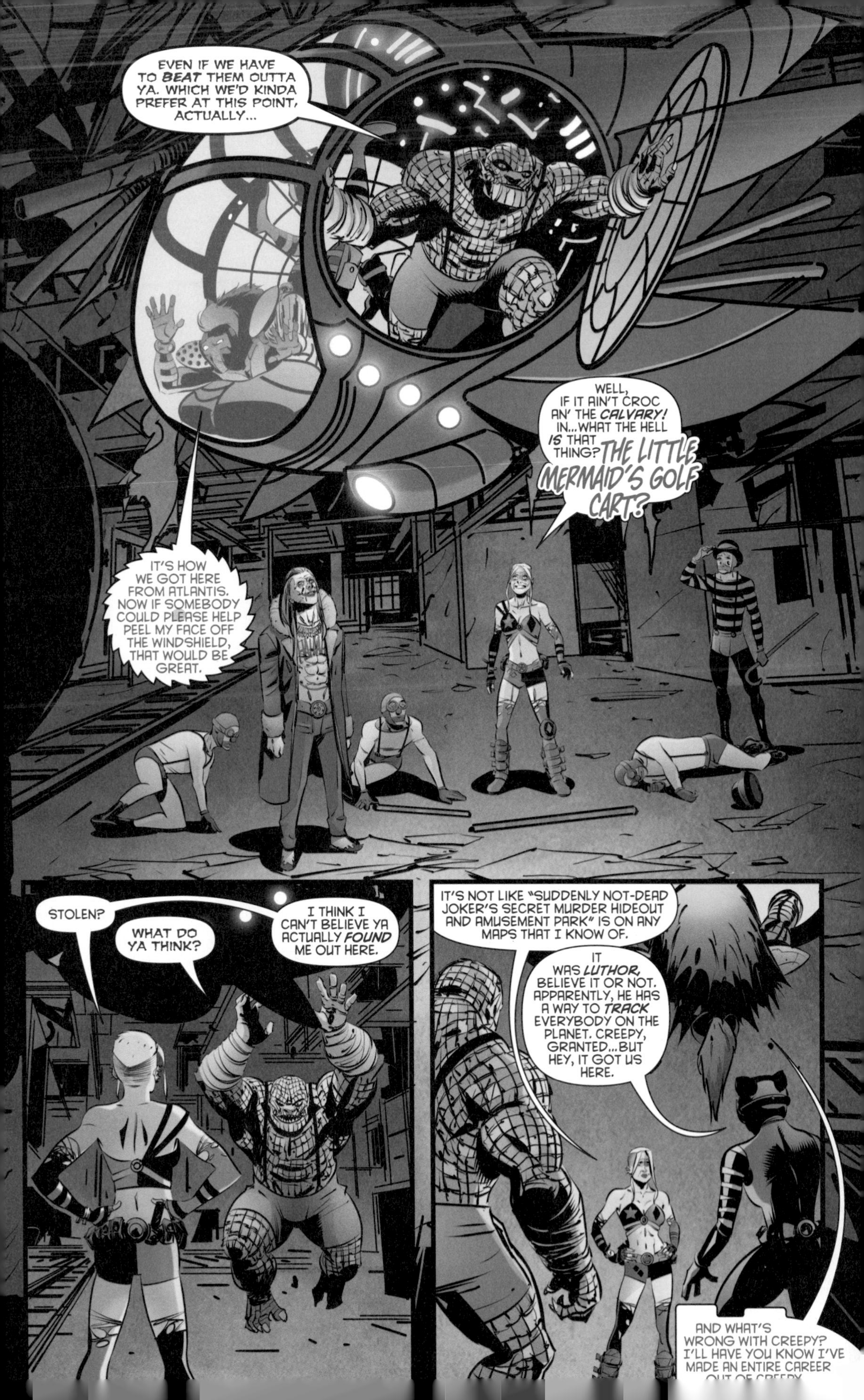
EVEN IF WE HAVE TO *BEAT* THEM OUTTA YA. WHICH WE'D KINDA PREFER AT THIS POINT, ACTUALLY...
WELL, IF IT AIN'T CROC AN' THE *CALVARY!* IN...WHAT THE HELL *IS* THAT THING? THE LITTLE MERMAID'S GOLF CART?
IT'S HOW WE GOT HERE FROM ATLANTIS. NOW IF SOMEBODY COULD PLEASE HELP PEEL MY FACE OFF THE WINDSHIELD, THAT WOULD BE GREAT.
STOLEN?
WHAT DO YA THINK?
I THINK I CAN'T BELIEVE YA ACTUALLY *FOUND* ME OUT HERE.
IT'S NOT LIKE "SUDDENLY NOT-DEAD JOKER'S SECRET MURDER HIDEOUT AND AMUSEMENT PARK" IS ON ANY MAPS THAT I KNOW OF.
IT WAS *LUTHOR,* BELIEVE IT OR NOT. APPARENTLY, HE HAS A WAY TO *TRACK* EVERYBODY ON THE PLANET. CREEPY, GRANTED...BUT HEY, IT GOT US HERE.
AND WHAT'S WRONG WITH CREEPY? I'LL HAVE YOU KNOW I'VE MADE AN ENTIRE CAREER

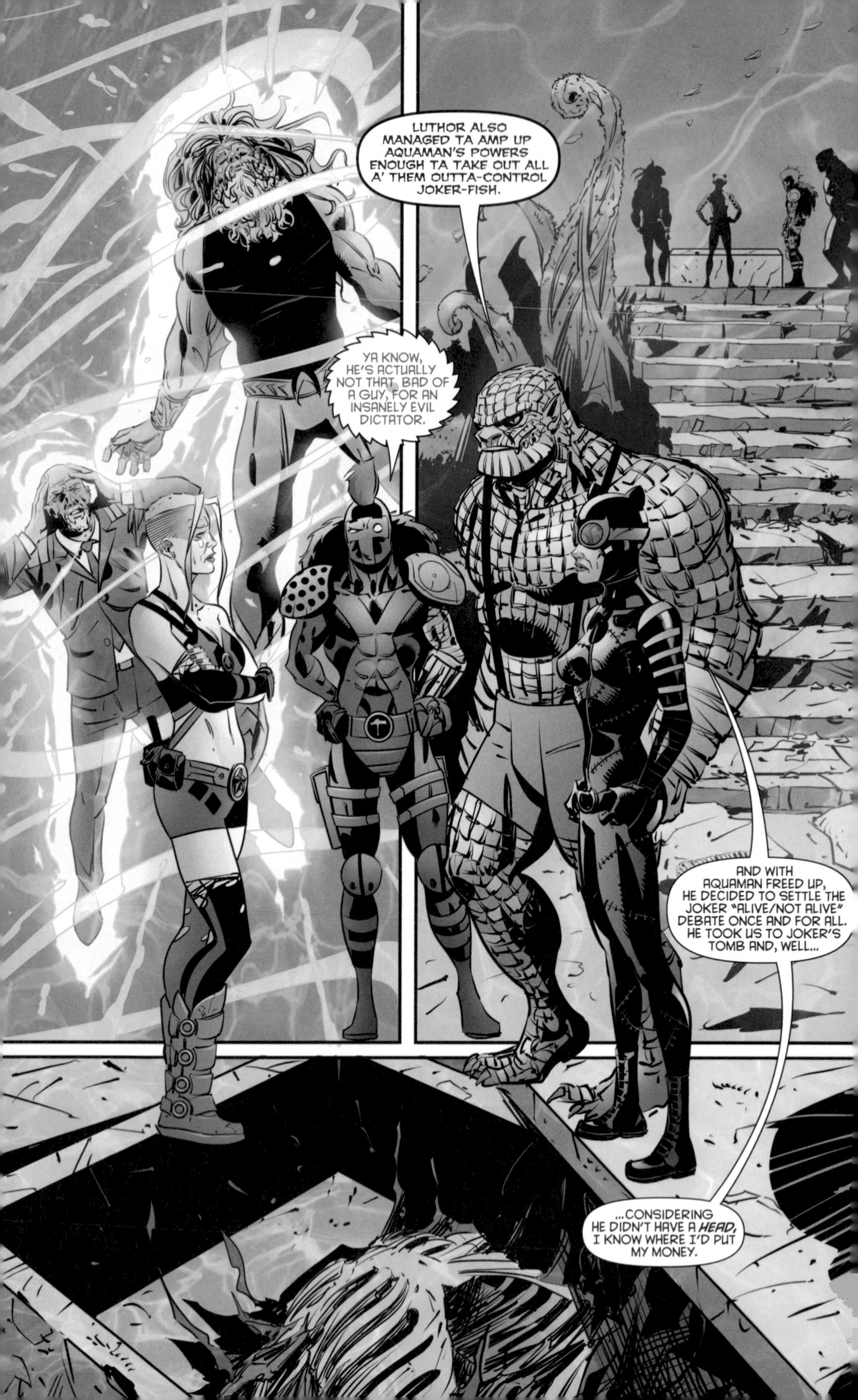
LUTHOR ALSO MANAGED TA AMP UP AQUAMAN'S POWERS ENOUGH TA TAKE OUT ALL A' THEM OUTTA-CONTROL JOKER-FISH.
YA KNOW, HE'S ACTUALLY NOT THAT BAD OF A GUY, FOR AN INSANELY EVIL DICTATOR.
AND WITH AQUAMAN FREED UP, HE DECIDED TO SETTLE THE JOKER "ALIVE/NOT ALIVE" DEBATE ONCE AND FOR ALL. HE TOOK US TO JOKER'S TOMB AND, WELL...
...CONSIDERING HE DIDN'T HAVE A HEAD, I KNOW WHERE I'D PUT MY MONEY.

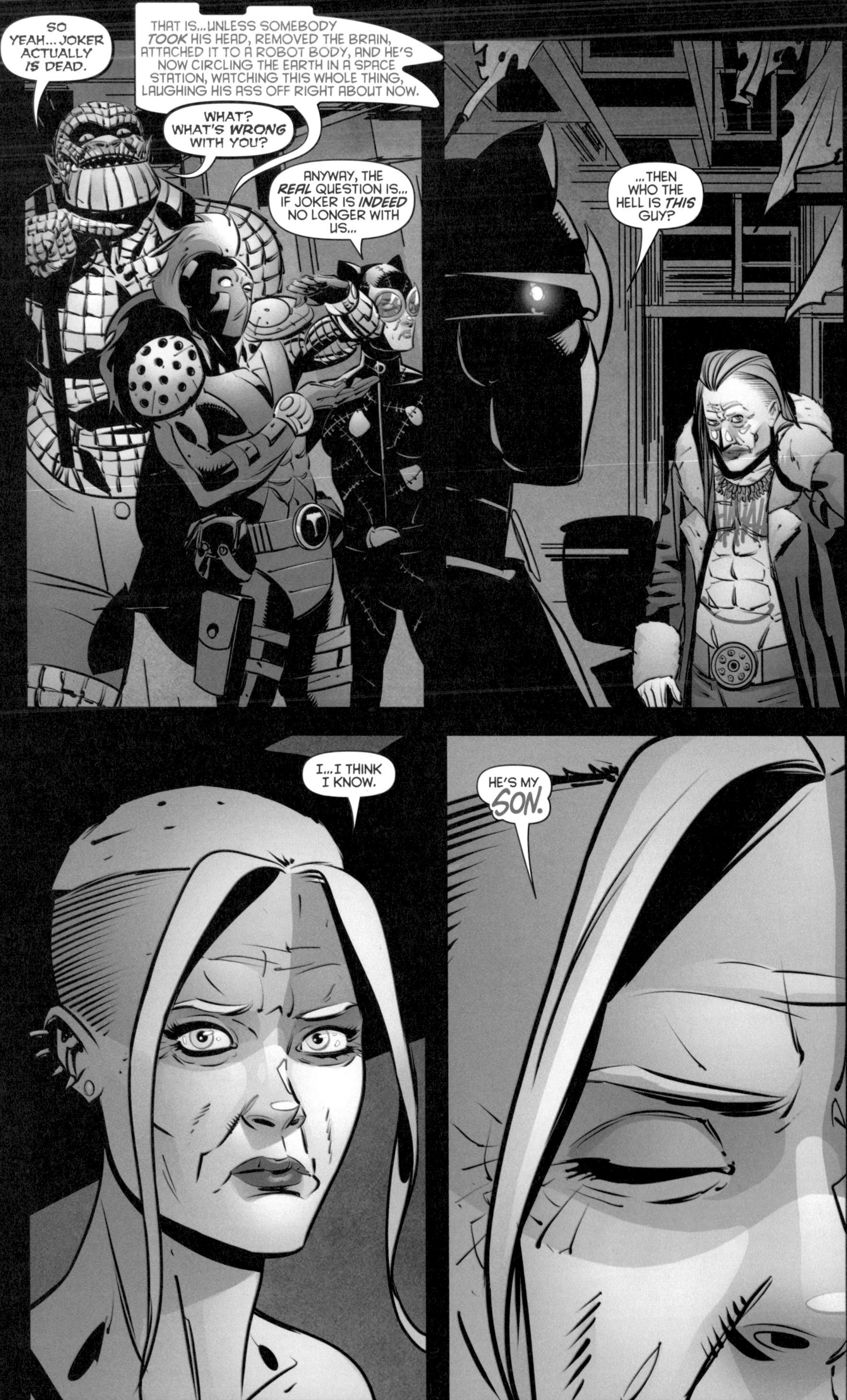
SO YEAH... JOKER ACTUALLY IS DEAD.
THAT IS...UNLESS SOMEBODY TOOK HIS HEAD, REMOVED THE BRAIN, ATTACHED IT TO A ROBOT BODY, AND HE'S NOW CIRCLING THE EARTH IN A SPACE STATION, WATCHING THIS WHOLE THING, LAUGHING HIS ASS OFF RIGHT ABOUT NOW.
WHAT? WHAT'S WRONG WITH YOU?
ANYWAY, THE REAL QUESTION IS... IF JOKER IS INDEED NO LONGER WITH US...
...THEN WHO THE HELL IS THIS GUY?
I...I THINK I KNOW.
HE'S MY SON.

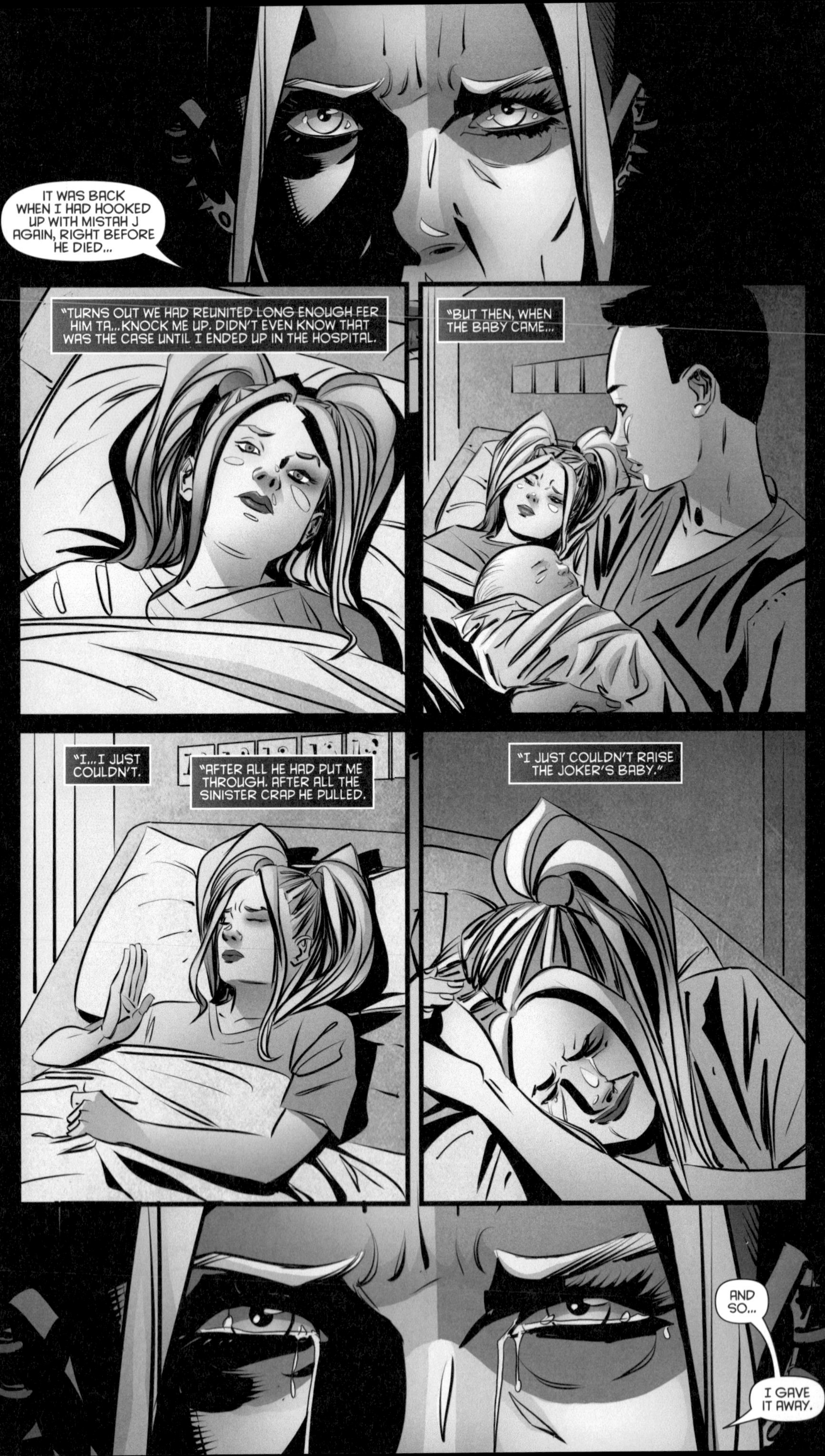
IT WAS BACK WHEN I HAD HOOKED UP WITH MISTAH J AGAIN, RIGHT BEFORE HE DIED...
"TURNS OUT WE HAD REUNITED LONG ENOUGH FER HIM TA...KNOCK ME UP. DIDN'T EVEN KNOW THAT WAS THE CASE UNTIL I ENDED UP IN THE HOSPITAL.
"BUT THEN, WHEN THE BABY CAME...
"I...I JUST COULDN'T.
"AFTER ALL HE HAD PUT ME THROUGH. AFTER ALL THE SINISTER CRAP HE PULLED.
"I JUST COULDN'T RAISE THE JOKER'S BABY."
AND SO...
I GAVE IT AWAY.

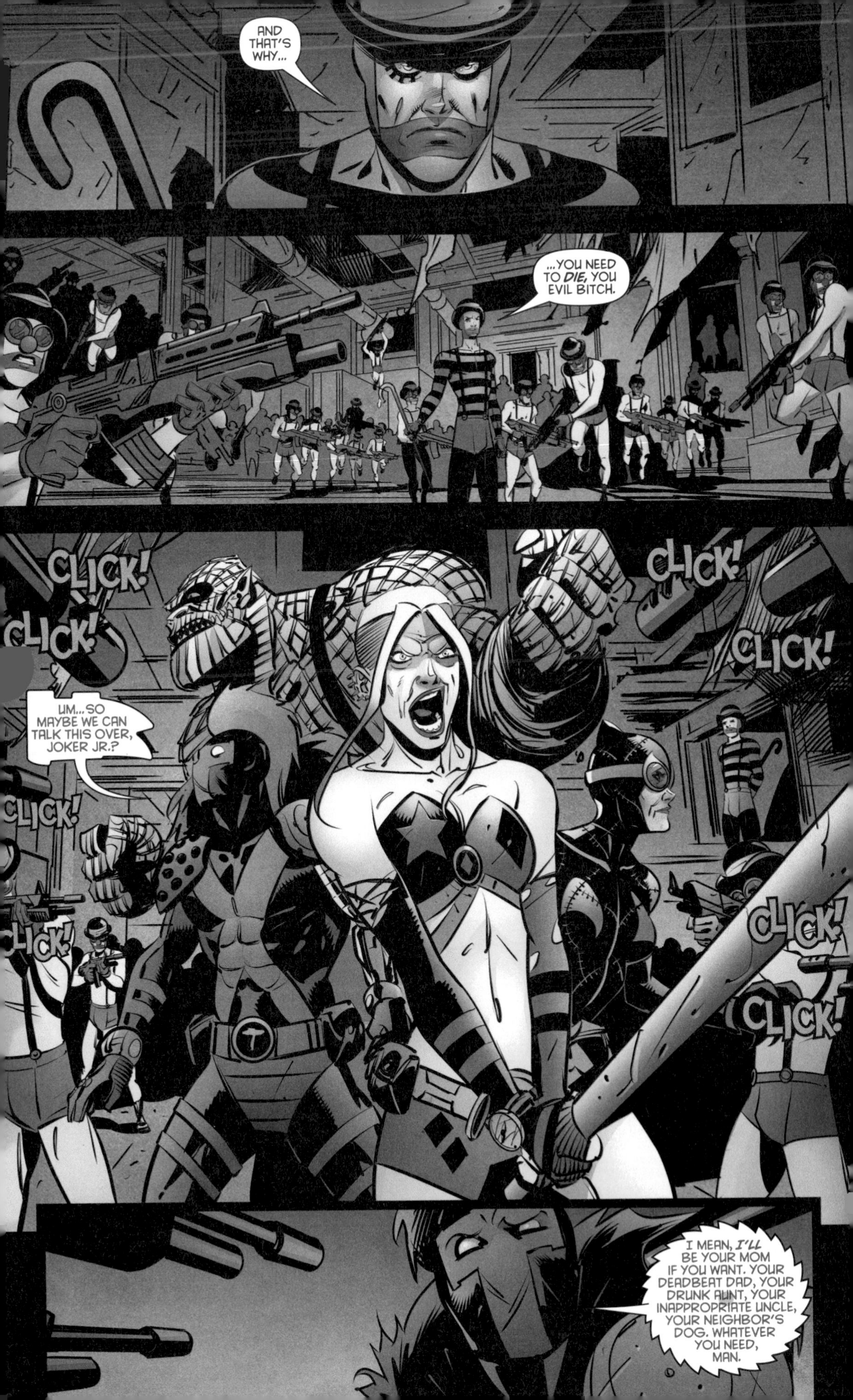
AND THAT'S WHY...
...YOU NEED TO DIE, YOU EVIL BITCH.
CLICK!
CLICK!
CLICK!
CLICK!
UM...SO MAYBE WE CAN TALK THIS OVER, JOKER JR.?
CLICK!
CLICK!
CLICK!
CLICK!
I MEAN, I'LL BE YOUR MOM IF YOU WANT. YOUR DEADBEAT DAD, YOUR DRUNK AUNT, YOUR INAPPROPRIATE UNCLE, YOUR NEIGHBOR'S DOG. WHATEVER YOU NEED, MAN.

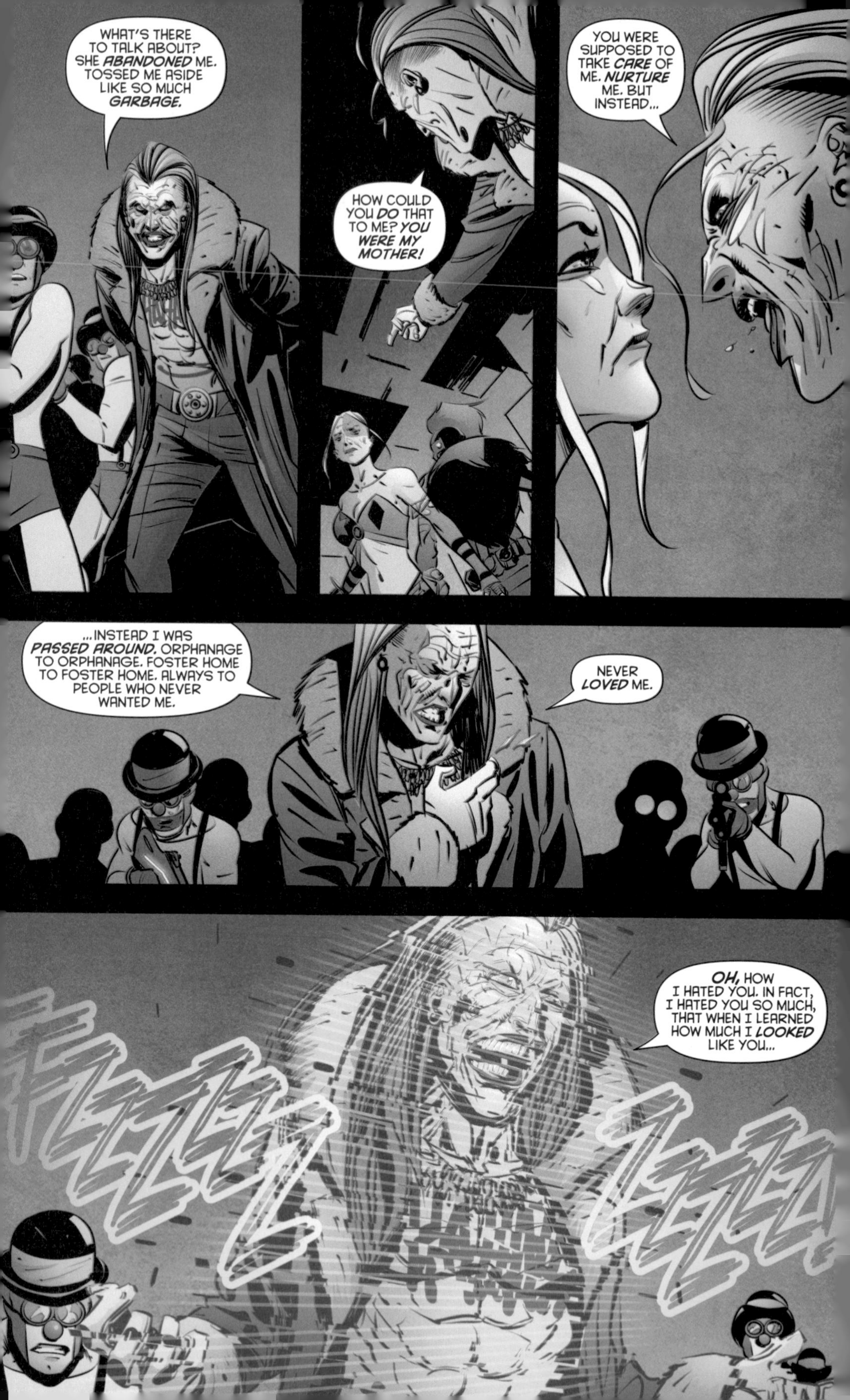
WHAT'S THERE TO TALK ABOUT? SHE ABANDONED ME. TOSSED ME ASIDE LIKE SO MUCH GARBAGE.
HOW COULD YOU DO THAT TO ME? YOU WERE MY MOTHER!
YOU WERE SUPPOSED TO TAKE CARE OF ME. NURTURE ME. BUT INSTEAD...
...INSTEAD I WAS PASSED AROUND. ORPHANAGE TO ORPHANAGE. FOSTER HOME TO FOSTER HOME. ALWAYS TO PEOPLE WHO NEVER WANTED ME.
NEVER LOVED ME.
OH, HOW I HATED YOU. IN FACT, I HATED YOU SO MUCH, THAT WHEN I LEARNED HOW MUCH I LOOKED LIKE YOU...

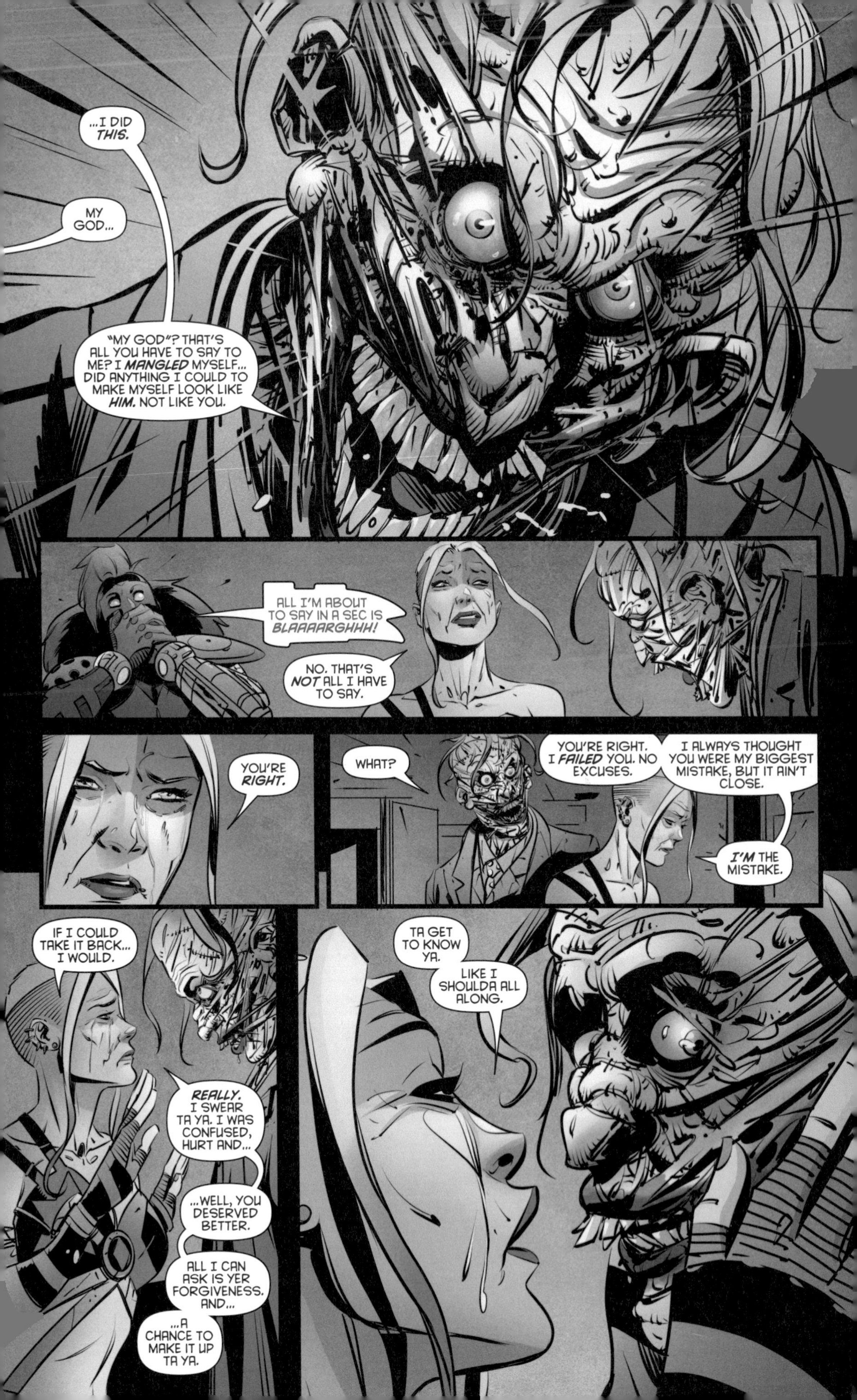
...I DID THIS.
MY GOD...
"MY GOD"? THAT'S ALL YOU HAVE TO SAY TO ME? I MANGLED MYSELF... DID ANYTHING I COULD TO MAKE MYSELF LOOK LIKE HIM. NOT LIKE YOU.
ALL I'M ABOUT TO SAY IN A SEC IS BLAAAARGHHH!
NO. THAT'S NOT ALL I HAVE TO SAY.
YOU'RE RIGHT.
WHAT?
YOU'RE RIGHT. I FAILED YOU. NO EXCUSES.
I ALWAYS THOUGHT YOU WERE MY BIGGEST MISTAKE, BUT IT AIN'T CLOSE.
I'M THE MISTAKE.
IF I COULD TAKE IT BACK... I WOULD.
REALLY. I SWEAR TA YA. I WAS CONFUSED, HURT AND...
...WELL, YOU DESERVED BETTER.
ALL I CAN ASK IS YER FORGIVENESS. AND...
...A CHANCE TO MAKE IT UP TA YA.
TA GET TO KNOW YA.
LIKE I SHOULDA ALL ALONG.

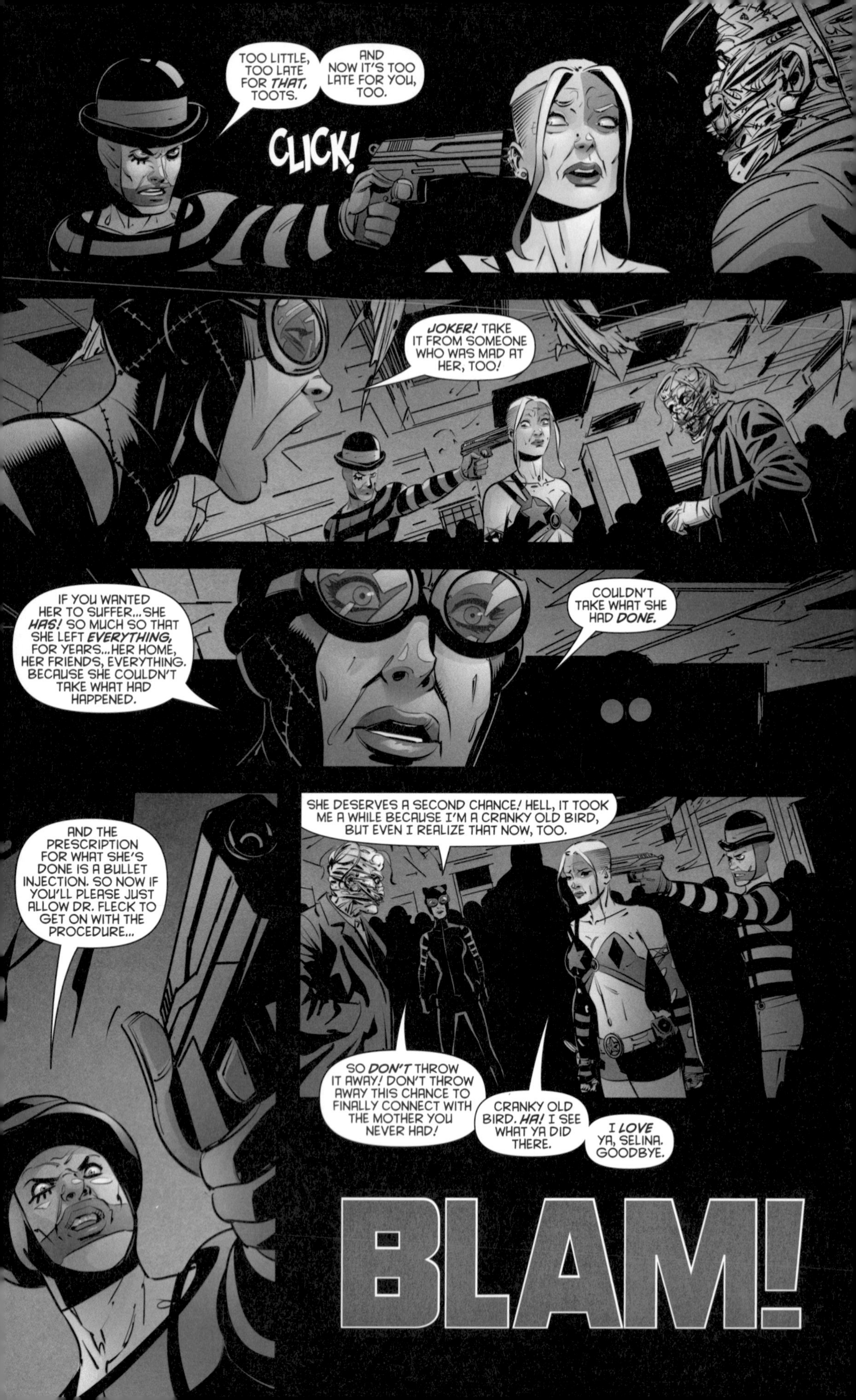
TOO LITTLE, TOO LATE FOR THAT, TOOTS.
AND NOW IT'S TOO LATE FOR YOU, TOO.
CLICK!
JOKER! TAKE IT FROM SOMEONE WHO WAS MAD AT HER, TOO!
IF YOU WANTED HER TO SUFFER...SHE HAS! SO MUCH SO THAT SHE LEFT EVERYTHING, FOR YEARS...HER HOME, HER FRIENDS, EVERYTHING. BECAUSE SHE COULDN'T TAKE WHAT HAD HAPPENED.
COULDN'T TAKE WHAT SHE HAD DONE.
AND THE PRESCRIPTION FOR WHAT SHE'S DONE IS A BULLET INJECTION. SO NOW IF YOU'LL PLEASE JUST ALLOW DR. FLECK TO GET ON WITH THE PROCEDURE...
SHE DESERVES A SECOND CHANCE! HELL, IT TOOK ME A WHILE BECAUSE I'M A CRANKY OLD BIRD, BUT EVEN I REALIZE THAT NOW, TOO.
SO DON'T THROW IT AWAY! DON'T THROW AWAY THIS CHANCE TO FINALLY CONNECT WITH THE MOTHER YOU NEVER HAD!
CRANKY OLD BIRD. HA! I SEE WHAT YA DID THERE.
I LOVE YA, SELINA. GOODBYE.
BLAM!

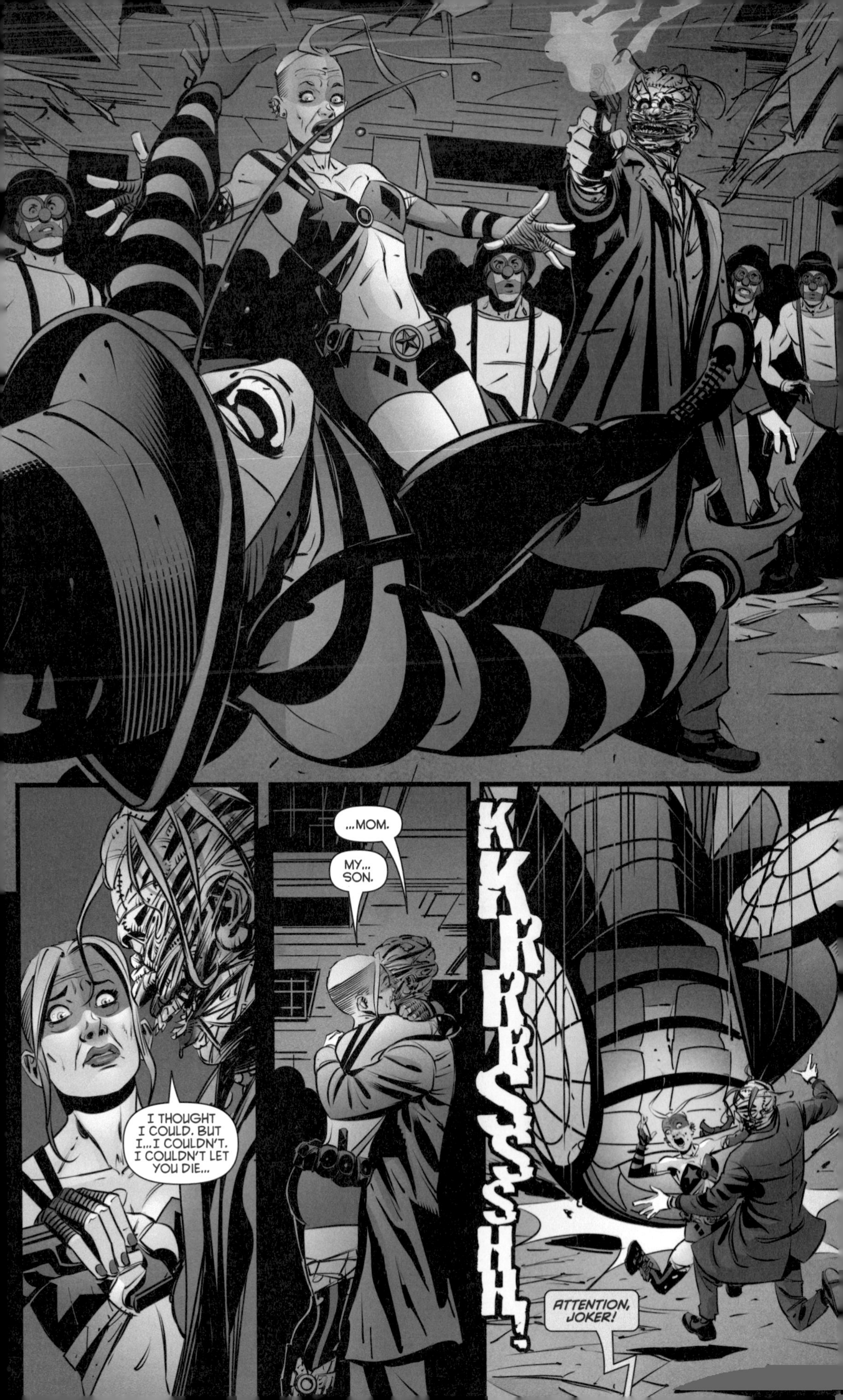
I THOUGHT I COULD. BUT I...I COULDN'T. I COULDN'T LET YOU DIE...
...MOM.
MY... SON.
KKRRSSHH!
ATTENTION, JOKER!

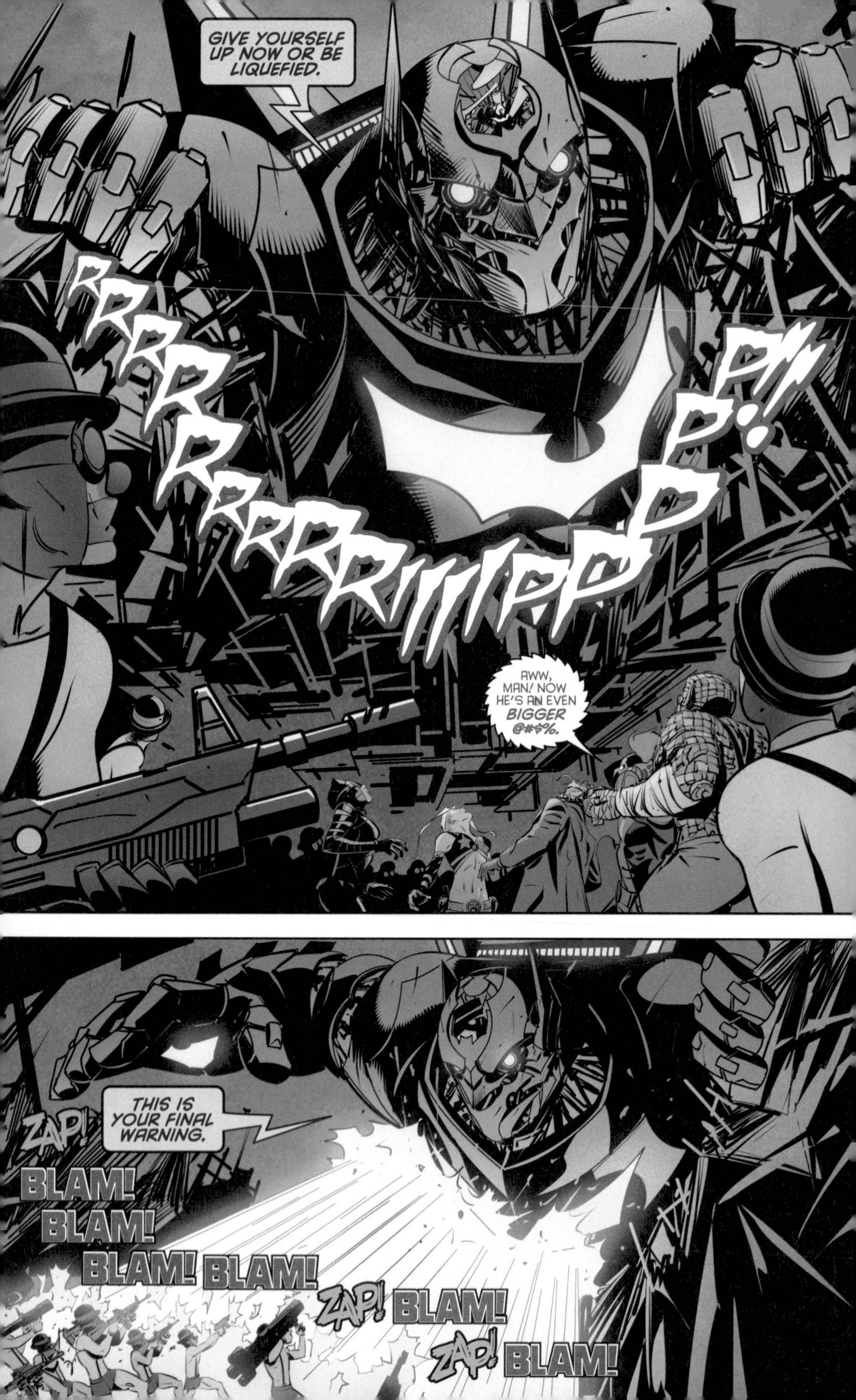
GIVE YOURSELF UP NOW OR BE LIQUEFIED.
RRRRRRRRRRRIIIIIPPPPP!!
AWW, MAN! NOW HE'S AN EVEN BIGGER @#$%.
THIS IS YOUR FINAL WARNING.
ZAP!
BLAM!
BLAM!
BLAM! BLAM!
ZAP! BLAM!
ZAP! BLAM!

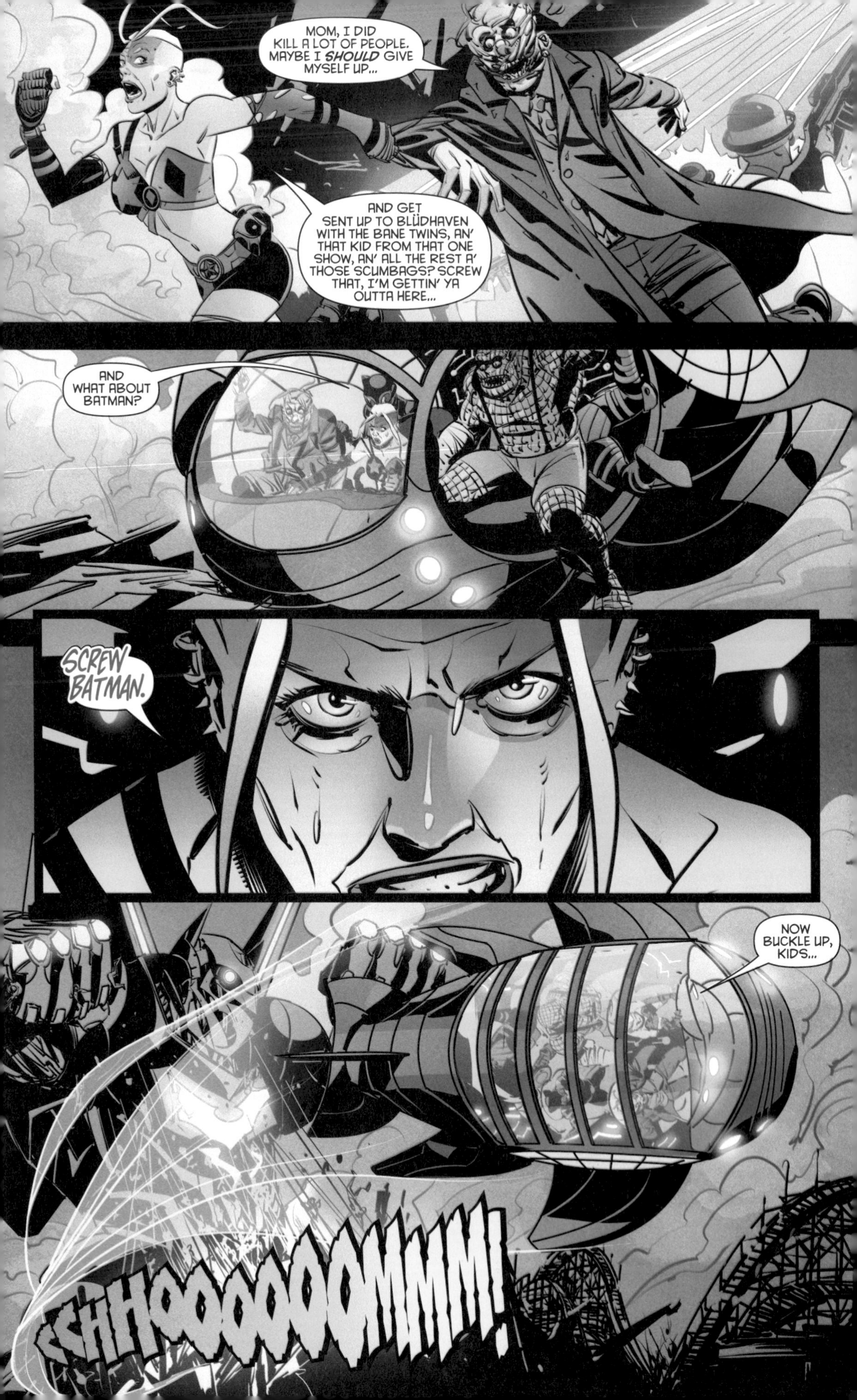
MOM, I DID KILL A LOT OF PEOPLE. MAYBE I SHOULD GIVE MYSELF UP...
AND GET SENT UP TO BLÜDHAVEN WITH THE BANE TWINS, AN' THAT KID FROM THAT ONE SHOW, AN' ALL THE REST A' THOSE SCUMBAGS? SCREW THAT, I'M GETTIN' YA OUTTA HERE...
AND WHAT ABOUT BATMAN?
SCREW BATMAN.
NOW BUCKLE UP, KIDS...
SCHHOOOOOOMMMM!

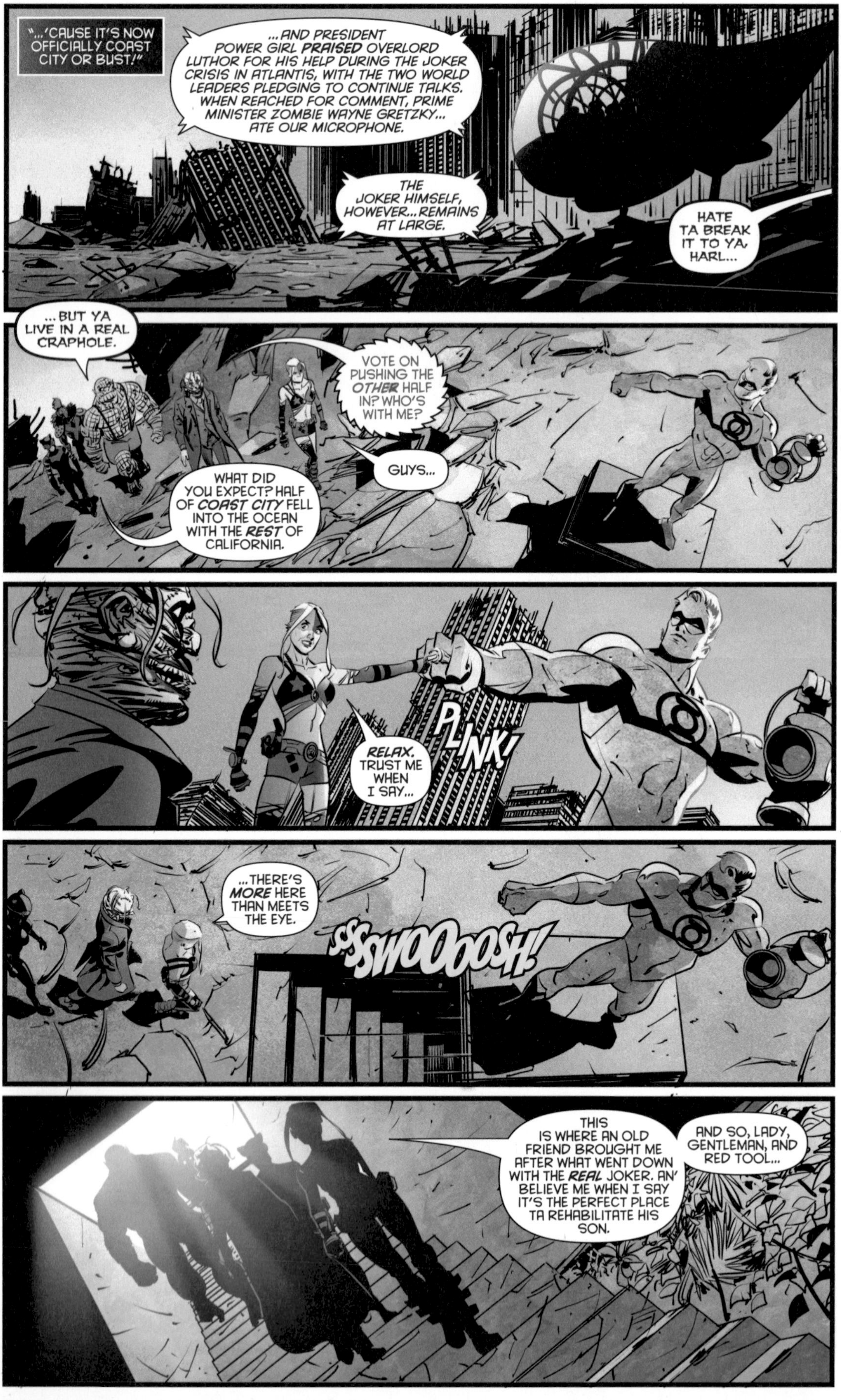
"...'CAUSE IT'S NOW OFFICIALLY COAST CITY OR BUST!"
...AND PRESIDENT POWER GIRL PRAISED OVERLORD LUTHOR FOR HIS HELP DURING THE JOKER CRISIS IN ATLANTIS, WITH THE TWO WORLD LEADERS PLEDGING TO CONTINUE TALKS. WHEN REACHED FOR COMMENT, PRIME MINISTER ZOMBIE WAYNE GRETZKY... ATE OUR MICROPHONE.
THE JOKER HIMSELF, HOWEVER...REMAINS AT LARGE.
HATE TA BREAK IT TO YA, HARL...
...BUT YA LIVE IN A REAL CRAPHOLE.
VOTE ON PUSHING THE OTHER HALF IN? WHO'S WITH ME?
GUYS...
WHAT DID YOU EXPECT? HALF OF COAST CITY FELL INTO THE OCEAN WITH THE REST OF CALIFORNIA.
PLINK!
RELAX. TRUST ME WHEN I SAY...
...THERE'S MORE HERE THAN MEETS THE EYE.
SSSWOOOOOSH!
THIS IS WHERE AN OLD FRIEND BROUGHT ME AFTER WHAT WENT DOWN WITH THE REAL JOKER. AN' BELIEVE ME WHEN I SAY IT'S THE PERFECT PLACE TA REHABILITATE HIS SON.
AND SO, LADY, GENTLEMAN, AND RED TOOL...

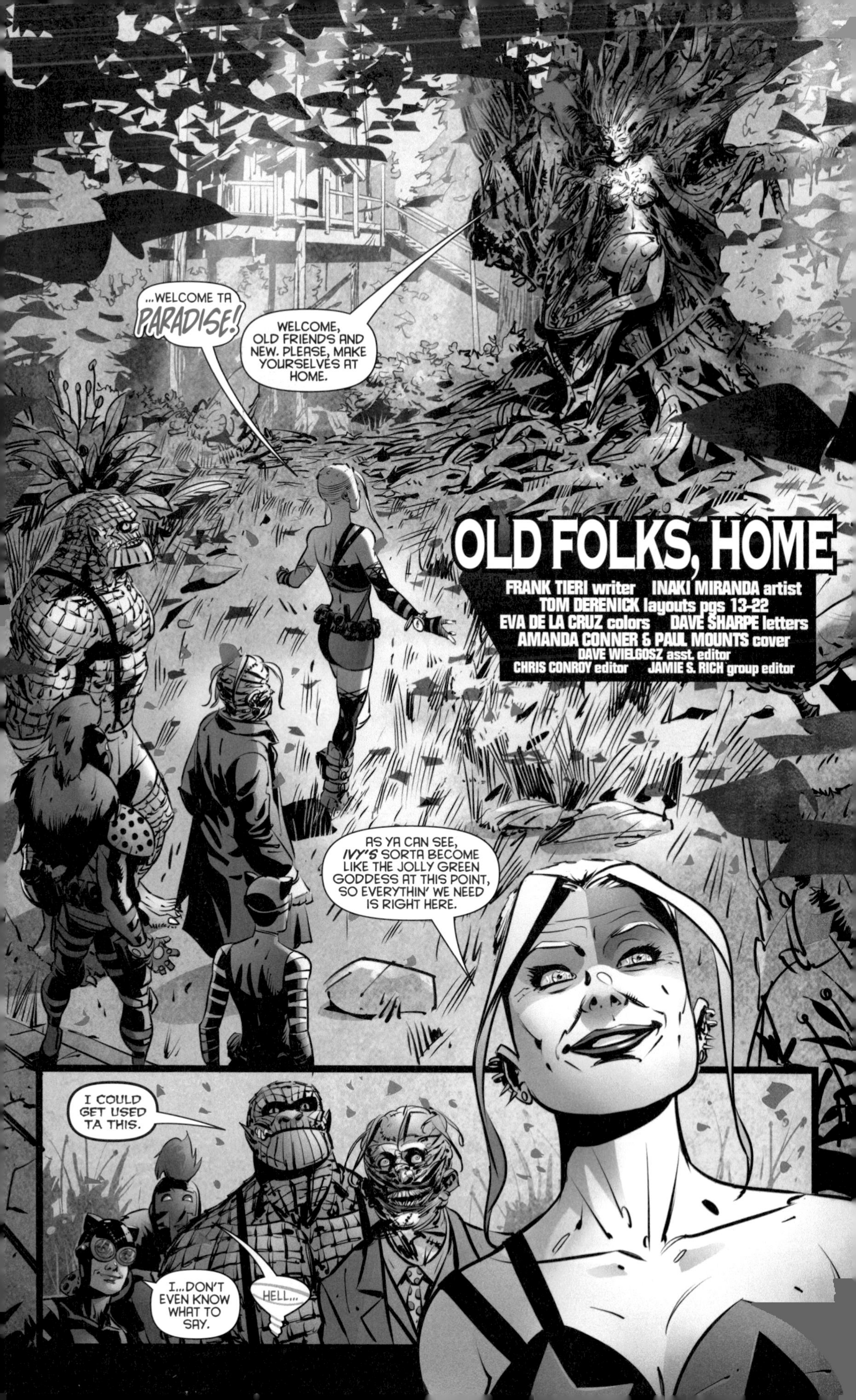
...WELCOME TA PARADISE!
WELCOME, OLD FRIENDS AND NEW. PLEASE, MAKE YOURSELVES AT HOME.
OLD FOLKS, HOME
FRANK TIERI writer INAKI MIRANDA artist
TOM DERENICK layouts pgs 13-22
EVA DE LA CRUZ colors DAVE SHARPE letters
AMANDA CONNER & PAUL MOUNTS cover
DAVE WIELGOSZ asst. editor
CHRIS CONROY editor JAMIE S. RICH group editor
AS YA CAN SEE, IVY'S SORTA BECOME LIKE THE JOLLY GREEN GODDESS AT THIS POINT, SO EVERYTHIN' WE NEED IS RIGHT HERE.
I COULD GET USED TA THIS.
I...DON'T EVEN KNOW WHAT TO SAY.
HELL...

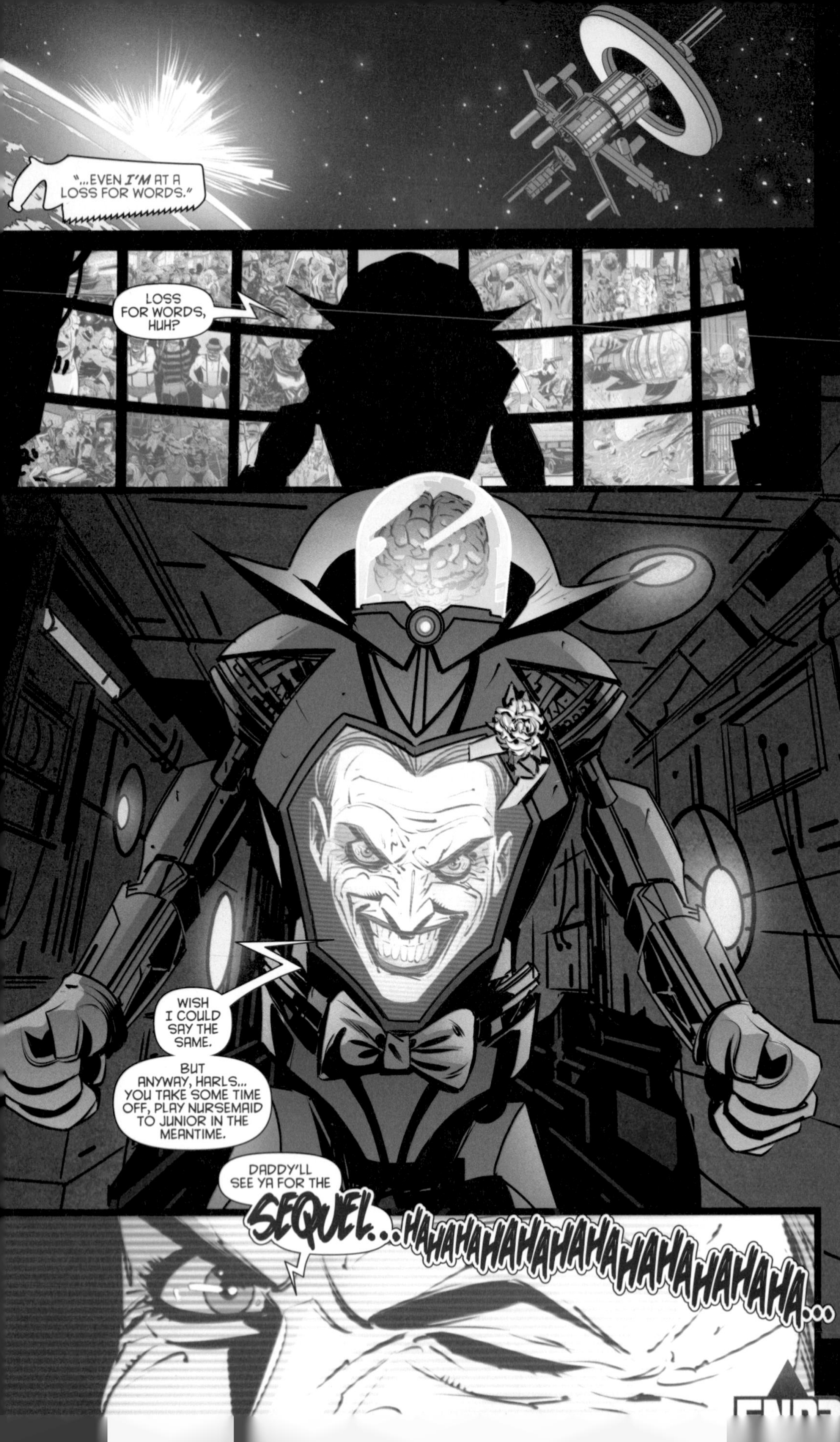
"...EVEN I'M AT A LOSS FOR WORDS."
LOSS FOR WORDS, HUH?
WISH I COULD SAY THE SAME.
BUT ANYWAY, HARLS... YOU TAKE SOME TIME OFF, PLAY NURSEMAID TO JUNIOR IN THE MEANTIME.
DADDY'LL SEE YA FOR THE SEQUEL...HAHAHAHAHAHAHAHAHAHAHAHAHAHA...

OLD LADY HARLEY *#1 variant cover*
by **AMANDA CONNER & PAUL MOUNTS**

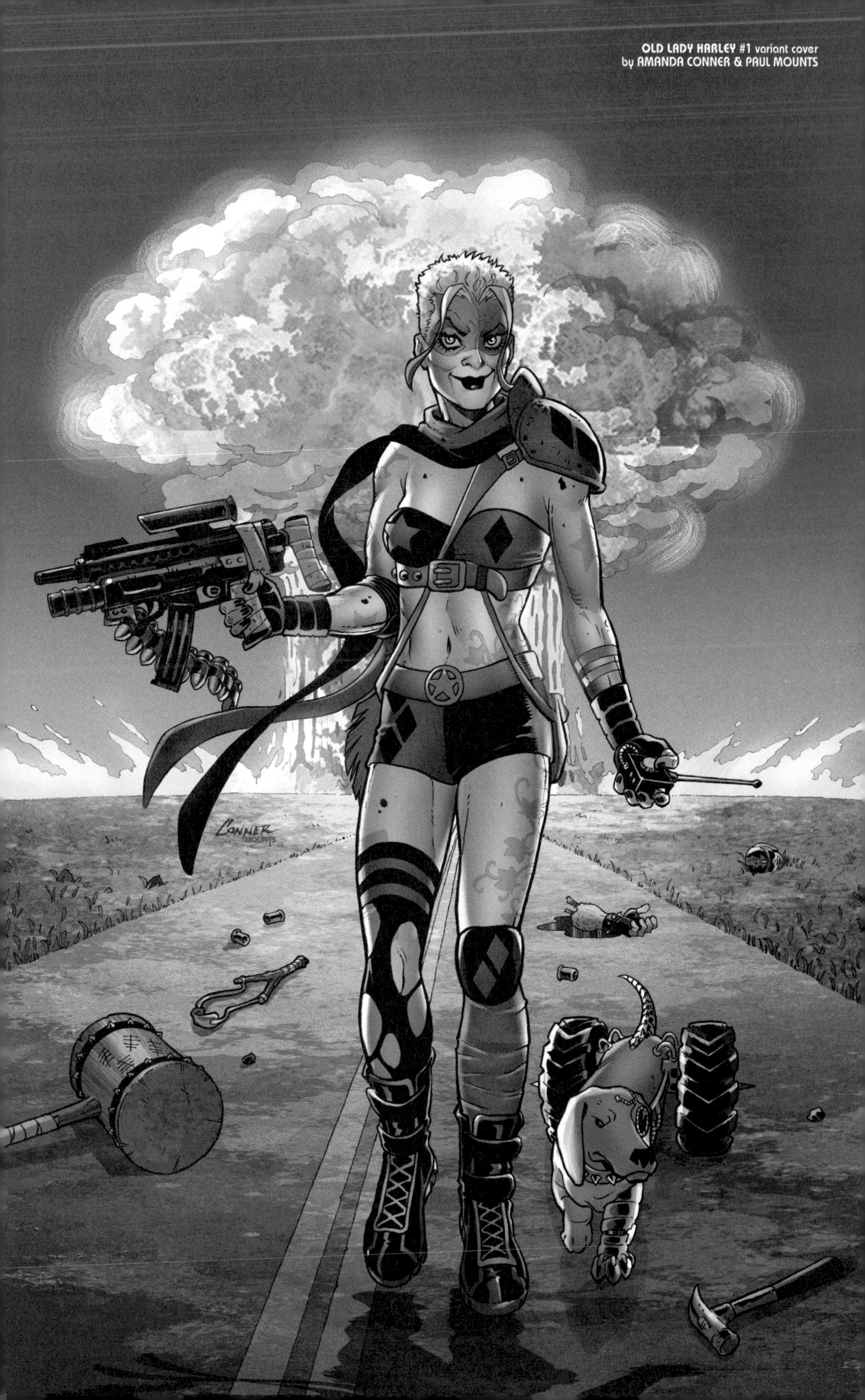
CONNER
MOUNTS

OLD LADY HARLEY character studies by INAKI MIRANDA

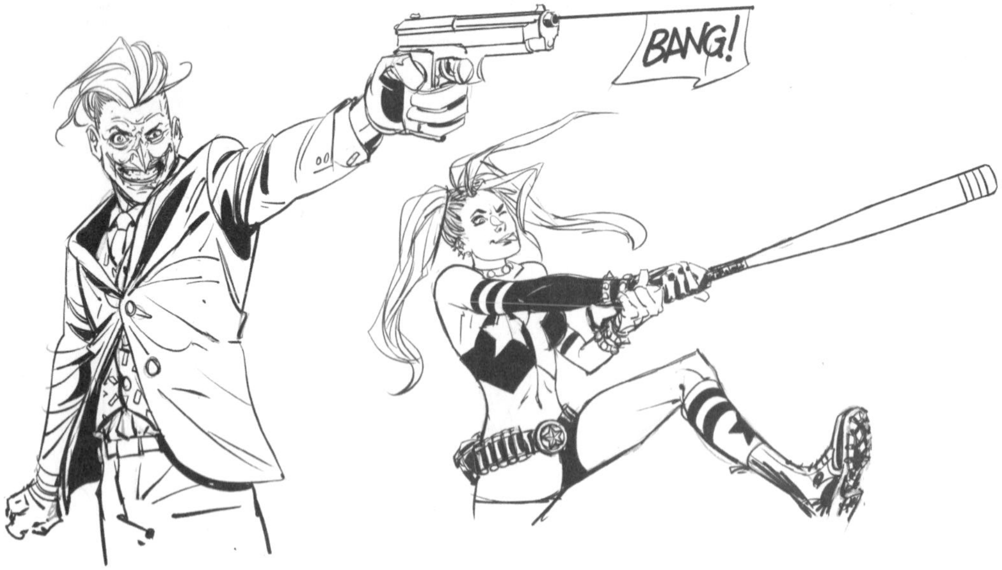
BANG!

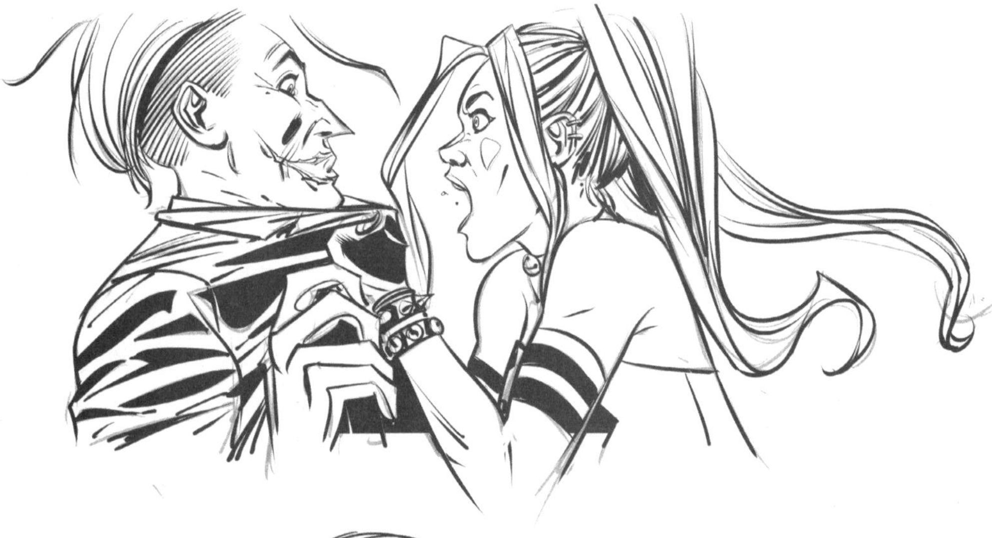

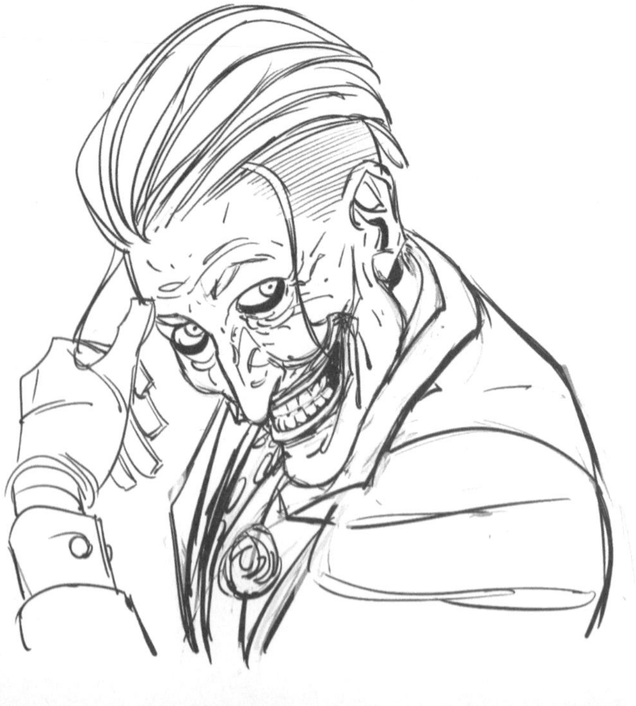

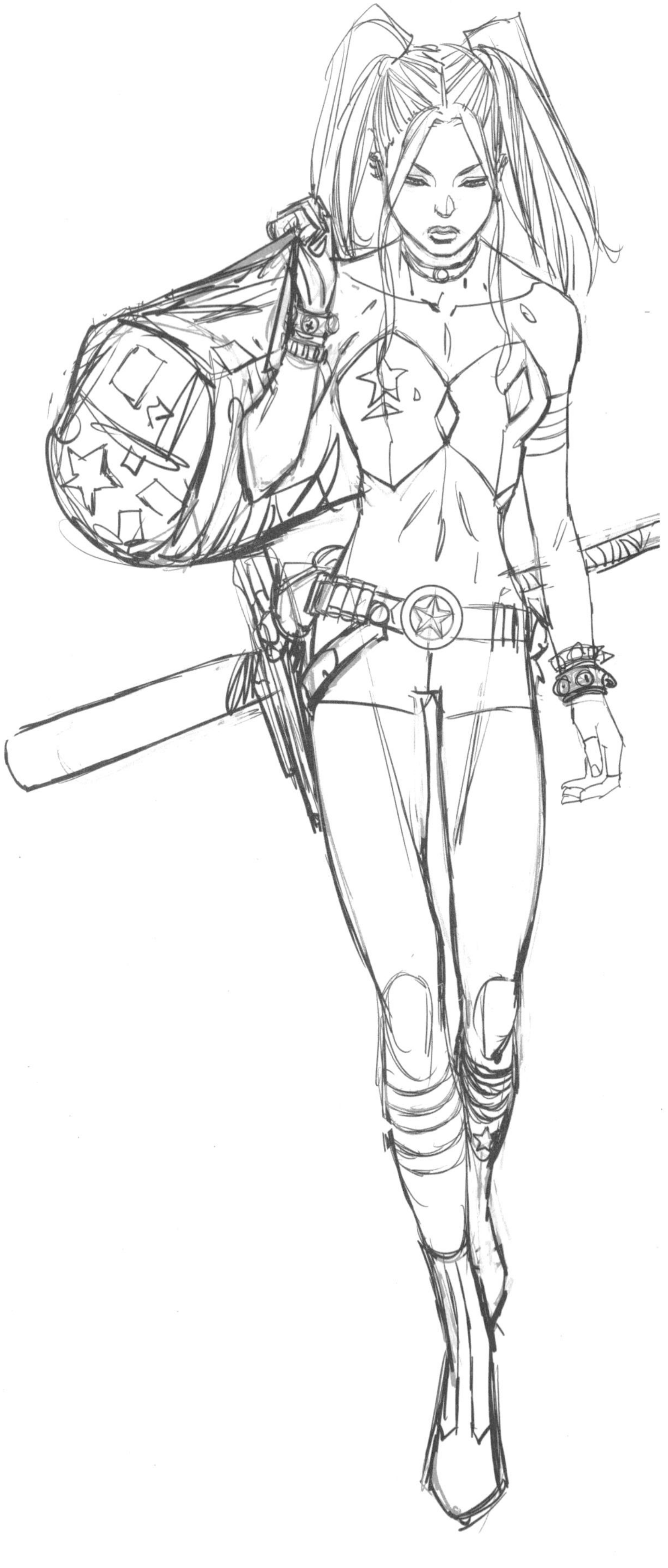

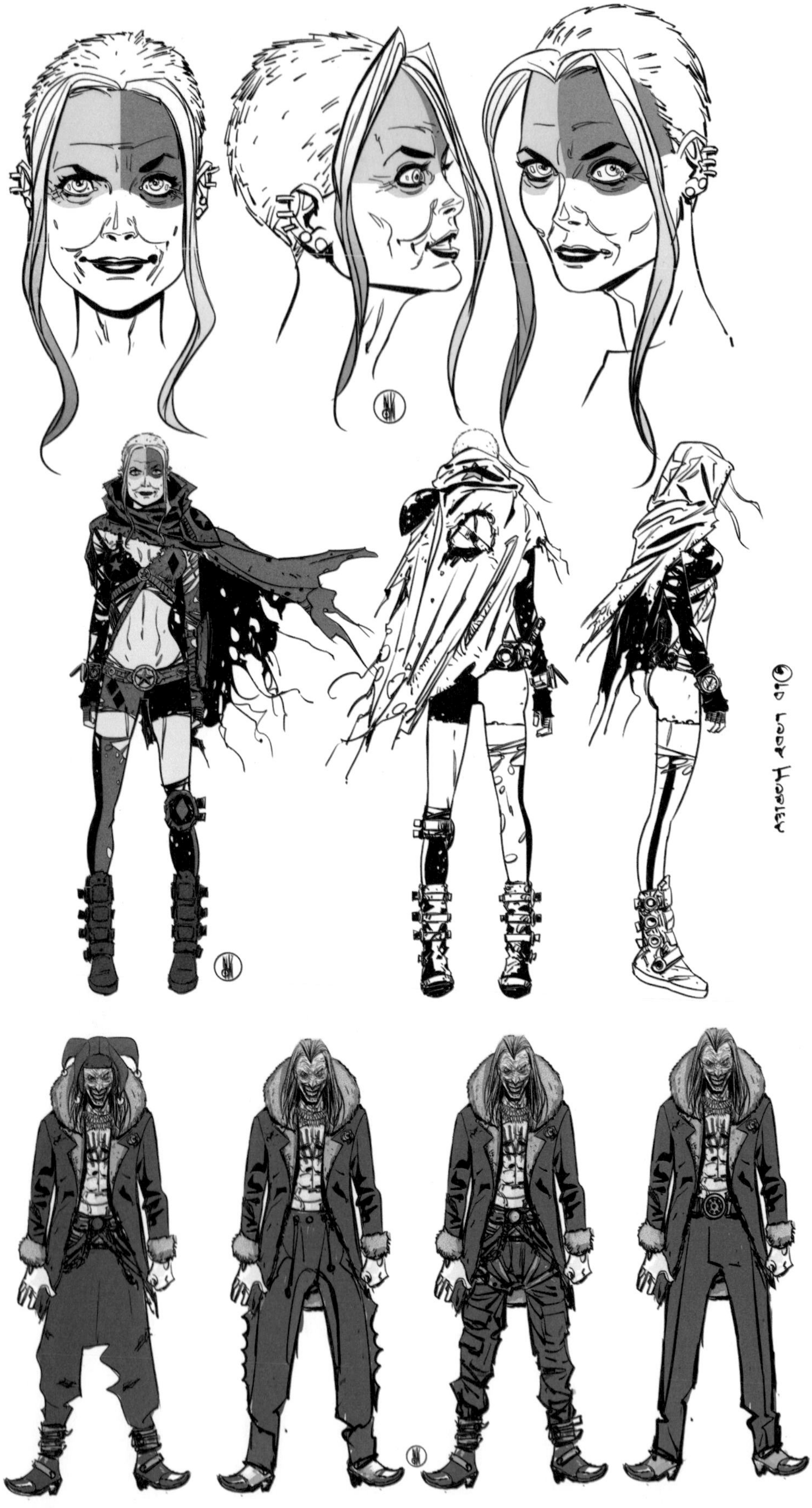
OLD LADY HARLEY ©

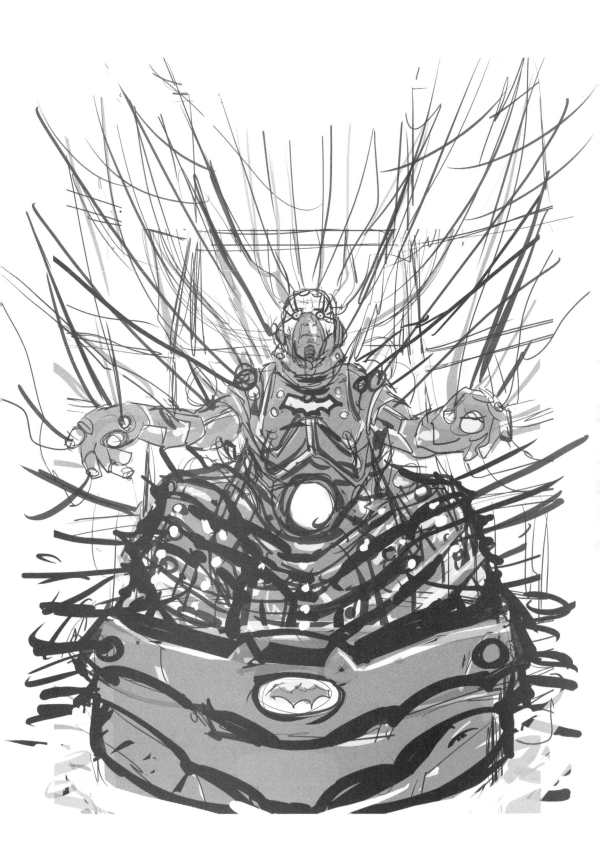

In-process pages for **OLD LADY HARLEY** by **INAKI MIRANDA**

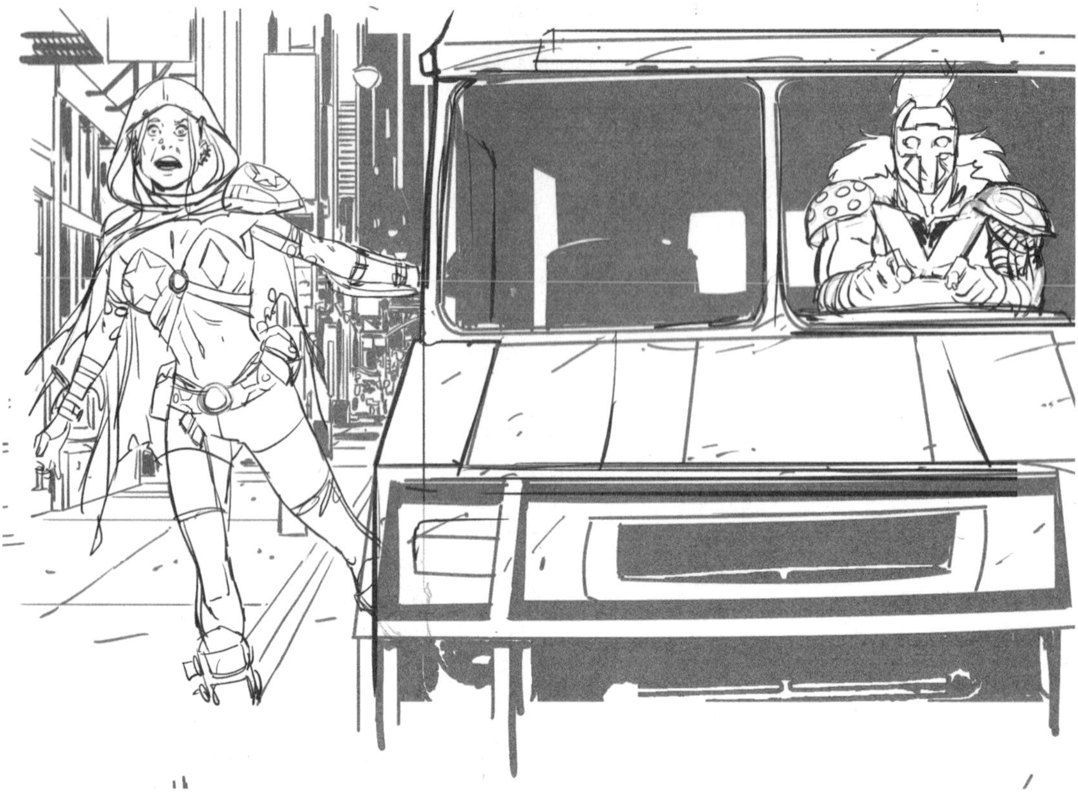

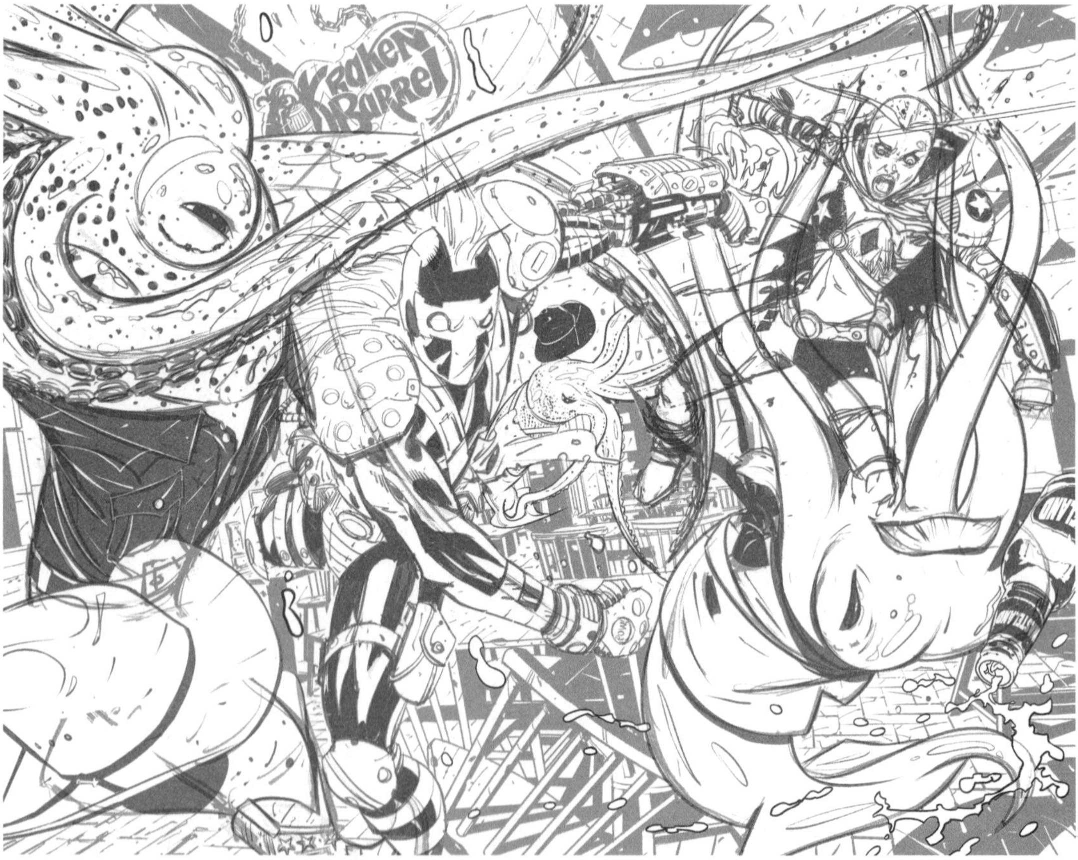
Kraken Barrel